MTV RULED THE WORLD

The Early Years of Music Video

BY GREG PRATO

Printed and distributed by Greg Prato
Published by Greg Prato
Book design and layout by Linda Krieg [myspace.com/lindakriegdesign]
Front cover painting by Theresa Dudley [theresadudley.com]
Book proofreading by Catherine Hensley [CLHediting.com]
Copyright © 2010, Greg Prato. All rights reserved.
First Edition, November 2010

ISBN: 978-0-578-07197-8

Contents

Introduction

"You'll never look at music the same way again" was an early ad slogan used by MTV. And throughout the early '80s, I couldn't agree more. When MTV appeared in my home in the summer of 1982 (a year after it was originally launched because Long Island, New York Cablevision didn't get MTV until then), suddenly, there was a new way to discover bands. Radio at that point had completely lost its pizzazz, and here was a new outlet that didn't seem to cater to one musical genre. Men at Work, A Flock of Seagulls, Duran Duran, Prince, Def Leppard, Quiet Riot, Madonna—the list is endless of artists who became household names thanks to MTV.

But as the famous saying goes, "All good things must come to an end," and by the mid '80s, MTV had become as regimented and predictable as radio was before it. Instead of continuing to be a reaction of sorts against the standard, it became the standard. And when MTV decided that "hair metal" was the most happening rock genre in the late '80s, it was time for me to tune out. But in all honesty, I didn't completely tune out. Instead of going to MTV to constantly discover new bands as I did during their early days, it was more about trying to catch videos from bands I already liked, rather than just soaking it all in like a sponge.

For me, the golden years of MTV were always 1981 to 1985. And I've always wondered, why hasn't anyone done a book that focused on this MTV era and spoken directly to the people (both behind the scenes and the actual artists) that were there during the channel's formative years? The wait is now over, dear readers ...

I want my early '80s MTV!

Greg Prato

p.s. Thanks to all my family and friends, as well as Nina Blackwood, Alan Hunter, Bob Pittman, and Les Garland for hanging in there during my seemingly never-ending list of questions. Also, special thanks to Richard

Galbraith, Bev Davies, and Mark Weiss for the great pictures, and to Theresa Dudley for the great front cover artwork.

    p.p.s. Questions/comments? Email me at gregprato@yahoo.com.

Cast of Characters

Jon Anderson [Yes singer]

Pete Angelus [Video director: Van Halen's "Hot for Teacher, David Lee Roth's "California Girls," etc.]

Carmine Appice [Rod Stewart, Ted Nugent, Ozzy Osbourne drummer]

Art Barnes (aka Bill Mumy) [Barnes & Barnes singer multi-instrumentalist]

Steve Barron [Video director: Michael Jackson's "Billie Jean," Dire Straits' "Money for Nothing," etc.]

Toni Basil [Solo artist, singer, dancer, dance choreographer]

Jello Biafra [Dead Kennedys singer]

Nina Blackwood [MTV VJ]

Eric Bloom [Blue Öyster Cult singer/guitarist]

Sergeant Blotto [Blotto singer]

Ricky Byrd [Joan Jett & the Blackhearts guitarist]

Gerald Casale [Devo bassist]

Ken R. Clark [PA to original VJs/manager of on-air talent]

Ken Ceizler [MTV director]

Phil Collen [Def Leppard guitarist]

Bootsy Collins [Parliament-Funkadelic bassist]

Stewart Copeland [The Police drummer]

Cy Curnin [The Fixx singer]

Chuck D [Public Enemy rapper]

Martha Davis [The Motels singer]

Paul Dean [Loverboy guitarist]

Warren DeMartini [Ratt guitarist]

John Doe [X singer/bassist]

Thomas Dolby [Solo artist, singer/keyboardist]

Geoff Downes [The Buggles, Yes, and Asia keyboardist]

Jonathan Elias [Co-writer of MTV's theme song]

Joe Elliott [Def Leppard singer]

Rik Emmett [Triumph singer/guitarist]

Lita Ford [Solo artist, singer/guitarist]

Les Garland [MTV executive]

Bob Giraldi [Video director: Michael Jackson's "Beat It," Pat Benatar's "Love is a Battlefield," etc.]

Rob Halford [Judas Priest singer]

Daryl Hall [Hall & Oates singer/keyboardist]

Greg Hawkes [The Cars keyboardist]

Colin Hay [Men at Work singer/guitarist]

Alan Hunter [MTV VJ]

Debora Iyall [Romeo Void singer]

Oran "Juice" Jones [Solo artist, singer/rapper]

Bruce Kulick [Kiss guitarist]

Geddy Lee [Rush singer/bassist]

Julian Lennon [Solo artist, singer]

George Lois [Advertising executive, creator of "I Want My MTV!" slogan]

Dave Marsh [Music journalist]

Eddie Money [Solo artist, singer]

Angelo Moore [Fishbone singer/saxophonist]

Jeff Murphy [Shoes guitarist]

John Murphy [Shoes bassist]

Aldo Nova [Solo artist, singer/guitarist]

John Oates [Hall & Oates singer/guitarist]

Wally Palmer [The Romantics singer/guitarist]

Mike Pelech [MTV cameraman]

Bob Pittman [MTV CEO]

Roger Powell [Todd Rundgren/Utopia keyboardist]

Derek Power [Stewart Copeland's manager]

Marky Ramone [The Ramones drummer]

Richie Ramone [The Ramones drummer]

Herman Rarebell [Scorpions drummer]

Mike Reno [Loverboy singer]

Stan Ridgway [Wall of Voodoo singer]

Todd Rundgren [Solo artist, singer/multi-instrumentalist]

Michael Sadler [Saga singer]

Rudy Sarzo [Ozzy Osbourne, Quiet Riot, and Whitesnake bassist]

Mike Score [A Flock of Seagulls singer/keyboardist]

Rick Springfield [Actor, solo artist, singer/guitarist]

Frank Stallone [Solo artist, singer]

Frankie Sullivan [Survivor guitarist]

Mickey Thomas [Jefferson Starship singer]

George Thorogood [Solo artist, singer/guitarist]

Glenn Tilbrook [Squeeze singer/guitarist]

Tommy Tutone [Solo artist, singer/guitarist]

Kathy Valentine [The Go-Go's bassist]

Dave Wakeling [The English Beat singer/guitarist]

Fee Waybill [The Tubes singer]

Mark Weiss [Rock photographer]
Verdine White [Earth, Wind & Fire bassist]
Ann Wilson [Heart singer]
"Weird Al" Yankovic [Solo artist, singer/accordion player]
Robin Zorn [MTV producer]

The Early '80s Music Biz

GERALD CASALE: Around that time, it was the last hurrah of the "old order." No one knew that. No one saw what was coming and how fast it would come, but that's when labels still operated with a lot of power, controlled the means of distribution of music, since music was physically distributed. Had major relationships with radio, where they actually did use payola and whores and blow. And interesting—if not nefarious—characters running these labels because they came up through the ranks ... like gangsters. And they knew music. A lot of them were quite smart and knew how to play the game. It was definitely where the artist was a "plantation worker," who had the chance of making millions of dollars, and when they did, the artist would always turn around and screw the record company that screwed them.

So it's the old paradigm, not interesting, but unfortunately, they set it up so there would be no other outcome. It's where you got an advance, you got maybe ten or twelve points on your record. From those ten or twelve points, you had to pay back everything they gave you, so that they were in the black long before you could see a penny ... and they would pretend that they were in the hole. So that was the situation. And there was plenty of money being made. It was good times, those kind of "Gordon Gekko times." We'd go into the office with a meeting with our A&R man, and at 5:00, he'd open his desk drawer, because people still sat at these old-style desks, as if they'd have typewriters, and he'd yank out a vial, and just casually while he was talking, tap out some lines, and kind of gesture, like, *"Cocktail hour, anybody?"* It was common. Everybody successful thought this was the drug of privilege. No losers did it. It wasn't addictive. It just was great [laughs]. There was a restaurant called Roy's, where you could have a booth, draw the curtain, and the waiter would bring you lines. It was an arrangement where you were paying a big tip for a "white dessert."

We made a deal with Time-Life for [the home video] *The Men Who Make the Music,* which we took all the videos we had at the time and all the interstitial bits of our in-concert films, where we had created this world where there was big media, and there was one monolithic record company run by "Rod Rooter." Rod Rooter was this nefarious record exec, who basically was an amalgam of everybody we had met and been horrified by. And the best thing about Rod Rooter was everything he said was real! I didn't make up one line of dialogue for Rod Rooter. I just took everything that we were told that we were horrified by, and put it in his mouth.

DARYL HALL: There was a new music that was happening. 1980, there was a shift in music, and the sound of the '80s started happening. It started in the late '70s, and it sort of came out of the punk scene and the R&B scene, and it coalesced into new wave music. I found it to be very "New York-centric," east coast-centric as opposed to west coast. It was the first coalescing of what we had always done, R&B music and European music ... Afrocentric and European music all put together, which we pioneered ten years before that, that was starting to come together. The Talking Heads, us, Prince, and people like that—they were part of a new music sound, a new sort of coalescing of what had gone before.

STEWART COPELAND: It all seemed very "mom and pop," compared to the way it is now. The record companies and the radio stations, even the big record companies, had a guy that you could talk to, and the chain of command would go up to a president somewhere. And certainly, in our case with A&M, it was a much smaller company, and it went up to Jerry Moss, and that was it. There is no higher authority than him. And also, with each radio station, it would go up to the owner of that station in that city, and it wouldn't go any further than that. The MD and the owner of the station— they were right there in your face. Nowadays, the record company A&M is owned by Universal, which is owned by Seagrams, which is owned by Halliburton, which is owned by the dark planet. And there is no upper-echelon that you could even get to. It's sort of like it disappears off into the haze, the hierarchy. Directives come down, and it's difficult to make requests that go up, to get permits, licenses, or decisions.

So in those days, it was much more connected. You could actually meet the people who determined your fate, both within the record company and outside the record company with the media—the papers, the stations. More recently, maybe ten years ago, I was on tour with Oysterhead, and I was saying to the guy, "Hey, let's hit the radio stations!" He gave me a pitying look. "Uh ... sure, we can go visit the radio station, they'll put us on the air, but they can't put us on the playlist. That decision is made in New York by some expert. They've legalized payola, and all these stations are owned by a corporation, and they've decided what the very narrow cast demographic for this station is, and the list comes out of New York. You can schmooze all you want." So in other words, in olden times, it was much more do-able. You could do it yourself. You could get yourself out on the road, you could get yourself to the gig, you could call up the station, you could get the guy to come down, and it would make a difference. Nowadays, I don't even know what the levers are that you pull.

ANN WILSON: That was back at the end of the era of payola, I believe. So the music business at radio was not yet quite as pigeonholed as it is today. It was beginning to be, but not quite as much. People relied really heavily on FM radio—there was only AM or FM—and they relied on FM radio to be their big crossover. The only way you could really come into the American living room was sometimes on HBO or Showtime, they would play rock videos between movies. There was the *Midnight Special* and a couple of other shows that you could be seen on. But it was all about touring. There was no other option really than those that I just mentioned to be seen.

DAVE MARSH: It was a hell of a lot healthier than it became, for the simple reason that they had developed an ability to coordinate album-making/concert-touring/radio-airplay. And that required certain kinds of coordination, and it required fairly hefty budgets. One of the budgets that everybody talks about was a payola budget. There's no doubt that came into it. I doubt if there were many "bagmen" at AOR radio even in its heyday. It just worked a different way. People might have been carrying around bags of joints! [Laughs]

PAUL DEAN: We were kind of the guinea pigs. When we came out, Columbia was trying to make a stand against the independent promotion guys at radio stations, and they said, "Screw it, we're not going to pay payola anymore. We're bigger than that. We don't need to do that." All the independent record promoters said, "Fine ... don't pay us! You can kiss Loverboy's ass goodbye." We were just on the verge of breaking through. To me, we made it in spite of that, but who knows if we hadn't have been the guinea pigs, if they had been playing ball as normal. I support their decision on trying to do that. I'm sure it's still going on now. I heard people are using American Express gift cards now for payola, because you can't trace them.

"WEIRD AL" YANKOVIC: That was in the days before peer-to-peer file-sharing sites and BitTorrents ... you know, when people *actually bought music*. But still, it was the general consensus at the time that the music industry was in a serious slump.

FEE WAYBILL: It was obviously a completely different business than it is. It was actually a viable business. This is back before even CDs, and everybody wanted to buy an album. It seems like the attention span has just gotten so much shorter now with the Internet. People used to look forward to those obscure tracks on the b-side. Now, forget about it. Nobody cares. They'll download the one tune from iTunes that they hear on the radio, and that's it. And you had a bigger window of opportunity to have a hit or pull it off. We did five albums with A&M before we ever had a hit, before we ever sold any records. So you don't have that anymore, either.

HERMAN RAREBELL: The big difference in the record industry back in the '80s was that they really backed the artists. Let's say one album didn't go as well as it should go. They'd go, "OK, make the next one. The next one will be 'big time.'" They'd be sitting there, choosing the songs with you together. It was a like big family "build up," where the record company and band built the future together. Where now, the record company is more like betting one song, if the song makes it to the charts, then the band continues. If not, "Goodbye guys ... see you." Everything has become really short-lived, so to speak. Back in those days, everything was long-term planned.

RICK SPRINGFIELD: Everything was still being done the usual way, with record promotion. You find a band, you record them, you go on the road. It was still all about selling little black pieces of plastic. It could still be a very lucrative thing. A great song could still break an artist. Although everyone was complaining at that point, it still had the spirit of what radio was founded on originally. It hadn't become the complete corporate nut-job that it is now.

EDDIE MONEY: Now, you buy everything on the Internet. But in those days, people used to go to record stores, and you'd have to have a diamond needle and a turntable that worked. They act like it's the age of the dinosaurs, but people used to buy albums. I used to work at a record store when I was a kid. In those days, I came out of Berkeley, California, which is a college town. We had a large college following—San Jose, Berkeley, Richmond, Oakland, Freemont, San Francisco. I think we were the first band to get a record deal off a VHS tape. We did a show called *Sounds of the Cities,* which is amateur night, at the Winterland. I told everybody, "They're going to film us. Everybody, get up to the front!" It was a rainy Tuesday night, and it looked like the place was packed. We did a great set and wound up getting a record deal with Columbia Records and Bill Graham Management.

TOMMY TUTONE: It seemed to be a period where they had plenty of money, and they were signing a whole bunch of bands. They would sign 40 bands, and by the time they'd get done, maybe 15 of them would get started on records, and they'd get down to ten records, but they'd only promote one or two of them. The record companies were trying to be cool. I think there was a mixture of the old guys that did it the old way and new people. I know there would be people at the company that thought they were hip but didn't know anything about the record company. The guy who wrote a great column in the college newspaper, they might make him an A&R man.

CARMINE APPICE: I was just getting ready to release my solo album, *Rockers.* Solo albums were easy to get. You released it, and you hired radio people. I had like 90 stations playing my solo record. It was a business. It was great. You were out there on tour. It was easy to get tours. In those days, I wouldn't leave LA unless I had my drums, my drum riser, the road crew, and the whole shtick.

PETE ANGELUS: Of course, it was a completely different animal, a completely different world. The early '80s, in regard to Van Halen, it was really like a free-for-all, because once that record [*Van Halen*] got out of the gate, everything started moving very quickly. I think there was much more freedom for the artists, much more creative control from the artists back then, much more money being thrown around, much less—at least it was my experience—control from the label. Whether it was video or stage production or lighting design or marketing ideas or publicity stunts we pulled off, we really had complete creative control and a blank canvas to paint on. We really didn't have anybody standing in our path with too many objections or too many ideas that contradicted the way we wanted to go. So I would say it was a completely different world from where the music business is today. And in my opinion, it was a preferable world, only because there was so much more money being put up by the labels and so much more freedom in that regard.

ALDO NOVA: It had a lot of record companies. People were actually looking for talent, rather than a fast buck like now. If you're over thirteen, you can't get a record deal. Now, if you're not Miley Cyrus or the Jonas Brothers, nobody wants to sign you. Back then, it was great. I got signed by a publishing company first that heard my stuff. Then, my demos became the record.

TONI BASIL: I wasn't signed by a record company. I was signed for a video album deal, from Europe. So I wasn't really dealing with the American record scene. I made actually seven videos before the songs were really released. I didn't make an album. They released a song, and I made a video for that. And I did it through a European company, so I had nobody breathing down my neck. They just sent me money to do videos. I did three, they loved them, I did more, and then I got a recording deal, out of those videos.

THOMAS DOLBY: The music business was very locked into radio and the *Billboard* chart. And the only way to break as an artist was to get massive radio play, and then chart, get more radio play, and so on.

GLENN TILBROOK: The music industry ... certainly, radio seemed behind the times, as far as I was concerned in America. Now, several factors played into that. I think stuff that was happening, radio wasn't really ready to pick up on. There were honorable exceptions—KSAN in San Francisco and WNEW or WPLJ in New York. Squeeze was getting airplay in some key markets. But a lot of bands that were part of the same sort of music couldn't get airplay.

DAVE WAKELING: It was as though college radio was busting to go main-stream but couldn't do it through radio because they already had its own lock on it. And it seemed that video was the vehicle. There was a lot of stuff that had been "college darlings" for a few years were now some of the first acts to get the audio/visual side down.

DEBORA IYALL: College radio was really the only way to get airplay when we first started. The first time we went on a tour, we pretty much only went to college radio stations to make visits. In San Francisco, we had two really strong college radio stations—KUSF in San Francisco and KALX in Berkeley. In L.A., there was college radio out of Long Beach that was big. I can't remember a lot of others, but I sure remember going to campuses and going down into basements to do interviews. It was kind of a great social thing for us, too. We felt a lot of kinship with the fandom with the DJs that we'd meet, because we were all discovering the same bands at the same time. We didn't hear what we were listening to on the radio.

MARKY RAMONE: In '79/'80, the music business was bloated. Stadium rock, over-indulgence, who could play the fastest guitar, who could do the fastest drum solo. Songs on an album were like eight minutes long. You saw an album, and they only had like five songs on it. It was the end of the disco era, basically.

PHIL COLLEN: I think it was nearing the end of a little cycle. You always have these cycles. When punk rock emerged in England, everything had gotten really safe and staid and a little bit boring. There was a need for a change, and there always is. Whether it's socially, politically, or whatever, music just reflects that, really. But I think you had a bit of a doldrums thing.

KATHY VALENTINE: It just seemed like the music industry was on the tail-end of realizing that the scope of music had changed. That taste had changed. There was an audience for bands in the late '70s—the Eagles, Yes, Genesis—and all that big, over-produced stuff. It seemed to me that the music industry by '81 had woken up and realized that there was a new thing going on.

JOHN DOE: There's a lot of revisionist history about punk rock. People *wanted* to have impact and wanted to make a living and be an artist. If I were to sum it up, I'd say the music industry was pretty naïve at that point. There were so many fewer bands, so many fewer media outlets. It's like the reverse of now.

STAN RIDGWAY: There were independent labels that were popping up, because there was a scene that had started in 1975/1976 with punk rock, so there were a number of people that were just enthusiasts more than business people that were putting out records, even singles. Labels like Dangerhouse in Los Angeles. Greg Shaw had his Bomp! Records thing going on. And once that grew a little larger, people tried to hook up with distributors, and I remember one of them being Greenworld Distribution. It was pretty exciting, because we were all just starting out.

JELLO BIAFRA: In the early '80s, the "business side" of the music business was at least as ugly as it is today, but the biz and the underground were a lot less friendly towards each other. There seemed to have been a pattern, if not a policy, starting in early '78, where there was a "We don't want another '60s. We will not sign any punk bands ... but *new wave* is OK. So if you want your record contract, you better put on those skinny pink ties and become a little more harmless, or you'll be pushed out to the fringe." And the beauty of that was punk and some of the related, more artsy music got more unusual and extreme in response because there was no more constraints. "Getting signed," so to speak, was no longer an option anyway, and some of us never wanted that to begin with. We'd seen how strong the independent scene had become in Great Britain, to the point where it was penetrating the mainstream on its own terms. So we thought, "Even if we don't penetrate the mainstream, why not just continue to operate on our own terms?"

WALLY PALMAR: We were just trying to find our niche, and the record company was trying to find the niche for us. And sometimes, that came from categorizing, "Where do we fit in?" They were always trying to label us at that point. Us coming out in '77, we were a punk band but didn't really fit the punk "image." We were then classified as a new wave band and then a power pop band at some point. Trying to put labels and trying to fit you in a certain category.

JOHN MURPHY: The bottom sorta fell out in mid-'79. Returns were pouring in, and it seemed record companies across the board weren't selling what they thought they had, after a flush few years during the phenomenal success of albums like *Rumours*, *Frampton Comes Alive*, and the debut Cars LP. By the time our record, *Present Tense*, came out in the fall, they were banking on two long-awaited albums to "save" the industry, *The Long Run* and *Tusk*. So the early '80s were a bit tentative for the record companies. Tastes were changing, the tried-and-true dinosaur acts had gotten a swift kick in the pants from the already-fizzled punk movement, and everything coming down the pike was labeled new wave. A lot of fresh and exciting stuff was popping up, but the companies had to figure out how to market it…I mean, what was a song like "Heart of Glass"? New wave? Disco? Rock? Bands like Talking Heads, Devo, the Ramones, and Cheap Trick were mixing it up as well. Disco music per se had finally been kicked to the curb, but the beat survived, and a rash of synth bands with extreme haircuts were prancin' around. It really felt like a period of transition.

ART BARNES: That time period is certainly not a great one. Lots of cocaine floating around the big money companies, and many vintage artists seemed to dry up then. I liked what the Stones were doing ... Bowie was interesting then. Springsteen, the Pretenders, Devo, Tom Petty and the Heartbreakers, the Police ... all that was good and musical and interesting. But there was a lot of fashion bullshit, and it was the dawn of drum machines, which, looking back, was really lame. It eliminated dynamics, created a template of sterile perfection, and made it easy for non-musical people to have dance hits. There was also a lot of disco still being made and overblown arrangements on big hits. Not my favorite era at all.

MARTHA DAVIS: But the '80s, everybody just went their own way. Nobody wanted to sound like anybody else. Nobody wanted to look like anybody else. Everybody wanted their own identity. And I think the diversity of the era is what made it so fantastic and wonderful.

JEFF MURPHY: The industry was in flux, as it always seems to be. There was a growing backlash to the success of the Knack, mainly because of the overt Beatles marketing approach, and a lot of "pop" bands were being dismissed off-hand. New wave—whatever that was—being tossed around as the latest musical term for almost any new band, regardless of musical genre. LP sales were on the decline, and the industry blamed tape copying. Bands were encouraged to be more flamboyant and flashy, neither of which we were comfortable with.

BOOTSY COLLINS: The music business was changing, a lot with the sound of it and the way it was exposed to the public. For the raw street music, it started to get more difficult to get play for your music, because it had to be more polished than previous years. But the change was good for some that fit this mode.

ORAN "JUICE" JONES: It was like the Wild West. Music was a mecca you could just come to and take your shot. It was like the "gold rush days," going to California for the gold rush, that's what the music business represented for inner-city cats, especially. The music business was like the Wild West. Cats went to the West to try and strike it rich, and they got there, and there was no blueprint, no guideline, no floor plan. They just got in and did whatever they could do and hope for the best. But a couple of cats had a little more going for them. What I think happened is when music was on the street—especially with hip-hop—a lot of cats that really could have blew up huge as far as the music was concerned, they lacked the tools necessary to take them, as far as their ability, to handle business. So that's why the mentality wasn't really geared towards handling business at that level, because cats were used to going to work or hustling or whatever.

ANGELO MOORE: It was a time of innocence. We got raped, we were taken advantage of and were just paying attention to our music, and we didn't know how to pay attention to the money. And a lot of people ripped us off, like the record company, the management, and probably the agent, too. You're an artist, and you don't know what the fuck is going on, and they're just booking you, and you're making this money, and you see all the thousands of people out there, and you come home, and the accountant says, "You ain't got no money." Somebody's fucking up somewhere. Somebody's stealing from somebody. We signed a contract with Sony/Columbia. We signed contracts, and we didn't know what the fuck we were signing. We didn't know we were selling our soul to the damn devil, all kinds of shit. Getting into contracts that last up to 15 years, and you can't use your own music. It's just the education, man. Being in the music business was, and still is, an education. "The education of hard knocks." Reading in between the lines, because we didn't read in between them lines. They've got shit in there that says, "For perpetuity," and you know what that means ... that means *forever.*

COLIN HAY: The record label that we signed to was CBS, which then became Sony-CBS in Australia. I supposed we had a mistrust of record companies, and we were very suspicious of their motivations. We were given reason for that, too. I mean, we had almost a criminally bad record deal, even for then. It wasn't as bad as the acts would have gotten in the '50s and '60s, but our deal was horrible. But it was the only game in town. It was the only label that was interested in us, and it was really one of the only labels that we were interested in.

We had supporters from CBS affiliates in different parts of the world. There was a convention around that particular time, and they played "Who Can It Be Now?" at that convention. And there was the CBS label in Switzerland, the CBS label in Israel, different countries around the world that saw the potential of our band and released the album, and it did very well. But the country that really was the hardest country to crack was the United States, because our album was actually rejected twice. The A&R department didn't want to release our album, because they didn't think there was a hit on it. Even though it was gaining all this success in different parts of the world, they couldn't see it.

We were amazed at the level of idiocy that we struck with record company executives, who were in strong positions of power. We just thought, more than anything, the music business was like an obstacle course. It had nothing to do with what we were interested in, which was to be as creative as possible and get to as many people as possible. This was an obstacle course that had to be maneuvered and negotiated.

Todd Rundgren Has an Idea ...

TODD RUNDGREN: I had a video studio at the time. It was a fascination I had, and I leveraged a lot of the initial royalties that I got from *Bat Out of Hell* [which Todd produced for Meat Loaf] to build a video studio in Bearsville, New York. We started producing videos of all kinds and allowing other people to come in. Most of it involved more conceptual or experimental things, in that we had a big green screen up, chroma key, and other effects-oriented stuff. At one point, I think we did a Utopia [video], and we had a very highly choreographed and conceptual sort of approach to it. I remember sending it to England, where the record label wanted to have some promotion, and them just being incredibly upset. It wasn't the typical kind of stuff of either singing a song or getting a bunch of pretty people around while you sang the song. Essentially, that was what the expectations were out of video.

ROGER POWELL: We started experimenting with video technology in the late '70s. Todd and I were "the technologists" of the group. He built a two-million dollar, state-of-the-art video studio. Albert Grossman was the manager of the band and Todd. He was also Bob Dylan and Janis Joplin's manager. I had a contact at EMS Studios of London, which was a company that made very early sound synthesizers, around the time that Moog was first becoming popular, and the resident genius there in London had put together a video synthesizer. A digital video synthesizer. I hooked Todd up with EMS, and he got one of the first digital synthesizers.

So then he started accumulating other equipment. He got Umatic tape recorders and cameras. First, it was in his home, but then it got so that there was too much stuff, so the thought was to start a company, Utopia Video. Then it got to the point where it was, "We should build something with a soundstage." So we had a pretty big soundstage, 43 x 41 feet, everything all done up, the latest cameras, a mini-computer controlling things, computerized lighting. So we were starting to make videos at that time. Actually, the first thing that he was going to work on was a video disc project using Tomita's *The Planets*. This was before the record companies had any inkling of what was going to happen with video, and they didn't have anybody in the record company departments who knew anything about all this or could see any market for it. So they just couldn't figure out what they were going to do with this. He pitched it to RCA, I think. RCA and MCA were the earliest video disc companies. And they were like, "We don't know what to do with this." So it remained as a demo.

But that got the whole studio thing started. And then we did a handful of videos. We were one of the first bands to do music home videos. This was negotiated by our manager, Eric Gardner. One of them I know came out on Sony. These are VHS or Beta tapes. This is '78 and '79. So then we started thinking there might be a market for these things on TV. And by the way, I'm refreshing my memory by a book by Billy James, *A Dream Goes On Forever: The Continuing Story of Todd Rundgren, Volume Two*.

TODD RUNDGREN: The irony is that my business manager at the time, Eric Gardner, after I made the investment, got the idea that we should get a satellite channel and collect all these promotional videos. And [we] came up with this idea of a VJ, as opposed to a DJ. Somebody who would sit there and just play all these videos. And we actually put a $10,000 deposit down on a transponder channel for a satellite. This is when there were very few video satellites. Video was still, in many places, being transferred over landlines. In any case, this whole idea of satellite-based televisions and more channels being available, this was happening in the industry, where every couple of months, another satellite would go up. And essentially, all of the channels on them were pre-sold. I think there were 24 channels per satellite. So we got on a wait-list to get a satellite channel.

ROGER POWELL: Todd put a deposit down in '78 for a satellite transponder that was going to be launched in '79. We were looking at hiring VJs, and we hired a guy named John Zacherley, who was a radio personality and did vampire characterizations. So we were all set with the video studio. We were going to do live concerts from there. We were going to bring people in. And because of fate, it didn't go down that way.

TODD RUNDGREN: What happened was, at a certain point, one of the satellites got lost! They sent up a satellite, and it didn't find its orbit, or the rocket had to be self-destructed or something like that. And everyone got pushed down on the list. At a certain point, we said, "This is taking too long."

ROGER POWELL: I should also mention that we were one of the first bands to make separate deals for video rights in our contracts. That's the other thing that I remember about the music business. All the record company contracts, like if you were signed up by a major, the wording was they would retain the rights to "aural and visual." And everybody thought, "Well, that just means that they own the artwork for the album covers or the promotional photos." And that ended up tying up a lot of people when the video age was ushered in. These guys went, "Uh-oh ... we could have made a separate deal for these videos."

TODD RUNDGREN: So my manager and I took a meeting with Viacom and took this idea to them, because they already had the transponder channels. And they kind of didn't—or *pretended* that they didn't—hear the idea. They didn't think it was a cool idea. And then it seemed like, within months, Viacom announced this MTV channel. So maybe when we took the meeting, they already had the idea, but they weren't ready to talk about it or something like that. But essentially, it was at a time when the idea was just ripe to happen.

Bob Pittman/Preparing for Lift-Off

BOB PITTMAN: I was born in Jackson, Mississippi. I consider my home-town Brookhaven, Mississippi, but I moved around Mississippi a bit as a kid. As a teenager, I was a radio disc jockey and wound up programming radio stations by the time I was 19 in Pittsburgh. Went to WMAQ, which was the NBC station in Chicago, when I was 20, and then they gave me the FM station. The AM was country; the FM was album rock. And then I came to New York to WNBC when I was 23. It was when American Express bought half of Warner Cable. They formed a company called Warner-Amex Satellite Entertainment Company, and they recruited me as their head of program-ming. So at the age of 25, I went off and did the Movie Channel. And the Movie Channel did very well at first, before HBO figured out what we were doing and created Cinemax, to do what we did. The company wanted to build another network, and I had done a TV show on NBC called *Album Tracks*, which ran after *Saturday Night Live*, which played a little bit of music videos, some music news. So I pitched the idea of, "Let's do a video radio station." My boss, a guy named John Lack, loved the idea, loved music, and thought it would be wonderful.

John had this vision. John was the executive vice president of the com-pany and had been a sales guy through the sales rank and had been at CBS and ran the rep firm. Really came out of that "old CBS executive mold." And unlike the CBS executives, John thought, "If this company narrow-casts, I need a radio programmer here to be my programmer, not a TV programmer." And that was a big fight. John was the executive vice presi-dent, in charge of sales, marketing, and programming. And Jack Schneider was the CEO of the company. Jack had been the president of CBS, a very big, important figure in the TV business. John wanted to hire me, and Jack didn't. So John had a great idea. There was a legendary TV programmer at CBS, Michael Dan. They had Mike Dan on retainer, so they send me to see Mike. Mike interviews me, calls Jack Schneider up, and says, "Yes, he can do the job. You should hire this kid." So off I went to put together the team, which included John [Sykes] and Tom Freston. Les [Garland] wasn't there originally—Les joined a year later—and Fred Seibert.

We were also all kids. We were all in our twenties. I think Freston may have been 30/31/32. We were out trying to convince people that we were serious. One of the hallmarks of the MTV guys was, every time we went anywhere, we wore suits. And we wore suits because nobody would take us seriously otherwise. So we said, "OK, we're going to be the guys that always dress up, so it's going to be a suit and a tie." We'd go to concerts in suits and ties. That was sort of our deal. And it came about because we were trying to be taken a little more seriously than a bunch of kids trying to start this network.

GERALD CASALE: Bill Gerber, who was working for Elliot Roberts [Devo's manager] and was our personal guy at management, he was young and gung-ho and "in the know." Plugged into all the right people. And he said, "There's this cool new thing that they're going to do, and I want you to meet these guys. I want you and Mark [Mothersbaugh] to come to lunch." I think it was at Giuseppe's in L.A. We're sitting there, and two guys walk in, completely looking like preppie, east coast businessmen. You know, navy blue suits, Brooks Brothers shirts but without the tie on, cordovon shoes. And it was Bob Pittman and John Sykes. They were very caffeinated and very up and very articulate. They started telling us about this great new thing they were going to do, but they needed our videos because they hardly had any programming. They were going to make us "huge stars" ... but they weren't going to pay us anything. They were going to expose us to millions. And it was just such a strange meeting, because they were so preppie and corporate and talking like ... *trying* to be hip about music. And what made it even stranger was, just before lunch, Bill says—and this is like a set-up, like a joke on *Saturday Night Live*—"Each one of these guys has one glass eye, so don't look at them funny. Don't blow it. *Act normal.*" Of course, once somebody tells you that, it's like when somebody has a big mole, you just stare at it. And plus, it was so bizarre that these two guys that would kind of revolutionize the business of music would each have one glass eye! It was really wild. And then we find out that Bob is the son of a Baptist preacher or something, and it got even stranger. So we were elated that so many people would get to see us.

BOB PITTMAN: It's funny the way it sort of feels like today, except instead of the Internet, it was cable. Cable had not been in the major cities. It had only been in rural America, rebroadcasting distant signals for markets that had no broadcast signals coming into it. The '70s were about beginning to build out the major cities. I think, when we launched MTV, only about 20 million U.S. households had cable. They were just beginning to build out Dallas, Houston, and towns like that. So we were right there at the beginning. Everybody was trying to figure out what it was going to be. Every cable convention had a panel about narrowcast, and Kay Koplovitz from the USA Network was on the panel, and I was on the panel. And we'd argue about, "No, no, no, it's going to be one channel for one subject, and the consumer will watch different channels and put together their own array of programming, a little bit of news, a little MTV, a little sports, or whatever they want. Instead of the network programmer programming this, the consumer will." And they would say, "No, no, no. You have to do the big rating, so everything looks like ABC, NBC, CBS." FOX didn't come along yet. So that was the tone of the period.

And, by the way, everybody was talking about every subject matter was a narrowcast channel, so it wasn't like we dreamed up music out of nowhere. As a matter of fact, there were already people doing it. There was a service called *Video Concert Hall* that was already on the air. It was sort of hard to claim credit for "We figured out music on TV." But I think what we did was figure out how to make music on TV *work*. We were more "Henry Ford" than "the inventor of the automobile." And I think one of the primary things we did was we were the first network to really make the network the identity, as opposed to the show. The second thing we did was everybody had tried to make music work on TV by making music fit into the TV form. We said, "No, no, no, that's backwards. What we're going to do is change TV to make the TV form fit music," being that TV was all about story arcs and shows, and music was about mood and emotion. So we said, "This is going to be about mood and emotion. *All attitude.*"

MIKE PELECH: I was a staff cameraman at a company called Teletronics in New York, which was just a great, high-end videotape company. The company was on the east side of New York. We purchased a film studio, called Flickers, and converted it into a video studio, with the lighting grid and air conditioning. We were probably going to keep doing television commercials and industrials, until the MTV people were looking for a studio. I forget the exact connection. I think it was a salesperson by the name of Shelly Reiss that brought them in to look at our facility. We were doing videotape from beginning to end, so the editorial process was very important also. We wound up using that studio on 33rd Street, between 10th and 11th. The studio is still there. I believe it is owned by a company called NEP. It's right behind a McDonald's, the only drive-through McDonald's in Manhattan. The neighborhood was terrible when we first moved in, a lot of prostitutes and derelict buildings. It was an awful, awful neighborhood. But it was a great little studio. We worked that whole spring and summer of '81, so probably around January of '81, we threw a lot of stuff out and got ready for all the renovations to make it a functioning cable television studio.

ROBIN ZORN: I was the first production person really hired. Sue Steinberg was the original executive producer, and she was there before me, but I was the first person on the actual production team I believe that was hired. The production team are the people that did all the VJ stuff, all the segments in the studio. I got there because I had worked with some people at ABC as an intern. One interview led to another, and I met someone at Warner-Amex, and they were setting up MTV, the Movie Channel, Nick—there were four or five channels—and said, "You'd be perfect for a PA on any of these. Which one do you want?" And I was like, "I'm 22 ... *I want to work in rock n' roll!*" That's how I got to MTV. In the very beginning, it was just a few of us in a hotel. We were at I think the Sheraton, and what I remember about the early days is it was myself and Susan Strong, who was a woman who worked in promotions, and a few other people.

KEN CEIZLER: I was initially hired as a director. I graduated from NYU Film & Television, and while there, I had a good friend, Rene Garcia. While I was out in Los Angeles looking for work, he told me that there was a new cable company starting up. They were doing something with music, and they were looking for directors. And I happened to be coming home. I was born and bred in New York. I came back and got an interview with Sue Steinberg. We hit it off, and she walked me down the hall to meet with Robert Morton, who at that time, I believe was the creative director, and we also hit if off. The next I know, I was hired, and I was one of three directors. And the three of us were responsible for the VJ segments that would be recorded at the studio.

BOB PITTMAN: The challenge we had with VJs—and I'd programmed radio a good bit—what you realized is listeners/viewers want to bond with a human being. They don't want to bond with a machine. No one says, "They've got the best jukebox down at Bob's Restaurant." But they'd say, "Wow, Z100 is fantastic!" It has a human feel to it, and that's because there are human beings on it. And what we realized is we didn't need VJs. We didn't need human beings to play the videos. We could just play the videos. But then there would be nothing to bond to. We'd look like a delivery system or a vending machine. And so the idea was to hire human beings to give it something for the consumer to bond to.

ROBIN ZORN: We were in a room, literally, going through audition tapes of the VJs. That's how early I was there. It was totally arbitrary. "That one's cute. That one's not cute." A lot of people there didn't have a lot of experience with anything. I mean, I had worked in TV, but again, I was 22 and [had] not done a lot of TV.

NINA BLACKWOOD: I was born in Massachusetts, but I grew up in Cleveland, which is "the rock n' roll capital of the world." I just had a deep love for rock n' roll and loved radio. I had a manager [Danny Sheridan]—he's still my manager, all these years later—and you can only get so far with the things I wanted to do in Cleveland. So I remember one wintry day, Danny took out a map and said, "Should we go to New York or L.A.?" He hates cold weather, so he put the push-pin into L.A. We packed up our stuff, and he went out first. He found a house, and he also had a band. So the band moved out, and then I moved out, drove cross-country in my little MG Midget that was overheating every few hundred miles. Got to L.A. and started pursuing the same things, more on the acting front. Got the agent and studied at Strasberg. My day gig—which was actually at night—was playing my harp. I played six to seven nights a week. And then my manager met a guy, Michael

Seinherdt, who was already working with video. He had tapped into this video music thing that was happening in Europe at the time, promotional films.

Michael and I came up with this television pilot, basically, that I was functioning as a host, kind of like a VJ, but it didn't have a name. Interviewing and going out on the street. The punk and new wave scene was happening out there, so we'd go down to Chinatown at Madame Wong's, and do "man on the street" things. It was really much more punk-oriented. I don't like needles, so I never got a real tattoo, but I had this fake tattoo on the side of my arm that said "BAD." I was working on that, and then I ran into two separate other producers, one was a film student at UCLA, but he wanted to do a video show. I was working with him. His name is Brad, but I don't remember his last name, and another guy, Stan Neon. He actually came up to me and said, "I'm working on this idea of a show with music." It was this TV show that was music-driven but really out there, like had me playing harp and then hitting me in the face with a pie and working with visual artists.

So I was working on those three things, and I always read *Billboard* and the trades. One morning, I was having breakfast, reading the trades, and I saw this article about this 24-hour video music channel that was looking for hosts that they were calling "video jockeys." And I go, "Oh my God, that's what I'm doing!" I wanted to stand out, so I'm getting my 8 x 10 and my bio together, and my manager walks by and sees me. I had these crayons out. You know, trying to make it look real "punk." [Laughs] And I remember him saying to me, "You know Nina, there's such a thing called 'color Xerox'." So he doctored up the picture. It was cool. Sent that and hadn't heard from them ... then I got a call, and they were holding auditions. People from New York were coming to L.A.

I went down dressed head-to-toe black in L.A. I remember *sweating*. Did the first audition and thought it went well. They came back out and did another audition, this time with a mock interview, and I thought it went well. And then I didn't hear from them for a while. I'm not cocky, and I don't ever assume that I got a job or deserve to get a job, but for some reason, for this one I kept saying, "How many other people in this country at this period of time are even working on these projects?" Because, really, it was not even a glimmer in most peoples' eye—video music. So I said, "If they don't hire someone like me ... who are they going to hire?" And I don't mean that in an egotistical way. It was just like, *I was already doing it.* And sure enough, I got a call, and they said, "We want to fly you to New York and meet with Bob Pittman. We think we want to hire you." They said they were going to hire me, but the big thing was, "You have to move to New York." I didn't know that. I thought, "Satellite communication, you can do it from L.A." Moved to New York.

ROBIN ZORN: Alan's audition was really funny, because nobody there thought he would get hired. He wasn't great. He was funny and really cute, but he just didn't seem to really have it together and didn't seem really "rock n' roll-ish."

ALAN HUNTER: I'm a southern boy, born in 1957. I was born and raised in Birmingham, Alabama, and went to college in Jackson, Mississippi, at a place called Millsaps College, a fine liberal arts school. I got a degree in psychology and had every intention of becoming a psychologist, probably a counselor of some sort. But did a lot of theater, so after I got out of school, I did a year of theater in Birmingham. After that year [1980], I went to New York. I became a bartender and a waiter and acted in some stuff. It was less than a year that I got the job at MTV. The right place, right time. Because I went to school in Millsaps, most every state has some sort of summer picnic up in New York City, and they'll take over the park for a day and scare everybody. Obviously, the Confederate flag waving at the Mississippi picnic was scaring everybody else in the park! So I was at what was called "The Way Up North Mississippi Picnic," hanging out in my shorts, wondering what my career was going to be. And Bob Pittman is a fellow Mississippian. He just happened to be there, and we bumped into each other. I told him I was a lonely actor, and he said he was starting this new cable channel soon. I had no idea what he was talking about. But two or three weeks later, I got a call from the executive producer, who said, "Bob bumped into you. Maybe you should come and audition." It was total serendipity up to a point. If I wasn't in New York City, I wouldn't have bumped into the right people. That was the summer of 1981, I think May or June. And MTV started August 1, so I got hired the first week of July. I had three weeks to get my act together before we started on the air.

MIKE PELECH: Alan was in a music video, "Fashion," by David Bowie.

ALAN HUNTER: [Before joining MTV] I was an actor making the rounds, putting my headshots in every casting director's hands. I did a couple of little small bits in movies. I was in the movie *Annie*. My kids to this day love watching the DVD and catching me on three frames. I did a couple of way-Off Broadway shows, and I went to a casting session for a David Bowie video. They put me in a line-up in a cattle call, and they called a couple of weeks later and said, "You're in the video. Can you dance?" I told them I was a pretty good dancer, and I was one of the six featured dancers in that video. So I was nothing more than a face. I did get paid 50 bucks a day, and I got to meet David Bowie. It was totally worth it. But that was only about three months prior to me getting the job at MTV. Nobody really knew what video music was all about. It played on *Midnight Special*. That's where I got to see it for the first time.

BOB PITTMAN: We set about trying to find a somewhat representative group of people. Some people were very serious about music. JJ had been recommended by the manager of Queen, Jim Beach, who said, "Man, this guy does the best interviews. He's the most solid guy. He's a DJ in L.A." Mark Goodman had been on WPLJ in New York, which was much more mainstream album rock, but had the qualifications.

MIKE PELECH: Mark and JJ were the most knowledgeable. Both of them had a lot of experience in FM radio. Between the two of them, they almost had an encyclopedic knowledge of music. They would know the a-side, the b-side, the whole history of albums, what groups people had come from. [The others] did not have that background, so they had to rely more on the producers to give them information. But you could talk to JJ *for hours*. He just knew so much about the groups, knew so many of the groups personally. He was very good friends with Rod Stewart and Robert Plant. Those were his two closest buds. And I know he was very close with Aerosmith. They had even mentioned that he had broken them in Boston and that they were very indebted to his support. Mark at that time was married to Carol Miller, who was a radio celebrity also from WPLJ. So the two of them were a real dynamo couple. I would say that was the brain-trust of the music information, those guys.

ROBIN ZORN: JJ was like "the big dad." JJ took care of everybody, had a big smile for you, was in on everybody's secrets. JJ knew everything. JJ walked around with a long fur coat. JJ was larger than life, and his smile would knock you out. The fact that he was on MTV really established us, because everybody—especially on the west coast—knew who JJ Jackson was.

MIKE PELECH: JJ had the most spectacular radio voice and the most infectious laugh. I think everybody mentions that when they speak about JJ, what a wonderful person he was. We would just laugh with him doing stupid stuff.

ROBIN ZORN: And Mark was the same thing for New York. Mark was on WPLJ and a pretty established DJ. And knew a lot about rock n' roll but hadn't done as many interviews as JJ, I don't believe. But Mark was a good rock n' roller. Alan was this country guy. He just didn't seem to know much about rock n' roll, and he'd mispronounce names all the time. He came to the interview wearing a flannel shirt. He looked really cute, but I remember me and Liz were on the floor that day, looked at each other, and said, "No way is he getting hired." Alan became one of my closest friends. Alan was with me my first date with my husband. Alan and his wife came, because I didn't want to go by myself. Nina was this ditzy/sexy blonde, you never knew what was going to come out of her mouth. She was smiley ... but ditzy. Really, really ditzy. Had this effervescent, sexy personality all at the same time. That was definitely a draw, and we knew was going to be a draw for the teenaged boys out there.

NINA BLACKWOOD: They hired me first, then Mark, and [then] Meg Griffin. Meg Griffin decided she didn't want to do TV. She wanted to stay with radio.

ROBIN ZORN: I worked with Meg Griffin, before we went on the air. My recollection of this was that Meg thought she would have more autonomy and that she would be able to pick videos. Not that they do it anymore on the radio, but they used to. When she found out there was a list that was preordained, I don't think it was along her liking.

NINA BLACKWOOD: Martha was the last one. They hired Martha to replace Meg.

BOB PITTMAN: Martha Quinn was the last one, on the last day of auditions. I programmed WNBC in New York, and my assistant called me up, and said, "Hey, we got this intern over here who's really good and really talented. You ought to interview her for that thing you're doing." And I'm going, "Shit, OK, as a favor, if she can get there at 5:00, we can put her on tape." The next day, the guys came in and go, "Wow, that girl you sent was great. A lot of warmth, a lot of energy." So they brought me the tape and that was the way she got in. They all got in a little different way.

ROBIN ZORN: Martha was just this sweet, preppie, little girl. If you look at some of the haircuts ... she was there for the preppie contingent, people that weren't stoned all the time. And Martha was really excited about rock n' roll. *Loved* David Lee Roth. She had such a crush on him.

ALAN HUNTER: In general, I think everybody was pretty down to earth. I think there was a "gee whiz" quality for all of us, maybe more severe for me. JJ and Mark had been in the music business and had some notoriety before that, but for me, I was fairly awe-struck.

ROBIN ZORN: Everybody was pigeonholed. Like, Nina was the ditzy blonde/sex symbol, Martha was this preppie little girl, Alan was the sweet southern guy, and Mark and JJ were the rock n' rollers.

MIKE PELECH: Nina would get flustered, and then she would start bobbing her head. But she's a very endearing and engaging person. She's a good friend. Martha, also, is just a lovely person. One of my codewords to JJ when he needed some make-up, I'd say, "Can someone please get Mr. Jackson's bags?" That meant the bags under his eyes were needing a touch-up of make-up. We would just have things that we do with the VJs to either help them or annoy them or get them to laugh. It was a nice rapport with them.

NINA BLACKWOOD: [JJ] was the guy that gave us the tip, "If you have bags under your eyes, Preparation H works really well."

ROBIN ZORN: I would say Alan and Martha were probably on the outs at the beginning. They didn't have any background in rock n' roll. So not to say that Mark and JJ felt superior to them, but I think there was a little bit of, "This is a legitimate rock n' roll venture, and I want to be a legitimate rock n' roll guy ... *why are they here?*"

ALAN HUNTER: Mark and I didn't get along very well in the beginning. He was snobbish to me, and he'll admit that. He thought I was an actor, and he didn't like that I didn't have any expertise in the music business. And he thought that I was a joker ... which I kind of was. I relied on comedy, not musical knowledge. Nina and I got along the best, because she was an actress. She and I relate on that level. And she, in fact, would give me advice after my shift. My first three/four/five months were *horrible*. I just wasn't getting in the swing of it at all. And she would take me aside and give me some tips on how to relax and just be me. So I appreciated that.

Martha and I were ... I don't know. Everybody thought Martha and I had a thing going. And that did not make my first wife happy. She wasn't happy because I wasn't wearing my wedding ring the first little while because I thought this was "a part" I was playing. Until she said, "Oh no, you're part is *you're married!*" So, I had a little push-pull between the wife and the producers of MTV, who were begging me to keep it off. So Martha and I got along very well. I think, after a time, it became that she and I were going to be kind of "the kids next door" of the MTV world.

BOB PITTMAN: I think they were much more "middle America" than MTV is today.

ROBIN ZORN: Then we met everybody on the staff, and more people got hired—producers, directors, associate producers—and I think I was there less than a few weeks before I was moved from a PA to associate producer, because I could write. I was on the first team working with the VJs, and what we did was write the news break segments. I wrote interviews for the VJs, and we were on the floor of the studio producing the VJ segments.

NINA BLACKWOOD: The launch was scheduled for August 1, and they flew me in the fifth of July. So those weeks leading up to the launch were spent in rehearsal, working at the studio, from early in the morning until midnight at night. Working out the bugs with the technical aspect, working with the set. Figuring out what we were actually going to do. So it was a lot of preparation, rehearsal.

KEN CEIZLER: This was the invention of the term "non-linear television," so it wasn't programs and half-hour breaks. We were trying to break down what the channel would look like for an hour and where the VJ segments were going to be and what the role of the VJ segments were going to be. So there was a lot of discussion about that role that they had, as far as from my end, because I was working with the VJs in the studio, as far as what they were going to do.

And since we did the VJ breaks, it wasn't live. They were all integrated later in Smithtown. It was called NOC, Network Operations Center. What we were doing was we were creating the VJ segments kind of without context. The VJs worked with associate producers on the floor that would instruct them what music they were about to come out of, and they had to do a great job of pretending like they just listened to the music and saw what you did. In the same regard, they would have to do these lead-ins and lead-outs. That was certainly a learning curve, and it was always interesting to see when it was finally put together how much it worked.

MIKE PELECH: The studio was a former film stage. Film stages don't have the technological backbone of a television studio. It was pretty much just a pipe grid for hanging lights, with a hard cyc [cyclorama] and lights on stands. To turn it into a television studio meant that the [lighting grid] had to be electrified. We had to install a lot of air conditioning and build a control room with a switcher and video tape machines. The technical infrastructure was pretty extensive. And it was a real job to finish the work on schedule, because August 1 was just not enough time.

It might have been six months to turn the studio around. You would just walk in one day, and people were walking around. The pipe grid is on the floor, and there are people with ladders and equipment installing stuff. It was a madhouse. But we finally got it together, and we started to do some rehearsals. The schedule for taping would be Monday through Friday, and by the end of Friday, we had enough footage for the weekend, so that all that footage went out to the uplink, and the videos were integrated into the studio footage. By Monday morning, we were probably about a half a day ahead. So what we were shooting Monday morning would probably air Monday evening. Our end of it was pretty much 9:00-7:00 every day. It was fairly long days.

ALAN HUNTER: It was crazy. The preparation was insane. I was immediately thrown into a world that I did not know anything about. I was going to be an actor, for God's sake, and here I was, being asked to be a television host. I guess I fit the demographic bill. They had the Jewish guy, the blonde vamp, the girl next door, and the black guy, and I was "middle America," I suppose. But it was kind of like cramming for a test in college. I had three-ring binders. I was looking through all the bands that existed in the video catalog at the time. I was totally into music, but I liked a lot of jazz. I was a Joni Mitchell and James Taylor fan, loved the Who and the Stones, but I didn't know a lot about bands like Def Leppard. So I really had to "go to school."

We did tons of rehearsals. They were building the set. They were putting new potted plants on and taking them off. It was total chaos, because no one had ever done this before, and the entire crew, except for the tech guys who ran the cameras and did the stage managing, they had done television before. But in terms of the producers, the floor producers, and the content people, they were all throwing this stuff against the wall for months prior to the launch, trying to really figure out what was going to happen on day one. What was the format? What was going to happen? Were we going to just sit and read news all day? They didn't even know what the name of it was, up until a couple of days before we went on air. It was called "The Music Channel." No one had said "MTV," right up until the last moment.

BOB PITTMAN: The original idea was it was going to be "TV1." Not very sexy, but the idea of TV1 was it was a different kind of TV. So we tried, and we couldn't clear the name. There was some production company called TV1. But we could clear "TVM." So it was going to be TVM, and we sort of began to work on that a little bit. We were in a meeting, and we always did this "group brainstorming," and the driest, most research-oriented, least creative guy in the bunch, a guy named Steve Casey, who programmed the music, said in a very dry way, "How about *MTV* ... doesn't that sound better?" Everybody goes, "Yeah, MTV. That sounds better!" So it went from TVM to MTV, based on Steve Casey.

MTV's Theme Song/Launch of MTV

JONATHAN ELIAS: My background—I was more of [a] classical composer, still am. I have one foot in classical music and one foot in pop. At that point, I was working with John Barry, who was the James Bond composer, as an arranger and orchestrator with him, doing synthesizer/orchestration things. And I had also done a bunch of movie trailers, the original *Alien* trailer. So I had started doing a few things in the city. My brother [Scott Elias], we had just started doing some advertising music, too, some commercials. I had done a bunch of stuff for *Sesame Street* and a few logos. Somehow, he met Fred Seibert and Alan Goodman, and they were doing some of the marketing stuff [for MTV], the promo materials and whatnot.

So it was such a small project at the time, because none of us really believed it was going to happen. Who believed that you could actually do something where you were going to see videos all day and night, 24 hours a day? I think that was about the only 24-hour thing going on then, other than CNN. I had a loft, and it was a seven-story walk up, because our elevator was out, and having Fred and Alan come up to the loft was always a pain in the butt for them. [Laughs]

There were a bunch of different pieces we did for them, and eventually, they settled on this one. They ran a bunch of these different interstitial commercial logos for MTV. It was everything from the original moon landing, which is the one they ended up playing the most, obviously, but we must have done eight or ten that were running at the time. It was funny. I think it was my college roommate who played guitar. And the drummer was an old friend of mine, too. This guy, Alex, he's a microbiologist now. I don't even remember Alex's last name. And the guitarist was Ray Foote, another old friend. It was just like you put together your friends back then. I don't even remember who played bass. It was all kind of "low tech." Everything was low tech then.

BOB PITTMAN: We were trying to figure out what icon we were going to use to say, "This is a change in TV." So we had this idea that we were going to use the words, "One small step for man, one giant leap for mankind." Those were Neil Armstrong's words, so we sent a letter to Neil Armstrong, saying, "We're going to use this ... unless you tell us no." Sort of negative option. We had the video already cut. Every hour, it's supposed to say, "One small step for man, one giant leap for mankind" [then sings top-of-hour music]. Literally, the week before, we get a letter from him, saying, "No, you can't use it." Then we have the decision, do we have to scrap this whole iconography? And Fred Seibert convinced ourselves that it was OK to be more abstract, that we didn't have to *say* it. We could just still have the video there and the guy jumping around on the moon. We didn't have a face. You couldn't see a face, so we didn't have to worry about name and likeness. And that's the way we went. But the idea was to use the whole space motif, which was very hot at the time. You know, the shuttle was just coming out. To really say, "We're new, different, cutting edge, etc."

JONATHAN ELIAS: That was written exclusively for the MTV theme. There were a lot of things John [Petersen] and I were writing for the MTV theme at the time. Some I wrote on my own, and some I wrote with him. They were ten, twelve-second small pieces. So for a couple of weeks, we were just writing a bunch of things, throwing them against the wall. This was something that was pre-scored. We hadn't gotten the film of the moon landing yet. And frankly, I wouldn't have known how to synch it up back then, anyway. I didn't even have a 24-track back then. I think I was working off of a half-inch TASCAM deck. We went into this cheap little studio with a couple of friends and just knocked out a bunch of these things. They weren't polished studio players ... *we* weren't polished studio players, John and I.

We didn't make enough money to pay anyone. All the guys got 50 bucks or 100 bucks to play it. There was no money involved in this, because none of us thought it was going to amount to anything. I think in those days, they were paying a thousand dollars a logo. You get a writer's share [each time the song is played], which has been extremely lucrative over the years. It was funny getting a thousand dollars ... and becoming an icon. But it gave you instant credibility in the commercial market, which is what I went on to do, and becoming a rock producer. One of the bands I produced later was Yes, who were old burnouts, even *they* knew the MTV stuff. No one knew it would become an icon, especially me. I think we all were like, "Wow, a thousand dollars!" In those days, a bunch of us were living in a loft in Manhattan on 17th Street, between Fifth Avenue and Broadway, which was the costume jewelry district. It was no man's land when I was there, '80/'81. It was unexpected, and like a lot of things you do in your career, some things stick, and some don't.

BOB PITTMAN: If you go back to the early promos, it was all about attitude. "Don't watch that. *Watch this!*" It was all sort of parodying other TV and MTV. Visually, the guy I hired to be the head of the on-air look was Fred Seibert, who I hired from radio. And one of Fred's great contributions was, before MTV, everybody cut their video first, and then they rolled music under it. Fred and his guys cut the audio track first and then cut the video to the beat of the music. Now, that would seem pretty basic today, but believe it or not, it wasn't back then.

Back then, everyone was doing the sort of *Star Wars* logos—big chrome logos coming out of a star-field, starting small and becoming big—and we didn't have the money to do any of that. So Fred was the one who said, "Instead of trying to do a cheap version of what everybody else does, why don't we come up with a whole new style that we can do cheaply, but because there is no point of reference, we'll never look cheap. *We'll look innovative.*" And, indeed, we were. We broke all the rules at the time of design—logos can't change, they have to stay in the same position, the colors can't mutate. And we changed the logo color all the time, moved the logo all the time. It was animated. Completely new approach, and people picked up on that as an approach.

ALAN HUNTER: When it came time for the actual launch, we all got into a bus in Manhattan—because they didn't have it in Manhattan—and we had to go out to a little restaurant/bar out in New Jersey [The Loft] to watch the actual kick-off. So we got in this bus, we got totted out there, [and] there were hundreds of MTV employers and family members. My heart racing a mile a minute. We had all been drinking pretty heavily the whole night long, and we had to wait until 12:01/midnight. And at that point, the rocket blasted off, and it was drop-dead silence in the room. The guy said, "Ladies and gentlemen, this is rock n' roll," or whatever the line was. The rocket blasted off.

The funny thing was the order we were to appear on camera was I think Mark, Nina, JJ, Martha, and then me. I was supposed to be the last guy. But the people out at the technical center in Long Island that do the uploading of all the video footage—that literally load the tapes into the machines—they loaded the tapes backwards, so *I* was the first one to come on! That's the trivia question, "Who was the first VJ on MTV?" That would be me, but it was supposed to be Mark Goodman. So after the Buggles came on [the first-ever video played on MTV was the Buggles' "Video Killed the Radio Star"], we all just looked at each other and said, *"Holy shit!* This might just get big ... if we can last." Of course, the next day, we all had to get to work. So that was pretty painful the next day, I'll tell ya.

GEOFF DOWNES: We were told that "Video Killed the Radio Star" was used as the "launch track." I think it was more in hindsight. It was just something that they selected at the time. The impact started to progress as time went by. But nobody knew that this MTV channel was going to be quite significant.

NINA BLACKWOOD: It wasn't just the VJs. It was everybody that worked on MTV. The office people, the suits, the crew. And then the time came—that infamous rocket—that still gives me butterflies in my stomach. When that rocket went off, we were just ... I've never experienced everything like that. It was like a collective baby being born. There were tears, hugs, screaming, just such amazing energy. It was just an "Oh my God ... it's real!" feeling.

BOB PITTMAN: We click on ... *and it's a disaster.* All the VJ breaks were on a tape, a reel-to-reel, and all the songs were on a cartridge. And normally, they did automation the other way. We set it up backwards, and everything went wrong. One of the problems was no one had done "stereo TV" before. We had a stereo system rigged up, where we would broadcast the stereo system over an FM frequency, then you could get a splitter on your cable, hook it up to your stereo system, and get the audio in stereo. It seemed somewhat simple at the time, very complicated today.

Unfortunately, if you reverse the polarity of positive/negative, negative/positive in the wrong way, in mono, you can't hear it. And a couple of the production houses that we used had reverse polarities. So you'd look at something, and it would be silent. And you don't know what it is initially. It takes you a while to diagnose this problem. So every third or fourth little ID, we had no audio on it. We had a commercial break where we gave it to the local affiliate, but if they didn't have something, we ran music. Well, somebody had flipped the switch the wrong way, so if the local guy didn't have a commercial, it was silent. Everybody else was enjoying the party. I was on the phone having a heart attack, talking to the network operations in Smithtown, Long Island, trying to work all these problems out. I think I didn't sleep for about 48 hours after launch, before we got it settled down. I wished I had a couple of the drinks everybody else had had.

KEN CEIZLER: The one distinction that I brag about is that the first five hours of the VJs on the channel I directed. That's something that I try to get people to think I'm important.

ROBIN ZORN: But it was long hours and really crazy, crazy things that went on in that studio, with the people and the personalities. We were just making up things up as we went along ... and it was great. I mean, I was on the air once, put into a garbage pail. There's a segment with Nina Blackwood going, "Oh my God, Robin's in the garbage pail!" Because the guys just threw me in a garbage pail, and that went on the air. At the time, nobody does that. It was kind of reality before reality really was, I guess, because it was how we were living and what we were doing.

KEN CEIZLER: It wasn't like there was a lot of oversight in those early days. And there was a lot of fun, over-the-top, non-sequitur stuff that was going on down on the stage. We were having a great time. It was only until the channel started to get into Manhattan, where the executives could see what we were doing, that they started to go, "Wait a second ... you guys have got to cut that out." Certainly the first six months—before we got into Manhattan—it was pretty much a playground.

JONATHAN ELIAS: I always laughed about the fact that we were doing this stuff, and they didn't even have cable run to our building. It took a while to get cable in New York.

BOB PITTMAN: The reality was we launched into maybe a couple of million homes. Tulsa, Oklahoma, was one of our big markets.

ROBIN ZORN: There was an old guy named Leo who worked at Teletronics, and he was the "prop guy." He was great. He would appear on camera, handing props to the VJs. That was the kind of thing we would do. *The prop guy* was on the air. Things like that are done now, weren't done then. It was loosey-goosey. Whatever happens, happens. We would just go with it. We didn't re-do things. If they really made a bad mistake, maybe we'd re-do it. But often, we didn't. And that's why things went out on the air mispronounced. You'd think, "Oh my God, we can't have a VJ mispronouncing a name." But we did.

ALAN HUNTER: I was a huge Bowie fan, and as I said, I was in his video. When I was introducing Bowie, I said "Bough-wee" one time. The producers just thought, "Oh God ... *how did we hire this guy?*" I was fairly nervous the whole first year of MTV, no doubt. Certainly, that's why I liked interviewing the younger bands, because who were they, for God's sakes? At some point, a year or two into MTV, we were more known than these bands were, so that gave you a little bit of confidence. You were introducing *them*, which happens. Ryan Seacrest interviews everybody in the world, but he's like Dick Clark now. He's more well-known than these new bands. But it's weird. Bono is maybe three years younger than I am. And when I interviewed him, it was like '82. I think, "Wow, *how young that guy was.*"

ROBIN ZORN: One time we were on the air, and JJ had to describe why sometimes there were outages. Cable was really new then, so he was trying to explain how the Earth's rotation and the sun was blocking why cable couldn't come. He had a couple of us on camera. I was supposed to be "the sun" or "Earth." I can't remember which, but he would walk us around in circles. Basically, it was like a grade-school demonstration. Nobody was doing that kind of stuff on TV, and we were doing that. The first time that we did a contest, we had names in a thing, and I was out there with JJ, just sticking our hands in there, pulling names out. "I don't like this name. Let's pick another one." The feeling was we were just a bunch of kids making this stuff up as we went along. It was definitely TV production value, but it was just fun. Pretty much that was the definition of everything we did there. All of us went to concerts together. We hung out together.

BOB PITTMAN: We did TV a different way. The big fight was the guys who had done TV said, "Oh no, we can't do that. We have to rehearse. They have to stand on this mark." We'd go, "Why do they have to stand on a mark?" "Because there may be a shadow in their face." "We don't care if there's a shadow in their face!" So again, you're changing the production of how it was done. The hallmark was it was cheap. We decided we didn't want to own any facilities, because the equipment would change so quickly that we'd be stuck with old equipment, and we'd have to run that instead of being able to change studios for whoever had the newest equipment that could do cool effects for us.

NINA BLACKWOOD: We didn't have a whole lot of videos. I think the number was about 300. I seem to remember around that number. Which, when you're running a 24-hour video channel, you burn through those pretty quickly. I remember a lot of Rod Stewart, Pat Benatar, the Buggles, Nick Lowe, Carlene Carter, Aldo Nova, Iron Maiden, Lena Lovich. [Lovich] was one of the first people I ever saw a video of, and I just loved her. I think we were playing Blondie at the beginning, "Heart of Glass." When we play one of the songs that we played back then on Sirius, it just all comes flooding back.

ALAN HUNTER: It was a pretty limited library. When you have to include the Charlie Daniels Band, you know you're hurting. The majority was Rod Stewart. My favorites were David Bowie videos—"Fashion," "Ashes to Ashes"—because his were so dreamy and hallucinogenic. We had a lot of Styx, Journey, REO Speedwagon. The early days of video were pretty much a literal translation to song. Rod was standing in the rain next to a light pole, smoking a cigarette, thinking about his honey, y'know? Pretty right on the nose. I think of Barnes & Barnes' "Fish Heads," those type of videos. But it was really pretty lame.

CARMINE APPICE: Rod [Stewart] definitely had a good time with the videos. We all had a good time with the videos. We made *a lot* of videos. He knew the value of them at the time.

ALAN HUNTER: The other interesting thing about the channel that a lot people didn't understand is we didn't have any commercials the first year. MTV was literally not selling any ad space, because no one wanted to buy. The filler was stock footage of astronauts floating in space. And people thought that was great. "Wow, no commercials, and this interstitial material of cool graphics and just space people." And then about a year into it, when we started selling ads, people would come up to us in the streets and say, "MTV is selling out." I'm just like, "No ... they're just trying to make my salary!"

I don't know what the others were making. I won't quote a figure, but my only criteria for a good job was to get as much money as a good chorus boy makes on Broadway. That was my dream. I lived in an apartment on 55th and Broadway. I used to look out down Broadway and dream about being on Broadway some day. I wanted to be in musical theater. If I could just make 550 bucks a week, which was the going union rate for an equity actor, that would be just great. If I could make that, I'm home free. I made *better* than that. But I was not getting rich on MTV for the first year or two. I renegotiated my contract with them a year into it. We extended things, and I started doing a lot better. But I'll tell you ... we were like the early sports stars. We played hard, we got a lot of fame, and we started the whole business of MTV. But we did not enjoy huge salaries.

BOB PITTMAN: The other issue was trying to get the record companies to keep producing music videos. If you remember, in 1981, the record industry was in a slump. It was the first time in many years they'd got in the red ink, and one of the problems was the radio playlist had been so tight that they couldn't get new music exposed, and they were heavily dependent upon radio. So we went to them and said, "Look, *do MTV.*" We had to fight some of the record companies. MCA and I think PolyGram didn't give us their videos at first. They wanted to be paid for them. So we launched without them. A&M gave us their videos, and a guy named Gil Friesen, who's a good pal, said, "I don't know if this is going to work or not, but you've been really good to me, and you've broken a lot of records in radio, so I'll give you my videos." And we had other people say, "Yes, absolutely. We believe in it."

The record industry was churning over so much red ink. One of the obvious areas to cut back in the budget was music videos. And if they did that, we were going to be dead. So the risk we took was, we'll launch with 200 videos. It ain't enough to have a network, but if we work, the record companies will make more videos. If we don't work, it doesn't matter. We don't work. We took that gamble. So a lot of the fall was trying to prove that we were working. And one of the reasons we pushed the launch August 1 is we needed to be on the air before the budget sessions went on at the record companies, and they made a decision to cut the videos out of the budget. As soon as we launched, we ran in *Billboard* and *Radio & Records*. We'd do this "Case Study #1." And it was actually just stories. "Tulsa, Oklahoma: MTV Launches." We'd quote three or four record stores that had some records by the Tubes that weren't being played on the radio, sitting around, gathering dust. Suddenly, they blew off the shelves. So it was this music that only MTV was playing was selling.

The reality is we didn't have much quantity, but we were able to pick locations where it was beginning to create the understanding that we did sell records. I think the influence worked. Record companies kept it in their budget, and they produced more videos. In the early days, we begged everybody to make a video. In five years, there was more videos than we could play. You had the opposite problem. How do you tell people no? But in the early days, we were scrounging for almost every video we could get. I remember playing Andrew Gold and going, "Whew, boy, we've reached the bottom of the barrel."

ALAN HUNTER: Everybody else had dropped whatever job they had, but I kept my bartending job a month or two into the gig. I literally went and taped the show during the day, and then I'd go to a place called the Magic Pan—it was on 57th and Sixth Avenue—and I had a nighttime bartending job. I didn't let go of it in the beginning. I don't know why. I just thought, "We'll see how this MTV thing works out." So about maybe two months into it, I was mixing a daiquiri, and this guy was sitting at the bar, two sheets to the wind, looking at me. He said, *"You look familiar,"* and it still didn't dawn on me. He said, "Aren't you 'Mark somebody,' on this music channel?" And it dawned on me that he was talking about the gig I was doing during the day. I corrected him, and said, "No, *I'm Alan Hunter.*" Pretty much, the next day or two, I put my notice in and quit the job, because I thought, "I don't want to be here making drinks while people are checking me out." It was kind of hard to let go of that gig. I was going to be an actor, if not a TV host, so for me, I took a diversion in my career. I think I made the right choice.

GEORGE THOROGOOD: We did a rock n' roll Christmas video with John Lee Hooker, which they put on ["Rock and Roll Christmas"] exclusively for MTV. I remember talking to some of the MTV people, saying, "We've got this rock n' roll video we made about Christmas, and we want to get it on." And they said, "Sure!" They hired Dave Edmunds to produce the single, and then we made the video right there in New York at the MTV studio. It was real fun to be part of that whole time.

ALAN HUNTER: Collectively, the live New Year's Eve show was the most nerve-racking. Four hours. But ultimately, the most satisfying. I was much better live than on the pre-taped stuff. And the audience didn't know better. They thought we were all sitting there 24/7, anyway.

KATHY VALENTINE: What stands out a lot to me is MTV used to throw these big parties, New Year's parties. It was a big deal. For a few years, it was just the highlight of the year. They were amazing, great parties. There was one in New York that was really cool. I remember being there with John Belushi. I just remember getting a message at my hotel [from Belushi]—"Are we on for tonight?"—and going together.

ROBIN ZORN: My favorite New Year's of my entire life was the first New Year's concert. I was an associate producer in the truck, and I remember, at one point, people said, "Robin, go out there and see who's there." It was the first time we did a New Year's show. We didn't know if we would get anybody there. And I remember I walked outside, and John Belushi was just stoned out of his mind, sitting at a table with his head on the table. I was all excited, like, *"John Belushi's here!"* And, of course, he was stoned, and we couldn't even get him on camera.

Also about that first New Year's show, I was responsible for keeping us on track time-wise. We had to hit four midnights. The first midnight was right on, the second midnight was a little off, and the third and fourth we weren't even close to being midnight. Again, it was MTV, so we just had the VJs announce that it was midnight. That was very typical for us. We were way off, and yet, we were on the air going, "Yeah, Happy New Year, it's midnight out there on the west coast," and meanwhile, it wasn't midnight. We just flew by the seat of our pants.

MIKE PELECH: I was at the first New Year's Eve party, but I wasn't working. I was a civilian. And it was great. It was crazy. But just to give you an idea of how sparse it was for content, I think it was Jeff Bolton who was directing, and Chris Kelly, the stage manager, came running over to me on the dance floor, and said, "We need to fill a minute, so they want to interview you and want to ask what it's like to be a 'rock n' roll cameraman.'" That's how desperate everybody was for filler! They rolled the camera in, and they were just about to interview me ... and he wound up doing something else.

ROBIN ZORN: It was Karla Bonoff, David Johansen, and I think Bow Wow Wow. The New Year's Eve was really great but kind of hokey. We pre-recorded the opening, with fireworks in the background, and the VJs had to wear these really goofy tuxedos—the guys did—and they hated that. They were different colors. It was almost a high school prom. We were on the air live, they were talking to each other, and it was hard to hear, but it was great. It was really fun. We had cameras walking through the audience, and I remember a camera shot underneath someone's skirt, and the girl didn't have any underwear on. And I remember someone going, "Hey, that's my girl-friend. Get the camera off there!" We definitely got a crotch shot that should not have made air.

ALAN HUNTER: MTV filled a huge void. And it was unlike all those other programs. It was on as people's "friendly company," at all hours of the night, for college dorms or housewives in the morning. That was people's "feel-good hub."

Initial Impressions

GERALD CASALE: When it kicked in, it was like the beta model. People were writing it up and mentioning it, but nobody knew what to think about it yet. And they played the same ten videos all day long, because they had like four from us, and they were playing Rod Stewart videos, David Bowie's "Ashes to Ashes," "Video Killed the Radio Star," "Turning Japanese," and a few others. And it just kept rotating all day with these VJs, who were trying to act hip and who were totally out of it. We would laugh at them. It's like they came from radio, and they acted like what they thought was hip and were like ten years behind.

MICHAEL SADLER: That was the beauty of it. It was like guaranteed air-play, because they didn't have a huge library of videos to choose from.

RICKY BYRD: They were begging the bands for videos, because nobody knew what this thing was, and there weren't a ton of videos really being done.

"WEIRD AL" YANKOVIC: When MTV started, I was working in the mailroom at a radio syndication company, and there was a lot of buzz about this cable TV channel that was playing music videos 24 hours a day. My boss thought it was an idiotic idea that would never catch on, but I thought it sounded really cool. I was living in a one-room apartment in Hollywood with a Murphy bed that folded out from the wall. It was a big investment for me at the time, but I took the plunge and got cable TV, mostly so that I could check out this new thing called MTV. I also figured out how to hook up my TV in stereo, which their promos at the time were coercing people to do. Suddenly, my TV sounded *big* ... and my neighbors weren't happy.

I was completely mesmerized. I love music videos, so I would just sit and watch it for hours at a time. Even if I wasn't actively watching, MTV would always be playing in the background, kind of like "video wallpaper."

In the early days, they didn't have a huge backlog of titles to choose from, so you'd see a lot of the same videos over and over. You'd also see a lot of bands like Devo, bands who maybe didn't have a huge mainstream following but had the foresight to make a bunch of music videos before they were deemed mandatory. I also remember there being a lot of technical glitches and VJs messing up, which was actually charming. The channel had a wonderful guerilla "Hey, let's put on a show!" feel to it.

JOHN OATES: It looked crude. It was crude in the beginning, just like so many start-up endeavors are. And the videos were crude. The production values were crude. But then again, there was nothing to measure it against. But it was new and unique. It really did create a buzz. People really did like it. Right off the bat, people got into it.

VERDINE WHITE: It wasn't the first music channel, to be honest. Actually, BET was doing music videos first. They just hadn't come to prominence.

RIK EMMETT: I didn't take it all that seriously, to be perfectly frank, because my thinking about television and how it affected rock n' roll, it was never really done very well. Like, even when you'd see the Beatles on *Ed Sullivan* or the Rolling Stones, and you'd see shows like *The Monkees*, you had to go for an easy laugh, or it had to be dumbed down. And it always sounded like shit coming out of a television. I always thought that TV turned music into a bit of a cartoon—animated, goofy, sitcom-ish.

In its early stages, for Triumph, we were lucky that we had videos, because Mike Levine [Triumph's bassist] had the vision, because we were signed to RCA, and they were coming out with these newfangled VHS machines and really had a corporate desire to try and sell these things. The whole idea of the convergence of different branches of a large conglomerate—that kind of thinking hadn't really taken hold yet, but it was just starting. And Mike went, "Hey RCA, you've got a division where you manufacture these VHS machines, right? But you've also got a record label, right? Well, why wouldn't you have some concert footage of a band that you're trying to promote, put your machines in every record store you can, run a loop of these guys playing, and use that with an RCA television sitting in every store, and you'll be promoting the band, the television, and your VHS machine. This is a marriage made in heaven for you guys." And they went, "Oh yeah, jeez, that makes good sense." So we had these videos that we made in '78/'79, set up on a soundstage somewhere in Kleinburg, Ontario. When MTV started, they were desperate for content. They had very few videos. So they said, "Oh great, Triumph has some stuff? We'll start running it."

GEORGE THOROGOOD: People would say, "I've been thinking about doing this a long time ago," but you couldn't put it on *The Johnny Carson Show*, y'know? Everybody had a lot of great ideas about things they always wanted to do, but they didn't have an avenue to take it to. They had their doors open 24 hours.

TOMMY TUTONE: It had a good long-range thinking that "We're going to see how this works, but you've got to give them a while to go." It reminds me of what they say about Japanese businesses, where they have to show profit the first quarter. It seemed like it wasn't profit-driven, at first. It is in the long-range, but first, they have to stretch out and bait themselves. That seemed like there was some intuitive understanding that it was going to take a while before we can make these two be in line, so we have to give them their "sandbox" and let them play.

GEDDY LEE: In the early days, I would say it was pretty exciting to see. Everybody was watching it. Everybody was looking for what they would see in it. It kind of got you thinking about songs in a different way, both good and bad.

ANN WILSON: I was completely thrilled. I was really knocked over, because it was the same opening up of possibility that happened when silent films became talkies. It all of a sudden added a whole other dimension to the music.

JOE ELLIOTT: Not a lot, because I didn't live in America. In 1981, we were in the States with Ozzy for about six weeks and Blackfoot for about a month. And then we were gone. We were back home by September/October

'81, preparing for the next album, and didn't know anything about MTV. We'd shot three kind of ... I wouldn't call them videos, promo "movies" of three tracks from *High N' Dry*. Which for us, we knew the only chance we had of getting them shown was on *The Old Grey Whistle Test* on BBC in England or the equivalent shows in France and Germany. And maybe *Don Kirshner's Rock Concert* would show one, but normally, they'd have a band live. So MTV was new to us. We really didn't know much about it.

PHIL COLLEN: It was a little bit like how XM Radio is, because initially, there were no commercials. It was just a really nice mix of a radio station. Different genres and everything.

MARKY RAMONE: The other Ramones were older than I was, and I understood the vibe of doing a song and presenting the song video-wise for two minutes and thirty seconds. The story of your song, visually. I would explain to John, Dee Dee, and Joey what this was really about. I would say, "If you saw the Monkees, that's basically what it is, but it's going to be different. It's going to be more advanced, and it's going to be *our* songs, not that stuff. This is the new deal. This is what's going to happen." "Well, we like the songs on the radio." "Well, this is what it's going to be." "Oh, but now we have to travel. We have to go here and there." You had to put a prod on their behinds to do it, but then they understood it. Then they wanted to do more, because they saw themselves on this new medium. No one really at that time grasped the importance of what this medium would turn out to be.

STEWART COPELAND: It was brilliant. Up until that point, videos were not an art-form. The only place I'd seen them was in England, on shows like *Top of the Pops*. When there would be an American group that actually couldn't show up, they would send video, which was usually just a camera following the band around a park while they walk around, and someone says, "Hey, get an ice cream! Let's have all the lads eating ice cream!" They were sort of like *Monkees* videos.

ROB HALFORD: It just shook everything up. It shook the industry up from top to bottom, much like the invention of the Internet. Everybody thought, "What's this video thing going to mean to the labels? What's it going to mean to the bands? What's it going to mean to revenue? What's it going to mean to everything?" And it didn't take too long to appreciate that this was going to be a really important, exciting development, because primarily, you're going to have your favorite artists streaming into your home.

MIKE SCORE: I remember in England, we finished our album [*A Flock of Seagulls*], and it was basically sitting on the shelf, waiting for something to happen. And then Clive Davis, who owned Jive Records, which we were on, came to us and said, "We're going to do a promo clip, because there's a new company called "MTV," and they're looking out for promos from new bands." So we're like, "OK ... *what the hell is all this?*" They said to us, "Go out, go shopping, get yourself some clothes, and when you come back this afternoon, you're going to make this promo clip." So we talked to the guy that was going to direct. I can't remember his name now. Basically, he said, "Portray your image, and we'll set up a quick shoot." And I think the whole shoot took no longer than about a couple of hours. We either saw it the next morning or that night. It was that quick. And then the next thing you know, it was on MTV.

MIKE RENO: I think the first time I saw it, I was on it! Here's the deal, as far as I can recollect. We were playing I don't even know where. We were probably doing some kind of a promotional gig, maybe playing with the group Kansas. We were told that, the next week, we were going to fly to Albany, New York, and shoot ... they used the word "video," but we never heard it before. Video for us was when you put a video in the video machine and you watch it. So shooting a video went right over my head. They said, "You're going to play songs, and we're going to film you."

Now, you learn ten, twenty years later that these videos cost a fortune and they make or break your careers. But we were one of the first bands to deliver a video to MTV. We delivered *three videos* to MTV the first week they were opened. They were all done on the same weekend in Albany, New York, on the same stage. And apparently what they did is they spliced in clips of people doing funny things and whatever. So they filmed us live, chopped it up, made us look as best we could. We were all skinny rock stars at the time, y'know? Kids. So we looked pretty good. And I remember the first time I saw MTV, I was on it. [Laughs] I thought, "What a cool channel." It's 24 hours of music videos. That was the initial MTV. I thought, "What a great concept." And, because only a few bands were hip to sending in videos, we were on this heavy rotation, which just turned us into TV stars. So it went from us being unrecognized—unless you just did a gig and you walked down the street when the gig got out—to being like super famous TV stars. That's what happened to us. Overnight, I remember the difference.

CY CURNIN: First time I watched MTV, it was early morning. It was refreshing to see a video instead of a cheesy infomercial or a Bible-bashing preacher. Kids for once had their own channel to start the day. It was the first "national" music station, too, so a hit was a hit nationwide at the same time.

DEBORA IYALL: The first time we saw MTV, we were on tour for our first album [*It's a Condition*]. We were somewhere back east, you know where it's really verdant and brick buildings and smaller university towns. I can't even remember if it was North Carolina, outside Philadelphia, or where it was, but we got a motel that had MTV. We were leaving our doors open, because we would have MTV on the TV, and people would be walking in and out to watch it before we went to soundcheck. We were fascinated. I think the first thing I saw on MTV was "I Want Candy." I was pretty excited. It was like, "Wow, a band that we know and dig is on television.

ROB HALFORD: Each time I would come to America from 1981 onwards, whenever I was in my Holiday Inn in Duluth or wherever, my TV would be on MTV. All the time, 24 hours a day. You never switched it off. Even when you were asleep, you had it on, but with the volume down. There was just an endless display of music, music, music. And interviews. It was just an exciting experience for bands, and obviously, fans.

PAUL DEAN: I was in Wichita, and we were on tour. I guess it was 1981. I was slipping through the channels, looking for something to do before soundcheck, and I stumbled on MTV. I couldn't believe how amazing it was. I probably stayed in my room all day. I was really fascinated by it. I never saw anything like it.

RUDY SARZO: The first time I ever heard of MTV was when some of the execs came to visit the Ozzy Osbourne Band. They brought some merchandise—ties, shirts, and coffee cups with the MTV logo. And Ozzy's first reaction to the whole idea of MTV was he thought it was nuts! He'd say, "Who wants to watch a bunch of old geezers 24/7, running around on your television set?"

RICK SPRINGFIELD: I thought it was a good idea. I likened it to the video jukeboxes from the '60s, where you'd put a dollar or quarter in, and they'd play a really bad eight millimeter film of some guy surfing, while the Beach Boys sang "Barbara Ann" or something. That was my closest image to what MTV was and had been aware of videos because of that, but didn't really understand it would go any further than the little local video jukebox thing.

ROGER POWELL: My first impression was, "Hell, that should have been us!" But no, my thoughts were this was a perfect creative extension of what musicians were already doing with sound in the studio. And, of course, it was a superb method of promoting what you were doing. So it was really cool that you could make these little companion mini-movies to go along with the music, so people had a visual accompaniment. As an art form, it was really exciting.

GREG HAWKES: We were excited to do some videos. It's funny, because I remember on the other hand, I think especially Ric [Ocasek] being a little bit reluctant about jumping in a big way, because you've got that double-edged thing of, "The videos could make your song popular, but then, it's got that thing, 'Gee, I can't even listen to that song without thinking of the video.'" So it's got that thing where it sort of imposes a meaning to the song, that the author might not have necessarily intended, or in some ways, it can be limiting. It leaves less room for your own sort of "mental movie" of what might be going on with the song.

MARTHA DAVIS: I had that "video killed the radio star thing," because part of me is music is the thing where you close your eyes and you envision it. It's like reading the book rather than seeing the movie. So part of that is it's a double-edged sword. But it was so absolutely fun doing it.

MICKEY THOMAS: It was a new way to interpret the songs and the music. I think a lot of artists didn't like it because of that reason. One of the criticisms early on was, when you put out a song, you put out music, and it's something strictly for listening enjoyment. Then people can form their own images in their heads of the song, what it means to them. Especially if it's a more abstract lyric. Then, the video process, some artists felt, was restricted to the art, and [they] put out a pre-planned image of the way you were supposed to interpret the song. I didn't necessarily agree with that school of thought. Basically, what we tried to do was have fun with it. We did some pretty silly videos. [Laughs] And those were some of my favorite ones, the ones that were sort of abstract, goofy, and didn't have a whole lot of rhyme and reason to them. I'd like to think that we went with more of the sort Fellini-esque interpretations of our songs and videos.

PETE ANGELUS: I thought it was a very exciting opportunity for Van Halen, because Van Halen was such a visual group, and David had a great sense of humor. Once we started seeing what the videos were, I felt that when we had the opportunity, we could do something that was pretty different from what was being done on there.

ERIC BLOOM: It was watchable ... if you wanted to watch rock videos. And being in the business, I would watch to compare, to say, "That was cool" or "That sucked." So I had a different eye than just a person not in the music business watching MTV.

FEE WAYBILL: When MTV first started, it was so exciting, and it was such a great marketing tool ... although, I thought that pretty much it didn't suit the Tubes. We were just too weird. MTV was too straight. It was appealing to the lowest common denominator. It was like doing a "family show." And the Tubes were never really much of a "family show of a band," at least back then we weren't. We've gotten smart now, because like everybody else, we want the gig. We want the money. But it was a family show, and we weren't huge fans.

JELLO BIAFRA: There was still this grey area. For example, not knowing any better, the Dead Kennedys' guitarist, East Bay Ray, helped ram through a deal to hook the Dead Kennedys up with Faulty Product, which was the independent distribution arm of IRS Records, run by Miles Copeland. And around the time of our second album, *Plastic Surgery Disasters*, the word came down from our manager, Mike Vraney, that Faulty wanted a video clip of "Moon Over Marin," and they wanted the band to pay for it themselves. And he was all enthusiastic, even though the band didn't have that kind of money.

We felt that since they were already in arrears with our royalties—deliberately as it turned out—that Faulty should be paying for this, if they wanted it that bad. Plus, we noticed that our British label wasn't as interested in that, and that would have been the main area where something like that would have been played.

And the more I was exposed to MTV, the more I thought it was just plain stupid. I've never been a big fan of lip-synching, and part of what rekindled my desire to get on stage and be in a band was seeing live bands shot in the raw on shows like *In Concert, Don Kirshner's Rock Concert*, and even *The Midnight Special*, to the degree that *The Midnight Special* was bands playing live. But my favorite, by far, was *In Concert*, and that's what I thought good music video should reflect, is really hot performances in front of a real audience by live bands. I still feel that way.

JOHN DOE: We were part of a pretty independent bunch of bands and felt that MTV was just part of the corporate mess. I don't think any of the members of X had a whole lot of respect for it. [Laughs] For better or for worse, saying, "This is a bunch of bullshit. This is part of 'the man.'" Meanwhile, two years later, we signed with Elektra, which is part of "the man."

DAVE WAKELING: It was bright and sparkly, and it was new. So I couldn't see any of the pitfalls, particularly when they were showing one of our videos. It seemed like the most natural extension of the pop world ever to me.

And it did introduce you to another set of fans, like another level of mass-marketing. Because people would leave MTV on all day, like people would do with the radio on in the background. And sometimes, people would just leave it on all day with the sound down and then turn it up only if it was the band they liked or something that caught their eye enough.

GLENN TILBROOK: I always had an ambivalent relationship with video. I was much more of a traditional "let the music do the talking" sort of guy. However, we had fun with videos. I think there were some people who decided not to get involved at all. And really, it's like trying to say, "Stereo isn't coming" or "DVDs aren't going to work," or whatever the new thing that happens. You just have to go with it, because it's going to be, regardless of what you think about it. I think also the thing about when it started up, because it was a new medium, it was a new way of getting across. The rule book wasn't in place, the same way that it was for radio. So it was tremendously free. It could do what it wanted.

JELLO BIAFRA: Maybe I had too much of a gut-level negative reaction, but it occurred to me early on that the name "Dead Kennedys" was going to be enough that MTV would never play us anyway, so why bother? Plus, how can you turn a Dead Kennedys song into some sex, drugs, and rock n' roll thing ... well no, take out the "drugs"—*it's MTV*—with me as the silent film comedian, mouthing the words, trying to look cute. My stuff was never supposed to be cute, any more than it was supposed to be used in TV commercials or something like that. The purpose is to provoke, not to soothe.

Maybe I would have felt differently if I blundered into a video director who was so "out there" that we struck a chord from the very beginning, like I did with a collage artist, Winston Smith, who has done so many of my album covers. You never know what could have happened, but then again, who the hell would have shown it? The way they were laying it down then was, "This is the way music is going to go. From now on, there is no point in even writing a song unless you know what it's going to look like on TV." And that occurred to me instantly, "Well, even if that's what the major labels think, I think this is bullshit, and so do most of my peers, so I'm not even going to worry about it."

I've realized that I'm almost alone in how little I've cared about mainstream pop culture, ever since I discovered non-mainstream culture and got off the radio grid when I was about thirteen or fourteen years old. By the time I was 15, I was just buying records whose covers I thought looked cool or had gotten negative reviews in the mainstream paper. When the review critic of the *Denver Post* says, "Paul Simon and the Bee Gees are the greatest composers of the 20th Century," then turns around and says, "Black Sabbath is almost as bad as the MC5," someone like me is going to know immediately to run out and search for MC5 albums the same day. To me, it kind of smelled like major labels trying to bring back the era of Pat Boone and Connie Francis, and I wanted no part of it.

BOOTSY COLLINS: I thought of it as a very white *Ed Sullivan Show* that was in color but in style with the youngsters that could afford cable TV. It catered to that certain market. And for what it was, I think it worked.

DAVE MARSH: I'm a journalist. I train myself to see what's there and what's not there. And there were some pretty glaring absences. There was an absence of history, to start with. Pittman, who was one of the most idiotic PR people I've ever come across, made a big point of their all-white playlist. And I was outraged by that. The videos themselves weren't much. Now, my wife works in the record business. I've been around record companies since I was 19/20 years old, so I knew how new—particularly live clips—were and weren't. They were new to America, but people were making live clips for Europe for a couple of decades. And that never gets talked about.

ORAN "JUICE" JONES: It was unfortunate, but they were a bit strict in who they let in the club in those days. It got better as time moved on. But when I first saw video, I knew this was the next level. This was where it was going.

JOHN DOE: My introduction to MTV was them coming to interview us at our old rehearsal space. I clearly recall them asking me to do a promo and me saying, "Hi, I'm John Doe, and you're watching *'Empty TV'*" because I didn't have a lot of respect for television. I still don't. Television is kind of crap, and

I thought, "What, this is another means to remove fans from the music? Excellent. *Not excellent.* This is dumb." It's kind of like Facebook right now. It's another marketing tool, and marketing is always at odds with art.

DARYL HALL: My memories are almost like we were living there. We were so involved in MTV on so many levels. They would invent contests just to use us. Like John and I did this thing where John got in a jet in California, and I got in a jet in New York with MTV winners and we raced across the United States to see who would win the jet race with these people, and we raced to the center of the United States. Crazy things like that. And we used to do commercials for MTV. Like anything that's new, they didn't really know what they were doing. They obviously had an idea, a very strong idea, that it was going to be a show that was going to show music videos. In between, they were sort of clueless of what they were doing. They had all this time to fill in between.

They had their VJs, but they didn't really know how to script. They treated it as if it was it used to be in the early '70s, the underground radio format, where people would sort of talk. And at the end of whatever little conversation they had—stream-of-consciousness thing—they'd say, "Oh, and here's a Pat Benatar video." They had so much time to kill, they used to ask us with a certain amount of regularity to come on and just fill time. I remember a Christmas show where it seemed like we were on for four hours. I don't know how long, but it seemed that long, and we did a whole shift. We would just say pretty much anything that we wanted to, and they'd say, "OK, now it's time to introduce the video," and we'd just babble on and introduce the video. I remember one time, we had our band come on, and we all just cooked. We made scrambled eggs! It was really, really loose.

JOE ELLIOTT: It was brand new, the way it was edited together. The little stuff they did between [sings the "MTV top of the hour theme"], the big M and the spaceman holding the flag. They had some wacky little stuff between programs that probably gave a video director a break. Like, "We need you to make this thing. It's only going to be 20 seconds long." That's where a lot of people get their breaks to do stuff.

KATHY VALENTINE: That was back in the days where there were a lot of all-nighters, so it was great to have "somebody" to stay up with.

GEORGE THOROGOOD: Here's the scene in '81/'82/'83. In the early days of MTV, around the New York/Philadelphia area, if someone had an apartment and had cable, the thing to do is people would have MTV on the TV, and they'd turn the sound down. And then, they would play loud music, like the best of Motown or the Rolling Stones or something. You'd have trash cans full of beer, and you'd have these "MTV parties." People would all come over and talk. They'd have MTV on, but they wouldn't have the sound on. And people were so hooked on it, they were just watching it. "Oh, that's my favorite video," or "I saw this guy play in Detroit," or "This band, the Go-Go's, is going to be really big."

ANN WILSON: When you turned it on, you felt, "We can invite people over and sit down and have a party and have MTV on." It was a great gathering point for people. I can remember going over to England when it first came out in America—they didn't have it over there yet—and going out to dinner with a bunch of English record guys and just expounding the whole time about this brilliant new thing that's on TV.

JOE ELLIOTT: We used to watch MTV, and if you saw a video that you'd seen enough, you'd go and pour yourself a drink, come back, and sit on the edge of the bed.

JELLO BIAFRA: I didn't have cable in my house for 20 years, in part because, that way, no bands crashing on my floor could watch MTV on my time.

GREG HAWKES: Back then, it really was a *rock n' roll channel.*

VJs

GEDDY LEE: It's hard to say. They were personalities, and I think they wanted to establish these personalities in a way that would garner them a following, much like the early days of FM radio. Obviously, that kind of fell by [the] wayside over time. But I think it was very personality-driven in the early days.

COLIN HAY: Well, they brought *themselves*. They brought their own personalities. I think that they were quite largely responsible for the success of the channel as well, because people had someone they could relate to on camera. It wasn't just a face-less channel. They had personalities to connect to.

KATHY VALENTINE: They seemed more like fans than celebrities or people that wanted to be celebrities. I thought that had a sincerity to it that was really, really nice.

ANN WILSON: I loved those guys. They were all amazing. They weren't quite as sarcastic and ironic as the VJs are now. They were still really behind rock, and they really seemed like rock fans. Like, "We've got something in our pocket we want to show you."

MICKEY THOMAS: They just loved exposing the music, videos, and art to people and were truly excited about it. And were fans of all the bands and musicians that they were promoting.

STAN RIDGWAY: They were hosts, so you did get some information from them, about how something was made or what they were up to. My goodness, it seems really innocent and naïve at this point remembering it, almost like a fireside chat or something.

TOMMY TUTONE: They looked like they were picked by some committee somewhere. But I think they did a good of picking one of each kind of person. They were all completely different. They each had their own charm, but they were a nice mixture. I thought they were all great.

FRANKIE SULLIVAN: I thought that they were integral. I thought they were an important part of it, the way that they presented themselves. And they were pretty unbiased back then, just kind of did their gig, played videos, and entertained the audience. It was more about "entertaining" to them. We went from "DJ to VJ." We probably all didn't realize it, but when you look back on it, it's monumental.

RICK SPRINGFIELD: It was a tough call, because I think nobody knew exactly what to do. Again, it was an unknown quantity. Do you get someone who is more of a TV personality? Do you get someone who knows something about music, like a DJ? I think they did a great job of the first casting of the VJs. They covered a lot of ground with it.

PHIL COLLEN: It's just like DJs. What do you think of DJs? It's the same thing. It was just a visual version of that. Everyone was very polite and nice, and it changed a little bit as you went on. But you're on the air, so you can't be too edgy or cutting-edge if you're a VJ, really. You've got to just talk about the bands or the artists.

TODD RUNDGREN: I'm trying to remember if I was particularly impressed with any of them. [Laughs] I don't think I was. They are an "on air personality," and that's their strength. And in that particular sense, you never got any sort of gravitas that these people knew much about either the video and its comparative quality or the artists that were making the videos. You just kind of got the sense that they were essentially personality, there to set up a playlist that somebody else had come up with.

JELLO BIAFRA: I kind of had a *Beavis and Butthead* reaction. One of them came on, and I was like, "Who is this dolt?" And off went the TV. That's about all I know. Now, I'm sure they have every modeling agency pounding at the door, if they even have VJs at all. But otherwise, to some degree, they just scooped up the first people they could find and threw them out there. And consequently, none of them are anywhere to be found today.

JOHN DOE: I think everybody thought they were kind of silly. [Laughs] But I did know that Martha Quinn was pleasant, and she was professional. She was nice to us ... that's good. [Laughs] But it was an impossible task, to be on that and be a professional journalist and be hip. Especially at that time.

JOE ELLIOTT: I loved them all. I thought they were all cuddly and smart. JJ reminded me of Harry Belafonte! He was such a great guy to do interviews with. I was in and out all the summer of '83 with voice problems, canceling gigs and rescheduling them and coming on and telling everybody I'm alive and kicking and everything's fine. Martha Quinn—I remember our manager Cliff Bernstein had a crush on her big-time. They were great. They had great personalities. They were some great characters. They really were.

MICKEY THOMAS: The different personalities and the two cute little girls. [Laughs] When I say "little," I mean they were diminutive in size— Nina and Martha.

MIKE RENO: Nina was the sexy little thing, and everybody wanted to get an interview with her. Alan was funny. Alan reminded me of my brother. He could have been in my family. Martha was the "big sister" kind of thing ... that's probably why they were so very successful. They were kind of like big brother/big sister hotties that you want to meet. They had all their bases covered. JJ Jackson was in there, too. He was a very cool guy. He kind reminds me of that guy now who's on *American Idol*, Randy Jackson. It's almost like they could be in the same family. A very entertaining group of people. I always enjoyed going to MTV. It was a big rush. When we went to New York, we always were like, "Let's go on MTV and say hi to everybody!" It was a drop-in center for us young rockers. Whether the camera was going or not, we dropped in to say hi. I loved that big "MTV" logo. We always tried to scoop up some t-shirts or hats with the MTV logo on it, because MTV was becoming bigger than anything. It was becoming the biggest thing out there. If you had an MTV jacket, you were "the shit." So you'd try to get in there and get an MTV jacket and get one for your brother.

STEWART COPELAND: Martha Quinn was kind of a friend of ours. Rather, she was assigned to us, or we were assigned to her. I'm not quite sure how that worked. But anyhow, whenever we would talk to MTV, it would be her. And since it was her, we got along real well with her. Apart from dealing with the "business suit"—which was John [Sykes]—it would be her. She was nice enough. After a while, she knew the band. She knew what to ask. So I guess it was a good fit. She was the only one, for that reason, that we ever interacted with, I think. And usually, they were not highly regarded, the VJs. It was kind of a geeky gig. The voice on the radio, it's just a voice. You imagine somebody with great charisma behind the voice. But when you actually see the guy on camera, I seem to recall that they didn't have a lot of credibility in the beginning. I don't say because they were geeks or anything like that, but I think that's how they were regarded in the beginning.

GREG HAWKES: Probably my favorites were Nina and Martha, for obvious reasons. [Laughs] Nina Blackwood was sort of the "rock n' roller type." They seemed like they became part of the culture. They were like the face of the channel. Almost like TV personalities.

RICKY BYRD: The lovely Nina Blackwood ... which, of course, all the guys in bands had crushes on!

NINA BLACKWOOD: I guess you look at it as a compliment. But it's funny. In hindsight, you look at it, and you go, "God, why wasn't I more powerful with that?" But—and my VJ cohorts can vouch for this—at the time, I was just a much more fragile person. Now, of course, I would be able to be stronger about it. Because I didn't really consciously think about that. It was kind of strange for me. But then as I got older, and people would say stuff like ... I remember this one guy, I was interviewing Ozzy Osbourne at a show, and he goes, "I had my first sexual relationship watching you ... *but I was alone.*" It was like, "Oh God!" I could kind of laugh at it.

ART BARNES: I absolutely loved Martha Quinn. She was turbo-cute.

FRANKIE SULLIVAN: Martha I was closest to. I always liked her. She came out and did a thing on the band. MTV did a special on the band. She spent four or five days on the road with us. We had some really good conversations. She gave me a book on Buddhism. I still have it. I just remember she had some spunk to her and was kind of fun and bubbly.

MARTHA DAVIS: I've seen them since, and I've got to say, *Mark Goodman is looking good.* [Laughs] He was kind of a goofy guy on [MTV], but he's grown up all nice.

ANN WILSON: Mark Goodman—I've had the pleasure to speak with him a lot of times over the years since. What a great guy.

DEBORA IYALL: I remember I liked JJ. I felt like he knew the history of music a certain way. He had a real genial attitude toward discovering new things and being a champion of new music. Some of the VJs seemed like, "Where did they come from?" It's like, "This guy was on the football team one week, and now he's a VJ?" Or, "She was trying to be a model, and now she's a VJ?" I guess I was attracted more towards music fans in the VJs, ones who really loved the music and not necessarily were that photogenic or whatever.

JON ANDERSON: Over the years, I used to enjoy a lot of the VJs. They were just funny and comical. They made fun of the silly videos and made light of the good videos. Sometimes you'd watch MTV just for the VJs, because they'd have their show and in-depth talks about, "What does this video really mean?" or "Is this music any good?" They're actually very early *Entertainment Tonight* shows, very early *TMZ*. The music, a little bit of chat, a little bit of rumor, a little bit of gossip. But it was actually very fun, because it was fresh.

GLENN TILBROOK: They had a youthful irreverence I think, which all the best "presenters" throughout time have that, and they have that for their own time.

BOB PITTMAN: People would say, "Wow, I love Martha Quinn." "Why do you love Martha Quinn?" "Because she plays great videos." It had nothing to do with Martha. "I loved that contest." It had nothing to do with Martha. They attribute all the attributes of the channel to human beings. So that was why we needed them.

KEN CEIZLER: You're given the title of "director," but the reality is that I was a novice at that time. I think there was definitely "give and take." I was giving [the VJs] instructions probably out of context, because I wasn't going to be seeing the whole thing. People above me would say, "Do this, do this," and I would try to instruct them, and they would give me a weird look, like, *"Where did that come from?"* We all role play to a certain extent. I think that's natural. But I would say, for the most part, the thing about directing, it was mostly just about keeping the crew and everybody organized, to get done on schedule. That was a very important aspect of it. We didn't want to pay extra for overtime and studio time. So we had to be fiscally responsible. And I think the director's role was mostly that.

ROB HALFORD: I think they were really growing with the experience themselves. Massive rock n' roll acts were coming into that little studio, and I'm sure they were as overwhelmed as a lot of people were in that time. But I think they all had their own distinctive style. Everybody warmed to them immediately. They became stars very quickly. It was a bit of a mash-up, really, because they all did different kinds of things. None of them were exclusively into any particular side of rock n' roll. They just did everything that was thrown at them. That was a really cool, organic way to accept genres of all types of music from that time frame. It was just very unprejudiced, very open-minded. Anything that was hot or exciting was brought in.

FRANKIE SULLIVAN: Those VJs. I think about them sometimes, because some of them took a liking to an act. Some of them made a difference. I really believe some of them pushed a song over-the-top, enough to maybe it went to a number one spot, where it was sitting at number two. Because they liked it. And people would watch them and like them. They were fans and devoted, so they followed. I did like that beginning camaraderie and those original five. It's kind of like watching *The Right Stuff*, only musically. They were like the pioneers of that stuff.

"WEIRD AL" YANKOVIC: They became celebrities in their own right. If you were a fan of MTV, it's like they lived in your house. They were all fun and immensely likable. They seemed like people you'd want to hang out with. It's kind of like *SNL*. There have been many cast members over the years, but nothing ever quite matches up to that original group. There was something just kind of perfect about it.

Early MTV

ROBIN ZORN: [The VJs] all came at different hours, because they were on shifts. They came into the office, would look over the copy. Nobody had assistants, so they were just pitching in like everybody else. We did have wardrobe and make-up for them, but they really just came in and hung with everybody, and that's why we became so close. It wasn't like they were treated like superstars by the staff at all. It was just the same as everybody else. So our days were all long. There was a McDonald's right around the corner from Teletronics, and we would go grab french fries and milkshakes, sit on the roof of the building, and have lunch, all of us. That's a pretty typical lunch for us—milkshakes and french fries. We were working like 15/16 hours a day. And as much as it was fun, we were making very little money, and we were exhausted. I left to go work for *Good Morning America*.

KEN CEIZLER: We really were split in two. There was the world of the studio, and there was the world of the office. I can tell you that, certainly in the studio, a typical day was we started pretty early, and each of the directors was responsible for a certain amount of shifts, which was basically like directing five hours worth of VJ segments. Now, that doesn't mean that we were recording literally five hours. What we were doing was recording ... John Fisher was a production manager, who from my understanding, created "the wheel of the VJs," which meant that we had a full hour, and there were five or six breaks per hour. Those were in the prime time hours, and those VJ breaks were anywhere from a minute to two minutes long.

I think the first break after the hour was music news, and the fourth break was also music news. The ones in between were to promote on-air stuff or lead-ins and lead-outs to music. So early on, I think the directors were taking real care in doing these VJ segments, and we worked long days, because we wanted to make sure we got it right. But then once we got the hang of it, everybody started to know the drill. Through time, we were able to do these things pretty quick and efficiently. So our days got shorter and shorter. But in the beginning, it was full days. Each director was responsible for getting down at least five hours of programming a day.

MIKE PELECH: It would start around 9:00, and they would do the intros and outros. They would have a list of what the videos were or would be, so they could do a little bit of color commentary on the video. We would occasionally get some of the videos in, so we could see them, but that was a luxury. Usually, that stuff didn't come in until later, and that was usually integrated in an editorial suite or out at the uplink. The original format of the show was very stiff. It was very heavily blocked. It was almost like a very traditional television show. The executives didn't like the way it looked. Coming out of a video, where people would be running around and going crazy, coming out to a very stilted, formal, newscaster type of presentation just didn't work. So the blocking went out the window, and pretty much, they said, "Loosen it up. You can talk to the VJs off camera. You can do nutty stuff, whatever you want."

As the day would go on, we would just develop stuff. One of the things that I developed was something called "runaway camera," which originally, the director was Jeff Bolton, and I think Nina was in a funk. Her father was ill, and she had very little energy. So Bolton said, "Michael, *do something*. Get her animated." With two cameras, you were cross-shooting, so you were probably always 45 degrees away from each other. I just came up with the notion of runaway camera, so I started yelling, "Runaway camera!" And pushed the camera out between Nina and the second camera, so the camera rolled through the shot, and I chased it. Nina was totally surprised, and that became a semi-regular part of the schtick that we used to do there. People from the office would come down and dress in costume, and we'd do runaway camera. The camera would go running through the set. I would go chasing it and would be followed by up to ten people. So it became a thing that people really looked forward to and liked. We almost planned doing them, so people could get involved in it.

NINA BLACKWOOD: I was always first up to tape. So I'd be in there really early. In our first studios, for the first couple of years, I would take a cab down there, do my own make-up, and start with recording the show. About once a week, we'd get a reel of the new clips, and we would watch them and take notes on what we were watching, so we knew what we were talking about. In the early days, again, it took a long time for the bugs to work out. We sometimes were in that studio all day, into the night. But once the bugs got worked out—a year or two down the line—then it was basically you come in, do your show, and then you'd take care of whatever other VJ business you had for the day. Going back to the office, answering the fan mail. And as it progressed, we'd be going with a wardrobe person. You'd get your script—we called it "a log"—the night before. So I'd do all my prep work at night. For a while, everything was scripted. Then, everything was not scripted. Then, there was kind of a hybrid. I loved doing the research and the prep work. And then, in the evening, we're going around. Since we're in New York, we're seeing the bands that we're talking about. It really was a 24/7 job.

ALAN HUNTER: Early on, it was all day. We were all very vigilant, until we started taking the job for granted about three years into it. We were starting to "live the lifestyle" in the '80s, and it was hard to get up early. I don't know how I turned out to be "the early guy" on the stage. I just drew the short straw, I guess. For me, I was probably the first or second to tape my shows. I went to bed at a good hour and studied my news reports, which weren't scripted. In the very early days, we had some scripts, but they threw those out pretty quickly and just said, "Ad lib. Here's the news. Read the news. But everything else that you say about the song, it's got to be extemporaneous." Easier for Mark and JJ being in radio. A little harder for me, the actor, who needed a script. But I started getting into it.

There was a lot of homework. If I wasn't on the soundstage doing my show, I was up at our offices, pouring over the new videos and studying videos. Since we weren't sitting there watching them—we were just doing our little bits in-between—I had to have a good idea what I was coming out of. I was studying videos, going over material, looking at bios. So that was two, three, four hours in the middle of the day. Frequently, we'd have to go back to the studio across town to do another part of our shift or a weekend shift.

After a year, we started to get the hang of it. We were going out to rock n' roll shows every night. You bet I wasn't doing quite as much homework, because now, I was starting to really know what I was talking about. I knew all the bands. I knew the members. And if a new band came on, like a Kaja-googoo or a Haysi Fantayzee, they were new to the world as well, so it wasn't like I was having to bone up on something that everybody else already knew about.

The middle of the day meant that now I was starting to go to the gym, going to have lunches with people, and enjoying my life in New York, around the edges of taping my show. And towards the end, it was, "How can I get in and out of the studio faster?" Because it might have been that I did my morning shift from 8:00 to 10:00, then I'd have a noon interview with Frank Zappa or Andy Warhol or some other band somewhere in New York, where they would come into the studio, or I was boning up for that interview that afternoon. As happened a lot, we would have interviews at the clubs.

MIKE PELECH: Martha Quinn, her trivia questions, she would always ask the people behind the camera if they knew the answer, and we would yell out the wrong answer. The official wrong answer was "Trini Lopez," which nobody of that age group knew, but she would ask questions about Squeeze, the Shoes, or the Cars. She would ask the question, we would yell out from behind the camera, "Trini Lopez!" And she'd go, "No, no, no. It's not Trini Lopez." Those things just kind of evolved. It was from the executives loosening up the reins and making it a more freeform type of studio and getting us involved in the anarchy. There was a lot of anarchy behind the cameras that you kind of got wind of but never really saw. It was fun.

Then we'd take a lunch break, and everyone would usually go out to a bar on the corner called Sam's, and everybody would pretty much go to lunch together. Go to Sam's, have a cheeseburger, and they had booths. Everybody would take over Sam's. At that time, everybody had MTV tour-jackets, which were great. The Warner-Amex people were really nice. They gave us a lot of their merchandise for free, and we'd wear it on camera and walk around the streets with it. Everybody would have their black satin MTV jacket, with the original logo on the back. Everybody would be at lunch together and carry-ing on the conversation from the studio. Occasionally, guests would come in, like Joe Cocker or somebody like that, and we didn't really have much of a green room, so Mark would just take them to the bar and have a beer or something. It was a real typical Greek greasy spoon restaurant that we gave a lot of business to.

BOB PITTMAN: John [Lack] left about a year after we launched. When the business didn't do well financially, John I think got—unfortunately—the brunt of that. So he left, and then I took over John's job and a little more, became the chief operating officer [and eventually, Pittman became CEO].

Some Struggle in the Video Age

ANN WILSON: Suddenly, you had to be able to do some minimal amount of acting, and you had to be able to take direction from a "visual director." Some people just were a little bit too ... some of the southern rock bands, you saw them once, and said, "Oh, OK. I can go see them live, and that's who they are." Suddenly, there was a whole new role put upon you that I think some people couldn't handle. I keep alluding to the silent pictures and the talkies. Some of the big silent screen actors couldn't make the break because their voices weren't cool enough. Some of the bands couldn't make the jump because they didn't have enough creativity and wonder in their look or in their ability to act or translate the song visually.

GEDDY LEE: It suddenly shifted everybody's thinking, because bands that were not image-oriented—in a way, that was us—suddenly had to start thinking about doing a visual presentation. And I think, for some people, it came naturally. Obviously, the pop stars were more used to that, because it was "face first" for those bands and those singers, anyway. But we were a band that didn't think of ourselves in terms of anything other than guys that liked to play.

JOE ELLIOTT: It also wrecked a few careers, too. If you were one of them bands that had that horrible, balding bass player with a mustache, that was "career gone," because now, they knew what you looked like. It really was much more beneficial to Duran Duran than, say, Uriah Heep.

FRANK STALLONE: It wasn't even about the music anymore. It was like, Christopher Cross came out with one of the best break-out solo albums I'd ever heard [*Christopher Cross*]. But then all of a sudden when they saw him— and he looked like this truck driver—it killed him. I mean, I saw him at the Roxy. This guy had a beautiful voice, and you're figuring this really cool-looking guy will come out, looking like Charlie Sexton. And he came out looking like Bluto. I felt really bad for him because he was really good. So he was definitely not "MTV friendly."

DARYL HALL: There's the anecdote that I find offensive, but they always said that Christopher Cross was too ugly to be a rock star. Which I think is a terrible thing ... but I think there might be a little truth in that kind of thing.

JOHN OATES: I think some were better looking than others. After all, it is a visual medium.

ROGER POWELL: Some of those guys were just butt ugly. [Laughs] From the 40th row, it's OK, but once you start really *seeing* people ... it's kind of an odd comment, but whatever, God bless 'em all.

ERIC BLOOM: You might have a handsome lead singer that would carry the whole thing because he's hot. [Laughs] Maybe the music isn't so good, but he is, or she is. There's that phenomena that you would never know from the airplay, but now you see who's singing. And vice versa. I can think of a few acts that were just not particularly photogenic.

RIK EMMETT: I don't think it's any mystery that there are some people that the closer the camera gets, the more it loves them. That's why there's movie stars and people in daytime soaps, because they're beautiful people, and the closer the camera gets, you go, "Oh my God, her skin is flawless," or "Oh my God, look at how big and beautiful her eyes are," or "Oh my God, look at that guy ... does he have a flaw anywhere?"

MICKEY THOMAS: You mean, aside from the fact that we were just so damned good looking? [Laughs] I don't know. Looks is part of it. I think we had a pretty interesting looking band for the time. I mean, shit, *we had Grace Slick*. [Laughs] And then the fact, too, that most of us in the band were open to expanding our horizons visually and theatrically. I've always been interested in movies and incorporating other forms of art into the music. Paul Kantner was not afraid of that. Craig Chaquiço was very much into it.

Grace of course. So we were not afraid to take risks and some chances and not afraid to fall on your face and make a fool of yourself if you look stupid.

FEE WAYBILL: A lot of those bands—Grateful Dead and stuff—they didn't even look up when they played. They were playing in Levi's. They had their head down and half the time their back to the audience. They just didn't translate to TV. Whereas we—that was our whole deal. We were all about TV and doing a big theatrical presentation, and we're very gregarious kind of guys and really put it out there. A lot of people weren't.

DAVE MARSH: I think the prog bands had more trouble, because first of all, the prog bands didn't have concise songs. And secondly, they didn't have poppy songs. They tended to be more morose. It wasn't something that MTV was terribly good at displaying. No great loss.

JON ANDERSON: Some bands were just good musical bands, and video doesn't translate whether the talent is good on stage when you're on cameras, and you've got make-up, and you've got all that stuff. It puts people off, because they're not actors. They're musicians. So they couldn't "transfer." They weren't funky-looking. [Laughs] They weren't great looking. They didn't dress correct or whatever. They weren't hip enough to carry it over. Even though the song may have been very good, the videos generally ... 50% of the videos weren't very good, because it wasn't their forte. It wasn't what you become a rock musician for—to make videos? That's what movie stars do or pop stars or whatever. A lot of people—like Queen—worked amazing, because they actually started off as a visual event. "Bohemian Rhapsody" was a great video, and Bowie had great videos. Certain people were great videos. Yes, we're lucky. We had ten minutes of success [on MTV], but the music of Yes survives everything.

ALAN HUNTER: I think music was the key there. The other ones grew and evolved. I'm not saying they got different. The Grateful Dead didn't have to do anything different. But we played one of their videos, did we not? David Bowie was built for the video age. He was making videos in the '70s. "Ashes to Ashes" was one of the stalwart first ones. He was OK to evolve.

Bands like Yes were the ones that worried me. I was a huge Yes fan, but I didn't know how they were going to work. Not because of the visuals, so much as how was their "prog rock" going to work? *90125* came out in 1983, and mainly due to Trevor Rabin, their sound was so updated and cool that it worked, and I was happy for them.

ZZ Top—I don't know how they worked as well as they did. I love ZZ Top. I think they had a real good sense of themselves and knew exactly what they needed to do, and that was nothing but have fun little videos. Their little bearded personas were so fun. But it's amazing how much accolades their videos got. "Legs" was a Video Music Award winner. It's like, "Really? *That video?!*" And Heart—Ann and Nancy were so pretty and photogenic. I think they kept relevant musically with their music during the '80s. Whether they came from the '70s or not, they so updated everything. They were still vital. And Ann and Nancy were easy on the eyes. With their costumes and highly conceptual videos. They sold a lot of albums, so they had some pretty good budgets, and they remained relevant. I think if you didn't remain relevant with the music, you weren't going to live through the '80s anyway.

RICKY BYRD: Look, ZZ Top are not a good-looking band, but they're great, and they're cool as shit. What they did is they took advantage of the visuals and said, "What can we do to make ourselves look really cool? Dude, fast cars and women ... and fuzzy guitars!" And they took advantage of that. And look at Robert Palmer. Same thing with Power Station. That was *huge* MTV stuff. Always putting hot girls, half-dressed. I mean, look at "Hot for Teacher." The stuff that stands out is that kind of stuff. And then there's interesting stuff like Tom Petty.

GEDDY LEE: I think some bands were better at focusing on what they were, what they wanted to look like, and could exploit the whole image that they had already garnered. For a band like us, we didn't really have an image. We were "players," whose image evolved over many years. And I guess our image—even today—are one of players. And the fact that we don't really have a visual image outside of that, in a strange way, worked in our favor. It's the *lack* of image that became our image. [Laughs] I think that made it very difficult obviously in those "image-driven times." And other bands—especially hard rock bands that had the big hair and all the hard rock accoutrements—I think they leaned on that, and that was their image.

FRANK STALLONE: I remember Bonnie Tyler was at the Grammys with us, and she did "Total Eclipse of the Heart." It was such an amazing vocal. And she looked like a hairdresser. She looked like she could be at the Jersey Shore as a hairdresser. And she was a fucking *amazing* singer. But again, she didn't really translate to the screen, whereas you get someone with zero talent, and they translate wonderfully.

MARTHA DAVIS: I think it really just depended on the acts, and sadly, it was like if you're more visual, you got more out of it. And I think that's always a problem in the industry, like nowadays, if you're fourteen and have a good bellybutton. We're too wrapped up in that stuff anyway as it is, and that sort of heightened that aspect of it. The cuter you were, that came with it. And it's sad, because there are really talented people that maybe didn't have quite the stage presence or appearance that everybody was looking for. I think it probably did take a toll on some people. There was a downside to it.

PETE ANGELUS: When you say "They couldn't," I think maybe your point is that "They didn't." I think they could have, actually. Maybe they just couldn't figure out the proper way, which is really not so difficult, to present themselves in that medium. And I don't know why that would be problematic, because even for the bands that wanted to shy away from any humor and just present who they were, that could have been done in a very creative way, as well. I don't know why they couldn't, and I don't know why they didn't. But for the people that saw MTV for the opportunity that it was, a lot of people made a lot of memorable videos that had a lot of impact on a lot of people during those years.

JOE ELLIOTT: You have to remember there were a lot of people that were actually threatened by this channel. A lot of bands that were established before we came along looked at it with scorn. I've talked to them about it—

bands like Journey, Kiss, Styx, maybe even REO Speedwagon—they were like, "Why do we have to shoot videos? We never had to do this before." They took this ... I wouldn't say a *lazy* stance, but like a stance against it. They reluctantly shot videos, and consequently, they didn't make very good ones.

ROGER POWELL: I think some bands just didn't know what to do. You handed them this powerful power tool, and they didn't know where to plug it in.

Les Garland and John Sykes

BOB PITTMAN: There were two guys that really dealt with the artist community day in, day out—John Sykes and Les Garland. Les sort of dealt with the people who really wanted to go have fun, and just loved Les for being the pied piper. John hung out with the ones that were very serious about the business, and wanted to understand exactly how and where, and much more management-oriented on the business. They sort of split up the artists and the managers based on that approach.

LES GARLAND: Small town boy. Came from a little town in southwest Missouri near the Arkansas border, called Forsyth, Missouri, which is by Branson, Missouri. I was mischievous and a bit of a rebel at a very young age, out to express myself. I'll never forget as a teenager, when my father took me aside, and gave me "the speech" about, "Very few people are given this gift of what's known as 'leadership skills,' and you need to be very careful with that, because you can very easily lead people—including yourself—down the wrong path. And you need to find that right path, and you need to be positive about your leadership skills. It's a gift. It's like soul—some people have it, some people don't."

So now I'm a teenager, and I'm messing around with bands. I want to be in a rock band, and I'm booking rock bands in high school. Meantime, I'd go home at night and go to bed, and I'd have my little transistor radio, and I'd be dialing around and try to pick up distant radio stations. And the two that come to mind is one in Chicago, WLS, and another one out of Little Rock, Arkansas, KAAY. Those started influencing me. The music was really influencing me. So off I go to college. I'm supposed to go to school in Dallas, and I ended up hanging out at the local rock n' roll radio station down there, KLIF, one of the top radio stations in the history of radio. Then I decided I was going to secretly get my third class license, which was a license you had to have back in those days to be a DJ, because you had to read transmitters. So I snuck into a school and took a twelve-week program to get my radio license.

[After radio jobs in Los Angeles, Detroit, and Boston] I went to the pinnacle of it all, which I thought was the greatest radio station in America, a station in San Francisco, KFRC. I stayed over four years, and it was "Radio Station of the Year" three or four years in a row. I was "Program Director of the Year." We had number one ratings. After about four years in San Francisco, I had been approached by each of the major networks—NBC, CBS, and ABC—in various capacities. I felt that I had reached the top of the mountain, and there was nothing left to prove in radio. I was challenged to do something else. One night, I was with Doug Morris, who has been the most powerful guy in the music business now for a good ten years. We were having dinner in San Francisco, and he asked what I was going to do after my radio career. And I said, "It's funny that you bring that up, because I've been thinking about that. I don't really know, but I'm intrigued to do *something.*" And he said, "Would you be interested in coming over to the music company side? There's something going on at Atlantic that maybe we can talk about." He was with Atlantic, which at the time was the number one record company in the world. So that led to a couple of meetings, and the next thing you know, I was the vice president and general manager of Atlantic Records.

MICKEY THOMAS: Les was irresistibly lovable, a bigger than life character. He's one of those guys that seems like he can seamlessly and effortlessly do anything he wants in life and get away with it. Extremely charming, just *dripping* with charm. A lot of that might go back to that radio voice of his. The voice, the looks, the charm, the charisma—Les had it all. And whenever you were in his presence, you knew a good time was going to be had by all.

LES GARLAND: Bob Pittman and I had known each other for a long time. Bob and I had crossed paths when we were youngsters in Milwaukee, in the formative years of our radio career. Small-town southern boys that did well in radio and achieved a certain level of success. He came out to Los Angeles, and we were having dinner together one night. During the conversation, he says, "I want to talk to you about something. How many artists on Atlantic would you say are making music videos?" I'm like, "Not that many, actually." He goes, "So you think that music videos could work on television?" And it just hit me. I go, "You're thinking 24 hours a day, like a radio station? Yeah. *I absolutely do.*"

So we had another conversation, in the fall of 1980. Then came the spring of '81. The vote was coming down, whether to put up the funds to launch this music channel. Doug Morris became a very critical vote in that process, because it was Warner Communications, and don't forget, he was over at Atlantic. And of course, the smart people at Warner would want to know how the heads of the labels would feel about the company starting this thing to put music videos on television—would it benefit the artists, would it benefit the music company, etc. I remember Doug phoning me and asking what I thought. I said, "I think it's a brilliant idea. In fact, Pittman and I have been talking about it several times." He goes, "I should vote for this, right?" And I said, "Absolutely." Which he did, and then the green light was go.

BOB PITTMAN: Les was a promoter. Les was a great character.

LES GARLAND: So then they launch this crazy thing. I was still with Atlantic. In reality, the two markets that MTV had had at that time—it was a rollout, but it wasn't getting rolled out. The cable guys didn't get it. And it was in Des Moines and in Tulsa. I had gone through Tulsa as a youngster in my radio years, and I had a friend there that I had produced concerts with. I phoned him up and said, "Have you noticed this new channel that is playing music all the time? Do me a favor. VHS it for me once a week, 24 hours, and send me the tape." Which he would do, and I would ramble through them and check them out. I would call Pittman or send him a note—"I saw this, and I think you may want to consider doing this instead." Kind of constructive feedback. And he was intrigued with what I was doing.

Within 60 days of launch, I get a call. He's going to come to California and can we have dinner. By the way, a lot of what I was doing was talk our artists on Atlantic into making music videos for this new channel. And even people that *weren't* on Atlantic, for that matter. So Pittman comes out to Los Angeles, and he was aware that my contract with Atlantic was expiring soon, and he asked me what I was going to be doing. I was like, "Here we go again ... funny you bring that up, because I don't know if the music business is for me." I've done this for a couple of years, and I learned something about business in a sense. I learned that you can be on one of two sides. You could be a buyer, or you can be a seller. And I didn't even know until after I did it that I went from buyer to seller, and I liked the buyer side a little better. I said, "I'm considering things right now."

He's like, "Garland, would you be interested in coming to New York and running MTV for me?" I just looked at him, and I'm like, "Done. I'll take it ... did you just offer me a job?" [Laughs] He goes, "You believe that big?" And I go, "I believe that big, absolutely I do." He goes, "Can't pay you the money you're getting paid now." I go, "We'll worry about that later." We agreed that he would put the first call into Doug Morris the next morning, which he did. Doug phoned me around 7:30 California time. "Garland, Pittman called me. I think this is brilliant, and you've got to do this." Then we started putting everything together. I came down to Florida. We had some corporate meetings. That was in late November/early December of '81. I was on board by January, and off we went. I was senior executive vice president. I was the highest-ranking officer inside MTV.

ALAN HUNTER: Then Les came on board. I remember him taking the five VJs to lunch at Chow, the Chinese restaurant in New York. Very upscale. He was like—and I mean this in a good way—a vacuum cleaner salesman. Y'know, one of those door-to-door guys that could sell anything. He was a radio guy. I think Mark and JJ knew him from the radio days. He was slick, and I thought, *"I am in the big leagues now."* He took us to this huge, fancy restaurant, which was meant to show we were on a fast track now, and that he was there to make sure that we understood how big a deal this could become. But I'll tell you, Les was everybody's pal. He called you "pal" and put his arm around you. He was very huggy in a "radio promotion guy" kind of way. I never felt like I had to watch my back, but I definitely thought, "What's going on here?" I remember him and Bob Pittman, six months into it, sat me down and gave me a raise. Without my asking. They said, "We think you're going to be big here at MTV, and we want to give you a raise." It was their way—I understood later—of staggering the VJs out, so they could fire us five years later, in staggered order. [Laughs] He liked to play golf a lot. I figured, "You live in New York City ... *and you play golf?*"

KEN CEIZLER: Bob Pittman did have a glass eye, and then Les Garland did. Les Garland was "your rock n' roll guy." He was the antithesis of Bob Pittman. He knew all the rock stars and everybody. And he lived the rock n' roll life. In that regard, sometimes you have to pay the devil, and I think he had to pay the devil and give up an eye. He might have also given up another part of his body ... but I'm not too sure about that! Bob Pittman had a glass eye since day one when I met him, but it wasn't very noticeable.

ALAN HUNTER: The top three executives had fake eyes. They had one fake glass eye. So we thought, "Wow. Is that a prerequisite? ... or is that what happens when you get the gigs?"

ANONYMOUS: Les Garland—I didn't have a whole lot to do with him, but I just remember thinking, "He's just a blow-hard. He's so loud, and he thinks he's really cool. And maybe he is really cool ... but he's not as cool as *us.*"

ALAN HUNTER: Les would go out and let it down every so often, but always keep his "mature cool." Les was the party animal. Without a doubt. With Les, he was going to drink you way under the table and be out four more hours. We didn't hang that much with the executives—Bob Pittman and Les, and the upper guys like John Sykes. We'd always catch wind of a big party that they were at the night before. And early on, we were like, "Well, what are we ... *chopped liver?*" Like at the New Year's Eve show, the executives had on these fantastic tuxedo suits with these cowboy boots, with silver inlays. They were always edgy enough. The MTV executive suit—in the business—they were like the wild boys to the rest of the corporate community. There they were with Warner Communications and American Express. But Les wasn't "trying." The other ones were trying to exude rebelliousness in the corporate suit. But Les just *was.* He truly had fun with it. And if I hadn't seen him years later—way after MTV—down in Florida where he lives now, I would say that it was kind of a veneer. But it was wasn't. Les just loves life. He's a big gambler. I mean he'll *gamble* on things. But again, he could just sell anything.

DEREK POWER: Sykes was the person that was closest to Miles [Copeland, the Police's manager] and me. And he was the one who really was the guy that particularly saw the "videogenic" qualities of the Police as being absolutely identical with everything that MTV was looking to achieve at the time. And as a personality, he was always very funny and charming. He was somebody that was easy to get along with.

STEWART COPELAND: I have no idea what [Sykes] brought to the channel. I know that he brought a lot of laughs and good cheer to the dressing room. That's about it. I know that he was a "business shark." He would have had to have been. A&M was very noncorporate. I'd go hang out with Jerry Moss, and he was the boss, not just the president, but the owner. They would wheel Herb Alpert out every now then on ceremonial occasions, but basically, it was Jerry's gaff, and we'd go hang out with him, and he was a buddy. With MTV and John, he was a friend of the band, but he was very much a corporate animal as well, and that was our first inkling that giant corporations were invading our playpen, the music industry. And with that, we called it "the music industry," just to give ourselves a bit of gravitas. It didn't feel like an industry at all, until we would see Sykesy in a suit.

BOB PITTMAN: John [Sykes] was the on-air promotion genius. John would come up with contests like the one-night stand, where we'd send people out in a jet—at that time, it wasn't Gulfstreams; it was Learjets—and we didn't have much money, so we'd charter one, and we had a magnetic sticker that would stick on the side, that said "MTV." So when it came off the runway, John would jump out of the plane, put the magnetic sticker on, and taxi in, so we could get the press to see the MTV plane there. People would go to a concert, hang out with the band, have dinner with the band, fly home that night—2:00 or 3:00 in the morning—and they'd had a one-night stand with Fleetwood Mac. But those were John's deal. He got John Mellencamp to agree to paint a house pink and bought a house. So John was "that guy." And John slowly took over more and more of the day-to-day programming stuff there, too, in terms of the music and the contests, and eventually, the production stuff as well.

Tom [Freston] was great. Tom was originally our consumer marketing guy. When we launched MTV, I had all the programming and consumer marketing, so Tom reported to me, and he'd been one of our affiliate sales guys in Warner-Amex Satellite Entertainment Company, working on the Movie Channel. I felt Tom was terrific. As a matter of fact, for one moment in time, when we were spinning off the Movie Channel, we were going to bring in Paramount and Universal as partners, and I was going to go run that and leave MTV. So I sent Tom over to the Movie Channel as the head of marketing. Then we decided to merge the Movie Channel with Showtime, so then I had to get Tom back. But Tom was always my go-to guy. A great manager, real solid citizen. I put Tom in charge of affiliate marketing when I took over the whole company. And Tom did a great job of finally getting the cable operators to sign up and breaking through. And then I put him over as the general manager, which was over the programming and consumer marketing side of it.

Jack [Schneider, aka John Schneider] was the CEO of the company, from the time I was there until I took over as CEO in '85. And Jack didn't understand the business at all, but was very supportive of us and really pushed the board of directors of Warner-Amex to give us the meeting with Steve Ross and Jim Robinson, so we could really pitch it. He rarely gets credit and certainly deserves it. Steve Ross loved this business and was wildly supportive of it, and supportive of us as creative people, big business people. I would have never gone to the business side from the creative side had it not been for Steve. David Horowitz was the co-COO of Warner Communications under Steve and was our day-to-day liaison and watched over us, was our guardian angel. And was one of my real mentors. Was probably responsible for me becoming the COO of the company and moving into the business side. And David—when we went public—Jack left the company, and they decided I was too young for a public company. So David left as the co-COO of Warner Communications and came down as the CEO of MTV Networks, to be the grey hair and the steady hand and the older, experienced guy. Really loved everybody at the business, and it showed. And was a wonderfully supportive guy. He is sometimes forgotten but should be remembered.

MICKEY THOMAS: Les just happened to be a close and old friend of the manager of Jefferson Starship. We knew Les from his radio days in San Francisco. That helped us get an early foot in the door, as being one of the bands that got some of the most exposure early on, on MTV.

FRANKIE SULLIVAN: Look at Les Garland and what he came on to be and what he means to this industry, even to this day. He's irreplaceable. He's done everything. He's brilliant. He's iconic. He's one of my idols. He really did leave a huge mark on our industry.

LES GARLAND: [Pittman and Sykes] both brought a lot—a ton—to the channel. Again, it's like—sorry for the sports analogy—but it ain't just the quarterback. There has to be other players. There was a real *team* there. And Pittman and I fell into the role of leaders. We were the leaders of the whole thing. We did a very good job of sharing the stage with each other.

ROBIN ZORN: John Sykes was really nice. Bob Pittman was intimidating but so young looking, that when I remember I went in for my interview, he walked in the room while I was waiting to be interviewed, and I distinctly remember thinking that he was an intern. And then he walked around the table and started talking. I was like, "Oh my God ... *this is Bob Pittman?!*" It was not like "us or them," but we were definitely a different group than they were. The people that worked at Teletronics, we were really a tight, tight group. And unless you were there with the hours that we put in, you weren't in that group. And they were not.

ALAN HUNTER: I thought [Bob Pittman] was fairly genius. He was a fairly cool character. People called him "a shark," because he kept his cards very close to his chest, and his coterie of executives underneath him was pretty tight.

KEN CEIZLER: Bob Pittman is not just "a regular guy." He is a unique personality. His intellect can be very intimidating, and he absorbs information. What I always found fascinating about him was his ability to take a lot of information and complicated stuff, organize it in his brain, and then be able to explain it in a very simple way. Bob was always a very "suit-and-tie kind of guy," a very corporate guy. Although he was out of radio and rock n' roll, he wasn't your radio/rock n' roll personality. As a matter of fact, he hired certain people in the company to be those rock n' roll faces of the company. Although he came out of radio, he struck me as not being a rock n' roll/radio guy, as much as a Wall Street-type person.

NINA BLACKWOOD: [Pittman] was basically the executive that oversaw everything. He, along with John Sykes, who I loved, and Les Garland ... he was *a complete nut!* A complete party-man. We always laugh, because he was doing all the things they thought the VJs were doing. Just a "pedal-to-the-metal guy." They were kind of the "holy trio."

ALAN HUNTER: You had John Sykes, Tom Freston, Les Garland—they were really the barbarians at the gates. They were truly the "renegades of executom" back in the '80s. They were really the renegades in the offices of big business in Manhattan at the time, *because they could be.* They could go out drinking like all the rockers, but be in a corporate boardroom the next day, talking to American Express, Warner Communications, and Viacom. They were sort of everybody's idol at the time.

I Want My MTV!

BOB PITTMAN: We were out trying to get cable operators to carry us. Their first reaction was, "We don't want any of that damn 'sex, drugs, and rock n' roll.' It's nasty stuff, and it ain't going to be on my cable system." And the other ones that were more mercenary would say, "Well ... just pay me a lot of money," which we didn't have. One of my guys said, "That's called 'pull versus push' distribution. You create your consumer demand, and the consumer demands it."

LES GARLAND: We had one million dollars in our budget that year, which is really not a lot of money to do anything nationally. And we were trying to figure how we were going to best spend that million dollars to market the channel. By the way, the awareness to MTV in the target audience—which was 12 to 34—was somewhere just south of 20%. And we really needed to do something that was going to make a lot of noise. My idea that I was working on was no one at that point in time had ever given away one million dollars. And I thought, "The ink that we would get for giving away one million dollars would be worth *millions* ... and it would only cost us a million. Why don't we give away a million dollars in some crazy MTV way?"

BOB PITTMAN: So I hired George Lois and a guy named Dale Pon, who had been my promotions director at WNBC radio, and they had an agency together.

GEORGE LOIS: By the early '80s, I was big in the business [Lois—best known as an art director, designer, and advertiser—created countless famous covers for *Esquire* magazine in the '60s] and always on the cutting edge of advertising creativity. At that point, Viacom was looking for agencies for Nickelodeon, MTV, and the Movie Channel. And I think led by Bob Pittman's recommendations or ideas about what was going on in the business, it could have been other guys, because he had a lot of guys with him that were very bright and very sharp, and I think they talked to us. They chose us, and they said, "Which of the brands would you like to work on?" And I think they gave us an idea of the billings on them. The smallest billing of them, by far, was MTV. I think it was $250,000. Nickelodeon was a million something or two-million something, and the Movie Channel was larger, too. I said to them, "Well, I really want MTV." And they said, "MTV? Do you understand that MTV is *only $250,000?* We want a trade campaign." They meant a campaign to the cable operators. I said, "That's the one I really want. Don't get me wrong. I'd like them all, but that's the one I *really* want." And I think that impressed them. Maybe they thought I was a little nuts. I had a feeling they thought they had a real dog on their hands.

I ran into people many years later, who said that they were present at a MTV presentation in a cable convention. It was must have been '80 or something like that. And there were almost cat-calls in the audience. The audience sat there listening to this crazy fuckin' bunch of young guys talking about a 24-hour rock n' roll channel. It sounded like it would destroy the music business by giving away music for nothing. Ad agency people were laughing, saying, "Who the hell would want to advertise on that channel?" Everybody kind of laughed at them. And they thought it was the stupidest idea of all time. So when I said, "MTV—that's the one I really want," they said, "OK ... *asshole.*" And they also gave me Nickelodeon at the same time, so I was happy. When we went to talk to them, we did an ad or two talking about "cable brats," and then after a week or two of thinking about it, said, "These guys aren't going to be successful doing this trade advertising." Because if you talked to any of these cable operators, they still had the attitude that the whole thing was really ridiculous. You weren't going to convince them in any way, shape, or form.

BOB PITTMAN: They came, and we explained the problem. "We want something where we can pressure the cable companies to carry us. And rather than spend the money to get the cable company to carry us, I'd rather spend the money on advertising and make them carry us."

LES GARLAND: One afternoon, the phone rings. My assistant tells me George is on the phone, and he said, "Garland ... *I think I got it.* Can you get everybody together?" I go, "When?" He goes, "Today." I go, "Let me see what I can do." *Boom,* we set a meeting for around 5:30. From my collection, [it was] Pittman, Sykes, Freston, me, and could have been one or two others. George rolls in. You would expect an ad guy to come in with videos and easels and whatever. No, not him. *Nothing.* He just comes rolling in and starts this whole thing. He goes, "Let me ask you. Who does MTV belong to? Does it belong to Warner-Amex? Warner Communications? The advertisers? The artists? MTV is kind of like 'the color TV phenomenon.' It belongs to those who found it first. It belongs to them. If you're the only youngster on a block that has it, everybody goes to your house to watch it. They take a sense of ownership, those who find it. It's like when you find a new artist, it's yours."

GEORGE LOIS: I said, "Do you guys remember a campaign I did, where famous baseball players, like Mickey Mantle, say, 'I want my Maypo!?'" Maypo was kind of a baby cereal, and I told my client back then, "It's oatmeal. I don't know why it's just a baby cereal. Why can't I do a campaign that talks to older kids, so that you can do it from a baby cereal up to twelve or thirteen-year-olds?" So they're all looking at me and going, "Yeah, I loved that commercial." I said, "OK, now, all you sons of a bitches around the country are going to be saying, '*I want my MTV.*' Here's what we'll do. We'll do a TV commercial. And what we do is we fly right by the cable operators, because they don't give a shit. They smoke cigars and think all young kids are fuckin' hoodlums. I'll do a commercial and get a real visceral feeling about the thing. And I'll get footage of famous rock stars. And at the end of the commercial, I'll say, 'If you don't get MTV where you live, call your local cable operator and say ... I'll cut to somebody like Mick Jagger, who will pick up the phone, look into the phone, and say, *"I want my MTV!"*

They all looked at me and were like, "Well ... hold on. First of all, in a million years, you're not going to get a rock star. The rock business hates us and doesn't believe in us...in fact, thinks we could be destructive. No way." And I said, "Someway or another, I will get a rock star." And then they said,

"Even if you do, what happens then?" I said, "What will happen is thousands and then millions of young rock fans will look up their cable operator, dial it, look into the phone, and say, 'I want my MTV!' and maybe even make a second or third phone call to the guy." And they said, "Huh?! Really?" And then part of that thing was when I was describing the commercial, I said, "Right away, I'm going to take that logo that you've got, and I'm really going to make it work for you. Inside the 'M,' every time I show the MTV logo, I'm going to have a Rolling Stones logo coming out of it, a fist coming out of it, a picture of a star - every time you see the logo, it's going to be doing *something.*"

I think they thought I was full of shit. And at the same time, they knew I had a record of really exciting marketing and advertising breakthroughs. And finally, I think Bob Pittman said, "I guess we have nothing to lose. It's interesting." I said, "We'll do it. There will be an explosion of some kind, and at that point, we'll prove to the cable operators that something is happening." I think Bob wound up saying, "Give it a shot." Anyway, we ended up getting Mick Jagger. And they kept saying, "We can't help you get a rock star." I mean, when they hear a phone call from MTV, their agents say, "Go fuck yourself." So I called Bill Graham, who I knew, and I told him what I was doing. I said, "Can you help me?" He wound up helping me, and before you knew it, we had Mick Jagger. Not only did Jagger show up, but he shows up and says, "I've brought Pete Townshend and Pat Benatar. Would you like to shoot them also?" I said, "Holy shit ... I think so!"

LES GARLAND: He goes, "Garland, do you think you can get Mick Jagger to say, 'I want my MTV?'" And it hit me. I said, *"That's it!"* He goes, "We need the biggest rock star in the world first, and then we can get the rest of them to do it. Garland, you think you can get Mick to do it?" And I'd been friendly with Mick through the years, and I said, "I think so. I'd like to give it a shot, that's for sure." I go off to France in two days, and we're in Paris. I had Dale come with the production crew, I was so sure that I could talk him into it. I had my meeting with Mick, I went into the suite to meet with him, and it was very friendly. "Hi, good to see you again." We sit down, and he says, "Garland, you've come all the way to France. You must want *some-*

thing." I go, "I do," and I explain what we were about to do. I said, "I'd like to see if you'd be kind enough to let me roll the cameras, and you look into the camera, and say, "I want my MTV!" Mick says, "You want me to do a commercial?"

So we get into the discussion if whether this is a commercial or not. And I said, "No, I really don't believe it is. I think you, being Mick Jagger, with the greatest rock n' roll band in the world, are actually voicing your support for a new phenomenon, which is music videos. We just happen to be the venue where music videos is what you'd be doing." And he goes, "Yeah, *but that's a commercial."* I go, "Well ... not really." So we get into that for a minute. And I go, "So you're saying you don't do commercials? J van presented your last tour. And there you were, on a poster with J van. If that's not a commercial, I don't know what is." He goes, "Well, yeah. We got paid a lot of money for that." I go, "So that's what this is all about? This is about money?" And Mick says, "That would make it a little easier to do, yeah." I said, "Here's the problem. We've only got a million dollars to spend in media, so we don't have any money. We really don't. But if it would make you feel better at all ... " I reached into my pocket, pulled out a dollar, put it on the table, and said, "I'll pay you out of my pocket. I'll give you a dollar." He goes, "You're serious?" I say, "Yeah, I'll give you a dollar ... because I have to give everybody else a dollar." [Laughs]

He's laughing and goes, "Garland ... *we'll do it.* But, I want you to make out a little contract right there. We're doing this, and I'm doing it for a dollar, but I get final right of approval." I said, "OK, we can do that." I write out this thing, "I, Mick Jagger, hereby agree to allow Les Garland and the MTV crew to shoot 'I want my MTV!' at 2:00pm tomorrow—blah blah blah—for one dollar, with final approval." So we shoot it the next day, get back to America, and from there, now we're on the phone to everybody, that Mick is already in the can. Well, David Bowie ... no problem. John Mellencamp ... no problem. Pat Benatar—bam, bam —we had them lined up now. And we had the spot together within a week.

GEORGE LOIS: I've always called Mick Jagger the "patron saint of MTV." To me, I credit him with the fact that MTV made it and prospered.

LES GARLAND: When Dale and George put those babies together, the first time we saw them, they raised the hair on your arm. "America, call your cable company and demand your MTV!" It was a real "call to action campaign." Who would have known that the young people would actually do it? And they did. We hit the air with these things, and we were very smart. We bought cable spots around the country, for five bucks a pop. And it looked like we were *everywhere*. We threw the million out in about two weeks. The most important part of the whole thing was how effective it was. We went back out into the field, did another study, and the awareness to MTV had gone from south of 20% to somewhere around 88%. *Everybody* knew what MTV was. The cable companies couldn't believe the thousands of calls they were getting, and all of a sudden, MTV was totally for real, and we were being launched. We'd have weekly program meetings, and every week, I would walk in and go, "We picked up another 400,000 homes this week. We picked up another 500,000 this week. We picked up another 250,000 this week." It just took off, truly. Like that rocket ship every hour, it took off. And we were *rocking*.

ALAN HUNTER: Garland was instrumental in that whole thing. He was definitely the one who got Mick Jagger and others. When he got Mick Jagger to say, "I want my MTV!" we all thought, "Holy cow, this is big." It was like, "Yeah! *Mick Jagger* is hawking us now!" [Laughs]

GEORGE LOIS: I produced the first three commercials, and we run the first one ... I think it was in San Francisco. And I think they spent a couple of g's to run three or four spots. It was probably late night. The cable operator early in the morning—his 5:30 in the morning, gets a hold of Bob Pittman at 8:30ish—and he says, "Get that fucking commercial off the air! I'm getting thousands of phone calls." So what happened is basically what we had planned and did was we went into every market—mostly west coast I think at the beginning—and only ran a couple of days advertising in each market, and the same response was happening. Also, at that point, the buzz got around about this MTV starting to get cable operators, and the cable operators heard about it in the other cities, and before you knew it, we came up with the advertising.

I think six months later or something, it was so successful that *Time* magazine ran a front-page cover story saying, "America wants its MTV." And then, at that point, it turned from you couldn't get a rock star to do anything to all of a sudden they were calling, busting our balls, begging for us to include them in our spots. I think I shot a hundred of them, maybe more. We produced them. Sometimes, we had to shoot on the west coast; sometimes, we had to shoot here. People say, "What should a great campaign have?" And I said, "Two mnemonics"—mnemonics is a Greek word for memory—"One should be a visual mnemonic. You should see something you remember physically. And the other thing is there should be a mnemonic using words." So, Mick Jagger picking up the phone and screaming at the phone, "I want my MTV!"—that's two mnemonics. That's the words and copy working together that makes something so fucking memorable that you remember it all your life.

MIKE PELECH: You look back at that stuff, and you go, "Oh, it's so dated," but that stuff was really earth-shaking. The way the stuff was hand-tinted and really funky stuff. Nancy Paladino was the original art director. All the stuff was originally hand-drawn. The titler that puts the titles on the television image only had about ten fonts. Now, it's virtually limitless what you can do with different software packages for graphics. But a lot of that stuff was very labor-intensive, and I know she had to hand-draw a lot of those things. I know the "stereo hook-up" graphic she did by hand, and she would just hand-paint a lot of stuff. You really take for granted the technology nowadays, because you can do virtually anything.

GEORGE LOIS: About a year after the campaign ran and was incredibly successful, Bobby Pittman calls me up and says, "George, let's go out for lunch." "OK, where?" "21." "I hate 21." "Eh ... let's go to 21." We go to 21, and he says, "I don't know how to say this to you. 'I want my MTV!' saved our ass, but just between you and me, I want to stop using the line." And I said, "Why? It's so incredibly famous." He says, "Yeah, *it's too famous.* Wherever I go, if I go to a party, I say, 'I'm Bob Pittman from MTV.' They'll say, 'I want my MTV!' It's driving me crazy." So I had to do a new set of commercials. I did a commercial with a guy imitating Castro, and he's in the jungle, and he's talking about MTV. "MTV is gar-baggge." He's attacking MTV. And then another commercial was a born-again preacher talking about, "MTV is a disgrace. All they do is party, party, party!" So I had these guys attacking MTV because it was decadent. At the end of the Castro commercial, right behind him, there's a parrot. The commercial ends, and over his shoulder, the parrot says, "Awk ... I want my MTV!" Bob Pittman looked at me and said, *"Touche, George. Touche."*

ALAN HUNTER: That was all a major turning point, and it was an immediate success. That commercial didn't take but a few months to get people to wake up. The record industry said, "Oh wow, this is huge." And then advertising dollars started coming in ... and MTV started selling out.

Success!

NINA BLACKWOOD: All of a sudden, the fan mail started getting more and more. The VJs were also used as little ambassadors. Again, I have to reiterate the fact that this was the baby stages of cable. So we would be sent out on personal appearances to owner-operators of the cable channels, and MTV was actually used as a tool to get cable into certain parts of the country. As that happened, we still weren't in New York. I think it was two years that we were on the air, but we weren't on in Manhattan. So we didn't really have any idea, other than getting more fan mail. We were all trying to answer our own fan mail, and then it got so much that we couldn't.

I remember being sent out to San Antonio for a personal appearance. The limo is taking me to an autograph signing session at a record store. We're going into this shopping center, and I see this line wrapped all around. I'm going, "Oh wow, who's here?" And my minder says, "Well ... *you.*" I go, "WHAT?!" There were hundreds of people there. But because we still weren't in New York, we weren't really aware of it. And then once we got in New York, I'm flagging a cab, and I get picked up by the police, and they'll take me to where I was going, and the clubs all "opened." If more than one of us were together, like going to a concert...we used to go to Brendan Byrne Arena [in New Jersey] a lot. We couldn't sit in the audience anymore. We had to sit in the boxes, because we'd get mobbed.

ALAN HUNTER: I remember my first [personal appearance]. I can't remember if it was in Oklahoma or somewhere in Iowa. I was so excited. I got to get shipped out on someone else's dime, to have the company pay for your first class plane ticket. You arrive, and you've got a little bit of an entourage there. People are excited. It was totally foreign to me ... foreign to all of us. None of us had really been that kind of celebrity. But to have the local cable people just freak out to have you in their town, it still didn't dawn on me. I remember going in the limousine to go to the record store where we were having an appearance. And it was that clichéd moment, where I think anybody that is thrust into the limelight has, where they see 500 people lined up around the block and wonder who it's for. And the cable handler is like, "They're here to see *you.*" You're like, "WHAT?!" Just made no sense at all.

So I walked into a throng of people that just couldn't believe I was in this small town. Each of us had the same story when we'd come back from these appearances. We'd look at each other and go, *"This is huge."* Because we were living in Manhattan in a bubble. There was no recognition whatsoever. The occasional "bridge and tunnel" person would come in from Jersey and recognize us in a restaurant or something. But other than that, we were anonymous, and it felt just fine. When we went on those promotional appearances and it built bigger and bigger—every one we would go to later would be an even bigger crowd—and we'd come back with the tales of "This is huge."

MARK WEISS: They were all rock stars on their own. Wherever they went, everyone knew who they were. They were like newscasters, but I think everyone thought they were responsible for who got on there, so they were treated like gold wherever they went.

ALAN HUNTER: After a year, we realized that MTV was just driving Middle America crazy, because they didn't have anything else. It was CNN and ESPN when it came to 24-hour cable. When MTV came along, it was like the life of everybody's party. They were watching videos of bands they'd never heard of before, from the new wave in the U.K. to the Stray Cats. This was not albums or music that was being stocked in their local record stores. Imagine a kid in a small town with a little record store that was barely making it, and he sees these videos on MTV. The music business was tanking in the late '70s/early '80s, interestingly enough, kind of like it is now. They just weren't selling. And MTV absolutely revived the whole thing.

I think I kept my calm throughout my time, through today. I appreciated fans, but it didn't turn my head around. I really liked people, and I liked the people that liked me. I feel bad for bands or celebrities that have a job like Jerry Springer, where they must just hate their fans. Who would want to hang around with those kind of people? But I liked the people that liked what I did, and they all had their different taste. Every one of us had a different fanbase. They hated me and loved Mark, they loved JJ and hated Mark, and Martha was their favorite. It's just the way that goes.

LES GARLAND: People said, "Did you ever know?" Of course not. I really believed it could work. I believed people would like it. I believed it would be successful. We even made jokes, "If we really do this right, maybe one day, we'll have private jets." *But that was a joke.* We were all in our early 30s. We were youngsters. The average age at MTV was 24. So it was a bunch of young people not knowing that, in a lot of ways, we were changing the course of history. We were changing this landscape that wasn't just music. It was music, it was the presentation of music, it was television, it was advertising, clothing styles, hairstyles, film, international, the breaking of new artists. Nobody could have ever envisioned all of that. I remember—I don't know what year it was—but within two years, around '83, back in those days, it was like getting an Oscar, but to be called the *Billboard* magazine "International Innovator of the Year" was quite prestigious. To go to Greece and be handed such an award. Global, not just in the U.S. It was pretty amazing. I was in the greatest job of all time in that seven-year period that I was involved.

I told somebody, they were asking me about the impact of MTV, and I said, "Look, I hope this doesn't come off in any way egotistical. It's just my analysis of what I've seen, but I've never seen anything have the impact on the youth culture like this since the Beatles. What it did and effect and change people." And that comes with a great deal of responsibility. I think, hopefully, history will say that "There was Pittman and Garland," and "There was Pittman, Garland, and Sykes," and "There was a John Lack," and "There was a Gail Sparrow," and "There was a Julian Goldberg." There were so many other people that we could name that all contributed, and that's why it was this great team. I was the lucky guy who got to be the coach. And I don't take sole credit for anything. That's just not the way it is. I have seen where some have—or at least it got twisted that way—but funny enough, there is not one person. And that's good.

ALAN HUNTER: It was bizarre to be thrust into the middle of that kind of fandom. The young ladies were into Mark, JJ, and myself, and obviously, the guys thought that Martha was the cutest thing ever, and they wanted to sleep with Nina Blackwood. I was happily married at the time, so it was certainly not what I was looking out for.

NINA BLACKWOOD: It bonded us, because nobody other than the five of us knew what we were actually going through. We would share our stories, and we had each other as a family—to gripe about stuff, to complain about things. When the five VJs would get together, like say we'd go over to Alan's house, you could bet that, before the evening was done, there would be a huge gripe session. We'd be moaning, saying, *"This* should be done differently." But we all loved what we were doing, or else we wouldn't have been there. I think that's how we did get through that. For me, it was a complete dream job, combining things that I loved my whole life. If something like a VJ existed when I was a little girl, I would have said, "I want to be a VJ."

Living in New York and having the red carpet rolled out for you in a city like New York, it was just great. And for a shy person, it was a little bit of a double-edged sword for me, because I was shy, but it was kind of a cool thing, because any type of affair, I'm the one sitting in the corner getting up to get a drink and go to the bathroom, that's it. So it was kind of nice, because people were coming up to me, so I would meet people. I didn't have to move from my little wallflower corner. But it was phenomenal. I think all of us look back in the fondest way of that period. And very happy to be part of the beginning of it, not any other time, but the beginning was perfect.

LES GARLAND: I believe it was around '83 or '84, and Pittman and I did most of the interviews for the network—magazines, all over the world. I spent half my life doing interviews once we got to a certain point. I was being interviewed, and I forget who, but it was probably like a *Time* magazine or something. And the writer says, "Mr. Garland, do me a favor. I want you to look into your crystal ball, and tell me where you see the music industry in 25 years." No one had ever hit me with such a question. I'm like, *"Whoa."* I thought for a minute and said, "Well, here we go. I believe what I see in my crystal ball is that music will be up there somewhere. You won't be able to touch it. You won't be able to see it, but it will be there. It will be in people's 'devices.' Maybe it will be their telephone. It might be something on their wrist, but they'll be able to source it in all of their devices, whether it's their car, their home stereo, or their telephone. You won't have to pick something up, open it, put it in something, and play it. You won't have to do that anymore. I don't know how we're going to do that, but I think that's what may happen one day." And I remember almost being embarrassed, like, "I hope that reporter didn't think I was nuts." I don't even know where that came from. A little bit before the Internet, right?

BOB PITTMAN: The board of directors in the first couple of years made enormous pressure, because some people wanted to shut it down. It's called the civ. We were supposed to lose $20 million, and we lost $30 million before we broke even. And when it was getting close to $20 and we weren't breaking even, it was *howling*. And Steve Ross—to his credit—told the other people, "Look, the consumer loves it. We'll figure out how to make money." And I think we all had a consumer hit, but the money side and the market side was not happening. And again, that's where I went from the programming guy in charge of the product to being the guy who's supposed to make money.

There was a point in which a guy named Drew Lewis, who had been Ronald Reagan's transportation secretary, came in as the head of the Warner-Amex joint venture. I remember my first meeting, we were sitting around the table talking about something, and I mentioned Mick Jagger. And I just kept talking, and one of the people that worked with Drew a long time looked at Drew and said, "Drew, do you know who Mick Jagger is?" And he goes, "Uh ... no." "Have you ever heard of the Rolling Stones?" "Uh ... no." I go, "Holy shit, *I've got a lot of work to do here.*" And Drew gave me a mandate. He said, "If you can't get this thing profitable by the end of the year, I'm gonna shut it down." So there was a period of MTV—and I probably have a reputation of being the cheapest bastard alive—when I went through and slashed everything we could. And you know what? In 1983, by the end of the year, we were profitable.

ALAN HUNTER: The other moment that we realized MTV was a real powerhouse was probably year two. We sat down in a meeting, where we were told that this new band, INXS, was going to be "our baby," that we were going to break the band. It was going to show MTV's power, that we were going to work alongside the record company and try to break a band. Nothing nefarious—it wasn't Machiavellian or underhanded—it was just we were going to see if we really had an influence on people's music-listening. It was a little awkward to have to talk a lot more about INXS than any other band during your shift—promos, world premiere videos from this new band from down under, INXS. But lo and behold, INXS became a major, major band. And it was due to MTV's influence and the five VJs talking them up.

The "MTV Effect"

"WEIRD AL" YANKOVIC: I suppose it could also be argued that MTV had a profound effect on the TV and film industry as well, as the quick-cutting edit style found in many music videos made its way into movies and popular television series, i.e., *Miami Vice*.

BOB PITTMAN: The whole idea of the fast edit and "Let's just convey a mood, forget the words" worked its way into the movie business. *Flashdance* being a perfect example, where Jon Peters and Peter Guber said, "We had a bad movie. We didn't know what to do. We were watching MTV, and we said, 'Wait a minute ... *this* is the solution! Let's fix the movie by turning it into a big music video.'" Which they did, and it turned out to be a hit.

JOE ELLIOTT: About half-way through making *Pyromania*, we were starting to hear back from Cliff Burnstein, who was one of our co-managers, the one that was based in America, about this cable channel that was starting to play the video for "Bringin' on the Heartbreak." We probably just went, "Yeah, OK. Whatever." Because we were heavily concentrating on making a new record. But I guess it would have been about three months after that, we got a Telex—remember those?—from Cliff, saying, "*High N' Dry* has just doubled its sales in four months." We'd gone from like 250,000 copies to going gold. We're like, "Why?!" And he's like, "Well, this MTV thing."

ROB HALFORD: In a very short space of time, it was just huge, and everybody was clamoring to get on MTV. It became swamped. You had to get your timing absolutely right with the release of your single, album, or tour. Everybody was wanting to get on that MTV network. It was just *rammed*. It was like the 101 at rush hour in L.A. Everybody was crawling to get their slot and their time spot, because of its value and importance. We didn't realize it, but then when you come back to America, there are more people. There are more fans. You're selling more records. And that's "the MTV bump."

RUDY SARZO: Around 1981, if you wanted to build up a band, you had to do it city to city, radio station to radio station. I experienced that while I was touring with Ozzy Osbourne. Strategically, touring was a little different, too, because you would basically stick to one area. Let's say you play the Northeast. You would spend maybe four weeks playing that northeast area of the United States. Whereas, when MTV came, you could actually skip the "C markets" and some of the "B markets" and spread it around more to the cosmopolitan areas.

GLENN TILBROOK: By '82, we were playing Madison Square Garden. We had momentum in New York, and we had radio play in New York, but I think that was the thing that pushed us over the edge—the amount of exposure we got on MTV.

"WEIRD AL" YANKOVIC: ["Weird Al's" earlier videos] didn't change my life or my bank account very much, but the third one did. That one was "Eat It," and the day that video went into heavy rotation on MTV, my anonymity disappeared. Literally overnight, I became a celebrity. The "'Eat It' guy." After that, my albums went platinum. My concert tours sold out ... the money I spent on that video production was the best investment I ever made.

GEORGE THOROGOOD: You'd be walking down the street, and somebody would say, "Hey man, I saw you on MTV." That was very groovy. It wasn't, "I saw you on TV." It was, "I saw you on *MTV.*"

COLIN HAY: I think that radio was still the thing that really created the success with the band, certainly the initial success. And then MTV "rammed it home," if you like. It reinforced that and gave a really strong visual to the band, that really did help. Because I think our videos had some sort of personality that people responded to.

RICK SPRINGFIELD: The difference that I saw was, before MTV, you'd have to be on like your third successful album before people started recognizing you at the airport. But once MTV hit, you had that one hit single, and you were as recognizable as if you were around for three or four years. It was so instant. That was the power of television. And I had already had the *General Hospital* thing going, so I already had a pretty strong onscreen identity. Some of my videos were good. Some of them were awful. I think they helped, but they certainly never made a record successful. All my hits I felt would have been hits without MTV. But MTV was just an addition to radio. They had to be played on "saturation play" on radio, and MTV was just an added bonus. It could really catapult a song certainly, if it caught on.

TONI BASIL: Without it, I don't think ["Mickey"] would have been a hit. Even though I recorded the song in 1979—and I don't think it was really nominated for a Grammy until 1984—I think that I was lucky that they never released it in America until then. Because without MTV, I don't think it would have happened. The song being a hit was truly a product of the merger of the visual and the audio. When I got the American deal, that was exactly the time MTV started. So the timing worked out. It was definitely a product of timing, because if the song would have been released in America in '79/'80, I think it would have been confusing. I don't think radio would have known what do with it or how to handle it. But you see the video, and you understand the whole concept.

JOE ELLIOTT: Once ["Photograph"] hit MTV, over a period of three or four months, it just blew up. It literally went *apeshit*. The traditional route of breaking a band through radio was still very much alive and kicking, but this additional kind of media that was available now was pushing an album from two million to five million, an album from three million to six million. It was amazing.

STAN RIDGWAY: What happened with "Mexican Radio," it was kind of a musical accident. A "happy hit," which never really got above the top 40, but it floated around, and to this day, still floats around. It became an accidental MTV hit.

MIKE SCORE: I would say about 99%. The only other 1% is if we never had made the video, then it wouldn't have been on. They were so important to us at the time, because they put us in living rooms in Kansas and Boise, places like that, where the chances of getting out there to tour before that were probably zero, unless it was some horrible little undersized club, playing for next to nothing. But suddenly, because you were on TV, you were worth something. And every town with 5,000 kids, 500 of them would go see you.

RUDY SARZO: 200%. I'm completely honest. At the time of "Cum on Feel the Noize," it was only in selective cable systems in mostly urban areas. But I would say that everybody that had a cable system watched MTV, and our video was on every half hour. We went to number one, and we had to bump off *Thriller* to get to number one. Do you know what an achievement that is? We were at number two for about six weeks, with having *Thriller* or *Synchronicity* exchanging spots, and Lionel Richie the same thing. It was amazing. Finally, one week ... BAM! We went to number one. If it wasn't for MTV, it would have been impossible. In the old days, in order to go to number one, you had to sell one million records in one week. That's what "number one" meant—one million records in one week. Not like nowadays, where it's far less than that.

THOMAS DOLBY: It made a huge difference, because once it had hit on MTV, people wanted the product in their hands. Record companies, being what they are, hurried up and repackaged [*The Golden Age of Wireless*] and got it into the stores, saying, "Featuring the hit MTV video, 'She Blinded Me with Science.'" The album went gold, and it was really because of the success of the "Science" video that I put that down to. And I had mixed feelings about it, because on a certain level, it's not very representative of me and my music as a whole. On the plus side, it was a springboard that made millions of people discover the other aspect of my music. And it wasn't for everybody. Some of them just wanted a lot of wacky pop hits. But a percentage of them discovered the more mellow songs like "Screen Kiss" or "Airwaves." And that was the audience that I really wanted to reach. And long after my 15 minutes of stardom had faded, I still had a core audience who believed in the more mellow stuff.

RICKY BYRD: "I Love Rock n' Roll" became a huge hit before the video came out. It was a radio hit first. The video kept kids coming to the concerts around the world. People knew who we were, what we looked like, what to expect. It was just a whirlwind, the whole thing.

GEOFF DOWNES: In regards to the Buggles, MTV did not come out until maybe two years after the Buggles' single had been released ["Video Killed the Radio Star"], so we didn't really have the benefit to utilize that as a promotional vehicle. It became more of a history, Trivial Pursuit question—"What was the first video ever played?" But when it came to Asia, yes, it was very much part and parcel of our initial success, that we had another outlet, in the visual context we were being seen in.

MICHAEL SADLER: We hit the States with I think about four or five tours in a row in that one year, jumping from Jethro Tull to Pat Benatar to Billy Squier. We would just finish one and start another one. Between that and MTV, MTV was very instrumental with getting us a kick-start in the States, for sure.

SERGEANT BLOTTO: It was very big. Our first record—which had "I Wanna Be a Lifeguard"—came out in early '80. We'd gotten a lot of airplay on radio stations across the country, but once it was on MTV, it really broke open a lot of doors, as far as it made touring a lot easier. And the name recognition. Several members of Blotto had been touring around the country for five or six years. We would always get new fans wherever we went, but you were clawing and picking them up one at a time, as you were touring around. And we'd get radio play in towns we were coming in, and we'd have some records in the stores. But MTV really helped change all that. It was like having a national radio station. We'd go to towns we'd never been in before, and there would be people in the front row singing along, which was a very strange experience for us at first.

GEORGE THOROGOOD: I think it played more in making a success of George Thorogood and the Destroyers rather than the song ["Bad to the Bone"]. I have to be honest with you, the song came into its own when they launched classic rock radio. It was about eight years later that they started classic rock, and that's when "Bad to the Bone" took off. But the video itself helped our career visually *immensely.* Not just the song—the video itself. The video was so good, the song was almost like secondary. People looked at the video and said, "Wow. I want to go see this guy play." It was a great advertisement for the act.

ORAN "JUICE" JONES: This was a means that you could make crazy money and crazy visibility. And everybody would know you. You'd just be a hero in the neighborhood. MTV, when the videos came, man, they gave the cat who was hero in the neighborhood to be a hero in the rest of the world. So the impact that it had was incredible. Unfortunately, in those early days, they weren't playing too many urban artists. But we had BET, and even they were a bit selective, because they wanted a certain type of artist I think at that time—especially black. They didn't want artists that were scaring black people. [Laughs] They wanted to stay in the game, so they were a bit selective, too, so a lot of the underground artists didn't have the advantage of videos, because they didn't have the image to go along with it.

Fashion

MIKE SCORE: For everybody that watched MTV, to see what kind of fashions were happening, and the fact that they didn't just have to wear jeans and t-shirts anymore—I think that was a revelation to American kids. MTV was such a groundbreaker in the way it not only showed you the music, but it showed you what was going on in the rest of the world as far as fashion. I sometimes think about how many of those kids that came to see us and were dressed a bit gothic or a bit '80s or a bit wild and crazy, would have been forced into jeans, cowboy boots, and t-shirts if not for MTV. It opened up a whole new world for them.

THOMAS DOLBY: I remember meeting a guy once, who lived in some little town in eastern California, in one of the "test markets" for MTV. It was in like Owens Valley or somewhere like that. And he said every household in his town had MTV as a teenager, and when they would go and play football against neighboring high schools, they suddenly realized they were in a different "class" really, because they were experiencing MTV, and these other kids seemed like hicks to them all of a sudden. There was a rapid export of "cool urban culture," from the cities out to the provinces. So that I think was a huge influence.

GREG HAWKES: It just enhanced the pop radio sense of fashion, because then you could see it on TV, and see what artists were wearing. It just sort of carries over and affects regular fashion. It probably just made it more intense with MTV, because it was right in your face now, and you could see it all the time.

ROGER POWELL: Even if you couldn't attend a band's concert, you could get the flavor of what rock n' roll was all about by watching MTV. It was a way to "get backstage," if you will, or up to the front row at a concert. Now, all of a sudden, there was all this additional exposure to the rock lifestyle and rock fashions. You didn't have to guess that something you bought was going to be cool or not. All you had to do was double-check it against what was on MTV. So it had an enormous effect, because this thing was happening 24 hours a day, compared to getting a fashion magazine or *Rolling Stone* every month or whenever it came out. You're being bombarded, and it was always the latest whatever was there. And it started to differentiate the genres of music a little bit more, because the visual element became a reinforcing brainwave thing of, "Now I've got the whole picture of the band I like and what they're all about." The subtleties and the not-so-subtleties of it was much more reinforced and allowed you to feel like you were participating more.

RICKY BYRD: Oh, come on man, it led *everything*. Billy Idol was great with videos. People would see them and start dressing like him. Look at Madonna. Would Madonna be so big if video wasn't around, so people could see what she does? If you were a kid, and you just heard one of those songs on the radio, would you be as impressed as if you saw her rolling around on the floor? Shock value is hard to put across on the radio, unless you're Jim Morrison or something like that ... if it's just outward sexual appeal that's in the words. Listen, Elvis was amazing, but when they shot him from only the waist up? Dude, *that was his ticket.* Look at the Stones. When they told Mick Jagger he couldn't sing "Let's Spend the Night Together," well then it became a thing. "What was he saying? 'Let's fuck tonight?!' *What did he say?"* That's the mystery of rock n' roll that's totally not there anymore. When all of a sudden you could see everything, it kind of put everything in front of everybody. It took a lot of the mystery away. But some people took advantage of it and made whole careers out of being video stars.

JOHN OATES: I see the parallel between what *American Bandstand* did for teenagers in America, in that for the first time—even back in the '50s—teenagers in different parts of the country saw what teenagers were doing, what they were wearing, what they looked like, what dances they were doing in Philadelphia. And all of a sudden, Philadelphia became the arbiter of style for teenagers. It became kind of the benchmark of "Hey, this is what cool teenagers do," because they were on TV. MTV kind of took that to another level. All of a sudden, kids all over the country could see their favorite groups and what they were wearing. You didn't necessarily have to see them in person and wait until they came to your town, or if you lived in Topeka, Kansas, they may never come to your town. So this was an opportunity all of a sudden to see what English bands were wearing, and the clothing and the hairstyles. It was so much easier to all of a sudden be part of a new music culture.

MARKY RAMONE: That all started in the '50s, with Jerry Lee Lewis, Elvis Presley, Little Richard, and Chuck Berry. Fashion and music go together. It was obvious in the videos. Cyndi Lauper—look what she wore. The Ramones—leather jackets and jeans. Everything was more colorful, just to enhance the situation of the video. Remember, it's only two and a half/three minutes long. You have to put everything you have into that. You want to set trends, purposely or not. That was definitely a reason to integrate the two, the fashion and the music. And to set a standard, to who you were trying to appeal to.

PHIL COLLEN: Music is an art-form, so it's had very close links to fashion anyway. But all of a sudden, it was brazen. It wasn't just, "Oh, I saw this band in a magazine." *You were on TV.* So everything from Duran Duran to Prince, you had an automatic influence, and it was far-reaching. TV is the biggest thing out there. It just took over from all the radio stuff and was totally influential.

DAVE MARSH: Probably the worst thing that came out of MTV in one way was the idea that models should be taken seriously. Where that idiocy came from has to be MTV. It made no sense to me.

GEDDY LEE: Well, we've never been a very fashionable band, never been a very trendy band, so it's hard to say. But certainly, bands became much more conscious of what they looked like. I think management was much aware of assembling bands that would look good on TV. It didn't obviously affect us, but I could see it around us, with the kind of bands that were starting to open for us, that management was looking more towards what they could sell via television.

STEWART COPELAND: They must have had an effect on trends. But my sense is that it was the other way around. The guys making the videos would pick up on the trends and try and get them into the video. Certainly in our case, I don't recall Kevin and Lol [Godley & Creme] saying, "Hey look guys, plaid is in this year. Let's get you dressed in some plaid." I think it was the other way around. We'd show up wearing something, and the next thing you know, everyone else is wearing it. But we were never conscious of any of that, actually. We would *shoot ourselves* if we ever discussed wardrobe.

ROB HALFORD: I'm sure that people were frantically looking around their local store, dashing off to some place where they could pick up a bit of this and a bit of that, and try and emulate what their favorite act was wearing. Because they'd seen it on MTV. I think that, right from the get-go, the MTV execs probably realized the potential of the influence of that side of what they were about. Previously, you had *Creem* magazine, *Hit Parader* magazine, and *Circus* magazine. They were across America, so people would buy them and flip through the pages, look at the pictures, and copy it. But when you actually saw the stars in the studios or the stars on the screen, that again was an influential moment. All the fans try to emulate the way your favorite artist looks on stage or on video.

ORAN "JUICE" JONES: When you can see it, a picture is worth a thousand words. Well then, a video is a bunch of moving pictures, so how many thousands of words do you have? It had an impact not only on fashion, but *everything*. Because as opposed to just hearing it and visualizing it in their mind, it was right there in front of them. The impact that hip-hop especially had on people, and plus with video providing a visual, then it became obvious to them ... people want to identify with their artists, and they want to live next door to them, or act like they can reach out and touch them. They want to look like them, talk like them. That's what hip-hop proved.

On the record, he's describing the shirt, the pants, the sneakers, the hairstyle, the lifestyle, or the attitude. But the video allowed me the opportunity to actually *see it*. I can see the mannerisms and the characteristics. I can see what swagger is, as opposed to just hearing about it. And I think that little suburban kids, although I feel they identified with the music from an audio aspect, when they saw it visually, it gave them more ammunition, because now they didn't actually have to think about how to look, how to dress, or how to act. Now, they could see it. "Oh, I know what to get now." So the impact that video had on fashion, it's the same impact that fire had on cooked food. Before you had fire, you had to eat it like it was. And then when you had fire, you could cook it now. So, same food, just better. Same fashion, just better now. It had a positive impact.

DEBORA IYALL: I was watching, too, and saying, "Oh, I like the way she puts that scarf in her hair" or whatever. I guess there were more people jumping on "new wave fashion," and that became pretty dominant for the next five years—once people saw musicians on stage wearing more graphic clothes, more skinny jeans. I remember it was huge when the fashion changed from flares to skinny jeans and from long hair to short hair. In the punk scene, a longhaired kid in flares would have to have a lot of courage to come to a punk club, because they'd probably get a lot of shit. But after a while, it was kind of weird to see new wave fashion in the Macy's window. It kind of ended up being shocking a little bit, how fast the marketplace could co-opt an underground shift.

GERALD CASALE: Basically, videos became a fashion ad. And then, everybody in the country started dressing like what they would see. Specifically, all the sexy women that were in the videos. That more than anything, more than even how the bands dressed. That's how you'd see girls dressing in every town you went into, and every club you went into. There's just no doubt about it.

"WEIRD AL" YANKOVIC: I never was a slave to fashion ... I'm sure that's a shocking revelation to you! But I've certainly noticed how entertainers and their music videos have had an impact on fashion and culture. You really don't really need to look any further than Madonna. She famously changed her look every 15 minutes, and her throngs of followers and wannabes dutifully changed right along with her.

MICHAEL SADLER: Video—especially with the women—they would dress the way that they felt like dressing as artists, so that would influence a generation or that fan base. Girls would dress like Madonna did in "Like A Virgin." But on the other hand, a lot of times the artist is just reflecting what's on the street, anyway. So it's a tough call. Unless it's really extreme—like a Lady Gaga or a Björk—I think, ultimately, it's just reflecting what's going on on the streets anyway.

CY CURNIN: To give you my best example, when Madonna was about to launch her video in which she was wearing a tartan mini skirt—can't remember the song as much as the skirt—Wal-Mart were flooding their stores with cheap Chinese copies of the same dress. The market was feeding all the pigs at once now.

TOMMY TUTONE: We were coming from a very style-conscious generation. My parents thought I was a rebel, but really, I don't think we were *real* rebels. The look was very important. When we got signed in San Francisco, how you looked was almost as important as how you sounded. We got signed because we were more into music and songs, rather than haircuts and stuff. But still, the look was important. It had to be a new kind of look, so it wasn't like, "Go out and find somebody handsome or 'movie star/tv-like.'" They're looking for anti-heroes really. Well, "Let's try these guys. These guys are *really* off the wall!" I'd say there was a feeding circle from MTV to fashion and back again. Fashion goes through cycles where people try to invent stuff from the top and push it down, and other stuff springs up from the bottom. People find something in second-hand stores, and it becomes fashionable. This $2 item is $100 at Macy's next year. So it all met right there in the middle in a very interesting way, and they had a big effect on each other.

SERGEANT BLOTTO: I don't like to admit it ... but yes, I had a pair of red leather pants. Whether it was Loverboy or Boy George, when you can see that on a regular basis, and you're not just seeing that at a concert situation, it has that same impact as being a national trend. So if you saw Simon LeBon with his sport jacket sleeves pushed up, you thought, "Oh OK, *that's a cool look.*" And the next thing you know, the next 27 bands you see had their white sports coats with the sleeves pushed up.

MIKE RENO: I wore a bandana around my neck, and sometimes, I took it off and put it around my head. And the reason I did that is because the lights were so hot that I started sweating, and I wanted to keep the sweat out of my eyes. Well, now it's *a fashion statement.* Still to this day, people say, "Where's the headband? Where's the red leather pants?" The funny thing is, in half the videos, Paul was wearing the red leather pants, but they always come to me, like, "Where's the red leather pants?" They tied it all in with an album cover and our live show.

PAUL DEAN: I wore a headband the first night, and Mike liked the idea and stole it off me ... the son of a bitch! [Laughs] But I don't care. He still wears it. We don't wear the leather pants anymore ... somehow, they "shrank" or something. [Laughs]

MIKE RENO: I guess it's just what happens. You see somebody do some- thing, and that's the way you think of them for the rest of their lives. I just thought it was funny, because what people don't understand is the reason why we had the leather pants to begin with was because our manager, in the office, they had a publicist. And her husband owned a clothing store that made leather clothes. She said, "Go down to the leather shop, take whatever you want, and we'll make a note of it. When you make some money, you can pay for it."

So I went down and picked out a few things, and the only reason why I picked out the red ones was because they fit best. So it's not like I sat down and said, "If I wear red leather pants, I'm going to be hugely famous ... and I'll even be more famous if I wear a headband." I didn't plan any of this. I wore headbands because the sweat would go in my eyes and I couldn't see. At first, I started cutting off the sleeves of my shirts, because a shirtsleeve fits right on your head perfectly, a t-shirt sleeve. And it's also made of cotton, so it sucks up the moisture. So if you look back at a lot of the videos, actually what I have is a sleeve of a t-shirt on my head. It's not an official bandana. I just created it with whatever I had.

FRANK STALLONE: That's why I wore it [in the "Far from Over" video]— Mike Reno! Mike was a friend of mine, and that's exactly what I did. He used to wear a red headband and red leather pants ... when he could get into them. Mike's put on a little weight since then. Yeah man, I told him that. I bumped into him a few years ago. And that's why I wore it, because I thought it looked cool—black leather pants, a red headband ... and also, *red wristbands.* I thought I looked pretty good at that time, but now I look back on it ... you'd never see Clapton do that. But Clapton also had some clothes that would look a little dated now.

SERGEANT BLOTTO: To be honest with you, I don't remember a whole lot of Loverboy videos. I remember the headband and red leather pants.

MIKE RENO: I'd imagine we did a little of copying ourselves. We were swayed a lot by the group the Cars. I used to listen to their music and say, "This is great," and they wore all kinds of cool, weird, handmade clothes that I'd never seen before. So it wasn't like I created any of this. I was just going with the flow of what was going on out there, too. As soon as you wore it on TV, that's when the general public starting going, "I'm going to do that 'Mike Reno look.'" And even to this day, people come up to me and say, "I had the Mike Reno look down pat. I got laid *so many* times!" We did have a plan to wear some colors, as opposed to wearing just bland black and whites. Paul and I did discuss having some colors, so we said, "Let's wear some red, some yellow, and some black. Let's work with those three colors." I think we actually got that idea, though, from the Cars, to tell you the truth. I don't think it was an original idea. If it was an original idea, it was motivated by the Cars, because they were way ahead of their time—musically, sound-wise, the way they looked, their haircuts, the whole nine yards. I think we looked up to the Cars. I know I did.

PAUL DEAN: It's funny. There are a lot of people that show up in red leather pants and headbands—and still do! Especially if they have an '80s theme or something. We did a show a while back with an '80s theme, and everybody showed up like that. I had a big curly wig on, like Dee Snider. But I think videos still leave a very big impression on people style-wise. Van Halen was a huge influence, because I don't remember seeing ripped jeans until Eddie was wearing the ripped jeans.

ALDO NOVA: I don't think anybody borrowed the "Flock of Seagulls haircut," but it was definitely a fashion statement back then.

MIKE SCORE: I was a hairdresser for years and years. I was a punk hairdresser, fashionable hairdresser. To me, it was part of my world already. I was in hairdressing. I was doing all kinds of weird styles. I had a shop called Oz the Magic Hairdressers. Anybody that was a little bit crazy or wanted to be a bit different came to us, and we styled them up by chopping all their hair off. [Laughs] And if they didn't like that, we just colored it green and kicked them out.

JOE ELLIOTT: Things that become iconic are totally accidental, like the Union Jack shirt. It became the biggest-selling t-shirt of the *Pyromania* tour. But it wasn't like we had sit-down meetings about, "We've got to use the Union Jack." I had a £25 budget to dress myself for this video ["Photograph"], and I had £8 left. I had bought the trousers and boots or whatever. And the shirt was £7.99. I thought it was loud, bright, British ... it'll do. No great thought went into it. It was just instinct. But the way that David Mallet edited the video and what we called "bled out all the colors"—he made the whites whiter than white and reds redder than red and the blues bluer than blue—it just *leapt* through the TV screen. And I think that really set up an entire look that lasted a good 18 months to a year on MTV. All the rock bands seemed to copy that theme, because it worked. We were just very lucky that we were one of the first to do it.

PHIL COLLEN: It wasn't a conscious effort. It was just what we were wearing at the time. I actually think we were pretty interesting when it came to our look, because we didn't really have one. It was kind of culled together with bits and pieces from Kensington Market, this place that used to be in Kensington, High Street. And King's Road—whatever that was floating around. Joe had bought a Union Jack shirt, and Rick had bought some Union Jack shorts. When we got to America and we started doing videos and we were wearing them in our videos, it really crossed over. Us being British and everything. Totally unconscious, but it struck a nerve somewhere.

RUDY SARZO: I'm not like the most fashionable guy. I do most of my shopping at malls. I was on tour with Quiet Riot, and I needed to get a shirt. So I went to a shopping mall, and there was a store called The Merry Go Round. And I saw a shirt that had a target. That's what I wound up wearing in the "Cum on Feel the Noize" video. That shirt kind of became an iconic shirt for metal or Quiet Riot. So then The Merry Go Round started running their own ads on MTV, but instead of having us, they had Slade! [Laughs] It was their song, and I guess that was the only way they could get permission for "Cum on Feel the Clothes" or something. So if you're talking about fashion, my contribution to fashion on MTV was that round target shirt from Merry Go Round.

FRANK STALLONE: Olivia Newton-John and the ankle warmers and all that stuff like that. And I think Pat Benatar wore that type stuff. It was kind of a "stretchy period," a stretch material period.

RUDY SARZO: Metal bands were wearing spandex before MTV. The tighter the trouser the better, whether the cameras were rolling or not. And nothing is tighter than spandex. You can date David Lee Roth wearing spandex way before MTV was around. It's just that MTV was able to bring it to the home, rather than just leave it at the arena. It's like going to ballet. You see a dude wearing tights and say, "Hey, I think I'm going to wear that to the grocery store." *No.* But if you watch him doing that on MTV, then it becomes fashionable.

FRANKIE SULLIVAN: Duran Duran set the tone for all that stuff. It overshadowed a little bit how good they were and how good musicians they were, because they're really good players. But they were more on the fashion side of it, in a cool way. You had other bands that had very different looks, like Flock of Seagulls, but I think the pinnacle of it was what Duran Duran did with it, because they were a very stylish and hip band. They set that tone and ruled in that area for a long, long time. I think Robert Palmer did a great job. He was on the style end of it.

STAN RIDGWAY: People started to *view* music. They literally started to hear music with their eyes. And I always thought that there was a downside to that, because it kind of allowed more of the "false marketing" to come into play. Whether something was really musically challenging was questionable, but if someone was dressed up in a provocative way, then the audience thinks, "This is really edgy." I remember once, listening to—and I have nothing against this guy—Boy George, when Culture Club first came out. I heard their song, and my head was turned from the TV. I thought, "My God, *what is that?* It just sounds like middle-of-the-road mush." And then I turned to see the video, and of course, Boy George is dressed up and has all these things on, outrageous combinations of fashion. And that was an example right there, kind of an edgy look, but the music was starting to go backward in terms of challenging. But I still think music is best listened to, *not watched.*

ART BARNES: Ugh. *Heinous* fashion in those days. The dawn of new wave fashion or whatever you wanna call that was awful. Bad hair, bad shoes, over-the-top looks, too much make-up, and sadly, a lot of weak songs, lame synths—not all of 'em—guitars gone missing for the most part. *Lame.*

MARTHA DAVIS: It may have taken something that was already over-the-top and pushed it a little. It was almost like everyone escaped from art school. For some reason, that decade was kind of an indulgent decade in a lot of ways.

MICKEY THOMAS: We have a lot of laughs looking back at our videos and photo shoots from the mid '80s, because I'm buddies with a lot of the guys that were caught in the same "video trap" that we were. Mike Reno from Loverboy is a good buddy of mine, and Bobby Kimball from Toto and Jimi Jamison from Survivor. We look back now, and you're like, "What in the hell was I thinking?" I guess I *wasn't* thinking. It worked at the time, but boy, some of the clothes I was wearing in the mid '80s ... now, it's frightening for me to look at it. But a lot of it was the effect of MTV and the effect that MTV had on the fashion world. A lot of the more popular bands, like

Duran Duran, were really having a big effect on fashion. And it had an influence on us, too.

I think with being the singer, [being considered a "sex symbol"] comes with the territory. It's kind of understood that the singer is going to be featured in the video, or the singer is going to be the one who's going to do most of the interviews. And I think most of the guys in the band understand that, but you can't help but have a little animosity along the way. It always reminds me of *Almost Famous*, which is a great movie for capturing that behind-the-scenes competitiveness and resentment. Usually, it's competition between the lead singer and the lead guitarist, because those are two kind of "out front" positions and sort of ego-related. [Laughs] But like I said, it comes with the territory. I try not to take it too seriously, myself. It's like, "Alright, this is the way it's got to be. Somebody's got to do this ... *but I'm not a sex symbol."*

DAVE MARSH: There are no "ugly people" in American mass media, whether you're talking movies, television, or anything else. Ugly doesn't exist, unless it's grotesque ugly. And there's not even any "average," really. Look at the background figures in *North by Northwest* [a 1959 film]. You'll find a group of people that were quite a bit better looking, slimmer, and well-groomed than you would have if you actually had been in a Mt. Rushmore cafeteria or wherever the hell they are. It's just a fact. And the idea that that began with MTV? *No.* What began with MTV maybe is a more libertine take on "look," but that was going to happen anyway. I think MTV proved to be a real driver of it, but I don't think it was an initiator of it. I think what initiated it were changes in the society, that had something to do with the fact that women were freer to use their bodies for display, and men still controlled the media.

DEBORA IYALL: It's the marketing people. Not everybody can think of music as art. That's the bottom line. I still do. A lot of us still do. Probably most of my fans do. But there's this structure that's between you and your fans. That's the marketing people, and they just don't get it. They're too busy being creeps. What can I say? It's funny, too, because like, Bob Dylan, if he had come up during the video age, they would have gone, *"AHHH!"* [Laughs] It's like, those of us with ears, that care about culture in a personal way, we've just got to keep hammering it home that we're here and not going away, and we're going to find our fans, because they're out there.

PETE ANGELUS: I remember thinking that people were trying to push fashion as far as they could push it. And I also remember when choreography and a lot of dancers started to rear its ugly head on MTV. I specifically remember those two things, thinking, "Man, they are just pushing it and pushing it." And to me, at some point, it crossed a line where it became humorous. And I think I pointed to that in some of the videos that I did.

BOOTSY COLLINS: It told that particular crowd exactly what to do, to wear, to say, and more importantly, what was cool to play on their boomboxes while out with their friends and their parties. You had no choice in the matter. MTV ruled the world. Well, at least the world that bought into it.

MTV's Policies

LES GARLAND: When you're a DJ or an air personality, maybe there would be the desire to control the music in your show, because a lot of people still had the memory of freeform radio. But everybody was smart enough to understand that we needed to have an editorial stance. We needed to have a direction. What MTV was going to be was a hybrid version of AOR meets pop. There was no radio station like MTV. It would have been a hit if it was a radio station in any major market in America. It was differentiated from everything else out there. It wasn't just AOR; it was wider than that.

GERALD CASALE: When it went national, the joke was on Devo, because they had *immense* power. And they were laying down the terms, like a vanquishing army. And the rules kept changing every month—what you could and couldn't do. And before we knew it, they wouldn't play Devo videos because they were citing the fact that we weren't in the top 40. And yet, they would still play "Whip It," because it was "grandfathered in" and had been a hit before MTV existed. So then, we were thrown into that ghetto where unless we were getting a certain number of stations added with a new release, they weren't going to run our video. So it was like a cat and mouse game. It was like, "Yeah, but if you run the video, all the stations are going to add it."

LES GARLAND: We were people who, being born young in the '60s, etc., were a bunch of freedom fighters. We didn't believe in censorship, on any level. We hated the concept of censorship. So, in the very beginning, for the first few years, there were no rules. We accepted it as our responsibility. And sometimes, that requires making judgments. When it's all said and done and finished, someone has to ultimately be responsible for what goes on this television network. And I'd tell people when I programmed radio stations, [that] that was my job. Ultimately, it was *my* ass hanging out there. Rule one, protect the license. Rule two, get the highest ratings you could get. And that was the way we looked at MTV. We have a heavy responsibility here, of what is OK and what isn't. And we used just good, old fashioned, gut common sense.

But you can imagine how that started becoming after the first couple of years, people started analyzing everything. "Why did you turn that video down, and you're taking this one then?" They would get right down to the specific scene we found to be questionable. And then people started accusing us of messing around with the art and changing the scenes. We hated it. We just hated it. We were being attacked in the media. "What are these standards?" They forced us into doing something we never wanted to do. We created "standards and practices." And every network has such a department. And that, in some ways, was done for protection, to say we had such a department. And, in other ways, it was done because it was meaningful, and we felt like we needed to have such a department. It was kind of a double-edged sword in a way. As much as we had a disdain for that sort of thing, *this is censorship.* I don't give a shit how you paint this. When it's all said and done, it's censorship. And you're talking about what I consider to be art, which made it even more difficult. I didn't like it.

GERALD CASALE: It came to a head in 1982, with a song called "That's Good," where Warner's was really high on the song, and we were really high on the song. Radio was liking it, and we made this video. We sent it to them, and this guy that I had not met yet, who I would get to meet—Les Garland—who was kind of like their version of the Taliban ... the *corporate* Taliban, says, "We're not playing this." He goes, "We know what you're trying to say." And we go, "What are you talking about?" He goes, *"Let's talk about it.* You've got a cartoon donut flying through space, and you've got a cartoon french fry going through it. And then, it cuts to a girl with a smile on her face. I know what you're saying, OK? Let me tell you something. You can have the donut, you can have the girl ... but you can't have the french fry. Or, you can have the french fry and the donut ... but you can't have the girl."

We were unfortunately artists with integrity, like Martin Milner in *Sweet Smell of Success*, who screws himself by standing up to JJ Hunsecker. So we cite four or five other videos that are on the air that are so over-the-top sexual, not even with humor or animation. It's like hardcore crotch and rubbing ... plenty of tits and ass, which was de rigueur. He goes, "Have it your way. *That's it.*" Elliot tried to lobby him and wasn't getting anywhere, so we edited the video, put our tail between our legs, and swallowed the load. Sent the video back. But the process back then, it wasn't like Final Cut Pro. You had to go into a studio, and there were layers in that video, composites early on. It cost us a lot of money. I think by the time they got it back, they had this thing where they only accepted videos once a week. We got it to them within ten days, and then they let it float over into the next "acquisition day" or whatever. So 17 days later, he checks radio adds and says, "We're still not running this, because you guys aren't building a story for us here." [Laughs]

DAVE MARSH: They don't want anything that's too emotionally down. They don't want anything that smacks of danger. They just wanted to sell tits and ass, and they were willing to reduce the music to that to get their way. That was why I hated them.

LES GARLAND: I tell people, "You've got to understand something. I'm a programmer. I think I'm born to do that and to build these media entities. Whether they're radio, TV, whatever. But being a censor is being a whole other assignment." I'm just a curator of this art museum called "MTV." These "pictures" come in, and they fit the feel of our gallery. We don't judge them. We just say, "That fits. It's got a good feel," and we put it on the wall. And if people like it, we know that. If we don't, we take it down. It's not our decision. We're just doing this for people. We're not doing this for our satisfaction. Censorship is a very scary thing. So here comes standards and practices. Now, you can imagine the battles we used to get in, because standards and practices starts feeling like a pretty powerful little department. And where there comes a little power, there might come some abuse. And then it started getting silly. There would be fights—who could over-rule who? Could standards and practices over-rule programming, or could programming over-rule standards and practices? Because you would have to over-rule sometimes. So that became very, very difficult. It became time-consuming. It became difficult to manage. It was a bit of a nightmare, but it had to be done. So the first couple of years, it was wide open. We just used good, common sense, and it was a responsibility that we had.

DAVE WAKELING: You lived in mortal fear of this "woman," who I don't know if she actually existed or she was an archetype. But she supposedly sat in this room, with a list of 30 things, ticking them off as she watched your video and how many of those 30 ... that was how much editing you had to do, if you wanted to be on "her MTV." Unless it turned out that you were Madonna, because she had all 30 in every one of her videos! That was the benchmark. So there was that part to it. The quality control could be lowest common denominator.

FEE WAYBILL: They constantly censored us. We tried to do the "She's a Beauty" video, [and] they censored a whole bunch of stuff. We had a top-less mermaid, and of course, that was right out. We had to change that and a bunch of stuff. It was just a little too weird for MTV. We had a great big paper breast, a big screen with an air-brushed breast on it. And the guy in the ride for "She's a Beauty" would go crashing through it. Well, that was too weird, and they had to kind of soft-focus that whole thing, so it looked like a big fuzzy ball. For bands like Duran Duran, that changed their whole career, and they spent a fortune on exotic videos and locations. And they wouldn't let us spend the money. At that point, Capitol Records was worried that we weren't selling enough records to outlay that kind of money.

Originally, we were going to do the "She's a Beauty" video as this kind of freakshow/sideshow thing. Kind of a la Tod Browning's *Freaks*, have like "the chicken woman" and "the sausage man" and "the bearded lady." Sideshow freaks. That was too weird, *way too weird*. They said, "Nah, forget about that." Then we had to rethink it and came up with this idea of the kid on the ride. And that kid was Robert Arquette [who later became Alexis Arquette], because Rosanna was a friend of ours. She was the girlfriend of one of the guys in Toto, and we were at the same management company.

MARKY RAMONE: There was controversy [surrounding "The KKK Took My Baby Away"] because of the subject matter. A hornet's nest. I can see that. Today, it wouldn't be a big deal, it was a humorous song. It wasn't "pro-KKK." It was just *a song*. Then when I was out of the band, they did "Psycho Therapy," that was the next video. And that created controversy. They stopped playing it because, obviously, a lot of people got agitated because it was supposed to be inside of an insane asylum.

STAN RIDGWAY: I had a video of my own, from my first solo record, *The Big Heat*, where I made a video for "The Big Heat," and it was a film noir-ish, dark video, about a chase. I thought it came out great and was very intriguing. There was one point where somebody—and in a melodramatic way, almost like a 1940s film—gets stabbed in an alleyway. Kind of in a shadowy way. And MTV said that they couldn't play it, because "it was too violent." And we looked at that and knew, "That's not *really* why, because it's not really any more violent than these other examples over here. In fact, those are even more." Suddenly, the mix was changing, and certain things weren't fitting in.

WARREN DeMARTINI: I continued to be surprised that we were played at all. If we were on there, it was like, "Can you believe it? They're still playing this video?" I think on the record company's side—from hearing stuff in the hallways—there was a real shift of ... it was MTV that decided what was going to be played and what wasn't going to be played. But I guess we were helping to cause them to get big advertising dollars, so we were a mainstay on there for quite a while.

LES GARLAND: We looked at heavy metal music as just another category that was made up by music companies. Radio stations like to categorize things. We tried to destroy all the categories. If it was great, call it what you wanted to call it, we didn't care. It was great. If it was Iron Maiden and it was great, play it. Now, we never got into day-parting. Day-parting is an old game that was always played in radio, where back in the early days, top 40 radio stations have different demographics at different times of the day. So they might not play something that was really appealing to a young, hardcore male—like Iron Maiden or something—they may not play that during the daytime, because they had more women listening during the day, for example. We believed if something was on MTV, it was "on." On is on, and it plays in all day-parts.

As we became bigger, more viewership, we found ourselves applying some of the old "sciences" that we had learned in radio. And there were certain instances where things might be day-parted a little bit. But for the most part, if something was on, *it was on.* We didn't have *Headbanger's Ball* yet. We didn't have specific shows that were dedicated to one thing. The only "shows" we had back in those days ... a lot of people thought that the second generation team at MTV put all those shows on. But I remind people, we did "stunts." In my seven years there, we called them stunts. A lot of people came up with wacky ideas to make shows, but I said, "This ain't about shows. This is a music channel. That's why it's called MTV: Music Television." We wouldn't even consider it. Somebody would come up with a wacky show, and we'd go, "That's really cool, but that belongs on another network, not one called 'MTV.'" So we turned down a lot of that stuff. Instead, we did stunts, and we did some fun things.

BRUCE KULICK: I thought we got a fair amount of coverage. We weren't always the darlings, but it all depended. I had no complaints about our support from MTV. Unfortunately, every year, there was a different flavor of the month. Where one year, it's Whitesnake they want to show. But we used to get a fair amount of coverage.

DAVE MARSH: It's funny. When they did let metal in ... metal's like hip-hop. They didn't want metal, because look, what's the problem with metal and hip-hop from the point of view of an advertising-driven medium? They're down-market. Who listens to heavy metal? Poor kids, whether they're Anglo or Mexican-American, that's always been the "metal audience." Who's the "hip-hop audience"? Black kids who are mostly poor in this country. And MTV just didn't ... I mean, Bob Pittman didn't want that. He couldn't sell it. And what it was really all about was selling, because that's what broadcasting in America is about.

LES GARLAND: We did a show called ... I ripped it off *60 Minutes,* the show from CBS that had been number one forever. We used to do things irreverent against the networks just to fuck with them. So I came up with *120 Minutes,* which was two hours of music, and we did it on Sunday nights at midnight. That thing developed an audience. People loved it. Then we had *Basement Tapes*, because we knew there were tons of young people out there making music in their garage—get a camera, shoot it, and send it to us. We'll create a show. So we started having a little fun like that.

NINA BLACKWOOD: There was an acquisition committee, and there were various members at various times. We would call them "the suits." And as time went by, I think they opened up. This was a little later on, but we had a VJ assistant named Ken Clark. And he was part of the acquisition committee. And nothing against Ken, because Ken was a music aficionado, but go figure, they have *the VJ assistant* in there at the acquisition, but the VJs aren't even invited to the damn meeting! You had to pick your battles on stuff like that.

BOB PITTMAN: No, [the VJs] had no say. It was a guy named Steve Casey, who was the one that sort of figured out ... once the song was known, we'd sort of figure out which audience liked it and how did it go. Now, in the early days—because we had such pressure on the "sex, drugs, and rock n' roll"—we actually had a standards committee that would review it to see if it met our standards. And, actually, there were some videos we wouldn't play because they were—it might sound ridiculous today—*too raunchy*. We said, "There can be something about drugs, but it can't be glorifying it. It can have a little bit of a sexy situation, but it can't be abusive or demeaning."

Again, it's a 30-years-ago standards versus today. So that was sort of a veto on it. And then on the new music, we were trying to figure out what we should play, and a lot of that was working with the record companies, to figure out what they were really going to get behind, and what there was a good shot at working.

We used a lot of research. We made phone calls, random surveys to people's houses, asked them if they knew these songs, if they liked it, rate it on a scale. And from that, we had all kinds of scores. As it turns out, when you went through the Nielsen stuff and looked at the meter, the thing where you lost most of your audience was not commercials. It wasn't "I hate the song and change the channel when it comes on." Actually, the one that people tuned out the most was "I like it, but I'm tired of seeing it so much." Called burnout. So we'd always try to calculate when to get a video off the air when it has 10% burnout, 20% burnout. It was all sort of statistical stuff.

ALAN HUNTER: We were part of a committee of people that sat down, along with some executives and programmers. So we had a say, and every time they would sit down on a weekly basis and review all the new videos, we had a seat at that table. Sometimes we made it; sometimes we didn't. To be honest, we got so busy that we just didn't have time to do it, and we had to rely on the programmers. A record company would send a video to the programmers. Obviously, that was a big department. So we weren't likely to be getting a hand-off of a video in a coffee shop or a club by a manager. But quite frequently, a manager at a show or out and about would say, "Hey, I'm about to send Mellencamp's new video. I want you guys to see it." And it would already be in the hands of the higher-ups that were making those choices. So we really didn't have any say in that.

But we got great record service. The record companies knew that the VJs were the face of the channel, and we were the ones who were going to be excited about the music or not. Certainly, we were nonpartisan, but you could bet that I was going to talk about one artist more than I was another. I might come out of Mötley Crüe making fun of the video—and have a yawn —but I was probably going to really talk up the new Howard Jones video, because I really liked his stuff. So people got to know the kinds of music that we liked, because of what we would talk about, and they would identify the various differences between all of us jocks. But that didn't bother me at all that we didn't have a say-so in it, because the pool of videos, there was very little that was rejected. To be honest, it wasn't like programming a radio station.

LES GARLAND: Anybody could offer their input. A production assistant could come in to me and say, "Garland, I love this new band, Echo and the Bunnymen." And I'd be like, *"Who?!"* Anybody was welcomed to put their input in. The VJs could come in to put their input in. If the VJs wanted to come in and attend the music meetings, they were more than welcomed.

NINA BLACKWOOD: I remember Mark Goodman, in fact, raving about Stevie Ray Vaughan. He went to see Stevie Ray Vaughan down at the Bottom Line, and he said, "The second coming of Hendrix!" I went down the next night, and he was wonderful. So our opinions were stressed, but they had a whole acquisition committee that just did what they wanted. And that was frustrating to us individually to certain degrees. I think more so to Mark and JJ, because they came from FM radio, in the days that you could have some say. And with me, I was probably in the middle of that, because being a musician and all that, I had a strong say. And Alan and Martha, as we went along, I think would be frustrated, because then they started seeing things that they wanted to play. But it wasn't our call. It's like radio is now. Jocks don't get to play what they want. I found that frustrating.

LES GARLAND: Ultimately, it was my responsibility. I had what was called the "programming and acquisitions." Acquisitions acquired the videos; the programming department decided what to do with them. And we put everybody in the same room together, and that represented a good eight people, at least, in what was known as the official "music meeting." Don't forget—I was a longhaired hippie from the '60s. And I believed in this real "openness." The door was always open. People could come in and enjoy the music. We were all about the music. As a matter of fact, I am quite famous for the sound system I brought in. I had some Altec Lansing studio monitors that were just *badass*. Big furniture models, as big as your desk. And I had two of them in my office. That just rocked.

When we had music day, it was like a party going on down there, because it was the way I was born and raised. If we're not having fun here, it's not going to translate through that TV set. And it was the same way with my radio stations. What goes on inside these walls is what's going to come out through those speakers. So if you're not having fun, you should go home. Tuesday was the official music day, but honestly, every day was music day. If something new came in on a Wednesday ... if "Hungry Like the Wolf" by Duran Duran came in and it blew my mind, I'm calling everybody in. "Get in here, *you've got to see this video!*" And we'd crank it. We'd play it off and on all day long. By 7:00 at night, we'd be rocking. We'd have video parties in my friggin' office.

The MTV Studios

ALAN HUNTER: The two hearts that beat at MTV back then were certainly the corporate office and the studio.

BOB PITTMAN: We were spread all over. My office was at 75 Rock. First, it was at what is now the Fox Building. Then we had a lot of MTV programming people down at ... RCA was in that building. It was the Durst Building. I can't remember what number it was, like 44th Street and 6th Avenue. We went primarily between those two. And until we actually launched the service, we had the original group of people working out of hotel rooms in what is now the Omni Hotel. It was the Sheraton then.

NINA BLACKWOOD: The first studio was Teletronics. It's by the Jacob Javits Center. But at the time, the area surrounding it was all burned-out warehouses, and it was "hooker city." Martha and I, when we'd have to go out and flag a cab, people would think we were flagging something else. Our publicist finally put her foot down, and we got Communicar.

BOB PITTMAN: You'd have to kick the winos out of the way, and the heroin addicts, and the hookers out of the doorway to get in.

ALAN HUNTER: I remember auditioning down in Hell's Kitchen. 33rd and 10th was the original studio. It was kind of a hole in the wall. In 1981, New York was just coming out of a horrible slump, and Hell's Kitchen was truly that. It was *tough*. When I came back from the audition, I said to my wife at the time, "Oh my God, this is in a terrible part of town. But when you walk in the door, it's got a nice little set. It looks to be the real thing." We had three or four lovely years at 33rd and 10th. The early years—really for the VJs—was all about having to be in one dressing room for the first year. It was a ridiculous feeling that you were the face of this groundbreaking new entity called MTV, and we all had to dress in the same damn dressing room! Nina and Martha certainly were friends of ours ... who thought we were the luckiest guys in the world. And then I remember they built these junky little dressing rooms upstairs for the guys and the girls, so at least we had division there.

MIKE PELECH: [At Teletronics] there was full brick and kind of an arched window and a built-in storage area with records. And there were gold records on the wall, musical instruments. I guess the artifacts of a cool Manhattan loft. There were two cameras that we used that would be intercut, and we would do all the wraparounds. I'm still in touch with the other cameraman, Jerry Romano. The technology was not as sophisticated as it is now, with all the computerized graphics. Any of the albums that were going to be referred to in the copy, the album had to be shot on camera. And that meant physically taking the album cover, putting it on the wall, taking two lights and framing is so that, when it was played back from tape, the technical director could dissolve to it in a position over the VJ's shoulder. Nowadays, everything is done electronically. It would be repositioned easily. But we had to shoot it exactly where it was going to appear. The graphics PA would come in around 9:00, have a bagel, set up the product shots. The guy who was the graphics PA was Joe Davola. Joe moved on through the ranks of MTV very successfully. Him and Lauren Corrao were very instrumental in the creation of a show called *Remote Control*. Joe moved on to Fox, and I believe he met Larry David, who was pitching a show called *Seinfeld*, and I think they turned him down. But Larry liked Joe so much, he created a character and asked Joe if he could use his name. So Crazy Joe Davola—the crazy writer on *Seinfeld*—is based on the original graphics production assistant, Joe Davola. You can see Joe's credit on *Smallville*.

ROBIN ZORN: The floor of the studio was a big open space that we decorated with that brick wall and the monitors. And there was the ride there for us to sit on and stand in the middle. There were some neon signs. And there was a small control room. There wasn't a whole lot else. There wasn't a green room. In the beginning, it was *nothing*. It was just a space that we decorated. We came right off the street, walked right into the control room, and right out into the studio. Honestly, it was just our home.

KEN CEIZLER: Somebody had written a previous book about MTV, and I was amazed to read how they were talking about what they considered conscious decisions by the channel, as if they were thought out. And one of those things was, when we first built the TV set, it had its shortcomings in terms of accommodating interviews or the different variety of things that were coming into the studio and the stage. We were just starting to get some money, and at that point, I forget what my title was—I think I was creative director/executive producer—but I was working with others on it. And we hired a guy, David Morong, to build the set.

I had read in this other person's book how the set was conceived, how it was executed, and how all this thought was put into making it look like "a young person's loft." Wherever this person got this information, I don't know, but the truth of the matter is that first set—which was gigantic—David Morong did, which was a beautiful job. It was like most everything else. It was crisis management. We had a deadline. We had to get it done. Most of it was, "We have little time and little money." What's interesting is sometimes you get lucky with that stuff, and I think MTV did get lucky with that. Because on a daily basis, we were doing crisis management, and there was a "fire" here and a "fire" there. And, fortunately, we were probably able to make more of the right decisions than the wrong decisions—and survive it. There was no architecture of the channel. It was trying to keep the building from falling down.

JOHN OATES: It was just nothing there. It was a small, tiny studio. Everything was small and kind of homey. A bunch of young people working together. It was very low-key.

STAN RIDGWAY: They didn't look like anything out of the ordinary that a studio wouldn't look like—two cameras, lights. The overall impression I remember is that it was welcoming. People were loose. There was just a looser quality about things. I'm talking like '82/'83. I guess the huge, corporate marketing monster had not shown up in full-force yet. So people felt confident in their jobs and felt like they were doing something good. There was a good vibe.

GLENN TILBROOK: We'd drop into the studios from time to time. It just seemed like quite an anarchic place to hang out.

SERGEANT BLOTTO: It was pretty loose. Again, it was this real sort of "anything goes/do what you want to do" kind of thing. There are some MTV clips on the Blotto DVD, *Play Something Good*. There was one time when we went in—I think it was with Martha—and she was asking us, "Where are you touring next? Where are you going to be?" And our bass player, Cheese, had shaved his head, so Broadway leaned over and grabbed Cheese and stuck his head down, so the top of his head was facing the camera. And then took a magic marker and started drawing all over it. "Well, we're *here* ... and then we're going up *there* ... and then we're going down *here.*"

STAN RIDGWAY: Stewart Copeland and I [visited MTV to promote their collaborative song/video, "Don't Box Me In"]. That was another thing, when you were in New York City, you would get a call from MTV or whoever was promoting you at that point, and would try and get you on. You'd have to get the call at the last minute, go up to the building, and show up. Well, Stewart and I did that one day, and we ran right into Rodney Dangerfield! He was on the same segment that we were on, so we all went on together. That was a great, fun time. I remember Rodney being just a great guy. He was perspiring a lot and was saying things that we were laughing at, but the crew and the rest of the MTV people were kind of preoccupied. I remember him turning to me and saying, "Stan, am I funny? Is this stuff funny? Is this funny at all?" I'm going, "Rodney, it's really funny. I think they're not even listening." And he goes, *"Those motherfuckers!"*

STEWART COPELAND: I remember Rodney Dangerfield! I can't remember anything about the interview. I just remember him being ... he's exactly the same way in the green room what he is on the screen. That's him, completely him. There are so many like that. Ricky Gervais—another one, he is that character. Stan Ridgway is that character, too, by the way.

DEBORA IYALL: I met James Brown at the MTV studios. It was cool. I came in, and I was going to do my interview with JJ, and they put me in a little kitchen or something. It wasn't even a green room. And there was James Brown and his wife! They were getting ready to do some interview before me. So I got to meet him and hang out for a few minutes—I got his autograph—and then he went to do his interview, and that was it. But I remember I was pretty much walking on air. I had seen James Brown at that time probably four or five times.

[The MTV studio] was pretty low-rent, because like I said, we weren't in any fancy green room or anything. I think we were in a kitchen, waiting to be interviewed. There was a table. It wasn't like all these plush couches and a plate of fruit or whatever. They were like, "Wait in here, and then you're going to do the interview down a hall." You open up the door, and it was a pretty small, little stage. I would have to say, if the room was 20 x 20…it wasn't maybe even that big. They sat us on stools I think, and I'm pretty sure that one camera was set up, some lights, and a sound person, probably just one. It was very modest.

ALAN HUNTER: And then I remember when our studio producer said, "We're thinking about moving to a new studio uptown." The set was going to be like four times bigger, three-dimensional, and just really exciting. We were really stoked about that.

MIKE PELECH: In '84, they moved to a competitor, a company called Unitel. They wanted to change the studio look, to be larger and give more presence to the set. They wanted something much more elaborate. We were looking to get another piece of property to develop them, but unfortunately, they went to Unitel, which had a larger studio. We knew they were in nego-tiations. It was very disappointing. The wrap party was almost like a funeral. It was really like breaking up a family. It was real rough. It was at a place called Shutters, on 34th Street, right down the block. No party atmosphere at all. People that had been working together for three years, five days a week, and really evolved into a great team, dispersed. It was very rough.

For us, business-wise, it was a big blow, because the problem with hav-ing a long-running show, you're really out of the business, and people forget that you're in the business. A lot of our clients left for the west coast. The business had changed. And you're kind of out of the public eye. We were really dead in the water as a studio for almost six months. But we got another little show, called *National Geographic Explorer*, which became a phenomenon in its own right, so that got us back in the mix. There was a lot of work after that, but MTV leaving was a blow. It really was. You're losing friends. But a lot of people stayed in touch.

NINA BLACKWOOD: Unitel was right around the corner from where I used to live. It was great. I could just walk down the street. It was on 57th between 9th and 10th, right across from CBS.

KEN R. CLARK: The Unitel Studio was luxurious and very new. And keep in mind, back then, the location of the MTV Studios was a *hugely* guarded secret. Now, it's in a big glass box over Times Square. But back then, they were in the bowels of a television production facility. Nobody knew where they were, and that was a good thing, because all those celebrities could come and go, and nobody even knew. It was very anonymous. By the time I got there, everybody had their own nice dressing room, and they had make-up rooms, a VJ lounge, green room, and all that. The first studio didn't have any of that.

    Things worked like a well-oiled machine. MTV did not want to own their own studio facility, because MTV was completely non-union. If they had owned broadcast facilities, they would have been forced to unionize all of that, and they didn't want to go there. So from the very beginning, MTV leased studio space. The tech people—the camera operators and people like that—actually were provided by the studio, although MTV had a say in their selection and approval. But they were technically employed by the studio, so MTV didn't have to deal with the unions.

KEN CEIZLER: The first set was very plain-looking, and as we were "living" there, it started to get filled up with this clutter from crew and staff. The second one—and this really shows a big mistake on our part—we made it two stories. We thought that, by making it two stories, we would have the ability to do all this stuff up top and shoot through things. While some of it was true, *it was overkill.* We really didn't need the second story. For what we got out of it, we didn't really get the bang for the buck. But it had some nice features in it. It had a diner set up, which was probably too *Happy Days*-ish, but we were trying to make it "youth culture." It had kind of a desk, where the VJs gave some news. It had a set up interview area, so it was always there and ready to go when somebody would walk in. The second set had defined areas for certain things. The first set was just kind of an open space and a background, [for] which we would have to drag out chairs.

KEN R. CLARK: It was definitely in an unmarked location. The building said "Unitel Video." Nobody would have had any idea what was going on in that building. It was a very blank facade building. You'd walk in, and there was the main Unitel front desk. You went down a hall, and there was a glass door you had to be buzzed through. You walked into our reception area, where you were typically greeted by Carmen Walker. I don't know if any of the other people you've talked to have mentioned Carmen, which was our receptionist. She had nothing to do with the programming or what happened on that channel, but that woman *ran that studio.* She was a feisty elderly black woman, who would chase you down the hall and smack you upside the head if you looked at her wrong or pissed her off in any way. She was fabulous with all the celebrities that would come in, because everybody would walk through that door.

She was usually very well behaved when celebrities were in the building. It was everybody else that she would give hell to. [Laughs] The only Carmen story that I recall off the top of my head that was funny was often, we'd have to give tours to big ad sale executive clients. So if we did a big deal with Pepsi, for example, the Pepsi president's kids would want to come in the studio. Some very important ad executives had come into the studio, and a guy and a woman were standing right in front of Carmen's desk. They were literally three feet in front of her face, and they were talking about stepping out to get a coffee. The guy had said, "It's alright. They can just leave a message with 'the switchboard,'" and he literally put his arm out and gestured. His hand was about six inches from Carmen's face. And I was in the VJ office right next to the reception area, and I could see Carmen there. She just shot out, grabbed the man by the tie, yanked his head down to the front desk, and said, *"Do I look like a switchboard to you, motherfucker?!"* [Laughs] She pointed at the phone and the desk and said, "That is a phone and a desk. That is a switchboard ... *I am a receptionist!*" I think I just leaned over and closed the door.

ALAN HUNTER: We all had our individual dressing rooms, and we couldn't have been more excited about that. I remember looking at the plans at the old studio for the dressing rooms. That's really all any of us cared about. We had to draw straws for the dressing rooms. There was one big one, and then three or four that were about the same size. And guess who got the one big one? Martha Quinn. Up at Unitel, it was more like we were in the "real world" at that point. We were closer to the hubbub of the other studios and the television production world. We were near David Letterman. We all felt more in the game.

KEN R. CLARK: Off reception, there were a couple of executive offices up there and the VJ lounge, which was their research area, and all the videos, and it was the studio screening room. Then you went down a long hall, and we had a big green room. The MTV green room was a cool place to see, because every celebrity that came in spent time in the green room. There was a pool table and a great big neon MTV logo on the wall, and I'm sure untold debaucherous behavior went on in there over the years.

We would have probably three to five celebrities a week coming through that building, and I say, "I wish to God I was keeping a list or just the taping schedule of everybody that came through," because I'm sure anybody who was anybody on the channel during that period of time was through that building. And we had signed photos all over the walls in the green room. Just down a long hall was a series of little hallways where the VJs had their dressing rooms, and there were make-up rooms. Then at the end of the hall, you went through the big double doors and into the studio. I have to say that the original MTV set was almost as famous as the people that graced it over the years. It should have been preserved. I was actually there the day they tore it down and threw it in dumpsters, and people grabbed little pieces of memorabilia from it. The actual set was destroyed, which it ought to be in a museum, frankly.

It was a total environment. It wasn't just the set on one side and the cameras on the other. The whole thing was a huge circle, so you came in through various doors onto the set, but no matter where a VJ was sitting, you could see more of the set behind them. It was very three-dimensional. And it was a large studio. They actually took that studio and cut it in half. MTV retained the lease on half of it, and the other half was leased out to Sally Jessy Raphael. [Laughs] Which was fun, because then we'd end up with Sally Jessy Raphael fans roaming around the building. But they actually started doing a lot of things with blue screen and chroma key and trying to not have the expensive sets. I think, for a while, they thought that was going to be a good way to save a lot of money. And it just never really clicked. People never really liked it. Eventually, they went back to a full-blown set, and that was after the third move, which was still in the '80s, probably '88/'89 they left Unitel, and went down to National Recording Studios on 42nd, which was where the movie *Tootsie* had been filmed. That was another big set.

Big '80s/Party Animals

ANONYMOUS: What's the saying? "If you remember the '80s, you weren't doing drugs"? I would just say that the mores at MTV reflected what was being done on the outside. There were a lot of drugs at the time in the '80s, especially in the music business. It was very prevalent, and it was very accepted. And it was very accepted in not only the music industry, but we were on set doing commercials or something, [and] it was just all over the place. But I am reluctant to go into details.

KEN CEIZLER: I never saw anybody at the studio. Artists ... listen, I probably smoked pot with a lot of people. But as far as up in the office, I know that it was definitely part of the time, and there were a lot of after hours, where we would congregate in somebody's office, and we'd be snorting. And for whatever reason—I'm not really sure—but it was referred to as "donuts." People would walk around and say, "Do you have any donuts?" I'm not really sure why. I'm speculating that there are donuts that have white powder on them.

LES GARLAND: It was a real party scene ... but there were no drugs. There had been stories, but there were no drugs. Drugs were not allowed on the inside of MTV. What went on outside of MTV, I'm not a cop. But inside, we didn't do that—never. If it happened, I never saw it, and I never did it. I had experimented in my life, and I never held any secrets about any of that. We grew up in the rock n' roll world, survived it, and had a lot of fun in it.

NINA BLACKWOOD: Not in our studio. That was not happening at all. Maybe for lunch, or after we would go to this little Greek diner and have a beer or Courvoisier or something. As far as the studio and what we were doing, nothing. Clean as a whistle. Just clean, clean, clean. But certainly, living in New York and being in the world of rock n' roll, I witnessed the clichéd things. I was not a druggie, so I did not partake in that. You know, I *did* like to drink. I will admit that. [Laughs] But those were especially the days of cocaine, so I would see that just rampant in the clubs and bathrooms. Some of the artists would come in—and I don't want to name names about that—pretty loaded.

Well, I can actually mention one, because he did get clean and sober, and he's the first one to talk about it. I remember Steven Tyler coming in. It was during the period of time that Jimmy Crespo was in the band. They had *me* do his make-up. It was like, "What am I?!" He was upstairs, and he didn't act out of it, but he looked at me and said, "Oh, your pupils are as pinned as mine are." He was *wired*. And a famous punker with a "whiplash smile." I did an interview with him, and he was gone. But he too straightened himself out years down the road. But there was a lot of excess, definitely.

Even with the artists' managers and record people ... people didn't think cocaine was dangerous, so they were doing it like no tomorrow, and it really affected business decisions, and people's careers fell by the wayside, because they made stupid decisions or did not handle business. I saw some of that type of destruction. But as far as the personal part of that, like I said, I pretty much steered clear of drugs. I was around people that did it, but I wouldn't preach to them. I just really didn't partake in it at all. I'm too hyper. With coke, I would have been dead! Why do I have to be any more hyper? I'm already hyper.

KEN R. CLARK: For the most part, the gang at MTV that worked there were pretty professional folks. I don't recall an inordinate amount of drug use amongst the staff, other than going out to the bar up the block after a long day of shooting, and having a few cocktails. There were a few potheads that would step out to the loading bay and smoke a joint in between things. But there wasn't rampant drug use going on amongst the MTV staff, at least that any of us were publicly aware of at that time. There were a number of the artists, though, that came through that were obviously fucked up, and a few of them in general spent a lot of time in their dressing room, with loud snorting noises coming out.

And a couple of them were so fucked up on set during the interview that we were afraid they may just sit there and have a heart attack. Chaka Khan, for example. [Laughs] Buckets of sweat pouring off that poor bitch. [Laughs] She later did admit that she had a raging drug problem. David Cassidy—after he had supposedly had gone through rehab—was in for something, and he was obviously just blown out. I remember bands like Poison and the really raucous hair bands of the day—Mötley Crüe and stuff—there were empty booze containers and residue from what looked like blow on the pool table after they tore up the green room a little. But nobody ever caused mass-destruction. Most people were respectful of the space. I don't recall any real rampant, crazy drug use. It was a relatively professional environment.

MIKE PELECH: One thing I do remember about MTV were the parties. And the parties were usually impromptu. Usually somebody had tickets someplace, and we were invited to go to a lot of parties or concerts. The extracurricular stuff on MTV was just great. There were always passes or backstage entrances. And Mark and JJ were always very generous with that stuff. I'd go to concerts with Mark.

ALAN HUNTER: I remember those executives, man, they were throwing back the shots like nobody's business and got up the next day, before everybody. They were *machines*. They were cool cucumbers. They knew how to party, pretty highfalutin' lives. John Sykes was dating Carly Simon for a while. That was the other weird thing. We grew up with these people. And three years into it, it seems like they were the ones that were really benefitting from MTV's money-making machine. They were starting to date the stars, hanging out. I remember Les Garland was dating Maria Conchita Alonso. And we were like, *"Les is?!"*

MICKEY THOMAS: Starship had a spring break concert in Daytona Beach, Florida. So Les came down, because he would sometimes meet up with us on the road and hang out a little bit. We stayed over in Daytona for an extra day, and we were going to have a game of golf. It was myself, Starship's manager Bill Thompson, and Les. At the time, he was dating Maria Conchita Alonso, so she showed up with Les, not to actually play but to ride around in the golf cart with us. So Maria Conchita is riding around in the golf cart, we're having a golf game, we get up to the green, she starts walking out on the green, and she has these spiked heels on. So the marshal comes over and tells Les to tell his girlfriend that she can't walk on the greens with her spiked heels, because she was "air raiding" the greens. So I guess the fact that Les got kicked off the golf course because of Maria Conchita Alonso's shoes ... that's a story at least I can tell.

LES GARLAND: Are you asking me, as Les Garland, if I lived the rock n' roll lifestyle? The answer to that question is ... *yes, I did.* [Laughs] What's interesting is it wasn't new to me. In some ways, as a youngster, what, 31 years old I think, was considered quite young, really. But not in the rock n' roll game. Probably more considered to be in my prime. And I tell people, I'm so glad that I had the past that I had. I'm glad that I was wild as I might have been accused of being, and as wild as I would admit that I was. I had a very serious side, too, that understood responsibility, creative, and the business.

I grew up in this rock n' roll world. And I admit, I lived the lifestyle that went along with that. And I just carried that on through MTV. That life that I had already been living probably got a little ... "bigger" is not the right word. I had curtailed things. Let me put it to you this way. I have never ever in my life—and I say it to this day—been addicted to anything other than fun. Love, fun, family, and golf—those are my addictions. I've never been addicted to booze. I've never [been] addicted to a drug or anything. I experimented. I did things for fun. I'm a social guy. I tell people that I've never had a drink by myself in my life. If I did cocaine, I never snorted a line all by myself. I was more of a social kind of a person, and I knew when to moderate things.

I've got to tell you, the passing of John Belushi [on March 5, 1982] was a huge change in my life. He was a friend of mine. I had been with him in that hotel room seven to ten days before he died. Attending the funeral and seeing the sadness and the loss of a great, great star to something that we nicknamed "the enemy." Those horrible, hardcore drugs that were killing people and ruining people's lives. Being around that ended for me about the time Belushi went to the other side. Not that I had anything personally to worry about. I just realized how evil that really was and how far away from that we needed to get. To the extent that, honestly, if there had ever been any detection of that sort of thing going on within the walls of MTV, someone would have had to be toasted for it. There's no way that I would tolerate it. I saw it ruin lives, and it was not going to ruin MTV. What you do when you go out of here, and if you're at a club at 2:00 in the morning, I don't care about things like that. Creative people get things done in their own way, just get it done. I don't judge you. Don't come crawling into MTV hammered, drunk on Scotch with a gram of blow in your pocket, because you'll be asked to go home. You don't do that.

BOB PITTMAN: I'm sure whatever was going on, I didn't see all of it. But it was the typical '80s. If you go to a concert, you'd smell weed in the audience much more so than you do today. Beyond that, I don't know. The problem of being the guy who runs the business is you're the last guy to know.

The US Festival

— September 3-5, 1982: San Bernardino, California —

MARKY RAMONE: It was a precursor to the Warped Tour and Lollapalooza. That's really what it was. But the bands were much bigger. It was a one-off thing ... and then it happened again a year later. This was an experiment that went well. [Apple Computers co-founder/US Festival organizer Steve Wozniak] was a Ramones fan, and he contacted Gary Kurfirst, our manager at the time, and that was it. He probably felt that the Ramones deserved a little more at that moment, to perpetuate what they were doing. So that was a really nice thing of him to do. He could have got anybody.

KEN CEIZLER: [The shows] were hot, dirty, and dusty. They probably blend into all the festivals. What I remember is I would [be] driving around with our camera guy and producer. And as we would drive around taking pictures, there would be a lot of people screaming. I think MTV invented the whole thing of people getting on camera and just screaming, *"AHHH!"* I think I recorded about ten and a half hours of people going, *"AHHH! ROCK N' ROLL!"* In the beginning, when we showed up at these things, we didn't have much access to the artists, and that was always a big issue.

MARKY RAMONE: 115 degrees in the San Bernadino desert in 1982 ... with leather jackets on. I was smart. I went up there and put my leather jacket over my shoulders, and I had my black tank-top on. Me and Dee Dee decided we were going to wear black tank-tops. We go on, and at that point, there may have been 50-60,000 people watching us. There were other bands coming on that sold more records than us, but the audience liked us. It was a good show. We played very tight, but at one point, Joey's mic went out. That was not good, because we were trying to appeal to a larger crowd, and of course, the first impressions are very important.

After the show, there were oxygen tanks for pure air, because of the heat. I remember Johnny and Dee Dee using the oxygen tanks. They thought that was going to do something. It didn't. I tried it, and it didn't do anything, because the heat was still there. *It was blazing.* You could see the heat rise, a haze. And besides, the sand and everything else, the dust that was in the air. We felt weird that other bands wanted our autographs, and a lot of them were bigger than we were, not bigger in name but bigger in sales. So that was an unusual part.

DAVE WAKELING: We were lucky. We played both US Festivals. Only us and Oingo Boingo. That was very odd that new wave had now become "the establishment." You could see it because it was a quarter of a million people. So that I suppose was our own little Isle of Wight or Woodstock moment. There weren't millions of people there, but from the "millions" of people that told me that they were there, there was approximately between 15 to 30 million. [Laughs] We got to see a lot of our favorite bands.

STEWART COPELAND: We had to wait a long time for the Talking Heads to finish up. I remember that the B-52's "burnt down the house." They played at that magic hour, when the sun is just setting, and when the lights are beginning to have effect on the stage. And they were *on fire.* They completely rocked the joint. Then the Talking Heads came on and played for two hours. Then it was our turn, after a very long day. So I don't remember it being one of our most stellar gigs. For my little super-8 movie [*Everyone Stares: The Police Inside Out*], I cut some footage of it, and it actually wasn't that bad. It was just our sense that we were tired and didn't feel our most electric that night.

GREG HAWKES: I can just sort of picture being on stage now and looking out. It was huge, something like 300,000 people. I remember it being really hot and dusty, and down in front of the stage, the people pushed up. The front row always tends to get a little crushed against the front fence or whatever they had. And they had security people with hoses, just hosing down the people in front, because it was so hot. I do remember a scuffle with Bill Graham and the Kinks, because they kept trying to delay their set, because they wanted to wait until it was dark, so they could use the lights on stage. It seemed like Bill Graham was really having it out with their management. The way I remember it, Bill Graham eventually had one of his guys get a forklift and dump their manager's car on the other side of the fence! It was definitely the biggest we had played at that point. *It was huge.* Plus, Steve Wozniak was sitting over there in a lawn chair on the side of the stage, watching everybody.

— *May 28-30, June 4, 1983: San Bernardino, California* —

STAN RIDGWAY: We went on at like 1:00 in the afternoon, so it was pretty hot. I remember we got there the day before and stayed at a hotel about three or four miles away from the event. I did have an opportunity to helicopter in, which at the last moment, I turned down. So we drove in, and that was quite an adventure, because it was just a mass of really stoned-out people, out in the sun. The show was well put together and done well. I think all the bands thought to themselves, "Gosh ... *who's paying for all this?*" And, of course, we found out it was Wozniak, who was basically throwing his own party. He was a wonderful guy. Everybody had a little trailer they provided. I went out and walked around, just to get an idea of what was going on out there. There were a lot of people that were just really enjoying themselves. Some of them with no clothes on! And there were booths set up for computer types of things. Pretty damn innocent, really.

MIKE SCORE: The US Fest was presented as "The biggest show you will ever play." And it was. I remember flying over the crowd in a chopper. It seemed that the crowd went on for *miles.* As for the stage, it was so incredibly huge. I remember the other guys on the stage seemed only an inch tall, and our gear looked tiny. I don't remember much about the performance. Everything was so distant, and I was really trying to hear what everyone was playing. I remember going on ... and then being backstage. Also, we were exhausted by interviews and flying in from playing in Paris the night before.

Like I said, the crowd seemed to go on for miles. I remember thinking, "Where do they all take a piss?" and "How do you feed all these people?" As for crowd response, I don't really know how it was. I never do, really. I'm in my own little world on stage. If the front row is smiling and singing, I know we got it right. Backstage, we met a lot of people. Eddie Van Halen was one—he was super nice. But most of the time, I didn't really know who I was talking to. I spent most of my backstage time being interviewed by one mag or TV show after the other. There was so much going on, and we left quite early to get some sleep before leaving to start our own U.S. tour.

COLIN HAY: I remember a lot of people arguing—agents arguing—who was going to get paid the most, which was a little distressing ... and not particularly with the right spirit of things, since they called it the "US Festival." But it was great. We were on with the Stray Cats, who were really great, and I can't remember who else was on our night ... it might have been the Clash. But it was an extraordinary event, huge. I think it was the first time they had simulcast to the Soviet Union. It was a blur by then. I think that was probably the peak for us, and also, the beginning of the end, really. [Laughs]

DAVE WAKELING: We got to play with the Clash. We were on tour with the Clash, and it was sort of culminating with the US Festival. There was the big pandemonium on stage. They weren't going to play, then they were going to play. Then the stage crew and their crew got into it, and fights started breaking out. We all had our collars turned up and dutifully spitting at the floor, to distinguish that we were on the Clash's side. I don't think we did much apart from a few flurries, but a lot of posturing, a lot of spitting on the floor.

RUDY SARZO: It was before the summer. It was May. I don't even think the "Metal Health" video was being played yet. We got the spot on the US Festival about two days before it actually happened, because we were on tour with the Scorpions. We shared the same booking agency. So they stuck us in as an opening act for the Scorpions, who were warming up for that US Festival show. They didn't want to go in cold without playing. We did maybe a two-and-a-half week run with them. And by the time we got to Denver—which was one of the last stops before the US Festival—Barry Fey, the agent who was in charge of booking the bands for the US Festival, really liked us. There happened to be somebody that dropped out of the roster, and they had to shift people around. So there was an opening on the second day, and they asked us if we wanted to play. They said, "Do you want to follow Mötley Crüe, or do you want to go on before Mötley Crüe?" So we figured the first band is going to have the impact, so Mötley Crüe played after us.

We finished a show in El Paso. We were full of dust and sand, because it was an outdoor show. We went straight from the stage to the airport. I washed my face at the airport bathroom, got on the plane from El Paso to LAX, drove to San Bernadino, went to stay at the hotel, where everybody stayed for the show. As a matter of fact, when we were leaving, around 10:30 in the morning, because we didn't get the helicopter that everybody else got—we were in a van, and we had to go through traffic—Van Halen was just coming in from partying the night before!

What I remember the most about that show is that we had a "skeleton crew." Because that show was booked so hastily, we didn't have a real road crew. Our road crew, instead of coming with us to the US Festival, they went ahead to the next show we were supposed to be playing in Dallas. They just took the truck with our equipment. So everything was rented. First of all, my back-line—that was rented—did not work. I had to rely on the monitors. Fortunately, the company that was running the monitors was TASCO, which did all the Ozzy tours. So I knew everybody in the crew, they understood the problems, and they took great care of me.

Second of all, in the old days, we didn't have the type of guitar tuners we have nowadays. I mean, I have a tuner in my iPhone! Back in the old days, the calibration of the tuners could be knocked off very easily, which is what happened to my tuner. On the way from the dressing room to the stage, the calibration of my tuner was knocked off, and by the time I went to refresh my tuning during the guitar solo, I came back, and I was *completely out of tune* for the two songs that are the ones that were shown on TV—"Cum On Feel the Noize" and "Metal Health." So when you listen to the US Festival, listen to our tuning. I'm in tune with myself but not to the guitar. As soon as we finished playing, we got back in the van, headed to the airport, and got back out to Dallas, where Quiet Riot had scheduled a show.

ROB HALFORD: I was with Ozzy and Nikki last Friday in Hollywood [in 2010], and we were doing the press conference for Ozzfest. We remembered that [the US Festival] was the last time that Priest, Ozzy, and Crüe were all together on that particular day, almost 25 years ago. It was an extraordinary event. It was a three-day event, and the metal event had the biggest pulling power. You had figures ... was it 200,000 people? Was it 300,000? I think once you get past 200,000, everything becomes blurry. It's just too many people to consider. But the thing that I always recall is the only way the artists could get into the event—because it was rammed with traffic, it was just impossible—they flew us all by helicopter from a hotel that was like "base camp." So we all piled into the helicopter about an hour before the show, and it lifted off. It wasn't too far of a flight, but it was over the brow of a hill.

As we came over to the top of the hill, we could see thousands upon thousands of cars. It must have been a nightmare when you left the event. When you looked at each other and said, "Can anybody remember where we parked?" Because, literally, *a hundred thousand cars*, at least. And then when we went past that, we came over to the kind of natural amphitheater, and it was just a mass of humanity. It was just unbelievable. We landed and got off, and the fans were at the chain-link fence, and you do your "Hey, it's great to be here" thing, and then you rush to the dressing room. You go on, a boiling hot day. The fans were being sprayed down, and everybody was having the time of their lives. I think on that day you had Crüe, Priest, Ozzy, Triumph, Scorpions, so it was a fantastic day. And then the following day, we flew back to Spain, to start work on [*Defenders of the Faith*].

RIK EMMETT: It was an extraordinary kind of event. These kinds of things, you didn't get them all the time. Every summer, you'd get to play outdoor shows, but this was on "heavy metal day." Estimates run from 250,000 to maybe as much as 500,000 people. The helicopter flies in, and you just see *a sea* of people. And then you get into the backstage area, and there's sort of compounds for the headliners, trailers and stuff. And you realize that now you're in this area where, "Oh, there's the guys from Judas Priest," and "Oh, there's the guys from Mötley Crüe," and "Oh, there's the guys from Van Halen." It just never stopped. Everywhere you would turn and look, there were celebrities and television folks. I can remember seeing Valerie Bertinelli walking around with some other actress—her name escapes me—in the backstage area.

For me, those kinds of things become a question of, "I just want to get in my trailer, get a guitar in my hands, warm up, and get my game face on." You're in the circumstance where there's going to be bands all day long, but the only thing that's going to set you apart is whether or not you can perform really well. I think some bands around that time, their approach was more like, "This is one big party." So they'd be partying, and consequently, their performance might have been affected by the partying. [Laughs] Whereas my approach was, "No, no, no, I'm going to try and get out there and play as best as I possibly can. Because it's going to be out in the daylight. There's no special effects. There's no lighting cues that are going to enhance the experience. I've just got to get out there, and I've got play music, in a very larger-than-life kind of way. There's going to be cameras right up tight on my hands and my face."

Because that US Festival was being filmed, the barricades were so far away from the stage, that the audience was ... it wasn't intimate at all. It was very distancing. It felt like you weren't playing for any kind of audience; you were playing to this sea of faceless folks, that were a long way away. So the performance was really for these cameras that were swinging around on remote arms and a grip pushing a thing back and forth across the stage, which had to have its own platform built for it off the front of the stage. So that even pushed the audience *further* away. And there's these giant screens on each side of the stage—that was a relatively new development at the time—that would be showing what the cameras were shooting at the same time we were up there. You realized, "I'd better get my fingers in the right place at the right time, because it's going to be on a screen that's a hundred feet high!"

Wozniak was a really big fan of the band. He had come to the backstage area and had been hanging out. He and Gil were having long conversations and hanging together. He just loved the band, because Triumph was a little different, in the sense that a lot of our music was positive and motivating. The songs were about "holding on to your dreams" and "fighting the good fight" and "laying it on the line." We had this kind of positive bent to what we were doing, whereas a lot of the other bands, a lot of their songs were about raising hell and "rocking you like a hurricane." There's nothing wrong with that, but we were a little bit different from the standard kinds of messages and content of a lot of the other hard rock/heavy metal acts. So Wozniak, I think that's why he gravitated towards our band and wanted us on the bill on the day. My personal memory of that day is that it was extremely hot. It was somewhere between 90 and 100 degrees. And the air quality was really poor. All the smog from L.A. had blown up and got trapped against the mountains. You ran up and down the stage a few times ... and then you wondered why your lungs felt as if you'd been in some opium den or something. But we made it through. That particular performance has become one that is the legacy of the act. It was just one show on one day, but it was an extraordinary day.

HERMAN RAREBELL: Over 400,000 people. We played just in front of Van Halen. I thought for the Scorpions that was the big breakthrough in America. I mean, we already had a song in the charts with "No One Like You," but after that festival was over and we came out with "Rock You Like a Hurricane," that song went straight into the top ten, especially in California. As soon as we had done our show, we were flown out again by helicopter, just to avoid the amazing traffic that would happen after Van Halen's performance. A lot of people had already left after our performance. I could see this when we flew over all those people with the helicopter. So there was no time for hanging around with Van Halen. I just remember that David Lee Roth was completely drunk that night, and most of the other bands— Ozzy, Mötley Crüe—came and left already. None of those acts were hanging around. The party-time was actually later, in Los Angeles at the Rainbow. It was not one of those festivals where you could hang around. It was getting in and out, because of so many people and the traffic.

RIK EMMETT: As far as hanging out with other acts, Van Halen had their own compound, and those guys were having the greatest party of their lives. There had been this thing that had gone on behind-the-scenes—some of the other days, they had a "country day" booked and a "new wave" day—and the ticket sales were really soft for that. So at the eleventh hour, they decided, "We need a massive headliner." So they booked David Bowie, and Bowie had to get a million dollars. That was his price-tag. "No, I'm not available ... OK, I'll come and do it, *but you have to pay me a million bucks.*" "Well, OK."

Apple didn't care. It was "Apple money." Wozniak had so much money. They had this unbelievable year. They were either going to be paying it in corporate taxes, or they could use it to have some fun. So they figured, "Let's throw a party for America." That was the thinking. Well, they didn't realize that in the small print of the Van Halen contract, there was this standard clause, called a "favored nations clause," which said, "We don't play on any show where somebody else gets paid more than we do." So Van Halen's manager and agent came back to the promoters and said, "Bowie for a million, eh? Well, that means you're going to have to pay us *a million and one.*"

PETE ANGELUS: I went to that festival, because I was touring with [Van Halen]. I toured with the band from the time they got signed and went out on the road until the time they split up with Dave in 1985. So I was with them all the time. I was also designing the productions and the lighting. Van Halen was being paid a lot of money. I think it was $1,500,000 for a 90-minute performance.

And I remember Dave thinking that it would be a good idea to take a substantial chunk of that money and create a "backstage compound," that he could hang out in for like five days leading up to the event. And he could have his friends out there, and there were different trailers, and there were a lot of dancers that were coming in from strip clubs, that were being driven and flown in and out.

We also did a short film prior to the event of what was going on in the backstage area. Of course, that was a fabricated piece that we shot a month in advance of the event. But I do remember going backstage probably an hour before they were about to go on and realizing, "Oh man ... these five days of partying in this compound has caught up with Dave. [Laughs] *He's a little shaky at the knees."* Tried to figure out how we were going to deal with that and "wake him up" as quickly as possible. I don't say that in a negative sense. He was enjoying himself. But it was pretty evident in the footage that he was not 100% at his best.

"Billie Jean" and "Beat It"

STEVE BARRON: I did the "Don't You Want Me?" video for the Human League, which went to number one in America. Michael Jackson liked the look of it apparently. He was completing *Thriller* and was looking for people. I got a call from my partner, Simon Fields, who said, "Michael Jackson's manager is interested in the 'Don't You Want Me?' 'cinematic look' and doing something. Sort of a magical-story-type feel." And would I be up for doing an idea on it. They sent the track, "Billie Jean," no lyrics, no real idea, except the manager did say in terms of background, that Michael Jackson was very keen on Peter Pan and that sort of magic. Coming up with the story, as soon as they said "magical" and things like that, I think I had the "lighting up/Midas touch" idea for another artist that didn't happen. And immediately thought that really belonged to the atmosphere of this track, that it could be a strange land and some yellow brick road. I supposed I went into the yellow brick road thing a little bit in terms of Peter Pan, and that would be a good idea, to have everything he touched be turned … to the Midas touch, basically. So I wrote out a treatment, [and] they really liked it. They said, "Come over to L.A." I was in London at the time, flew over there, and met with Michael.

I had a storyboard and went through it with him, and he was really curious and very excited about it. Oh, and after I sent the treatment in, the manager said, "The 'new Michael Jackson' will be dancing. He's been rehearsing some dancing." He actually said, "He's been practicing in front of the mirror." And that was just an interesting image, of him practicing his dance in the mirror. But I didn't know what that dance was or what it would be. I didn't have any clue. There wasn't going to be any rehearsals or anything like that. So he said, "Leave some space for that." So, in the storyboard, I put a couple of panels and said, "I left this chorus for you to dance. It's up to you with what you want to do." Two choruses I thought it was. So I just drew a couple of panels of him in that "mode." He liked the idea of he goes by the camera shop, and the camera shop all comes to life, and the picture is taken of him. He said, "What about we do another store. It's a tailor store, and these mannequins jump out of the store window, and they dance with me?" Which I thought was a fabulous idea. This was literally two days before we'd film.

I go to the producer, and he said, "Well, we've got to change the shot, get some dancers, do some rehearsals, get a choreographer." And the budget of the video was like $55,000. That would be an extra $5,000. He went to the record company, and they said to him, "*No way.* This is already a high budget video." Again, this is six or seven weeks before the album had been heard by anyone. Nobody had any clue that it was going to be that big. They were excited about it, but there was no hint that it was going to be massive. So they said, "No, you can't do that." And I thought, "Well, I hope they're going to tell Michael, because that's a hard one for me to say no to." Funny enough, the night before we were due to shoot, I got a phone call in my hotel from Michael, saying, "You know, the idea of the tailor store ... I don't think I want to do it in this concept." So I just said, "Sure, whatever you think. That's fine." And I thought, "Well, I'm not going to tell him that they already said no ... now that we're not doing it anyway!" Later, I realized that he wanted to save that for "Beat It" to have the people dancing on "Beat It" and "Thriller" and to leave this one purely how it was.

It was two days. He was really sweet, really soft-spoken. I've got some nice photos of [him] on the shoot, just me chatting with him. Someone showed me the rushes recently, and there's a bit of me doing that "spinning dance" at the bottom of the stairs. There's a bit of me doing that, *to him!* Which looking back, it's like, "What are you trying to tell him?!" He knew I had a little baby actually, and he was really curious about [it], in a sweet, personal way, really interested.

BOB GIRALDI: I was a fairly successful commercial director, rolling along. And I met a young man named Antony Payne, who turned out to be my executive producer. He was a Brit, I think born here but raised there. He was hip to the new industry that was just beginning to start. He came to me and said, "Would you like to do a video or two?" I've always liked music and done some musical commercials. I was also at the beginning of the phase when Broadway advertising turned to commercials, and there was a lot of histrionics about that as well, a lot of negativism about doing that. But I remember Bob Fosse did the first *Pippin* commercial, and I think I came second with *A Chorus Line*, Michael Bennett's play. So I liked that genre of the commercial business. So I said, "Sure, let's go for it," and he made contacts with ... actually, we started with Michael Jackson, of all people. He was a very charming man, and [we] started a relationship with Michael's two agents at the time and got a meeting for us and showed him my commercial work.

Michael was taken by a couple of things I did, specifically one commercial. WLS TV in Chicago came to me, and they depicted something that was on their station one time. It's the story of an old couple in a sort of tough section, an area in Chicago where the white families left, the black families moved in, and an old blind couple refused to leave and stayed. And, in staying, threw a block party for the new kids of the neighborhood. So here I have all these African American boys and girls going to this block party, given by this white couple in their 80s, who can't even see. It was really quite moving. In all the years I've shot, I've never been that moved. I had to stop shooting, take a walk, and compose myself. And the two actors that I got to play the blind couple were very good and moving. Michael saw that and was taken with it, and was willing to meet the person that did it.

So we met, and he was very charming, and very smart. He asked me to come up with a scenario. We talked about ["Beat It"] and the anti-violence message of it. I remember going to the beach with my family, and instead of hanging out with my kids, I was lying on the beach with headphones, listening to the song over and over again and coming up with the scenario. Which over the years, most media people have written that it's a take-off/rip-off/knock-off of *West Side Story*. And it's absolutely not. It absolutely has nothing to do with *West Side Story* at all. *Nothing.* Not a movement in it. It was only about me and my childhood. As most people do when they write, they sort of personalize stuff, growing up in Paterson, New Jersey, and how everybody appeared to be and tried to be tough, when we really weren't tough at all.

So I depicted that sort of "street maneuvering" as I knew it and did it in dance. And luckily, found Michael Peters, who was the choreographer or associate choreographer at the time of *A Chorus Line* and *Dream Girls* and a lot of great things on Broadway. He worked exclusively with Michael Bennett. I was lucky to find Michael. Because I had shot the *A Chorus Line* commercial, I met him on the set and started a relationship with him. He was one of the biggest influences in my life of shooting videos, and probably everybody. Because let's not forget, that dance sequence in "Beat It" was not choreographed by Michael Jackson. "Beat It" was choreographed by Michael Peters and was the beginning of what was known then as "street dancing."

And the fight [sequence]—of tying their wrists and the fight—had nothing to do with *West Side Story*. It was a story that was told to me when I was working in a factory as a kid, by one of the tough guys that worked there, of a fight that he witnessed in the Bronx between two gang leaders, who ended up tying their wrists together and killing each other. It was pretty gruesome, and I utilized that in the sequence.

I worked for *weeks*. It was really great watching Michael Peters take these dancers and bring them into this sort of new kind of street dance. Less disciplined, just a lot more emotion. I'm not sure I know how to describe what it is or how it's gone on to become hip-hop/pop culture, but it was the beginning of it then. And Michael Peters created it. I always thought one of the nice anecdotes of the whole thing was Michael Peters played one gang leader—with the white jacket—and the other gang leader, played by Vince Patterson, went on to become Michael Jackson's favorite choreographer for many, many years. And he and Michael Peters were living together at the time. I remember him coming to me and saying, "I'm living with this dude who can really kick ass and dance, and he's white." So we gave him an audition, and he was incredible.

At the meetings, Michael ... when I came up with the idea of "Beat It" and explained it, all he asked was I get the real Crips and the Bloods from Los Angeles to be in the video. I said, "Michael, how am I going to do that? Who am I going to call?" He said, "Don't worry. *I'll take care of it,*" and he got a hold of the police department, who got a hold of the gangs. They were there on that first night—not the second night—in all of their glory and all of their hatred of each other. It was quite fascinating. The dance culture mingling with the rogue culture. In the early evening, everything was going right, because I think everybody's fascinated by film and crews and how you put it together. But like every time you watch a movie being made, you get terribly bored. It's like watching paint dry. It's boring to watch, and nothing really happens a lot. So the Crips and the Bloods—after they stopped flirting with the girls—started getting a little rambunctious, and there was an altercation. Two members of the opposing gangs started smacking each other around, and cops stopped it. It got a little hairy. It was late, and we were down in the barrio of Los Angeles. It was tough. We were in a warehouse. And I had not planned to dance for a while. I was waiting to do the big dance number on the second night, naïvely thinking that the Crips and Bloods would come back again.

But it was apparent that they weren't getting along, and the police came to Antony, our producer, and said, "I'm sorry, but I've really got to close it down. It's getting a little dangerous, and we're responsible for this. You don't really know what goes on between these two. They've really got some deep-rooted issues, and we shouldn't take a chance." I said to the police, "Do me a favor. Let me just try one thing. If it doesn't work, I'll absolutely close it down." I decided to dance, and I told Michael Peters, "Michael, I'm sorry, but get your kids ready. We're going to go in and dance." "Yeah, but we're not ready." "We have to be ready. The only chance I've got is if I start to play music. It maybe is going to calm the soul." So he said, "OK, let's go for it." I got everybody ready, and at the last second, I told Michael Peters to jump on that forklift and got somebody who was able to drive it, [and] that will be his entrance.

Now, you've got the Crips and the Bloods all lined up with dancers. That alone is a wonderful image, guys playing tough guys and guys who *are* tough guys. The music started playing loudly, and we started dancing. And we danced and we danced and we danced. I'll never forget the looks on the faces of those gang members, all lined up, watching something that they knew in their hearts and souls, that as tough as they were, they could never ever do in their whole lifetime. And it was beautiful, because admittedly, most of those kids dancing and kicking ass there are gay, and this is the complete opposite of who these people are, but the look of admiration and awe on their faces was something I'll never forget. Because they just saw something that their brothers could do, that they'd never be able to do. And then I got smart and cocky and changed the rubber knife to a real knife and gave it to Michael and Vince without telling them. I sprung that one on them—I made my AD make the switch without telling anybody—and that's what's in the film. If you watch it carefully, you'll see how really gingerly they were avoiding a real knife.

We shot well into the early morning. When the dancers come to you and say, "Bob, *the blisters are beginning to break,*" you know it was time to stop. But it was over then. We had won. We had gotten past that first night. We didn't need the Crips and Bloods again to tell the story. We didn't know we had history, *but we knew we had something.*

Black Artists and MTV

CHUCK D: They tried to run away from black music as fast as possible. The only thing black on MTV at that time was JJ Jackson, who was a VJ. They even said no to Michael Jackson.

BOB GIRALDI: I don't know if I'd say there weren't that many [black artists played on MTV]. There weren't *any*. No matter what you're being told by anybody, it was a racist station. A different point of view, they had a different philosophy, it was being played and marketed to white teenagers in the suburbs, and there was no place in their mind for what was pop-soul music. And Michael [Jackson], as always, bridged the gap. Made the change. Led the way.

STEVE BARRON: There was a weird moment where MTV saw the video ["Billie Jean"], and they said, "It's not really our demographic." And the head of CBS, Walter Yetnikoff, just went nuts. He said, "You're kidding me? This is a fantastic pop song and a really striking video, and you're MTV." They felt their audience was very "Midwest"—from what I remember—and that this would be not their demographic. And there was a couple of weeks where they weren't going to play it. Of course, the irony that turned that all around is Michael Jackson became the driving force behind MTV for many years. But there was a moment where there was a clash of demographics.

ALAN HUNTER: I remember hearing the news that Michael Jackson had this video, "Billie Jean," that was just blowing everybody away. We got the tape of it down at the studio. I think Mark and I were watching it as soon as it came to MTV. There was some debate early on I remember. The debate was still raging whether or not we were going to show it. But it didn't last long. There was not a whole long hand-wringing over that one. It was, "You know what? We've got to show this. *It's too extraordinary.*" The video was unbelievably great. It was Michael Jackson, it's a great song, [and] it just made sense. So it wasn't a painful decision on anybody's part. I remember being very excited. Mark and I were talking about how cool this was, how much it was going to change things and open up the doors. Everybody had that feeling. It was the first big premiere of its kind. That was another first for MTV, to premiere a video like that. The kind of promotion we put behind it weeks in advance. We'd get memos. "You've got to say this; you've got to do every break." After, we thought the doors were wide open.

BOB GIRALDI: I met with Bob [Pittman], and we had plenty of arguments. I think that history shows that they made a choice, and they were pressured to change the choice. And that was the right thing to do. Nobody bought as many records as they did *Thriller*. You can talk all you want about white bands, but it was the black artists that were selling most at that time. History was changed, and history was made. There's nobody to point fingers at. It's just the way it happened. And it was the right thing. It wasn't like it was a mistake, and history went with it. It was the right thing. Lionel came out with *Can't Slow Down*, Stevie Wonder had his, Ray Charles had his, Diana Ross had hers. Everybody had their moment. It was the time in history when the music business was the most glorious.

BOB PITTMAN: It started with Rick James. We had a review committee, and he didn't pass it for "Super Freak," which, by the way, today would be extraordinarily tame. So it didn't pass, and we wouldn't play it. He got in the press and said, "They're not playing any black artists." Which, of course, wasn't true. We *were* playing black artists. But just like white artists, there were a whole lot of black artists that didn't have videos, and there were a whole lot of white artists that didn't have videos. But the charge stuck. At first, our reaction was, "Of course, everybody will look at the channel and know that's not true." But they didn't look at the channel. They just wrote it. And this thing built up some momentum.

LES GARLAND: I took it quite personally—specifically, Mr. Rick James. He was the guy that I had the biggest problem with. He flat-out used my name one day. The guy had never even met me and accused me of being a racist. *I lost my mind.* And for people who knew me, knew that was absolutely not true. And then, finally, the confrontation with him came. It was a bit of a face-off, and I said, "Look, you don't even know me. You need to make some calls before you go around making statements about people." I was pissed. About a week later, he called and asked if he could come down and see me. He did and said, "Garland, I owe you an apology." I accepted it, we hugged, and became friends. I knew him—not a dear buddy, not a guy I hung out with—but we made our way through that. That guy made a mistake making statements like that, and he stood up like a man and admitted it. It got personal. The Michael Jackson story that flies around—that never happened. There were people of color on MTV. There just wasn't much selection of music videos coming from the music companies.

BOB PITTMAN: It's probably the reason Michael Jackson got so much attention. We started going out to black artists and saying proactively, "You've got to produce a video." Tina Turner was really big for us and Michael Jackson. And, actually, Quincy Jones is my son's godfather, as a result of Quincy and I becoming great friends through that process, because I began spending a lot of time with Quincy, saying, "Look, we've got to get this done. We've got to get Michael on the air." And, of course, they had "Billie Jean" and "Beat It," which were great videos.

LES GARLAND: It's become a part of Internet folklore, I guess. By the way, one of the guys that fuels it is one of my dear friends, Mr. Walter Yetnikoff. Walter Yetnikoff was the head of CBS back in the day, the most powerful music company in the world. And they had Michael Jackson. The story somehow got told that we said no to Michael Jackson. That MTV said, "No, we were not going to play the Michael Jackson video." Which couldn't have been further from the truth. I was the first person at MTV to see it, and I'll never forget putting it in my 3/4-inch machine, hitting the start button, hearing the bass beat to "Billie Jean" start up, and going, "Holy shit ... *are you kidding me?!*" I called everybody in and said, "You've got to see this. This is the best video of its time!" Pittman was on the west coast. I phoned him and said, "Bob, wait until you see 'Billie Jean.' It's going to blow your mind."

We put it on mid-week. It wasn't even a Tuesday add. But, somehow, this whole story erupted that we denied it, we weren't going to play it, and there were threats made by CBS that, if we didn't play it, they were going to pull all their music videos. This story just started gathering steam. Why? I don't know. Publicity? I don't know. I've got my theories. But it never happened, and I've dispelled this hundreds of times. It just never happened like that.

GERALD CASALE: It was absolutely true. Those stories are true. When MTV tries to refute the way that went down ... no, it's absolutely the way it went down. Walter Yetnikoff basically forced the situation, forced them to play Michael Jackson, by holding some other stuff over their heads, since they had such a huge label with other artists. MTV was never hip. They were always the last to the table on anything. But, of course, when you control that media like that, you rewrite history. You get credit where credit wasn't due.

VERDINE WHITE: It was true. I think with MTV at the time, because the program dynamically wanted to appeal to rock audiences, I don't think we really saw a lot of African American videos until BET did hip-hop and things like that. And I think Walter Yetnikoff at the time really put his foot down on MTV to even play Michael Jackson, because at first, I'm not sure if MTV was going to play him. Because the first ads on MTV was "I want my MTV!" and the ads were the Police and more the pop groups, not the African American groups.

DAVE MARSH: They didn't play black artists until they were coerced into it by Walter Yetnikoff is exactly what happened. Pittman may deny it—he did at the time—but the fact is that Walter threatened to pull all the rest of the CBS videos if Michael's *Thriller* record didn't get played. That was it. Typically, there was resistance, and then when they finally broke the resistance—I can't tell you how much I love this—it became one of the biggest videos they ever would have, because it was the "Billie Jean" video. And to reject the "Billie Jean" video—which is what they were rejecting—they must have seen it.

Because the performer was black, that isn't even a close call about whether it's Ku Klux Klan-level racism. There was no other reason ever advanced why they didn't play that video, except the race of the artist. I mean, maybe they used some codified lip service about musical genre or something. And I don't think they even did that. I just think they said, "We don't play black records." And, of course, the same thing went down with hip-hop. That was the next thing that got banned. And when they finally broke their own ban on it, it became the driving force of a whole sub-generation ... I don't know if it was a whole generation, but several years worth of MTV viewers were lured there more by hip-hop than anything else.

CHUCK D: They were being typically racist. And the white artists at that time that took all their riffs and covered a lot of black artists before that. So there was no reason for it to have apartheid in music, and they just felt that was the music they knew, and the companies that were actually experimenting with video were experimenting with all their "rock moneymakers." So I think the genre of rock music has really been structured and organized. But there had been black videos at that particular time. "Give It to Me Baby" was done by Rick James, and "Super Freak." You had black artists doing videos as early as '78/'79. White programmers were afraid that if they played black music, that white people would not subscribe to cable or look at that program. So it was just paranoia.

DAVE WAKELING: They didn't play any black artists early on, did they? I remember them making a huge fuss about when they were going to put our "I Confess" video on. It was like, "Oh, look, there are loads of black people. Loads of you." The way they made such a fuss about it kind of made you know that it hadn't of been accidental, but then you can't really blame them, because it had already been determined that radio had been segregated. And so pop music fans in America had sadly already been trained to expect segregated entertainment. So I wasn't surprised, although I suppose it looks more obvious when you can see there are *no* black people. I remember it being a big fuss, and we were told that we were going to be one of the beneficiaries of it, "I Confess." They were going to play it all the more. In fact, I even said,

"I could get *more* black people in the next one if it would help." Anything to help, that's me! [Laughs] So we dressed one as the Pope. Our security man, John, was dressed as the Pope. Just wandered around, blessing everybody, for no reason at all. We just had him walking across the scenes arbitrarily. And every time he did it, we were like, "Oh ... there you go again, another black person on MTV, courtesy of the English Beat."

JOHN OATES: I think the parallel was it was very similar to radio. It was segregated the way radio programming was segregated. You had FM-kind of rock stations playing basically white rock music. And then you had top 40 stations, and then you had R&B stations and urban stations. They weren't called "urban" in those days; they were called "R&B" or "soul." And you had stations that only played disco. You remember "disco wars" and all that crap that was going on? I think that MTV followed that pattern. They viewed themselves as a niche for rock and pop music. Whether they were racially biased or not, I kind of doubt. I think they just saw it as that was the most viable way of getting on TV and having the major labels jump on board.

DARYL HALL: This all came out of the radio format, and I think MTV thought of themselves at that time as a visual arm of radio—pop radio, rock radio, whatever you want to call it. Which was to some degree still ... I won't say completely segregated, but it was. It's hard to remember what it was like and how "weird" we were in those days, because we had hits on black radio *and* white radio. There weren't that many people like that. So I think they tended to format themselves in that direction, the way radio was formatting themselves in those days. It was wrong, but it's what it was. I remember championing people. I remember bringing August Darnell of Kid Creole and the Coconuts on the show to be a guest VJ with me, because I knew he was a great musician, and I wanted to introduce him to the MTV audience. I did my little part to try and desegregate MTV in the very early days. And, eventually, they saw the light, of course.

GEORGE THOROGOOD: They played the black artists that were available. Mostly, of older black artists, artists that were already established.

Smokey Robinson. That's all there was. And the movement of the era of Michael Jackson had yet to come. The era of Prince had yet to come. I think those two artists, more than anything, were foremost in breaking contemporary black music at that time. If you look at MTV, it's been around since 1981, so if Michael Jackson or Prince got in there in '85, that's relatively new. It wasn't like they were passed over. It's just that they weren't emerging yet. But once they did, they were on there. You saw them.

LES GARLAND: The racism bullshit—I'm so over talking about it. We've talked about it until we're blue, y'know? It didn't exist. It was nonexistent. It was trumped up in the press. It was trumped up by other people making statements. It starts with who's making the music videos, and I remind everybody, the number of videos being submitted to us by the music company side by artists of color were very, very minimal. As much as we encouraged making music videos for all their artists. We had visions of launching other channels one day. Maybe it would be urban-based. Maybe it would be country. We were smart enough to know that we had to land our audience first, and either grow that audience or launch other channels and acquire new audiences. We weren't stupid people. We were award-winning radio programmers, who were artists with a bit of a scientific mind. Because I understood the science of ratings and television and appealing to people. Because I had gone through all that, and I had learned all that in my radio years. It's science meets art, but let's let art outweigh the science just enough. And you've got that "artistic/creative edge," if you will. MTV was that. It never had anything to do with the color of people's skin. To think that people said these things about us was a very painful time.

ALAN HUNTER: JJ Jackson—the one black guy in the troupe here—was a great defender, although in an interview, Mark Goodman was interviewing David Bowie one time, and David leveled Mark and said, "Why don't you play any black artists?" And JJ, I remember him saying [he] wished that he could have had a conversation with David to set him straight somewhat. We *were* playing black artists. There was Garland Jeffreys, Gary U.S. Bonds, Joan Armatrading, but they played more mainstream rock n' roll. Michael

Jackson represented the "pop world," and that just wasn't in the parameters. There was certainly no overt racism about the thing. It was just what their idea of the music that we were going to play was. But Michael was definitely a turning point. Did that mean that we were going to be playing R&B? Were we going to be playing Lionel Richie? It opened up everything at that point, which, of course, was great. That was what MTV was all about, this total mishmash of heavy metal up against Howard Jones up against the Commodores up against Sting. It was all over the place, and that's what people liked about it.

NINA BLACKWOOD: Bottom line—if you go back and you listen to rock radio at that exact period of time, you are not going to hear a lot of black artists. And initially, MTV started—as hard as it is to believe now—its initial intention was as an AOR music channel. More rock n' roll. So it was not a case of the color of your skin or racism. It was the genre of music. If there was some behind-the-scenes racism going on, I was not aware of that, because we did have Garland Jeffreys, Phil Lynott, Joan Armatrading, Jon Butcher Axis. I used to feel that I don't need to sit here naming the black artists that we play, because I never felt it was a racist thing at all. I mean, we had JJ for crying out loud. *Come on!* And then, when the whole Michael Jackson thing ... again, I was not in on the acquisition meetings. I have read several books that are supposedly in-depth about what was going on behind-the-scenes, and it was "Billie Jean" that they didn't want to play. I don't know if that was racist motivation behind that, but that was just plain stupid, because the song was great. For whatever reason they were reluctant to play that was just plain dumb, because the song itself was a genre that crossed over pop and rock. It was so tremendous a piece of music that it could be played on any channel. I mean, I'm sure if Jimi Hendrix had a video in 1981, we would have been playing it.

ORAN "JUICE" JONES: Looking at it from both sides, it's like, yes, they didn't play a lot of black artists ... it wasn't really a movement like that. I think it was incumbent upon artists to step their game up. To have a record and the music—the audio part—that's one thing. You can get away with that. You can look any kind of way. You can act any kind of way, when you put the music out. But when it comes to the visual aspect of it, you've got to step your game up. I think for MTV from their perspective, they were just waiting for artists—particularly black artists—to just step their game up and create a visual that was worthy of showing the world. I would prefer to think of that than, "We just don't want to let you in."

BOOTSY COLLINS: Just look at what they played. I am not mad about that, but they were going for a certain market, which I think in the end, was a perfect set up for rap music and rap's independence, because white people began to rise up and got tired of the "*Brady Bunch* punch."

JELLO BIAFRA: That helped harden my attitude toward MTV in a very big way. I read an article—I think it was actually in the Sunday entertainment section of the *San Francisco Chronicle*—where an MTV executive named Bob Pittman came right out and said the reason they didn't play black artists, country artists, or even women at the time, was quote, "We don't want to cater to fringe groups." As if your skin color suddenly made you a member of a certain fringe group. And I was outraged by that, and so were a lot of other people.

I'm not your best evidence on that either. I don't know if you've spoke to Dave Marsh yet or not. I highly recommend that, because he's tracked Pittman over the years. because that's not the only thing like that that Pittman has done. It's almost like having to track people who fail upwards, like Lawrence Summers, when he was cleared back at the World Bank, and the IMF said that, "Africa is vastly under-polluted and that we need to measure where to put toxic waste by the value of the local future earning stream." And that, "The toxic waste dumps in Africa is impeccable." And then Bill Clinton made him Treasury Secretary and Obama even made him his economic guru ... and now look what's happened!

People like that need to be hammered with the horrible things they did in the past, before they knew enough not to say that when a microphone was on. If I recall, Pittman cited Olivia Newton-John as an example of why women shouldn't be on MTV, because that was a previous generation's music, and he was trying to get the next generation of consumer, who theoretically would be embodied by something like Journey instead at the time.

DAVE MARSH: I did an article for *The Record*. Pretty much what I said in that article is what I said to you. I talked about the falsification of history, because to create an all-white past for the music was disastrously dishonest, as far as I was concerned. And I talked about the ban on black performers.

BOB GIRALDI: They should be on the air, black artists. The quality of Lionel Richie and Michael Jackson and Stevie Wonder and Ray Charles should be on the air. That this new thing is showing this new medium, this new phenomenon, this new art, then why wouldn't they be on the air? Because their music is just as good, *or better.* But it was always about, "Well, it's not the kind of music we're talking about." I used to think, "It's not the kind of music ... it's the kind of *audience* you're talking about." It was really about the audience. Why don't you say it and admit it? You're talking to a white audience. "Oh no, we only play white bands." No, you're talking to white kids in the suburb. You know what? White kids in the suburb are going to like that music, anyway. And it was proven quickly, as soon as *Thriller* came out, and "Beat It" and "Billie Jean" simultaneously hit the airwaves and hit the video-waves, it just changed the phenomenon. And then all of a sudden, Pittman changed his mind. "Oh yeah, you're right."

DAVE MARSH: I think it was slow [MTV playing other black artists after Michael Jackson's success]. There were kinds of black artists ... you weren't going to see Teddy Pendergrass there or whoever the big ballad singers were. So it was still segregated, but it was *less* segregated. And that changed very slowly, and it's probably to this day. They're still more comfortable with Justin Timberlake than [who] Justin Timberlake is working with.

JELLO BIAFRA: But who invented rock n' roll in the first place? It's still an outrageously racist statement. Does that mean that he would refuse to play Jimi Hendrix, Little Richard, Sly and the Family Stone, or James Brown? Yeah, let's go back to that very side of the racially segregated, right wing, McCarthy-ite '50s culture that he was trying to bring back. Remember when they wouldn't play Little Richard or Chuck Berry or Bo Diddley or Fats Domino or even Nat King Cole on white radio stations, because it was some kind of "fringe group," and the term for their music at the time was "race music"? But then if Pat Boone sang some horribly sanitized version of "Tutti Frutti," that got on commercial radio instead. And that is the culture that Bob Pittman came from and major labels and MTV executives were trying to bring back.

The tragedy of that was when the spirit of rock n' roll was brought back through punk. It was almost all white people. I mean, the Bad Brains or Pure Hell were African American, or the Zeros who were Chicanos and whatnot. That was a rare exception. And then by the time hardcore hit, it was even more segregated. So a Latino band like the Undertakers in L.A. was barely even on the radar screen. I never even got to see them. They never even put out a record. And that should never have happened, because look at the rich contribution of people like Jimi Hendrix, Otis Redding, Question Mark and the Mysterians, or Santana for that matter. Is that somehow a fringe group that we shouldn't have to listen to?

DAVE MARSH: MTV, almost all of its greatest successes in running music videos came from kinds of music it *didn't* want to play. That's actually one of the single most important aspects of it, in the early years.

JOE ELLIOTT: Thank God Michael Jackson blew all that away. Had it not been for that, we had not got to see some really good rap stuff. Like all music forms, rap has got its bad stuff, just like rock has its bad rock bands. But we got the Run-DMC hybrid with Aerosmith. All these things were very important parts of music moving into a new era. I think urban music really got a great lift out of MTV finally dropping their almost racist policy.

Michael Jackson

ALAN HUNTER: "Beat It" came down the pike pretty quickly thereafter ["Billie Jean"], and then it almost became "The Michael Jackson Channel."

"WEIRD AL" YANKOVIC: A lot of people credit MTV—and specifically, Michael Jackson's presence on MTV—for single-handedly resurrecting the entire industry.

CHUCK D: [Michael's videos] were as good as the records. They took the records to a further place.

BOOTSY COLLINS: Michael was our savior. When it came down to crossing over, you could not assemble any better talent than that. Thank God for Michael. Michael brought a new threshold for MTV to live up to. It's just like when they started to let blacks play in major league sports. When that happened, the game changed, and there was a different level of flair, style, and a new way the music is played and observed. Blacks have always been able to do a lot with a little, just because we grew up with very little and learned how to make more out of what we had. It's not magic; it's just fact.

RICK SPRINGFIELD: He showed us what you should be doing with videos, basically. Before him, it was just a bunch of hair bands pouting, pulling faces, and trying to look hot. That's when I really disliked the whole "poser aspect" of it, which musicians don't need to be encouraged to do. They're automatically freakin' posers. So when Michael Jackson came along and suddenly turned MTV on its ear, everyone said, "Ohhh, *that's* what you're supposed to do with it."

TODD RUNDGREN: "Billie Jean" set a new bar in terms of staging and choreography. It brought two things that soon came to characterize all of

Michael Jackson's videos and then anyone who wanted to compete on the same level. First of all, you had to hire Paula Abdul or somebody like that to choreograph the video. Videos suddenly became all dancing, and also, very high production, a la Gene Kelly MGM dance routines. The production level as well. This had a great effect on anyone that was capable of dancing, suddenly. And some people probably weren't capable of dancing but had to do their best, because the kind of music that they were doing fell into the same category as Michael Jackson ... I don't know what to call it, but I would call it a sort of "mocha-fied pop music." It's pop music made more funky and slightly more black, as opposed to black music being made more pop. And that became to characterize music, until Prince came out. Then it got more funky and black again.

ANN WILSON: Well, obviously, Michael Jackson brought his dancing—his body, his movement. There was nobody that danced like him. And all of a sudden, it wasn't just a band in different sets lip-synching their song and looking a certain way, poised to look beautiful. It was somebody who was just *all over* the screen. It was a whole new, miraculous thing that had occurred in Michael Jackson. And, of course, he was influenced by the dancing in *West Side Story*, when he brought that influence to MTV, then everafter, you saw dance videos influenced by *West Side Story* ... influenced by Michael Jackson!

TONI BASIL: He's one of the greatest street dancers ever. And certainly as a pop star, probably the greatest, in his youth. He did take his inspiration from ... I mean, if you look at "Bad," that's taken straight out of *West Side Story*. If you interview any of those choreographers, you'll see that Michael looked at *West Side Story* over and over and over again. If you put the song "Cool" from *West Side Story* up against that, you'll see *hunks* taken. Not that it wasn't great, but just the only thing about Michael is he would never say where he was inspired from. He studied with a lot of different street dancers that would come in and coach him and work with him. And he never really gave them credit, which was unfortunate. Absolutely [in response to if Toni thinks Michael got "the moonwalk" from street dancers]. It is really called "the backslide" in the street dance community. *The media* decided to name it "the moonwalk," because the moonwalk is a different step, actually. The moonwalk ... if you take the backslide and you did that type of almost skiing and skating effect, but you did it in a circle rather than straight back. Straight back, it's called the backslide. If you move in a circle, with that that similar kind of footwork, it's called the moonwalk.

DARYL HALL: Of all of us, he was a dancer as much as a singer. And when you're dealing with a visual thing like a rock video, if you're an unbelievable dancer—a Fred Astaire-caliber dancer—then you're going to draw eyes to your movements, as well as your music. And I think he legitimately did that. And of all these people with these "overblown videos," his were sort of relevant and valid because of that. Nobody needs to see Pat Benatar flying around in a million-dollar airplane through the clouds or see John Oates swimming through the clouds. The music was important, but when you see Michael Jackson dancing, that was *equally* important.

GEDDY LEE: He brought Broadway to the small screen. He melded and drew upon all those influences and all those people that he had access to, to create these hugely entertaining mini-musicals. And I think he was the first guy to successfully do that. Very few people have done it that successfully since, really. Maybe Eminem, in his own way.

JOHN OATES: He embraced the medium. Living in L.A., he had the infrastructure to do whatever he wanted, and he had the budget to do whatever he wanted ... and *he did* whatever he wanted. His videos set a certain benchmark. If you think about it, so many of the contemporary music performers, their live performances now are based on Michael Jackson's videos, if you really distill it to its essential elements. It's a singer, or a group of singers, with dancers and choreography. Michael Jackson basically invented that. Madonna and Michael Jackson invented that whole style of which, to this day, pretty much every contemporary pop act does in a certain way. Unless you're a rootsy sort of band. So really, I think they set the standard for that.

FRANK STALLONE: Fucking great, unbelievable, probably the best of all. He had everything he wanted—budget, anything. Michael Jackson could have done anything. And I'll say one thing about Michael. I knew Michael, and he worked his ass off. He didn't phone it in. He worked really hard. I thought "Billie Jean" was great. I thought "Beat It" was great. You can't not like them if you're a music guy. I don't think there's anyone that's come up with anything as good now. I mean, it was a minimal of special effects. Now it's *totally* special effects.

JOE ELLIOTT: Brilliant, absolutely brilliant. Again, you're probably a little jealous of his budget. You find out they got a movie director doing them. But that's the solo artist over the band. It's a different animal. Nobody was expecting us to do *Thriller*. It was only Mutt that said that we could make "a rock *Thriller*," when we came to *Hysteria*. "Let's do an album with seven hit singles." We copied the theory. But "Billie Jean" was a fantastic video. I thought it was just awesome. The pavement lighting up was very cool.

ROB HALFORD: First of all, I still can't believe he's gone. I'm a metalhead first and foremost, but there's no denying he was an extraordinary talent, and there will never be another Michael Jackson. He was flying high in his career around the MTV moment, and everybody was excited. When they had those world premieres for the Jackson videos, *everybody* tuned in. Everybody stopped what they were doing. Because each one of them was going to be sensational. Every one of his videos were just extraordinary and uniquely different of the previous ones. You could tell—much like when you watch his last piece that's out now [*This Is It*]—he's just so on the ball of everything. Every single tiny thing means a lot to him, because he understands the value that this particular song or video piece will last forever. It will be here for *centuries*. I can just remember tuning in like everybody else and seeing "Beat It," "Thriller." Just every one was mind-blowing. He led the charge for that type of experience, with the dancers especially. I think he was one of the first artists that incorporated that extensive kind of choreography. So he just blew everybody's mind. He couldn't put a foot wrong—musically, visually, the look, everything. Gigantic superstar.

STEWART COPELAND: I can't remember. I think MTV and videos had been going for quite a while, concept videos that were shot like "a shoot," as opposed to just shooting the band goofing off. But he took it to the next level, certainly. But the idea, I'm not sure if he preceded or followed Adam Ant, but Adam Ant took "the video" a step further. But then [the videos from] *Thriller* went way far in that direction. It wasn't so much seminal as it was an apotheosis. So I wouldn't say it changed the rules; it just maximized the application of what was going on.

PETE ANGELUS: I would start by saying, regardless with what happened with Michael and the tabloids and all that crap, I have a tremendous respect for his talent. And I think that the videos that he created on MTV were outstanding. I think they changed the face of the channel. Everything about them—just his talent, was undeniable. And he kept pushing further and further up through "Thriller." He was really creating something very special. I think that Michael Jackson was a very, very substantial part of the growth of MTV. I have nothing but respect for what he did in that regard.

GERALD CASALE: It was a different universe and aesthetic than what we were interested in. But I understood the artistry, and I admired his talent. I saw him, and I couldn't believe how incredible it was to watch him. And, of course, he had the money to do these slick, high production videos. I would find it hard to believe anybody that said they didn't like him. For some, it would be a guilty pleasure, but I mean, he's so incredible. There's nothing like him.

JELLO BIAFRA: I haven't seen a single one [of Michael Jackson's videos] to this day. I've seen little snippets after he died, but I just wasn't interested. I mean, I *hated* the Jackson 5 when I was kid, because I would much rather—at the time—listen to Black Sabbath or Steppenwolf or Led Zeppelin. "What's this crap doing on the radio? Get it away!" Of course, I was aware that a lot of other people disagreed with me. I finally figured I could forgive Michael Jackson for all that horrible music when he tried to buy the Elephant Man's remains. I thought, "Wow ... by the time he's gone, this guy is going to be even weirder than Elvis!" I just didn't know *how* strange.

FEE WAYBILL: To be honest, I was never a Michael Jackson fan. I thought he was just too weird, trying to be a white guy. He was just too weird for me. I mean, the songs were very well-recorded and well-crafted, but I was not a huge fan.

ROGER POWELL: I never was actually a Michael Jackson fan per se. I actually thought he could sing a lot better when he was younger. And that maybe they just didn't let him sing, but developed that percussive vocal style. There were no long, drawn-out notes. It always had this "vulnerability sound" to it. So I was never really impressed with him as a singer, but those videos just worked so well. Of course, I bought his album, but it was mostly to hear how Quincy Jones did the magnificent producing and arranging and hiring all exactly the right players to pull that off. It was the backing tracks I guess I was most impressed with.

DAVE MARSH: People talk about Michael's videos ... "Billie Jean" was beautiful. From "Thriller" onward, it just went into excess as far as I was concerned. And the music didn't stay as good.

ANGELO MOORE: As far as MTV goes, Michael Jackson was great all the way around. And as far as being one of the first black people to break through on MTV—as far as having your music out there—well man, Michael Jackson was doing what black people are supposed to do. They're supposed to play R&B. They're supposed to play funk and soul. They're not supposed to play rock. So Michael Jackson was doing what black people are supposed to do, and when Michael Jackson did play some rock, it was just a speck in the middle of all this R&B, soul, and funk, which is what the people know him for. So he wasn't causing any waves anyway. Bands like Fishbone, Bad Brains, [and later] Living Colour, 24-7 Spyz, and probably a couple more out there, those bands were going against the grain, as far as white America goes when it comes to rock n' roll.

DEBORA IYALL: I did write "A Girl in Trouble (Is a Temporary Thing)" as a response to "Billie Jean," and I also wrote it for a friend of mine who I wanted to cheer up. But I didn't like him saying, "The kid is not my son." I thought, "If any girl-pal friend of yours is in that situation, that's how you're going to act?" *What a jerk!* It's just another jerky male attitude. So I wrote "A Girl in Trouble (Is a Temporary Thing)" for her, in a way. I may be as fascinated by the production values, the amazing dancing, and great riffs of the Michael Jackson videos and persona, but I was always analyzing it for the content, to be true to myself, what I appreciate in our culture. He wasn't working in the same revolution as I was. [Laughs]

RUDY SARZO: To me, the most significant thing about Michael Jackson's videos was the fact that I strongly believe that people fear what they do not know or understand. And the fact that you might have somebody that represents to some people—unfortunately, who are racist—a "fear of," to bring into your home, to actually understand and realize that they are the same as everybody else, that we're all the same. To create that familiarity was an important factor that any MTV artist ever had, the fact that Michael Jackson was the great equalizer.

Now, beyond that, you take his incredible artistry and vision, and it just magnifies his contribution. And not only that, he brought it not only to the people of the same demographic, but also to those who grew up watching Michael Jackson and appreciated him as an artist and a human being, and not just because he happened to be of a certain color. So his impact transcended generations. It made people who may have had a different outlook of what a black artist is and finally realize, "Oh, we're all the same." Whereas the new generation that might have never had that thought come across, just took him for what a great human being and artist he actually was.

BOB GIRALDI: I remember [the "Say Say Say" video] was one of the great moments of my life. Paul McCartney loved the idea. I came up with this idea that would [be] the "Mack and Jack Hour," and I thought they would be great con artists, roaming the Wild West, because that's the kind of song it sounded to me. And it seemed like kind of a "period piece song." In all due respect to Paul, it didn't seem terribly contemporary. It was always in my mind, rooted in a period mentality. And I came up with this sort of throwback.

And two things I remember standing out in my mind about that shooting. One was that Paul was terribly insecure about appearing next to Michael, in terms of dance. And who wouldn't if you're going to go on stage and be choreographed next to Michael Jackson. You don't stand a chance, obviously. We went for a walk in the woods of Santa Ynez, where he was staying and where we shot. We talked about what I was going to do and how I wasn't going to do any dance at all, just a ten or fifteen second little romp, that was in the middle of it, when they were on the stage before they put the place on fire, to escape the police. And he needn't worry about it. He took me for a walk and got me high! It was one of the highlights of my life up until that time, being "turned on" by one of my favorite Beatles. He's notoriously famous for having the best smoke in town, and it sure was. We had a great walk.

The second thing that I remember—which turned out to be historic—was it was the first time that a little known fashion designer ... my fashion coordinator, a stylist named Faye Poliakin, went to Gianni Versace and asked if we could take what was then the beginning of his new collection. Which happened to be a Western theme. And she got those hats—those fedoras—old-fashioned sweaters, jackets, slacks. Paul was a little reluctant, but Michael went along, because Michael looked great in anything. The way he was built, he was so young, thin, supple, and beautiful, that he could wear anything. Linda talked Paul into it. And the stuff they were running around in all was lent to Faye for that video by Gianni Versace. It was the beginning of a couple of careers. [Laughs]

There was another incident that happened that was kind of funny, and I can talk about it years [afterwards]. I was interviewed then, because I was working with those two superstars. And somebody asked me the question of what it's like on the set with two enormous egos and two enormous and talented superstars. And obviously, they were leading me into a place that I didn't know where I was going in those days. I wouldn't answer the question the same way today. But I said in a very naïve way, "There's only one star on my set, *and that's the director.*" It was then printed a few days later, and it wasn't about ten minutes after it came out on newsstands that Michael called me from California, and it was one of the few times that he was lashing into me. He was telling me, "What the hell was that about?" We always used the same weak excuse, that we were misquoted, but I wasn't misquoted. It was exactly what I said. It was a very naïve statement and a very stupid statement, because while I had the authority as a director, the real authority and stars were Paul and Michael.

But however, having said that, there was never a problem. Michael Jackson had the most incredible respect for people and other artists. As you can imagine, in all my years of working in film and commercials, I've worked with some of the worst divas and superstars of all time. Paul and Michael were not that. They were gentlemen. Because they were so big, they didn't have to scream and shout. And Paul ended up dancing ... not dancing, *strutting* alongside Michael in that one little scene, and he did fine, because he was strumming on his guitar, like he always does.

BOB PITTMAN: Michael wanted to produce "Thriller" [as a video]. But CBS wouldn't pay for it. CBS said, "We're only going to pay for two videos per album." And for the only time I think in the history of MTV, we paid for a video. But we had to figure out, "How do we pay for it without starting a precedent that everybody wants us to pay for their video?" So we actually paid for "The Making of Thriller," a TV show, which I think Vestron had the video rights on. We ran it on air, and they sold it as a VHS. And it turned out to be a big hit, but embedded in the cost of that was actually the cost of making the video. That was how we got around paying for a video, but in essence, paid for it. And by then, Michael had become so important to us that we wanted more and more from him, not less and less.

ALAN HUNTER: "Thriller" came along with an even bigger premiere, and the floodgates were open at that point. I think we all decided that we felt good about it, because it opened up for a lot more videos. We had a lot more to talk about at that time.

NINA BLACKWOOD: We all remember the big world premiere of "Thriller," which we talked about for weeks on end. Everybody was at home turning in on their TV, to see this amazing piece of footage. That was *huge*.

KEN CEIZLER: For the premiere of "Thriller," they had a big party at a museum, and we were invited. And a big argument we had, because I wanted to wear jeans, and everybody said I couldn't wear jeans. And then we got there, and Michael Jackson came out. *He was wearing jeans.*

LES GARLAND: "Thriller" wasn't just a music video. *It was a short film.* "Thriller" ran at 11 minutes, and we said, "Wait a minute. This video is going to be so huge. Let's try something." We never did what was called "destination television" very much. We had world premieres, like, "World premiere, Duran Duran, noon tomorrow." "Thriller," we pre-promo'd every single time we were going to play it. "'Thriller' will be repeated at 4:00." It was unbelievable the spikes in the ratings we would see.

JOE ELLIOTT: The "Thriller" video was just insane. I don't care what music you're into. Everybody sat in front of a TV if they could get to one for the premiere of the extended version of "Thriller." We all just looked at each other and went, *"Whoa. That's just awesome."*

ALDO NOVA: "Thriller" was like nothing you had ever seen at the time. It incorporated dance, a plot, a storyline. He just totally reinvented the genre at that point, to really stretch the boundaries. Everything he did, he really stood out. How much he was involved in it, I don't know, but I'm pretty sure that he had some sort of vision that came out.

ERIC BLOOM: More money was spent. It was like making a movie. I mean, we spent like *ten g's.* [Laughs] We had no budget, and then he goes and spends a million on a video, and it's a night-to-day difference of how it was done and how it was made. It's the real deal. It's real Hollywood. It was inevitable, but he did it first. But you know something, Bob Seger and Rod Stewart had great videos without huge production. You didn't have to be Hollywood.

STAN RIDGWAY: When I would see a video like Michael Jackson's "Thriller," it came off fake to me. Like a bad movie or something. I would say almost *too much* cutting. When you cut a video and people are dancing, and you cut it every three seconds, there's really no charm in it, there's no joy in it, because I can't really ever see anybody complete a move much. So cutting in videos became rapid-fire, to a point where we were just cutting and cutting and cutting.

PAUL DEAN: My fondest memory of Michael Jackson was Cyndi Lauper, Mike [Reno], and I were at the American Music Awards. "And the 'Album of the Year' goes to ... Michael Jackson!" Michael Jackson walks up, *and I shook the gloved hand of Michael Jackson.*

MIKE RENO: I liked the fact that he brought in a guitar player from a rock band. He'd bring in Eddie Van Halen or Slash or somebody. I knew some of the guitar players that worked with him, and they didn't bring in the "rhythm and blues guys." They brought in the heavy rockers. That really bridged it for me.

PETE ANGELUS: As far as the Edward thing [Eddie Van Halen playing the guitar solo on "Beat It"], all I remember is getting a phone call that Edward was being asked to play with Michael. And then having heard that he did it. He had a good time, and it went well. There have been incredible musical collaborations prior to that. But I think that Michael Jackson being what he was and the perception of Edward Van Halen as a guitar virtuoso, I think it was a very significant pairing. And very significant to that time in music and very significant to also what was being present on MTV, where you weren't seeing those collaborations more often than not. I thought it was great. It brought two musical worlds together.

FRANK STALLONE: When I first met him, he came over to Sly's house. I've got a picture of him and I on my website, frankstallone.com. He's wearing a red sweater with a Mickey Mouse thing on it and Levi's with white socks and black loafers and a black fedora. He was very nice. I was telling him some jokes, and he was laughing. He had a good sense of humor about him. But he was *so* guarded. People were up his ass all the time. But he was very cool.

BOB GIRALDI: I worked with him three times—on "Beat It," "Say Say Say," and that ill-fated Pepsi campaign, which the world has totally misinterpreted and been misinformed. *It was an accident.* It was an advertising agency wanting more, bigger, and better. And me asking the effects people to make the spark that happens at the top ... when he comes up for the explosion behind him at the top of the stairs to be bigger. And "bigger" just exploded and got into his hair. What he had in his hair, mixed with the sparks, created a quick fire on his head, enough to really be injurious and hurtful. He went down the stairs trying to put it out. I was backstage watching the five monitors—I had five cameras going—and saw him completely out off-synch and realized, "This guy's *never* out of synch. Something is terribly wrong here." Then he fell to the floor, and we finally realized. It was put out and smothered, the police and ambulance were called, and the rest is history.

But it was an accident. Nobody tried to hurt anybody. Nobody was, in my opinion, being irresponsible. I think it was just unfortunate, and it happened. I know he went through a lot of pain. I saw him later in the hospital. The burning of flesh is not an easy thing to take. But he was marvelous. He ended up donating money to the burn ward of UCLA, the hospital where he really enjoyed how they treated him. He got better and went on to become even bigger.

There are not a lot of nice anecdotes on that shooting. Not only that, but the day before, when I did that wonderful commercial with the Jackson 5 and the young fellow that imitated him, Alfonso Ribeiro. They're both terrific commercials, actually, and you'd think you'd have a lot of joy. *There was no joy.* When you work with clients and an agency as high powered as they were, I remember it being contentious. And with Michael, too. There wasn't a lot of fun. There was a lot more pressure. I had a lot more fun making the videos. It's just the pressure of a client wanting it a way he wants it, an agency wanting it the way they want it, but also the way their clients want it. And a director wanting it to be the way I would like it to be.

And then on top of it all, Michael ... I think, in all honesty, Michael was embarrassed selling Pepsi Cola. I don't think he was comfortable ever selling Pepsi Cola. He never drank it. And that was also the time the brothers decided to wear shades, and the Pepsi client and the advertising client wanted me to tell Michael, Jermaine, Jackie, Tito, and Marlon to take their sunglasses off. And I said, "Why am I going to take them off? *You* tell them to take them off! They look kind of cool with them on." In a commercial, today, you can wear sunglasses. In those days, it was a barrier between you and the audience, so you didn't want to wear them. They eventually had to go and tell them themselves, and Michael didn't want to take them off, and then he reluctantly did. His father was involved, having been part of making the deal with Pepsi.

Don't forget—this is the biggest deal of superstars endorsing a product of its time. It was not a lot of fun. It was a lot of pressure, a lot of opinions, a lot of high-power people. And out of it came a horrible accident. I saw him a couple of times afterwards at affairs or in California, and that was it. And then didn't have any relationship with Michael over the last 20 or so years. And as we all know, became a different person. But that was my history with Michael. And mostly, if you don't count the Pepsi experience, a positive experience in my life, obviously. I'm associated with that piece of work, but I'm proud of that piece of work.

BOB PITTMAN: Before MTV, artists were not recognized. They didn't have Diamond Vision Screens back then, so if you went to Madison Square Garden, that person playing on stage, you had no idea what their face looked like, unless you were in the first ten rows. Maybe the first row. And the album covers were pretty abstract. You didn't have TV coverage of celebrities like you have today. So they walked down the street, and no one knew who they were. And we changed all that by showing their faces.

One of the early ways we got the music industry behind us was the artists would go, "People said, 'I saw you on MTV.'" And Michael Jackson and Madonna—you've got to give them *both* credit—were the first two artists that truly understood this meant that the performing artist needed to be different. They needed to have a show, a dance, a face, a look, in addition to the music. And those two really ushered in a whole new definition of the "music star." You've got to remember, before that, it was the Eagles standing on stage in flannel shirts, singing the songs. Madonna put on *a show*. Michael Jackson put on *a show*. By today's standards, everybody puts on a show. But back then, they were real standouts from what everybody else was doing.

LES GARLAND: Michael Jackson—may his soul rest in peace—was one of the nicest guys I've ever met in my life. He was the most gracious, grateful artist. It's funny. The first time I was ever with him was in his trailer, on the set of "Thriller." He went into this whole rap about how appreciative he was and how much he thanked us. And I was like, "Michael, this should be me speaking to you, thanking *you*. You are the biggest recording artist in the world. Look at what you've done for us." And I tell people, "Isn't it amazing what can happen when timing is perfect?" Here was the evolution of this new venue called MTV, as this star was evolving. Michael Jackson didn't start with "Billie Jean." That's what I tell people. "He had three or four number one albums. He'd released seven or eight albums before MTV. He was a *huge* star. He didn't start at MTV. He wasn't an overnight sensation. He was a big star already, who got even bigger." And he did—the biggest star of his time, period. Not even a question.

BOB GIRALDI: I remember one time on the Pepsi commercial, when we were getting ready to go on, just before the accident happened. I was with the brothers in their dressing room. Evidently, Michael went to the bathroom. We're getting ready to get up to go put the finishing touches on make-up and wardrobe and go shoot ... and we heard this blood-curdling scream—*"AHHHHHH!"*—coming from Michael. Everybody turned white and ran to the scream, and he was in the bathroom. I thought he was being accosted by somebody. We ran in, and what he had done is mistakenly dropped his glove into this sea of urine and was screaming hysterically. And then we realized that he was screaming because somebody didn't get it. [Laughs] We looked at each other and said, *"Not on your life, brother!"* A prop guy came to the rescue with a hanger and fished it out and dried it, and he went on to wear it.

Prince

BOOTSY COLLINS: Ah, man! Prince scared 'em for a minute because he was too close to their game. But they let him in, because they did not have much black artists to choose from. He gave off more than what they were funkin' for, and he fit in just like Sly and the Family Stone did back in their era. You got the mix in colors and the female/male thang going on, which was great.

GERALD CASALE: Oh God, I love Prince. He's almost like the last man standing from the era, but he's the finest performer I've ever seen. And unlike Michael Jackson, he wrote all his own songs and plays guitar like a champ on top of it. He's just so powerful. I love everything he did.

FEE WAYBILL: He was *real*, and he could really play. It just seemed like Michael Jackson was, I mean, obviously he was a great singer and dancer, but it just seemed so manufactured, so fake. The whole thing just seemed fake to me.

TONI BASIL: Who would have ever thought that between he and Michael, he would have survived? When Prince came along, he was different than Michael. His dancing was different. And he didn't dance quite as much in his videos. But he seems to be the sole survivor.

CHUCK D: I think Prince made MTV understand that, if MTV wasn't going to jump on it, Prince was going to make a movie. I think Prince also made people understand that it's not going to be the quality of the videos. You've got to understand the quality of the music. People were happy to see Prince in any configuration. Prince could have been up there in crayon, that's how good his music is.

NINA BLACKWOOD: I heard about Prince way back, from a guitar player in Ohio. He was saying, "There's a guitar player in Minneapolis, who's really amazing." So finally when he broke, it was like, "Well, *it's about time.*" He really is a musical genius.

TODD RUNDGREN: Prince ... a funny guy. He's always been an interesting guy. My first video experience with Prince was my first and only time I was a musical guest on *Saturday Night Live.* And even though I did my two numbers—this was in one of these "doldrums," where Jean Doumanian was producing the show [the 1980-1981 season]. It was when the show looked like it was going to go off the air, and the writing was so bad that they had to fill in the show with an extra musical guest. And Prince did—I can't remember what song it was. And they got him on there because they heard he was real flamboyant and was dressed in nothing but a long coat and tighty whities! Literally, little white underpants, and did the song. I had heard something of him, but I had never seen him play and thought it was hysterical. But Prince's whole thing became "costume epic." Michael Jackson's was mostly about the dancing. Prince's thing became more about the clothes and accoutrements ... and simulated sex acts with various women. So, in that sense, Prince's thing was much less about the dancing and more about the gyrating and simulated sex.

RICK SPRINGFIELD: I think his music brought more than his videos did. Once he got the "outrageous tag," I think everyone was looking to see what he would do next, outrageous-wise. I don't think his effect was as deep as Michael Jackson's, as far as what you could do with a video. I think it was, "Oh, he's the outrageous one" kind of thing. His music did that for him. He didn't really need the videos, but it was very powerful, because he's a great, visual presence, and he knew how to use them.

PETE ANGELUS: Even before I saw some of those videos, I had seen some of his live performances, where he was opening for the Rolling Stones. And I remember thinking, "Incredible talent. And also, he's pushing the boundaries quite a bit." Which I always like and always respect. I thought he was

pushing them creatively. Some people just push the boundaries to garner attention. But I thought he was an incredible artist, and an incredible MTV artist. He made a lot of impact on that channel. And it probably had a lot of impact on musicians to follow him.

CARMINE APPICE: Prince's videos were great. I used to know Prince in those days. Before he made it, I used to stay at a house while I was getting divorced one time—that I had bought into—and it was owned by a woman who was involved in the management. So Prince used to be there. I'd walk in at any given time, and there would be Prince in my bed with Vanity. He was cutting the album *1999*. That's the one that took off.

GEDDY LEE: A guy with that strong a visual sense of himself is going to succeed on the small screen.

RICKY BYRD: There were certain people that were just made for videos, because they were movie stars to begin with. Prince is just "a visual guy."

ALAN HUNTER: He counter-balanced some of the more frivolous aspects of MTV. Stars like that are what made people stay up and watch late. So you had to sit through the occasional Debbie Gibson or Tiffany to get to a Prince. Or really, bands like the Barnes & Barnes stuff, which was more of the experimental side of MTV. Just interstitial. Kind of the glue between the really good artists, that had good songs and knew how to work the medium.

EDDIE MONEY: He was a skinny little guy, Prince. Just like Michael— these little thin kids, who are very animated. I loved Prince's music. I've always been a big fan of his. I mean, for a kid from Minnesota, you'd think he would have come out of Chicago, L.A., or New York. I thought his videos were great. I thought *Purple Rain* was amazing. I heard he's not the easiest guy to get along with, but I've always had admiration for his music. I heard he's a real prick ... but that's OK. [Laughs]

PHIL COLLEN: *Purple Rain* was one of my favorite albums. I was the hugest Prince fan. Prince took the visual thing in a totally different kind of outlet with it, whereas we went along with the record company and video directors. It wasn't until later on that we started going, *"This* is what we want. We want it to represent *this."* But Prince, he got going with that pretty early. When you see the first few videos—which are pretty ordinary—then he had the whole concept for the *Purple Rain* album. It made that album. It was a "diamond album." The videos were a huge part of those massive albums— *Pyromania,* certainly *Hysteria,* and *Purple Rain.* It was one of the reasons why these bands sold so many copies, because of this extra outlet.

GREG HAWKES: I don't remember much about Prince's videos, except for them being sort of "performance pieces," almost. I remember being a little disappointed at the movie. Just the overall story was a little trite. But I do remember going to see Prince at that club in Minneapolis [First Avenue], and he was great. The band was great. They were super tight. I was surprised when I actually saw him live was how much of an influence James Brown was on him, all the moves.

STEWART COPELAND: I thought *Purple Rain* was the dumbest movie I ever saw, but that Prince is one of the greatest artists I've ever seen perform. One of the greatest performers, absolutely. *That's* how you do it.

ERIC BLOOM: Prince is my favorite. I'm just a huge fan of his. He's one of my favorite guitar players. A lot of people don't think of Prince as a musician. They think of him more as a frontman or "an act." But the guy can *really* play, besides his moves, besides the movies, besides anything else. When he's on *SNL* and he's playing guitar, it's breathtaking. That movie is rock history to me. It could be one of the best rock movies of all time. We were on tour in France, and somebody from the record company took me to see it at the premiere. It was kind of weird to see an American movie with French dubbing. Just fabulous. The only thing that I thought was odd about that movie was there were parts of the movie where people were down on his character, because, "Oh man, he's losing it. Listen to this song. His songs are crap." I'm like, "Are you crazy? These are great songs!" He's just a natural superstar.

JELLO BIAFRA: I'm still pretty unfamiliar with him, overall. I mean, grant-ed, at the time, I hated disco music so much that I didn't give funk a chance until recently. So finally, a writer/peer, Peter Belsito, who was about to inter-view me for an interview/compilation book he was making, decided one way to provoke me was to force me to see *Purple Rain* with him first. And all I got out of that was I kind of liked some of the songs, and he obviously was more than just a straight disco artist and an incredible performer. So I respected him for that. But it didn't make me run out and buy his albums.

ANN WILSON: To me, his videos always seemed like cuts from *Purple Rain*, or maybe *Purple Rain* was just an extended rock video. I don't know. [Laughs] But he was another one, sort of like Madonna—the male version of Madonna—who just totally dominated the screen. His fashion sense, his personal beauty, his talent—everything just came right out. There are some people that are made to be on screen, and not in movies. I'm talking about who love the camera and who the camera loves. He was another one.

DEBORA IYALL: I remember liking the narrative of "When Doves Cry." The father, the alienated son, the domestic violence alluded to, and all that. I thought that was touching, and it brought me a little closer to his music. And he did one which was pretty much all performance—"Little Red Cor-vette." I loved that.

MIKE RENO: Prince—I couldn't really believe what was going on with this guy. I couldn't figure out what his deal was. I was always saying, "Who does he hang out with ... guys or girls?" He was like "ambidextrous," if you get my drift. [Laughs] He was very extravagant, but I liked his songs. He was over-the-top, kind of like Little Richard. But his songs made me go, "But those songs are great." He wrote some really great rock songs. When I first came close to him, I realized he was kind of a small guy. You can't really tell when you watch someone on TV how tall they are. But what a little bundle of energy that guy is! You look up the word "talent," and you'll see Prince's picture right beside it.

ALAN HUNTER: My first gig in Los Angeles was to go and hopefully interview Prince when he was playing the Palace ... it might have been the Greek Theater. So I flew out one late afternoon, got to L.A. about 7:00, and went straight to the gig, where I got to meet the thirteen-year-old Drew Barrymore. She was backstage, along with the Go-Go's and a few other notables. I was interviewing all of them. But years later, I found out Drew Barrymore was hopped up on drugs. [Laughs] I never got to meet Prince. Prince is groundbreaking. Was so strong a personality that video was a medium made for him, and he knew exactly how to work an audience, just as he knew how to work the camera.

ANGELO MOORE: It was pretty much the same thing with Michael Jackson, except Prince was more a little bit of a radical. Prince has enough R&B, funk, and soul, and Prince played pop music, as well. A lot of Prince's subject matter wasn't controversial. Now, some of his "rated X stuff," they didn't play. But Prince has enough of that pop, soul, R&B, and funk stuff to where he's not causing any waves when it comes to the American way and who America wants to say, "This person plays funk, and this one plays rock, and the different cultures that play this, and the genres of music that are being played." So Prince wasn't really causing any waves either. Now, you get a black radical on there—Gil Scott-Heron perhaps, somebody like that—that's going to be a little challenging to society. And *then* you might have a problem. Hell, you might not even see him ... unless it's 1:00 or 2:00 in the morning!

ORAN "JUICE" JONES: Prince is a phenomenon. I appreciate his work, and I appreciate his contribution. He's an incredible cat. His approach to music, his approach to art is amazing. It's just incredible. He doesn't really represent any segment of any particular group of people. He's just incredible. It's like Michael Jackson, James Brown ... well maybe not James Brown, because he was really a representative of the people. But there are certain times in music, and they go beyond the scope of race and gender. They're just *great*. And I think Prince is one of those cats.

Videos: R&B and Hip-Hop

— Earth, Wind & Fire —

VERDINE WHITE: "Let's Groove" was done by Michael Schultz. That actually was out before MTV came on. BET broke that video first. That video was never played on MTV. And we did another video, "Magnetic," from that album, which was a great video, but that wasn't played on MTV. To be honest, Earth, Wind & Fire was never known as a video group. It was like doing a movie. We had done Sgt. Pepper [the movie] a couple of years before, so it was really just an extension of that. But when Michael Schultz did "Let's Groove," I thought he did a great job.

— Eddy Grant —

STEVE BARRON: When "Electric Avenue" and "I Don't Wanna Dance" came in, I had been shooting two videos a week in freezing cold London. And we got a call saying, "We've got this artist, Eddy Grant. He hasn't done much for a few years. He's in tax exile, and he's in Barbados. You'll have to fly out to the Caribbean and shoot it there, because he can't leave the country because of the tax thing." I heard both his songs, and I'm not a good A&R person. I know what I like, but I'm not good at judging what's going to be a hit and what's not. And I thought, "We'll go there for a week. We're not going to shoot every day. We'll just do it over a couple of days, and the crew needs a real break. Let's just chill out."

To be honest, I really did not think that these videos were going to go out very wide at all. I thought it was going to be something that might not get a lot of airplay, so we "crashed them out" a bit, did it a bit by the numbers, and then spent a chunk of that week having cocktails by the pool. And then I got my "just desserts," because a month later, both of these videos were on Top of the Pops, for five consecutive weeks. And I was like, "Oh my God, I wish we hadn't sat out by the pool. We could have done something much better than this!" So that was my comeuppance. I think at the time,

I always had a storyline, and sometimes—for reasons [like] budget, circumstance, or cutting room, things didn't work—and the storyline would be the last concern often. But I would have had a storyline for that, and for the life of me, I can't remember what it was. It would have had a whole set of reasons for things. But in the end, you end up with what you've got. That was probably too many cocktails by the pool.

— Herbie Hancock —

BOOTSY COLLINS: OK, no way were you not going to play this one. This guy just came in with a new sound that kinda dated the "English robot music craze." Now we had a real musical genius, who somehow came up with a smash that would fit the MTV format. Thank God Herbie stepped off the total jazz platform for a minute—as did George Duke and others—to get a foot in the door of the total market, that they so much deserve. This was a brilliant move on Herbie's part.

— Lionel Richie —

BOB GIRALDI: My real favorite is the dance in Lionel Richie's "Running with the Night." If you look at it, you'll see each male dancer strut out his arm, so a female dancer can grab hold of it. It was based on, again as I was growing up, I would go to a dance with a gal ... based on, "If you come to a dance with me, you go home with me." Lionel loved that. He thought that was right on with what was "Running with the Night." And I just loved the opening, when Michael Peters cha-cha's down that hallway in the apartment to knock on the door and put his arm out, for the beautiful girl to grab hold of it. The most beautiful dance or rhythm I ever watched, out of all the years of doing videos, is when Michael Peters and his date leads each one of the dancers and their dates up the stairs, as they crash this ridiculous wedding that Lionel's at. It's just mesmerizing to me, to watch them take those stairs. The symmetry, the beauty of dance—it's just marvelous. Lionel and I became pals. He was fun to hang with. He was very collaborative, very approachable. He, more than any artist I ever worked with, tried very hard to dance and do what was being done with that music in those days. Obviously, not being Michael, he tried.

BOOTSY COLLINS: He brought the more settled-down country-side of the upper class black hood, which I think worked very well with what MTV was doing at the time. He could not go in there singing "She's a Brick House" with the Commodores, but as a solo act, it was cool. He was a much gentler black fellow.

BOB GIRALDI: "Hello" was nothing to do with what he wrote, and he said to me—he called me "Mr. G"—"Mr. G., this has nothing to do with what I wrote, you know that?" And I said, "Of course I know that. It has to do with what I wrote. And if you wanted to do what you wanted, you should have come up with it, given it to me, tell me what was in your mind, and let me see if I can interpret it!" He said, "No, let's stay with what's in your mind, because you're the director, and you were inspired by it to this." And he went for it. He loved acting in it. And then they fell in love, and the world fell in love with them falling in love. And yes, I was criticized, especially by some of my English brothers. The Brits thought it was schmaltzy and saccharine, and there's "no place for that kind of saccharine in music videos." I disagreed.

— *Tina Turner* —

TONI BASIL: I actually did a couple of [videos] for her, and I was her first choreographer, after she left Ike. I was the original choreographer of "Disco Inferno." Her style, it's just incredible, and it's because she comes from street. And then she turns around and makes it so "her own," as did Michael.

VERDINE WHITE: Her videos were great. Now, prior to Private Dancer you know, she was great before. And this was a whole generation that had never seen her. The Private Dancer record was a great record for her. She looked great. Great legs. [Laughs]

DARYL HALL: I will include her in the "Michael Jackson world," because she's a fantastic dancer. I think that she revitalized a long career through that and showed what she could do. She's always been one of my favorite singers and she's—at least in those days—a hell of a dancer.

— Oran "Juice" Jones —

ORAN "JUICE" JONES: During that time when I was filming the video [for "The Rain"]—I remember this vividly—there was a meeting, with a bunch of cats, and I won't say their names, but they're all prominent in music and entertainment now. But they were saying I was privileged to be sitting at that table for a minute. It had nothing to do with the video, but it was most impressive because it had an impact on me. At this meeting, these cats sat down and said, "We have something here—hip-hop music. We've got to make this into a culture. We've got to make this into a lifestyle so that it will survive and it will last forever. What can we do?" And those cats sat down there, the same way that Willie Lynch described how to create a slave, that's how they described how to make hip-hop, how to create that and place that in the mindset of America and the world. And oddly enough, it had nothing to do with making the video, but it's the most memorable thing that I remember during that time, that one meeting. It was crazy, man.

Hip-hop was something that was intangible. It was a concept. I mean, these cats, to have that vision, I was just happy to be there. That took place in the trailer, making the video. And the cats were sitting there. At first, I'm amped, I'm hyped, I'm doing a video, I'm having a ball. And these cats sat down, and I could see what they were talking about was much more important than what I was doing, because this was something that was going to survive. I was just thankful to be a part of it, to see it. But that's why no matter what happens, years from now, nobody can tell me that hip-hop, just all of a sudden, you woke up and it was there. No. Cats actually sat down and planned and plotted. And from that instance, I understood a great concept of business and how this business runs.

Right there in Soho in New York [was the video's shooting location]. What "The Rain" represented was an alternative option—take the money and take the stuff back you bought her and kick her to the curb, but keep it pimping, keep it funny ... not funny, but clever. Because we're not gorillas. You don't go beating up. A lot of cats came after that with the same concept. The most important thing to me is I couldn't do it all, so I just tried to do it first.

The whole thing was a blast for me, because I'm from the hood, and we didn't have access like that. We were down in an apartment in a loft down in Soho that was like a million-dollar loft. We were shooting the video, and I'm looking around, like ... I didn't realize how broke I was until I made some money. [Laughs] That whole series of events for me was crazy, because I was being introduced to a whole new world I didn't even know existed. And I think that's what hip-hop provided for a lot ... not for a lot, for everybody.

— *Run-DMC* —

FRANK STALLONE: Probably one of the great videos is ["Walk This Way"], when you had Aerosmith and Run-DMC. What was interesting about it was Aerosmith was all but finished. And again, hip-hop and that type of music—which had nothing to do with them—was just dominating. I don't know if it was Jimmy Iovine or someone [Rick Rubin], but it worked. It really worked. Two different styles melded together for that song. Aerosmith really went on from there. That's all they needed, a kick-start on that situation.

ORAN "JUICE" JONES: Run-DMC—what made them who they are is the fact is that they really stayed outside the box. Russell [Simmons] had a lot of influence on Joey [aka Run], but he kept them outside of the norm. And I particularly remember Joey especially—Darryl [aka DMC], too, to some extent, but Joey more so—really being concerned with "What's next? Where is it going? I want to get there first. I want to do it before anybody gets there." And it's kind of dangerous when you do that. I mean, it's a good thing, to blaze a trail and set a trend. You're the first one there, and it's a beautiful thing. But the downside of that is there is no barometer by which you can gauge your success. You're the only one there. There's no telling, "Are you good? It's new, but is it worth anything? What does it mean?" There is nothing there to gauge it against. You're just the first kid there. For him, that was what they wanted to do. They wanted to be the first.

"King of Rock," "Rock Box"—I can remember the first day Russell came in screaming, "Oh, oh, you've got to hear this!" I'm like, "What the fuck?" It was me, Larry Smith, Kurtis Blow—a bunch of cats were there. He put on "Rock Box." "Oh my God ... what the fuck is this shit?! Yo, rock guitars?"

We didn't know nothing about that. But that's what they wanted to do. And, oddly enough, they weren't even sure about it, because "Rock Box" was the b-side of the record. I forgot exactly what the [a-side] was, was it "It's Like That"? I know "Rock Box" was the b-side, and then they turned it over, and they played those rock guitars. Russell convinced radio to turn the record over, and they played those rock guitars, and that was it. It was a wrap.

I looked at that and thought that hip-hop, one of the greatest impacts it's had is that it's taught us not to be scared. Hip-hop has showed us how to trailblaze, like Star Trek—"To boldly go where no man has gone before." That was hip-hop. But you never really saw it like Run and them did, because Run-DMC really went where nobody went before. They went culturally where nobody went before. The impact that had, they were trailblazers. They made their mark.

CHUCK D: [Michael Jackson was] kicking down a big door. And then Run-DMC kicked down the door with "Rock Box" in 1984. That was a really big thing. It did a lot, because it allowed rap music to be seen around the country. It also gave a lot of artists a chance to understand there was a reason to make videos.

I mean, [Public Enemy] intentionally didn't make a video for our first album [Yo! Bum Rush the Show], because we said, "Who the hell is going to show it?" BET had yet to come into serious video playing, and MTV didn't have anything until Yo! MTV Raps [in 1988]. It wasn't until Yo! MTV Raps that we decided to make a video. And back then, the label would pay half, and you had to cover half of the cost. So I said, "Why am I spending money on something that's not going to be seen?"

The only reason why I started to like MTV was Yo! MTV Raps, with Ted Demme, Ed Lover, and Doctor Dre. They were boosting our genre into the stratosphere. That was very important. Yo! MTV Raps was the only reason why I gave a damn about MTV. And also after that, the MTV News with Kurt Loder. People I respected a whole lot. I thought they did MTV News the way the were supposed to have done it. Information about music in the news was something that really made me pay attention to the rest of MTV.

ANGELO MOORE: They broke down doors, which is great. I can say nothing but good things about that. I just wish that a lot more of it would happen, man. If more of it happened, then the doors would be open a little wider. They would give the chance for the porthole of a lot of different cultures and genres of music to come through MTV, because it's still one-sided.

Duran Duran

ALAN HUNTER: Duran Duran was probably the first big "poster band" for MTV. Their video for "Girls on Film" was so groundbreaking, because it was so sexual. We only showed the "PG version." The "R version" we saw in the office, and they had to edit out various stuff in it. But it drove Middle America crazy, because it was so *out there*. That was in '81, our first year.

NINA BLACKWOOD: Duran Duran I absolutely loved right off the bat. When we would do interviews, they would match each of the VJs up with the artists they think they would click the best with to do interviews, and I got Duran Duran. I think they were so innovative, cool, and stylish. They were absolutely perfect for the medium.

SERGEANT BLOTTO: That's the first completely over-the-top, "Let's blow the budget on this sucker." But I think Duran Duran should always be recognized as the pioneers that they are and the inventors of the "turning over the table in slow motion" move [a scene from "Hungry Like the Wolf"], which I believe is probably one of the defining stylistic moments of MTV.

JONATHAN ELIAS: Certainly, their videos ... they broke ground on so many pieces of visual material. And they really thought about art in a more holistic way. They knew about artists, and they knew about film and painting.

PHIL COLLEN: I loved them. They were clean-cut pop guys, and girls were just going bonkers over them. Again, it solidified their image—these clean-cut, playboy guys, jetting around on yachts and on beaches. It created that image of what their sound was all about. So all of a sudden, you put them into a bracket, and you actually knew what they were about. Again, mainly down to the videos.

GREG HAWKES: Eh ... I thought they were fluff.

DEBORA IYALL: Who cares. I just didn't get it. For one thing, it was total-ly sucking up to upper class taste and sort of want-to-be-materialist class system. I just couldn't care less. I don't want to be on a sailboat with a bunch of models, and nobody I know wants to do that or is going to do that. That isn't our life, and we don't aspire to it. I'm one of those people who did not grow up wanting a house on the hill. So seeing that, it was just like watch-ing something embarrassingly "suck up." Sorry Duran Duran! We actually turned down a tour with ... if it wasn't Duran Duran, it was one of the other bands that was like Duran Duran. Later, we thought maybe we should have done it. [Laughs] But at the time, it was just like, *"No way!"*

CY CURNIN: Duran Duran had the big budgets to go poncing around in James Bond locations. But hats off to them. They made MTV look expensive and took us away from reality. In the real world, Reagan and Thatcher were busy sewing the seeds of dysfunction. Now we are reaping that crop. Fuck them!

MIKE SCORE: Duran Duran's first album [*Duran Duran*] was brilliant. It was right where we wanted to be and right there in that era with them. I didn't particularly like them much after that. I thought they went too commercial, and we probably went a bit too underground-ish, too electronic, more in the "Devo era." But we were fans of Duran Duran. We didn't have huge backing, but we knew they did. Once we started to do stuff and they were coming up, we knew they were going on to become *huge*. Because everything that they did was backed to the hilt, whereas everything we did was kind of like, "Well, we'll try this, and we'll try that." We knew we could go out, tour, and do it live, probably more than they did. So I think they needed MTV a bit more than we did at the beginning, until they got more established.

THOMAS DOLBY: I really liked Duran Duran. Because of their image, they were sometimes poo-pooed as musicians, but they're actually really good musicians. Some very interesting song compositions. What did I think of their videos? I was jealous. [Laughs] I wanted to be a poster boy, too, but I didn't look like Simon Le Bon, so I went the other way and did the "mad professor thing." If you can't compete in the handsome stakes, you might as well be a character. You had him, Sting, and Adam Ant. There were a lot of real heartthrobs at the time. I just thought I'd go the other way.

COLIN HAY: I thought their videos were great. I thought that was a band where they really shone, in terms of videos, because they're all good-looking cats. And if you like that kind of music, it really went hand-in-hand, the songs and the videos.

MICHAEL SADLER: Duran Duran's videos were absolutely stunning. The music was almost secondary to their [videos], because you are talking *film* at that point, especially "Hungry Like the Wolf" and things like that. It's a real emphasis on making it like a film and extremely entertaining. Really well shot. The band itself—it was so well-managed, and the image was so well-controlled that it was outrageous. Just attention to detail. If a music video is supposed to be 70% the song and 30% the visual enhancement, that brought it up to a 70/30 of the visuals. I don't want to say the song playing at the moment was immaterial; it was more like *a film,* where the song was enhancing this cool mini-movie that the director had come up with.

JONATHAN ELIAS: They always used to laugh about telling me, "You're the only one that's on MTV as much as we are!"

JOE ELLIOTT: I loved 'em. I thought Duran Duran were great. You see, back in the '80s, people would throw things out like, "How do you get on with Iron Maiden? How do you get on with Twisted Sister ... or Quiet Riot?" Because they were seen as "rivals." One of us had to be top of the pile. There was no rivalry between us and Duran Duran, because we were completely different musical types. So, consequently, when we were in Japan in '83, me and Phil went down there to do promo, and so did John Taylor and Roger Taylor. We were literally following each other all day through ten, twelve, fifteen TV channels, and we met up at Lexington Queen that night and got completely smashed! We would just talk about the bands that we loved when we grew up. Our careers were like a "Y." We were a stick for a while, and then we went left, and they went right.

We all grew up listening to Roxy Music, Bowie, and bands like that. But Phil liked Slade and Sweet a bit more than Duran Duran would, and that's literally where the difference was. Our Bowie was *Aladdin Sane*, and their Bowie was *Low* and *Lodger*. They were just a bit more "keyboard," a bit more arty than we were. We were bricklayers in comparison to them. They were still a bunch of kids from Birmingham, their local accents not that different to Ozzy's. They always pretended they weren't, just like Roxy Music pretend they're not from Newcastle, or at least Bryan Ferry does. I loved Duran Duran. I thought things like "Rio" was a great song and brilliant video. We were jealous as hell of them. We didn't get to go to these exotic places with all these chicks and shoot videos on a yacht. We were up on gas towers in the middle of Dublin, freezing our bollocks off!

RIK EMMETT: In some ways—an obvious example would be Duran Duran—they're pretty boys, they have certain kinds of hairstyles, and they're doing wild, exotic things. So a certain segment of teenage girls, that like the music that's married to that kind of imagery, go, "Oh, this is great! I just can't get enough of this!" And the station realizes, "Wow, are our numbers ever getting great. And boy oh boy, can we ever sell lots of soda pop and pimple cream."

The Police

ALAN HUNTER: I think the Police brought a lot of class to the place. They seemed to be "the real thing." I loved their stripped-down, three-man sound, that stuff from *Zenyatta Mondatta* and somewhat *Ghost in the Machine*, although it started to become more produced at that point. It was kind of like Rush, three guys make a lot of noise. A good, full sound. I thought it was amazing how you only had three instruments playing and Sting's voice, in those early days.

To me, the "Spirits in the Material World" video played at 2:00 in the morning really provided the kind of atmosphere that almost made MTV hallucinogenic in that first year. Coming in from a night on the town, to hear that song, and those chords in the beginning, kind of gave me chills. I still remember that video, along with things like "Once in a Lifetime," or even, for God's sakes, the cheesy "Abracadabra" from Steve Miller, or "Brass in Pocket" from the Pretenders. Lately, I've been hearing a lot more of those songs, and it gives me goosebumps.

CY CURNIN: My favorite videos were all the Police videos. They had a great sense of humor back then and did not make themselves out to be bad actors too often. They also had Godley and Creme behind-the-scenes as directors. That made a huge difference.

PHIL COLLEN: The Police are my favorite band. Loved what they were doing. You just wanted to see how they would play this stuff, the stuff that Stewart Copeland was playing on drums. It's your favorite band, and you could see where they go with it. "Every Breath" was great, the black and white and the upright bass. Just the imagery, *perfect imagery.* When you write a song, you're supposed to create an image as much as you can. Like a story or a book or a movie—like you're directing a movie. If you direct a video and it's along those lines, I certainly think with the Police videos, they were very cool. They weren't too far off from the mark of what the song was about. Obviously, Sting is a true artist, and he was pretty much aware of what was going on, and the band were. Like I said, we were a bit green, especially on the *Pyromania* thing. The *Hysteria* thing was different because we'd learned a lot by then. But we were just thrown into it. And I think you look at the Police stuff, and their approach is a bit more "grown up." They actually knew what they were doing.

DEREK POWER: I was a partner in the management firm, called Copeland Copeland Copeland and Power. I met Sting when I cast him in the movie *Brimstone and Treacle*, and as a consequence of that—and during a very long negotiation with Miles Copeland, Stewart's eldest brother—I ended up forming a very tight relationship with him, and he asked me if I would go into business with him. My job with the Police was, first of all, there was a big demand for concert films at the time. So I negotiated the deal we made with Showtime, to show the *Synchronicity* concert, to both produce and show the *Synchronicity* concert. But before that, I had introduced Godley and Creme to the band, and they had done a number of very successful Duran Duran videos. It seemed like they were a much slicker version of what the Police might be able to do. And, of course, they made the absolutely iconic videos that we remember so well, including "Every Breath You Take" and "Wrapped Around Your Finger."

STEWART COPELAND: We played the song live [the clip for "Roxanne"], and they cut the live performance to the track. Then there's "the red video," which I have seen the shots, and I think that was for the "Roxanne" shoot, but I have no recollection of the video shoot at all. All of our songs begin with the word "don't" or have the word "stand" in them—"Can't Stand Losing You," "Don't Stand So Close to Me." [For the "Don't Stand So Close to Me" video] Sting pulled his shirt off—unrehearsed. I'm sure he had it planned in his mind. But as I said, he would have been mortified to have discussed such a brazen tactic, and he would have pretended that it was spontaneous. Although he's very calculated about that sort of thing. I mean, to his credit, he's a professional. When we would tease him about this sort of thing, he would say, "Look guys, *we're professionals.* I'm doing my job ... how about you guys start thinking about it, too?" We'd catch him teasing his hair or something like that. He was right. It was his job, and it was our job, too.

GEDDY LEE: They were always good-looking videos. Because their songs were always very high quality, they were always nice to look at.

STAN RIDGWAY: *Fake reggae.* I don't know them. I'm not really close to any of that. Stewart had seen Wall of Voodoo play in London, and his brother, Miles, was the head of our little record company then, IRS Records. When Stewart got called to do this Francis Ford Coppola film, *Rumble Fish*, he started to do the soundtrack, and I guess at some point, Coppola wanted a song, so Stewart thought of me and called me up. I appreciate that. Wrote the song ["Don't Box Me In"], went in there, performed it, put it down, [and] Stewart put a bridge to it, so we did write it together.

STEWART COPELAND: ["Every Little Thing She Does Is Magic"] we shot in Montserrat, and it's strange how that was regarded as "The Who destroying equipment of our time," because we were trashing that Trident desk. And that desk, by the way, ended up at Studio One in A&M, here in Los Angeles, and I've been to five or six different studios around the world that claim that the Neve sitting in their room is the one that we trashed. And I don't know which one is which. One Neve is the same as the other, if you ask me. And we weren't aware of trashing it at all. We were in the habit—because we were all very fit—of climbing over it, because it was very long. And if you were over there and you wanted to get over here to hit a fader or do something, we'd just climb over it. Certainly, we were not cognizant of any abuse of the console. But we were just dancing around. We hired a truck, to go and perform some of it—to *mime* some of it—with the natives of Montserrat, who were, I remember, really unimpressed. *Absolutely unimpressed.* And instead of us dancing around with the natives, and, "They're all dancing and laughing and singing!" ... they were pissed off, because we didn't give them enough beer or something. They generally looked pretty grumpy, so there's probably not much of them in the shot.

COLIN HAY: I can't really remember [the Police's] videos ... there was one where they were kind of hitting each other in the control room of a studio. [Laughs] They were an awesome band. Everything about them was awesome, really. Amazing bass player, amazing drummer, amazing guitar player—they were almost like the perfect band. Because of its minimalism, too. Great power in three.

FRANK STALLONE: I thought "Every Breath You Take" was a great video. But some of their other ones aren't that great—"Message in a Bottle," "Don't Stand So Close to Me." They're just OK. They're generic.

JON ANDERSON: ["Every Breath You Take"] was brilliant, sort of like the Beatles' cover of the second album, very black and white and grainy.

STEWART COPELAND: ["Every Breath You Take"] was extremely high concept—Kevin and Lol again. It was based on another video that they had seen, and I think they've been public about that. They've credited that. Probably some French black-and-white director. It was very steady, very set up. Every frame of it was a concept, which they designed on paper. And we were very much "set dressing." Even Sting, although he was performing his song, the way they positioned the three of us and the way they shot it, each frame was like a work of art. Each frame was like a black-and-white photograph.

["Wrapped Around Your Finger"] was shot in A&M, on the soundstage they had there. They deny it, but I constantly hassle both Kevin and Lol about their stealing my idea that I actually did with Klark Kent—the other way around, where I had the music run slowly, so that I mimed in slow motion, and then when they synched it up to the music, I had this herky-jerky, kinda "fast-mo" movement, that was still in time with the music, only it was sort of jerky and strange body movements. Well, they did it the other way around, where they played the music fast, and we mimed to it fast, and then they slow it down, so we were all in synch with the music, but in slow-mo. And the set was very simple. It was just a row of candles. And then when we got everything, Sting got to have fun destroying the whole thing.

["Synchronicity II"] was a lot of fun. They filled up this soundstage with garbage, with big fans, so it would all be flying through the air. And the mountain of drums and the mountain of guitars. I'm not sure what Sting's mountain was made off ... well, *Sting*. And they designed these cool outfits for us to wear, which Sting carried on and wore for the next three tours.

DEREK POWER: Clearly, MTV was probably the significant reason that *Synchronicity* became as huge as it did. Because when they presented the tour—"MTV Presents the Police," that's how it was—I'm not sure whether they ever had presented any other artists in the same way they presented the Police tour. It was such a beautiful integration of a video-friendly act, such as the Police, and the timing of the release of its most successful album. John Sykes and Bob Pittman could see the value. It was a perfect fusion of a moment, where they really wanted as much profile as they could get, and one of the ways they were able to do it was obviously by running the videos, which in turn were requested by the audience.

MIKE SCORE: Touring with the Police was the "heavenly spot." The Police were the biggest band in the world, and we were opening up for them. I think we ended up doing 30 or more shows with them. All huge shows, all brilliant. Watching Sting and the Police was like watching a master magician at work. Certain things that he did, which kept the crowd on edge and kept them wanting more. Just things he said and his delivery and their timing. It was like going to school every day. The thing is, with the Police, it took them quite a while to become as big as they did, so they obviously learned a lot on the way. And part of our problem was we weren't even going for a year when we were suddenly catapulted into stardom. We didn't really have time to learn.

When you're suddenly out with someone like the Police, everything they do is from experience. When you start watching that, you start to realize why they're the biggest band in the world. And not just great songs, but the way they deliver them, the way they play, and the way they interact. And even though there was all that "stuff" between Sting and Stewart Copeland, that's the kind of tension that makes bands. It puts a certain thing in the air, and people want to see that. It's like going to a race, where you want to see the car crash, but you don't want to see anyone get hurt. That same kind of tension. To watch that and see the way the whole show was put together was a huge learning experience. Of course for us, you look back and you go, "Jesus, 15 months ago I was in Liverpool, and I was going to grotty clubs every night, just because we were bored. Now, we're standing on stage with the masters of the universe."

DAVE WAKELING: We did tour with the Police, for a long time. Stewart Copeland was the epitome of the "video generation," wasn't he? He used to run around with a camera in front of his face the whole time. His idea was just catching people in unguarded moments, which, of course, is exactly what you *don't* want. Otherwise, if you'd have known he was going to be pratting around with a camera, you would have perhaps been guarded. He would keep jumping in where he wasn't wanted with the camera. Eventually, I had to get rid of him. I said, "Y'know, you're pretending you're doing a documentary, but really, you're just hiding behind that camera, so you don't have to actually be involved in any of this, do you?" He was like the student with his arms folded in the corner of a party, thinking that he's observing everything, but in fact, the whole party is going, *"Why is that prat standing in the corner with his arms folded?"* [Laughs]

DEREK POWER: The Police were on top of the world [circa *Synchronicity*]. They were the biggest band in the world, and deservedly so. Creatively, I've always loved Michael Jackson for what he was, but he was *a pop artist.* I've always felt that the Police were something more. And I think you will find that there's a statistic that says that "Every Breath You Take" is the most played song of the 1980s. Michael Jackson sold more records, but I don't think he was creatively more interesting, neither lyrically and melodically. But he was Michael Jackson.

STEWART COPELAND: Really? [Stewart's reaction to being told that *Synchronicity* knocked *Thriller* out of the #1 spot on the *Billboard* charts]

I wasn't aware that we even came close to that. Well OK … I'm honored, because *Thriller* was the big one. I guess "Every Breath You Take" was pretty big, too, but I never thought it was in competition with *Thriller*.

DEREK POWER: Here's the truth of it [about how the members of the Police got along]. There's a combination of realities here. There was a degree of competition, evidently, between Sting and Stewart. But there was also a lot of playful affection. I refer you to my film that I made with Stewart, *Everyone Stares: The Police Inside Out*. I think that answers that question largely. I won't say that there weren't moments where there were indeed real resentment and hostility, but it wasn't all that. My own experience was that there were moments where they weren't getting along, and there were moments where they were getting along fine and having a good time.

STEWART COPELAND: We were just screwing around [regarding an infamous clip where Stewart and Sting get confrontational during an MTV interview]. We had just played a show. I think it was in Toronto, one of those big "picnics" that they had up there. And it was our first show after recording an album, so we got the obligatory "Martha Quinn/Police interview." The conversation was stalling, so I forget who provoked who, but we had a nice bit of jolly jinx, with me chasing Sting off camera. I think somebody threw some water, somebody else threw a sandwich or something. I don't know. Anyhow, we went charging off, forgetting we were still plugged into our mics. We heard later, "The Police broke into a fist-fight and almost killed each other! *Oh my God!*" We were just screwing around. In fact, any time we were ever observed to be fighting, we were just screwing around. The time I broke Sting's rib, we were screwing around. We certainly did fight and have genuine disagreements and shouting matches, but those were never on camera and never involved anything physical.

MICHAEL SADLER: Fun and zany when it had to be, and cool when it had to be. Sting is one of the great artists of our time. Whether you like him or not, whether you like his pretension or not, he's an extremely gifted, creative man. And it's always been handled very professionally since day one.

I know most of it was plotted out. You can just tell. Highly entertaining. Again, using the genre for what it was.

STEWART COPELAND: There was one [solo Sting video] that I thought was really cool—"She's Too Good for Me." I don't think it was one of his big hits, but it was a funny video, where he's all drunk and disorderly. I think he may have had Trudie—who I love—as the high-class woman in it. And he's just all fucked up, trashed, and getting thrown out of bars and stuff like that. I always enjoy Sting getting thrown out of a bar! [Sting's more popular '80s-era videos] is probably my "post-MTV days." I don't think I've probably ever saw them. I do remember that one, that I probably caught by accident, and thought that was a cool video. Because you know what? It accurately showed the Sting that I know, which is actually a very kind of loosey guy. He's always been very good at presenting an image of himself that is so *not* him. He is actually very humble, extremely casual, and not at all the figure that most people seem to think he is. I think that's why I enjoyed that video. That's more like the real Sting than the guy you see looking all serious, with his lute. He's really good at that lute, by the way.

JON ANDERSON: They were perfect timing for MTV. They sang it, *"I want my MTV"*—[Sting] sang that on Dire Straits. It's something that lingers with you forever. You wish, "God, I would have loved to have been in that band."

Videos: Punk and New Wave

— The Ramones —

MARKY RAMONE: I was the "teacher" in "Rock 'n' Roll High School," dressed up in drag. I had to walk five blocks from the costume store to get to the studio, because I wanted to get used to it. So we're in a classroom, and obviously, it was a cheap production. The cameras are rolling, I'm the teacher, and I wanted to dress up like the teacher I remember I had, a conservative grey suit. I come in there, but I'm also sitting in the classroom with John, Joey, and Dee Dee. The song is playing, and I'm there with a boombox, and the other guys are doing their thing. Johnny is on the desk. Joey has a boxing glove, and he hits the principal on the face on the blackboard which was drawn in chalk. And Dee Dee was the guy who made the bomb. There he is in a science class with test tubes and everything. And the "pinhead" is in there. He was one of our roadies. And at the end, the school blows up. It took all day to do. See, that was the beauty of it. It didn't take weeks; it took *a day* to do that. We were very hyper people.

We were in a hotel room [circa the "Rock 'n' Roll Radio" video shoot] at the Tropicana. Then we'd go to the studio, and it looks like a room with a TV and everything else. "Rock 'n' Roll Radio"—what do you have there? You're watching the TV, and there's Buddy Holly, and you have all these guys that started rock n' roll. And at the end, we're all watching, and then John puts his guitar through the TV. It was interesting. You want to act ... but you have to be yourself. And then, later on in videos, you *had to* act. Really, the song was about what wasn't going on at the time, or what punk was against—stadium rock/prog rock.

"We Want the Airwaves" was done I think on top of Joey's apartment building, on Second Avenue and Ninth Street. It was 1981. It was hot as hell. We're up there, and I'm in my wife-beater shirt, we have our leather jackets on, and I think we take them off at some point. All the equipment is dragged up to the top of the roof. We had to talk to the manager of the building to see if we were able to do it, and permission was granted. Then we had to walk down St. Mark's Place, in our leather jackets, in mid-summer. And then, of course, everybody starts coming around. "Oh, why are the Ramones walking down St. Mark's Place?" Then, *everybody* wanted to be in the video. I remember I was with Johnny Thunders before that, the guitar player from the New York Dolls, who was in the Heartbreakers at the time. He goes, "What are you doing? What is this?" I go to him, "Well, we're making a video." He goes, "Can I be in it?" I say, "No, you can't." And he punches me in the mouth!

We Want the Airwaves" ... we *weren't* getting the airwaves. You work your ass off, and no one wants to play you, because punk at that time, they didn't want to play it. Unless you went disco, like the Clash or Blondie. We didn't. We stuck to our guns. If there was any distraction from our usual style was the Phil Spector album [*End of the Century*]. What did we do? "Baby, I Love You," which was his song. He produced it. You weren't supposed to dance to it. It was just a modern-day version. It wasn't, "Oh, let's have a disco/dance song." So bands like that were accepted, because they were "radio friendly," and that's why we did "We Want the Airwaves." Because we didn't want to change, and we never changed.

RICHIE RAMONE: All I remember is, when I got in the band, that is the first thing that we did [film the "Psycho Therapy" video]. We flew to L.A. I was in the band for like a week. Marky played on the album, and then he was gone. That's what the director wanted, like we were all on Thorazine. [Laughs] Putting those robes on, nobody really wanted to do it. And the girls were dancing around and all that stuff. It was a quick "in-and-out shoot," like a one-day thing. We didn't know any of those girls. They hired them. Then we did "Time Has Come Today" in New York, around the same time. That was kind of cool, because we shot that in a church, down in the Village. We had a lot of extras and friends come. That was a really cool video.

[The "Psycho Therapy" video] was before I got my drums stolen, the original Ringo Starr/Black Oyster Pearl drum set. Now it's probably worth about $20,000. Our whole truck was stolen on [Richie's] first tour in L.A., right out of the parking lot. Everything went, except for Johnny's white Mos-rite. Right after [the video shoot], we went on tour. The first night, we were at the Holiday Inn. It's not the Holiday Inn anymore; it's the Renaissance, where they built the hall where they have the Academy Awards. We woke up, and the truck wasn't there. We had to go to Guitar Center and get all new instruments. It was weird playing new amps. And we had to buy four leather jackets!

It was the Ramones ... what are the memories? Dee Dee and John hated doing anything, really. It's no real fond memories. They didn't show any of our videos, really, maybe super-late at night once in a while. Joey always complained about MTV's stiffness. He was mad at them that they never played our stuff. He was disappointed with them. He hated them.

— *Talking Heads* —

ALAN HUNTER: David Byrne understood the video medium long before MTV came along. Little mini-films. My favorite, number-one video of all time remains "Once in a Lifetime." Everybody's got a different reason why a video is important to them. It could be timing, it could be where you were, it could be the song, it could be the video. To me, it seemed to be the whole package. David Byrne and the Talking Heads—I was living in New York. They were a New York-centric band. As much as I didn't grow up going to the clubs and watching early Talking Heads in the '70s, I understood their mystique.

"Once in a Lifetime" was a simple video, with David Byrne against a green-screen and fun, weird graphics going on behind him. And he did that crazy little African "choppy chop" on his arm. And the sound of the music—there was something about the opening, watery synthesizer sound that was going on, that really gave me the goosebumps. When I hear that song to this day ... I think that was "MTV" for me. The coolest place in the universe, and this is the coolest video. I didn't know David Byrne very well. I got to meet him thereafter. But I just felt that he was a well-rounded artist. He liked music, he liked graphics, he liked art. And he was centered enough to just stand there and act weird. Maybe it's just because I like that goofy quality of David Byrne. I felt like, "If I had to do a video, it would probably be just like that." [Laughs] And it's kind of why I like Devo, for the same reason. I like the bands that didn't take themselves so seriously, not withstanding artists of great passion and great quality.

TONI BASIL: David and I, together, co-directed "Once in a Lifetime," so of course I'm a fan of his extraordinary talent. He wanted to research movement, but he wanted to research movement more as an actor, as does David Bowie, as does Mick Jagger. They come to movement in another way, not as a trained dancer. Or not really interested in dance steps. He wanted to research people in trances—different trances in church and different trances with snakes. So we went over to UCLA and USC, and we viewed a lot of footage of documentaries on that subject. And then he took the ideas, and he "physicalized" the ideas from these documentary-type films. From there, we discussed how they could be placed and used in the video. Then we shot this video.

We shot it not on a white background, but on a blue screen, so that we could multiply him. Things were done pretty simplistically in those days. I mean, I did seven videos for my company in total for about $90,000. And, at the time, when I was making videos—whether it was with Devo, David Byrne, or whoever—there wasn't record companies breathing down anybody's neck, telling them what to do, what the video should look like. There was no paranoid A&R guy, no crazy dresser that would come in and decide what people should be wearing, and put them in shoes that they can't walk in, everybody with their own agenda. We were all on our own. I don't ever remember any record exec or anybody from any record company coming around any of us in the early days. *Ever.*

— *Elvis Costello* —

GLENN TILBROOK: Elvis Costello and the Attractions really managed to capture the essence of what they were about live and to transfer that to video. That was a good thing and a smart thing to do. The classic video—which is how the Attractions really were—was "Pump It Up." They were absolutely gakked off their faces, chewing madly, and spitting venom. And it's a brilliant rock n' roll moment. I think it's one of the classic moments of the '70s and '80s.

— Blondie —

KATHY VALENTINE: Blondie—I loved their videos. I loved that it was low budget, but the essence of the band just shone through. I loved "Rapture." I like videos that capture the essence of the band, where it's substance over style, of the band and not the video director.

— Adam and the Ants —

STEVE BARRON: Generally, 99% of the videos that we did, the director would write the ideas. The artists that really came up with their own ideas ... Adam and the Ants. I did their first video, "Ant Music," and Adam was completely out of art school and really creative. He came up with a lot of ideas himself and said, "I'm going to be unplugging a giant plug, and I want it to be on an under-lit disco dance floor," and that's what the basic concept was. Most of the other artists it wasn't really about that.

— The Clash —

GLENN TILBROOK: The Clash really had it all sown up as far as I was concerned. I think that the Clash's videos from that time absolutely are of that time and transcend it, which is the most you can hope for when you shoot a video. Their videos still seem really fresh to me and manage to capture the spirit of what they were about. I've got nothing but admiration for them.

ALAN HUNTER: It's hard to tell what the pedestal was for others. Artists like Michael Jackson, Madonna, and Prince were the stars of MTV, and all of the other bands just provided the platform, kind of the meat and the glue. The Clash gave MTV its credibility, along with the Peter Gabriels and the David Byrnes of the world thereafter, who were popular but also seemed credible. And U2 and any other band you can name, like Springsteen. But those were the people that classed the joint up a little bit. I think the Clash gave some of it street cred.

"Rock the Casbah" was, to me, so *not* the Clash. I'd read interviews where Joe Strummer said, "We loved that stuff," but to me, it was like, "That was just your more poppy stuff, wasn't it?" It wasn't their true punk roots. Nonetheless, they had so much fun with the video. It was kind of like a Madness video, it was so underproduced. Or, if you go back to Men at Work, it was like them hanging around the outback with a camera crew following them around, doing silly shit. That's what the Clash videos seemed to me. I think that goes hand-in-hand with their persona. "Oh fuck it, we're not going to be overproduced here." But still though, it seemed like they had a sense of humor, which surprised me. The Clash wanted to kill you ... but really, they just wanted to have fun.

— *Joan Jett & the Blackhearts* —

RICKY BYRD: We were on the beach [for "Do You Wanna Touch"]. We were on the boardwalk, in Long Beach [New York]. There was a bar involved, I remember that, and Joan was boxing some guy. Some "muscle thing" going on. I just remember doing it over and over and over, and they were filming us walking and Joan boxing and standing by the bar singing. It's very tedious work, as anybody that does any kind of videos or movies will tell you. It's certainly not interesting for the performers, because you do it a million times, so they can get all the angles they want. For Joan, she did way more stuff in the video than we did, because we're "the band." So focus on Joan, then a shot of Ricky playing the lead, him walking down the board-walk, him walking down the boardwalk with Joan. But a lot of my time was spent sitting around.

MARTHA DAVIS: Loved Joan Jett. I think everybody you've mentioned, more than anything I can say, they were *captured*. And each one is so diverse, from my video to Joan's video to Devo's video. You had such a diversity of direction, and it made it nice, because you didn't have the same video. If you look back ten years ago or the hip-hop thing, you see the same-same-same, even in the hair band thing you'd see the same-same-same. But in that sort of eclectic, weird '80s time—because everyone was striving for something so different—it became so unique in each band's representation. It was a glorious time. You could watch TV for hours and not get bored, because it was completely different. There is something about "I Love Rock n' Roll," it just kicks ass. She is amazing. I've known her since the beginning, when they were the Runaways, and the Kim Fowley days. I'm glad she survived, because those were dark times. But to emerge with this anthem, and to do it so proudly and beautifully, it's great.

DEBORA IYALL: I was always fascinated with Joan Jett. She's a true rocker chick, of the kind that I never really knew and wasn't. But I always felt like I really respected her. She's got really catchy songs, so you can't argue with that.

LITA FORD: God, honestly, I couldn't tell you how they go. I don't remember sitting there and watching a Joan Jett video.

RICKY BYRD: ["I Love Rock n' Roll"] was done at a place called Private's in New York City. It was on Lexington Avenue and 80-something Street, and it was a really cool club that was owned by Leber-Krebs. That's where Joan worked out of, where they sold her first record, *Bad Reputation*, out of a little office in the back of Leber-Krebs. But they owned this club, Private's. It was a big room upstairs, and then there was a bar downstairs, which I don't remember the name of, and that's where we filmed the video. I remember walking in the bar in the video, and all the fans were there.

ALAN HUNTER: She was the opposite of Madonna. She was not about glitz and glam. I don't think any of us understood what "bisexual" necessarily was back then. We didn't really know what she was. She just couldn't have been more appealing to a guy like me. I had a big-ass crush on Joan Jett. But she seemed to be one of the most healthy holdovers from the '70s. She seemed to be connected to "the real." Kind of like the Clash were. It felt like Joan Jett was the real deal. Certainly, I wouldn't say Madonna wasn't the real deal—she was—but she was *manufactured*. She was the one in charge of her manufacturing. So she wasn't like a boy band, created by a producer. But Joan Jett felt real. She—along with Chrissie Hynde and some other stalwarts—was kind of "pop Patti Smith." What Patti Smith might have wanted to be, if she wanted to sell a whole lot more records. But she's also just so sexual. I think she drove a lot of guys wild, there's no doubt.

— A Flock of Seagulls —

MIKE SCORE: ["I Ran"] is just basically being stupid. [Laughs] You know, "Stand here, the camera is going to be in the middle, and you're going to try and do something." And, of course, we had no idea what to do in a video. Videos were not the "mini-movies" yet. If it was up to the band, we probably would have just stood there in our wild gear and gone, "OK, we'll just pretend to play." But they wanted a little bit more, a little bit more angular and quirky. It seems to me that all the early videos had to be quirky. I guess nobody was taking them seriously until somebody dropped a million dollars on one.

I think "Space Age Love Song" we did on top of a club called Danceteria in New York. All of that era became a bit of a blur, because there was so much going on every day. It wasn't like, "Oh, we've got to wait a month, and then we'll make a video." It was, "OK, we've got *a day* to make this video. We're going to Danceteria. And then tomorrow we're going to do this TV show." So there was other stuff going on every day. For that video, I got my hair to stand up better than it had ever stood up before. It was like the perfect day for doing your hair up like that. [Laughs] And actually making a video more or less in public was a little strange. It was kind of like doing a live show but without playing anything—with cameras there, and people stopping you and saying, "Change this. Change that."

Like all videos, you really had no idea what it was going to look like until you saw it on TV. Whereas these days with digital, you can play back stuff immediately, look at it, and say, "I don't like my nose," or that kind of stuff. But in those days, it was still basically film or video, and they would take a quick look at it for quality reasons, but not necessarily for content. They seemed to do a lot of content and then just go into the editing room and pick it out. Other memories of ["Space Age Love Song"]—I was thinner. That was nice. [Laughs] I think we just partied out after at the club. That was our life in those days—do something, and then just spend the night partying.

Wishing" was a bit of a different spin for us, because they spent a lot of money on the video. It wasn't so much that the band was involved in it; the band was just part of what the director wanted. He could have made a video without us, probably. Some things that were put in that video I don't particularly like. Basically, what was happening was we were on tour, we had a meeting with a director, he went away, put the whole thing together, we came in, did our part. It was put together, everybody seemed to like it, and we just went, "OK, that's it. We're done with it." [Laughs]

— *Wall of Voodoo* —

STAN RIDGWAY: "Mexican Radio" came about by us sitting in our car, going to rehearsals, and we were really tired of listening to boring music that we knew all about, and [we] would try to find a Mexican radio station. I couldn't understand the language very much, and it was something on there that was like, "What is this?" It was almost like when Wolfman Jack would broadcast over the border, from Tijuana. We'd pick up stuff like that, and say, "Oh look, *I'm on a Mexican radio!*" So that's where the title came from.

Doing the video, we thought we would go down to Tijuana on Labor Day weekend and just shoot some shots down there. And that turned into a wild *bacchanal*, that probably is best left in the past. There it is, all on film. And the rest of it was shot in a very small office space that I had rented for the band, off Hollywood Boulevard, right by the old punk rock club, the Masque. All the props, we made it up in a weekend. When we were all finished with it—as these things go—personally speaking, the director and I were somewhat disappointed, because we got some of what we wanted but not everything. And we thought, "Oh God, this is just not working. This is going to go nowhere. We're just losers. It's time for us to all join bartender school and get out of here." But nobody else thought that after a while.

We pulled in a lot of people—our friends from Hollywood—to appear in the video as extras. We had quite a party doing that. The woman who pulls off the pot at the end of the video—where I come up from out of the beans—I think she was on acid for most of the night. Building up anticipation for her scene, which we did last. And I had to get underneath the table and put my head up through this hole in a big salad bowl and breathe through a straw for a while, until they got the camera ready. It was a "one-shot thing." We did it once, and that was it. It sounds kind of ridiculous, but leading to one of my disappointments, we also wanted to make a video for "Factory." And one of the ideas that we had for "Factory" was the character in the song, who's a zombie worker, would go to the kitchen, open up the oven, and pull out a meatloaf ... and that my face would somehow be plastered into this meatloaf, singing a line or two. A little like the old *Alice in Wonderland* black-and-white, the way they did make-up for Humpty Dumpty. We didn't have any opportunity to do that. There was no money to do it, and we didn't do the song at all. So we kind of transferred somewhat of that idea to the beans, you see.

STEWART COPELAND: Was that the one with the face coming out of the soup? Face coming out of the beans. That's the image that endures. They were great, I was a big fan of Wall of Voodoo.

STAN RIDGWAY: I guess it's bittersweet. I thought we made a pretty good video in "Mexican Radio" for them. They played the hell out of it. It was really when we made that video, I was thinking Salvador Dalí and Marcel Duchamp, their movies they made in the early parts of the Parisian avant-garde or something. So I was from that angle.

— *Squeeze* —

GLENN TILBROOK: We did a video for "Tempted," and the record company wouldn't let us use it. It was an excellent video. So we ended up with a very dull performance on stage, at some gig in Manchester, I think it was. It was a fair enough reflection of where we were as a band at that point. But I have to say, it's a pretty dull video. [The original version] was absolutely ahead of its time. It looks contemporary now. I haven't even got a copy of it. There's a copy of it in Australia that someone played me. It was directed by Barney Bubbles, who did the cover for *East Side Story*. And he was jump-cutting a lot, before anyone had done it. Also, he replayed the images through a TV screen and then messed about with the tuning of it, so it looked like it was fading in and out. It was a remarkable video, and someday it will be recognized for the genius that he was. By the time "Black Coffee in Bed" came around, it was the beginning of spurious plots with no meaning. I think that "Black Coffee in Bed" is a true kitsch video classic, in that it's absolutely devoid of meaning, but it caught the spirit of the time perfectly. I experimented with make-up on that video perhaps more than any other time. [Laughs]

— *U2* —

MICHAEL SADLER: Basic, straightforward—the way that they were trying to put themselves across at the time. A little political in the beginning. I think the band wavered from that at the right time. I think if had they pushed that political thing too long, they wouldn't be who they are today. They would have been dismissed fairly early. Because the music—quite honestly—is slightly unremarkable from a musician point of view. But it works for them. It works because it's built and built and built.

STEWART COPELAND: U2 were slightly different. We saw them in Dublin, and they played in the afternoon. They were way low down on the bill. But just hanging out backstage, they had a charisma about them. They had a buzz, even though they weren't on the charts. I don't even know if they had recorded an album yet, but U2 kind of stuck in our brains, just the vibe of them. I think we had a lot of affinity with them, as a matter of fact. I can't remember any of [U2's videos]. You get to the top, and particularly when the band broke up, we weren't really in that business anymore. I just stopped watching MTV. I became a film composer and was watching movies. I had sort of "been there/done that" with that world and really couldn't be bothered to watch MTV videos. Sort of didn't see any of them. I mean, if you talked to the people that came before me, none of them saw any of our videos. It's sort of a disrespect that is not meant disrespectfully, if you know what I mean.

ALAN HUNTER: When U2 first came along, I was watching a video, as we often were watching a new video in the green room down in the studio. I think it was Mark and I sitting around, watching "I Will Follow." I think it was kind of a live concert clip—Bono in his loose-sleeved, sort of French-cut shirt, looking very styled. But very passionate. I thought it was kind of lightweight. Mark thought it was fabulous. He said, *"This is going to be huge."*

I was like, "Really? You think this guy is going to be huge?" I was not a hit-maker. I had no real feel for it. I thought Madonna and her "Borderline" song was lightweight. I didn't understand what was coming, to be honest. Mark was in the music business longer than I was, for sure. So he kind of understood the ebb and flow. But I got to interview Bono and the Edge first. Again, when new bands like that came along, and the interviews got divvied up, I used to get the new guys, and Mark and JJ got the Paul McCartneys and Rod Stewarts and Robert Plants of the world. I liked the new wave, from Depeche Mode to Ultravox to the bands from the U.K. Anyway, Bono and the Edge came on, and I introduced them. As the cameras rolled, "Today with us in the studio, from U2, it's the Edge and Bow-No." The producer stopped and said, *"It's Bono."*

JON ANDERSON: I think I grew into U2. I went to see them play, and then I realized how good they were. It wasn't until *Zoo TV* [that] I started to [think], "Hey, they're making really good stuff. They're making really good movement and capturing the world in that period," the sort of late '80s/early '90s visual art on stage, capturing it on video. And the music fits perfectly. That's why they're still *the* big band.

DAVE MARSH: There was a fund of money, usually that got charged back to the act, that helped younger bands that didn't have a touring reputation to go out and work. And the reason I bring it up is what happened when MTV came in is the video budgets—every dollar in them—came from the touring. And what happened was you created a bunch of bands that didn't create "road reputations." You see it even now ... you see it even *more* now. U2 was one of the last bands to benefit from that type of support. And that's why U2 was one of the last bands with staying power. One of the things that MTV did was reorient the recording industry—not the music industry— much more intensively than ever, to hit singles rather than album projects.

—Thomas Dolby —

THOMAS DOLBY: "Europa and the Pirate Twins" was mainly shot on a beach in front of a nuclear power station in the east of England, and featured my friend who was a still-photographer and his girlfriend, who got dressed up in a bandage for that song. [Laughs] And "Airwaves" was sort of a post-apocalyptic, underground survivalist kind of thing, and was shot in the Docklands of east London, which, in those days, were very desolate. Now, they've all been tarted up. "Radio Silence" was in the studio, in front of a white site, with various artifacts of the radio age—fragments of giant radios and things like that. When it came to "She Blinded Me with Science," I actually wrote the storyboard before I even had the song finished. It was kind of like the song was a soundtrack for the video. I managed to persuade my record company to let me do it myself, because I wanted Steve Barron to do it, but he wasn't available, because he was making "Billie Jean" at the time for Michael Jackson. But the budget had already been assigned, so I talked the record company into letting me do it myself. And I think it made a big difference, because the personality of that video is a very single-minded kind of a feel to it, and I think that results in the fact that it's all me.

"She Blinded Me with Science" wasn't on the album [*The Golden Age of Wireless*]. I recorded it as a single after the album. And then when the American record company heard it, they wanted to repackage the album with "Science" on it. We shot it over a day. We had a budget of £10,000. So that gave us a day's shoot, a long day. I left early in the morning, and it was a location in the middle of Regent's Park in London, which is *not* actually a home for deranged scientists. [Laughs] It's some sort of building that we rented for the day. It was quite hard really, being in front of the camera and behind the camera. I was still pretty new to the whole language of film. But what would happen was the crew community for videos in the U.K. at the time were basically feature film crews, who would work cheap because you would upgrade them. So like a key grip could become a camera operator, or a camera operator would become a director of photography, and so on. And they would work cheap, so they could get some work on their resume, in the slot above them. There was a sense of fun about it. You had to work quick and improvise things. You didn't have the luxury of going back and reshooting and getting lots of coverage. You had to get your shot and move on. And there was music playing all the time, which was nice [for the crew]. Usually when they do films or commercials, there's no music. So it had a party feel to it.

Dr. Magnus Pyke was a TV celebrity scientist for the BBC. He was a real personality, a real English personality. And I'd hired him to do the voiceover on the recording and said, "Would you come do the video as well?" He was willing to do that. He'd never been asked to do anything like that before. He seemed to enjoy himself, although the next time I saw him a couple of years later, he kind of cursed me, because he said every time he went to the U.S.A., people would sneak up behind him on the sidewalk and go, *"SCIENCE!"* And my father was in it. He was one of the "mad scientists"—he had on a pair of jet-propelled rollerskates. I think the rest of the scientists I picked out of an extras catalog, including "Miss Sakamoto." She just had the right look. I just thumbed through a bunch of 8 x 10s and picked people out.

— *The Fixx* —

CY CURNIN: There was an Eastern religious sect that had predicted the end of the world on the day we made this video ["Stand or Fall"]—April 12, 1982. We had great fun running around on the beaches of Dorset, trying to look like many. When I say many, I mean that we needed to create a battle scene, but we were a small army of five. Shot in 35mm, it looked—and still does—amazing. Jeanette Obstoj and Rupert Hine did us proud. Those guys always put passion into everything they do. I think it was an enormous part of our success. ["Red Skies"] was taken from a live performance for the BBC at the Riverside studios. I am actually singing live over the backing track. That's why I'm the only one who looks like he's concentrating.

We had Brian Grant chosen for us to shoot ["Saved by Zero"] by the record company. By this time, MCA had woken up to the fact that videos were important. They had been penny-pinching our earlier efforts, but now opened the vaults and in came the "professionals," with huge expense accounts that afforded us lunches, massages, and fourteen stylists to make us look like proper rock stars! The aftershock of the huge pricetag to the "Saved by Zero" video was that the record company agreed that Ostoj and Hine were in fact very talented at a third of the cost [for "One Thing Leads to Another"]. So with very clever storyboards, Jeanette was able to create a very memorable montage that still sits in people's minds. Goes to show that a good idea costs nothing. Superbly edited by Rupert Hine, who knew the song backwards, because he produced it, too!

— *Romeo Void* —

DEBORA IYALL: What was exciting was we hired a filmmaker [for "Never Say Never"] who was used to shooting in film, and he wanted to shoot in black and white. He was slightly doing a take-off on Godard in the video, but it only comes up at the end, where there's a little gesture of rubbing the thumb across the bottom lip, which is a lift directly from Godard. I think we thought it should be artistic, and the person who does it should be someone who knows how to make an artistic statement out of it, and see that in the band. I think it turned out quite beautifully, and it served us quite well all these years later, because it captures us as individuals making our sound together and obviously having a good time doing it, in our environment. We filmed that video in San Francisco, in our rehearsal studio. We got the local cafe in on it, because we had that scene where we walked by the cafe, and *that's* the cafe I used to hang out in all the time. And we filmed one of the scenes in my bedroom. It was sort of that "homegrown thing."

["A Girl in Trouble (Is a Temporary Thing)"] was filmed at the California College of Arts and Crafts in Valencia, and the director was Julia Hayward. She had also worked on the "Burning Down the House" video, which featured the projections on the house and the projection on the road, where it looks like the road is going into his mouth. I had met her through the San Francisco Art Institute, where I went to school. She was a lecturer there. So I said, "We've got to use her, because I think she's got a neat vision." It was fun to collaborate with the art students on that, and we got a lot of art student interns to help make the "starry sky" and things like that. It was actually a pretty fun experience. Originally, I wanted to have the skateboarder as the girl in the video, because they wanted us to have another lead girl. We went along with it, because it was, "Get your video made ... *or not.*" That's because they didn't think I was attractive enough to be the only girl in the video. So I thought, "OK, we can go along with that, but let's have a girl who is fierce."

So I had arranged to have this girl skateboarder be the other girl in the video, and then at the last minute, she just didn't show up for the shoot!

So we were literally at the shoot, with everybody—all the crew and every-thing—and it's like, "We don't have another girl … what are we going to do?" So we went running around the school, looking for people. We did a couple of little tests, looked at them, and decided on the girl, who in some ways, has some resemblance to me. She's not white, and she had big, fluffy dark hair. I think Julia is just amazing for being able to think on her feet, and we did that whole mirror sequence, where I turn into her and she turns into me. That was done by using a one-way mirror, somehow. Sort of early special effects. Also, the last scene I always loved. I loved filming that scene, see-ing the golden California hills and oak trees in our video. I've always really identified with California. I grew up here and looking at the foothills all the time. It was nice to integrate that.

— X —

JOHN DOE: We worked with Ray Manzarek on that video ["The Hungry Wolf"], because he had some film experience, at least film school. I remem-ber going into a soundstage, setting up, and playing. And our roadies up in the rafters, pulling a string with a bat on the end of it. We thought that was very "B-movie" and "kitsch." We had some grand ideas. I actually thought of a much more cinematic [idea], having a wolf coming down through the Hol-lywood Hills, and having this sort of horror element to it. But we couldn't afford that. We had one day, we sang it four or five times, they edited it, we made some notes, and [we] tried not to be embarrassed. [Manzarek] had the cameraman on roller skates, rather than having a dolly, because it was cheap. Rather than the wheelchair trick, he used the roller skate trick. Elektra was not willing to put the money into making a big production.

— *The English Beat* —

DAVE WAKELING: "Save It for Later" was at a crypt club in London, an underground crypt club to try and keep teenagers off alcohol. They made coffee bars under the churches, and filled up the coffee awfully strong, because the teenagers were all taking speed but not telling them! That "espresso culture" was born, and it wasn't just too much coffee. It was the burgeoning birth of mod in the '60s with these crypt clubs. And one of them had actually had groups that played there. So we had it done up as part of the budget of the video, and Julien Temple recreated this kind of '60s beat ambience. Messing with the other "beat," the Beat poets of the '50s and '60s. So there is a guy reading Jean-Paul Sartre upside down. And a little dance bit that was in that video ended up being a big dance for the band. You sort of wave your hands and wiggle them as though they're wet. We did the same sort of live thing with Julien Temple again with the song "Doors of Your Heart," a couple of days before the Notting Hill Carnival in London, with a float that had been made for that year and a rent-a-crowd. Edited the video together and brought it straight out. So people were amazed that we brought a video out of the Notting Hill Carnival like the day of the carnival.

— *Fishbone* —

ANGELO MOORE: "Party at Ground Zero" ... the video ... I remember it was somewhere in L.A. The band was together, we got ourselves painted up, and it was fun. I think it was the first [Fishbone] video that may have gotten on MTV, but it wasn't the first video that we did, though. The first video was "Voyage to the Land of the Freeze-Dried Godzilla Farts." There's always some waiting around between shots, with video preparation and all that kind of stuff that goes on. How is it filming a video compared to how Fishbone plays live? When we play live, there ain't no waiting. We blast right through the set. There's no time to get the camera ready, set the tripod, focus, or make-up, or any of that shit. *That's live.*

— *The Cars* —

MARTHA DAVIS: The Cars were a blast. A very distinctive and classic sound of the '80s, for sure. Also, really interesting videos. And they had a good sense of humor, which I think is a really great thing about how they came off in the videos.

GREG HAWKES: We asked [Gerald Casale to direct two videos from *Panorama*], because we loved the Devo videos. He was easy to work with. He's a funny guy. He had a partner, Chuck Statler, who co-directed the films with him, who was more "the camera guy." For "Touch and Go," we went out to this amusement park in Lunenburg, Massachusetts. It's called Whalom Park, which is no longer there, sadly. I remember that was a hot day. Elliot had to do his guitar solo while riding on this teacup saucer ride, so he was spinning around, and it was hot. He got somewhat nauseous from the experience. And "Panorama" was fun. We shot it in Boston. The idea was to make it like a little spy/James Bond/spoof kind of thing. It was sort of a little series of almost chase scenes. We got to go up in the helicopter for that one, for the shot of Ric at the end, when he's pushed out of a helicopter.

GERALD CASALE: [Devo's manager] Elliot Roberts had acquired the Cars, and they were a band that was kind of "anti-video." They were a band where Ric Ocasek and Ben Orr were incredible songwriters, and then they hooked up with Roy Thomas Baker, and they knew how to make a hit record sound. But they weren't performers. I mean, if you watched the Cars, it was the old "watching paint dry"—they just stood there and played, and it was incredibly boring. And they were really leery of this "video thing" that started happening. But Elliot said, "Hey, Jerry and Devo have done all these videos - they know all about it. If you don't want to spend a lot of money, use him!" And so we got off tour in Europe, and I stopped in Boston, and we spent a week in Boston doing "Touch and Go" and "Panorama." And of course, those were two of the least commercial Cars songs ever written! So it was very difficult on this tiny budget to even come up with something to do for those songs, that people would watch.

GREG HAWKES: The "Shake It Up" video we did in Los Angeles. It was directed by Seth Justman's brother, Paul Justman. I'm not a big fan of the "Shake It Up" video, to tell you the truth. The thing I mainly remember was doing the indoor shots, where it was a pseudo-garage, just because I remember with all the smoke how uncomfortable it was and how everybody was coughing and gagging afterwards. Paul did ["Since You're Gone"] as well. I remember doing it in Los Angeles, and it was probably within a month or two of doing the "Shake It Up" video. I remember there are little animated shoes in that one. That to me was the high-point of the video. [Laughs]

DEBORA IYALL: We were starstruck with the Cars a little bit, because they definitely had some real success, financially, so they all had leather jackets and stuff like that. I don't think I saw it in any objective way at all. I was just a fan of Ric's artist side and artistic intentions. And to that end, one of the reasons why we wanted to work with him [Ocasek produced Romeo Void's *Never Say Never* EP] was because he had worked with Suicide. So we knew he isn't just "The guy from the Cars." He's a music fan, too.

GREG HAWKES: ["You Might Think"] is my favorite. I think it's the best one we did. I remember meeting with Jeff Stein, the director, who showed us a demo reel of the Charlex guys. Charlex was this company in New York, which was run by two guys, Charlie and Alex, thus the name, "Charlex." So Jeff's idea was to do a somewhat animated video, in the style that these guys at Charlex sort of developed. They used this thing, I guess it was the "video paintbox." It gave it that cartoon-y look, and we shot everything on video. We went down to the Charlex Studio in New York and pretty much shot everything in front of the blue screen. Then they would put in all the backgrounds. And since it was shot on video, as soon as we would finish shooting a scene, they would have a crew that would start putting in the background and things. So we could see it being put together while we were there, shooting other scenes. I liked working with those guys a lot.

Now, the only bad thing is it seems like the Charlex guys and Jeff Stein had a falling out after that and never worked together again. I think it was somewhat over who deserved the most credit over that video. At least from my viewpoint, Jeff was the guy who had the idea of doing it and bringing Charlex in and was sort of the "big idea guy." But then Alex Weil was really the hands-on director and came up with a lot of the ideas for the various individual scenes. And we did end up working with Jeff Stein again on his own. He did the video for "Tonight She Comes," which I also liked.

Andy Warhol was, you'd probably call him the "executive director" [for "Hello Again"], where the actual director was this guy named Don Monroe, who worked for Andy Warhol. At the time, they had a New York show, called *Andy Warhol's TV*. It might have been a public access show. I think it at least started out as a New York public access show, and this guy, Don Monroe, was one of the directors for that show. So he was really the de facto director on the "Hello Again" video. That was fun. We shot that in New York. We did it at some club in Greenwich Village. Andy Warhol seemed like a somewhat shy, quiet guy. Seemed very pleasant. There was that guy, John Sex, with the snake, that does stick out a little bit. [Laughs] And the girls with the Jell-O or something.

The "Magic" video, again, I wasn't crazy about it. It's the one where Ric is walking on water, and there's a lot of odd characters hanging around the pool. We shot it in Los Angeles in an afternoon. To me, it's just fluff. Timothy Hutton directed ["Drive"]. In fact, that's where Ric met Paulina [Porizkova] and started, y'know, *that*. [Laughs] [Hutton] brought a sense of seriousness about it. I remember I was in the background, shooting pool or something in a scene, and he would talk to us each about, "OK, move your arm, and do the shot like this. *You've got to be thinking this."* It was pretty serious. I thought it was shot really well. The camera work was beautifully done. He had a good cameraman, and he worked with the cameraman a lot. He knew the technical stuff, as well as the acting stuff. [Ric hitting it off with Paulina] was the start of a certain amount of turmoil. [Laughs] I mean, with Ric personally, first of all, he was married at the time, so there was that "complication." That's just where they met, and it developed from there. I remember shooting ["Tonight She Comes"] in a big airplane hangar or something in Los Angeles. It wasn't as innovative as the "You Might Think" one, but I liked the look of it.

MIKE RENO: What I remember the most about the Cars was their sound. They had come up with a mixture of rock and synthesized music that was very interesting for me. They had sounds that I had never heard before, so they must have really dug in and created new sounds. They were definitely innovators, of synthesized sounds and cool rock grooves. The drums sounded *amazing*. And they looked cool. They had one guy that was kind of the geeky guy, and one guy who was really handsome, and one guy that was really scary. The whole thing was very interesting to me. But I loved their songs. Their songwriting is what really got me, and the sound of the songs. It really had nothing to do with video for me. Watching a video wasn't as special for me as it was for a lot of people. I liked the sounds and the songs. The Cars were right on target.

Def Leppard (and Mutt Lange)

MIKE RENO: As far as I'm concerned, Def Leppard had one of the best sounds going. I know now they used the same producer [on their biggest albums, *High n' Dry*, *Pyromania*, and *Hysteria*]. But back then, I didn't put two and two together. I just thought, *"How could they do that?"* They had this great sounding set of drums, huge vocals, and great songs that just seemed to be masterpieces. And they were running around with flag shirts and flag shorts. They were very British. Really cool looking guitars. It was a magic time. Those guys were awesome. And the greatest thing about it is today they're my friends. But Def Leppard just made me open my eyes. I couldn't believe a band could sound *that good.*

They had these harmonies, and they reminded me of the sea, *a wall* of harmonies. I said, "I've got to start trying to do that." And I realized it's hard to reproduce that stuff live. So we didn't use it much, because I didn't want to have people say, "They sure sound good on record ... but they suck live." So I always cut stuff in the studio that I knew I could recreate. But I didn't know how Def Leppard were going to do that, and then I realized that all five of them were singing all these harmonies.

They had some great songs, too, some *classic* songs. I'd have to put them up in the top five for classic songs, along with Foreigner and the Cars. Foreigner was hugely great, too. Lou Gramm—his voice was so great. And the guitar riffs by Mick Jones and the production. And it turns out that the same producer that produced the Cars and Def Leppard also produced Foreigner. So we ended up trying to get close to this guy. We wanted to work with Mutt Lange. So we ended up having a short but sweet experience with Mutt Lange [Lange wrote Loverboy's 1985 hit single, "Lovin' Every Minute of It"].

RUDY SARZO: The way I look at Def Leppard comes from the point that I knew them personally. Def Leppard was the opening act for Ozzy in 1981. And at the time, they had a guitar player named Pete Willis, who was having an alcohol problem. The sound of the band ... they had great songs. They were a great band, very young, very energetic. They really kicked us in the ass every night. It was a great bill, great people. But a little bit rough. They weren't as polished as they should have been. It wasn't until Phil Collen came into the group that he brought in that very balanced sense of presence, not only musically, but also as an individual. I mean, I'm not saying he was *a saint*. We all hung out and had a good time, but he was very professional, and he raised the bar of the group overall. And by the time that *Pyromania* came out, it was a whole different band. It's amazing how one individual can make such a contribution, that just becomes the paradigm shift in what the group is known for. By then, that album, great songs. Those are all gems, every single song. And the videos really sold the band, which to me, that is the ultimate outcome of making a music video—to promote what the group is really all about. Those videos were perfect. They sold the band.

PHIL COLLEN: The thing we always wanted to do in Def Leppard is just be a hybrid of a lot of other things. In England, you don't really do the "cover band thing." When you start up, you start writing songs before you can even play an instrument, in most cases. So America's the complete opposite. We were creating our own thing, and I think it was going to combine a lot of different rock bands—Thin Lizzy, T. Rex and the glam thing, along with the punk stuff, and Zeppelin. It was a total combination. We tried to do it with the music, and when we met Mutt Lange, he's great at creating "the hybrid." Obviously, what he did with Shania Twain—bringing country to a much larger audience. It crossed over into pop, and Taylor Swift is the next example of that. There's very little country. It's more pop than it is country, but it obviously has its roots in it. And that's what we were, a rock band, but we didn't want to be like a lot of the American bands. Which we thought were great—Journey, Foreigner, and stuff like that. We still wanted to have that hard-edged thing that AC/DC had, but we still wanted to have the harmonies, a bit like Queen. So again, it's just an absolute hybrid. Nobody had really done what we'd done until the *Pyromania* album came out. It was still kind of hard-edged. It had harmonies, but they weren't sung sweetly like, say, some of the American bands.

HERMAN RAREBELL: They make very commercial, pop-oriented, heavy, melodic rock. And with that formula, you can't fail on American radio. Very commercial, simple melodies, which go directly in your brain. Very catchy lyrics.

ALAN HUNTER: Def Leppard was easy for me to embrace. They weren't just heavy rock n' roll. I didn't love the heavier stuff. I mean, look, I got into Mötley Crüe ... but they were so lightweight, it just didn't get me going. It was fun to see a band like that, that had been kicking around for a while, that finally, across the ocean, found great success on MTV. And it was really only because of MTV. No one would have heard about them on radio. I don't think they were being played on radio at all at the time. So that was the other "weirdo phenomenon," that MTV was the first portal for so many bands, and they didn't even bother with radio. I thought Def Leppard was a classy heavier band. It was easy for me to talk about them, because I valued good production and good musicianship. Thank God I wasn't hawking music in the '90s, y'know? Nirvana and REM ... I'm not a "grunge rocker" at all.

JOE ELLIOTT: By the time we were wrapping up the recording of *Pyromania*, we'd gone in and shot ["Photograph"] for the lead-off single. This time, we were lucky to work with a director, as opposed to somebody who just filmed us and edited it together. We'd turned up at this soundstage someplace in Battersea, in London, and there was David Mallet. Now, I didn't know who David Mallet was really, but I knew that he worked with Queen. *That was good enough for me.* We walked into this pre-built stage. We had nothing to do with it. We can take absolutely no credit for it. But Mallet had put this thing together—mesh flooring with lights coming up through it and these cages with all these girls in it with torn stockings and ripped tops and stuff. [Laughs] Hilarious now, but back in the time, it was like, "Wow ... this is cool!" I remember Steve Clark was sick as a dog the day that we shot the "Photograph" video, and I think it was Sav's birthday, the second of December, 1982. We were still mixing the album at the time, so we probably actually lip-synched it to a rough mix. The album wasn't done, but we knew that this was the first single that we wanted to put out.

So we shot the video, and we also planned to shoot one for "Rock of Ages," so it was "in the bag" while we were all together in one place. That was going to be the second single, and we did that on Phil's birthday, which is the eighth of December. And it was David Mallet again, but a different soundstage. By the time we got to doing that one, we felt like we were troopers, and we knew what we were doing. For ["Photograph"], we just went in there blind, and if David said do something, we'd do it. I remember there's one bit where the "Marilyn character" stabs her heel through a Polaroid of me screaming. The first thing I had to do when I walked in at 8:00 in the morning—before I even had a chance to have a cup of coffee—David comes in, and he calls everybody "dear boy" or "darling." "Dear boy, I need you to scream into my Polaroid." So I did this kind of scream thing, and he's like, "OK, *done.*" You got pulled along. You got directed, because we didn't know what we were doing. He just said, "Be yourselves. Leave it all to me." And we just went out there and threw all the shapes, because you don't have to sing, so you can concentrate on the visual rather than the performance.

PHIL COLLEN: Do you know the Pink Floyd sleeve, *Animals*? It's the Battersea Power Station. That's actually where we'd done the videos, in there somewhere. David Mallet, who directed those two videos ... I guess ["Photograph"] wasn't really about Marilyn Monroe. It kind of hinted at it. He took the whole thing, and then all of a sudden, *the whole video* was about Marilyn Monroe! A lot of them back then, it was someone else's vision of what the song was about, which was cool. It turned out great, actually. And they really had a look to them, those videos.

WARREN DeMARTINI: Oh man, "Photograph" was right there when we got MTV in the first place. At that time, I was finishing high school. It was my senior year in San Diego. I think San Diego was one of the last cities to get MTV, so on that day when you get that new cable box ... and back then, it was on a cord with this box that had all these keys on it. And towards the end of the box, it was "MTV," and it had its own little icon. It was killer! "Photograph" was just starting to get into some real rotation. I thought it was great—great recording, great production, great song. I felt it was a very well-done conceptual/performance video.

JOE ELLIOTT: It was the ridiculousness of it, which is exactly what the video ["Rock of Ages"] needed to be. [Mallet] was like, "I want you to walk down this drawbridge holding this sword." It's like, "Oh, fuck off. Don't make me do that!" Of course, like an idiot, I submitted to his blinked eyes, looking at me like some long-lost dog. David Mallet's got a great way of manipulating people like that. I was young and dumb and went, "OK." I look at that now, and I think, *"What the hell was I thinking?"* But the things that make me laugh is the beginning bit, where there are these people—most of our road crew—laying in this dry ice, with these ridiculous gloves on with nails coming out of the back of them, clapping along to the song. It's hilarious!

And there's a couple of shots where Phil was clapping along on the verse—because there's no guitars—and he's standing directly behind me, so I look like I've got these "clapping antlers" coming out of my head. Watch the video carefully. I'm wearing a bandana and a yellow shirt, with the immortal Neil Young phrase, "It's better to burn out than fade away," which we stole for the song. And the bandana, for one version of it, it's got the "V" at the front, and it started to spin slowly around, so the knot was at the front. By the time he'd edited it together, the bandana just keeps going front, back, front, back. I didn't notice for five years, probably pointed out by somebody else going, "Look at your bandana!"

PHIL COLLEN: Pretty funny when you look back. The "robe thing" took about 30 seconds to film. You kind of forget about that. It's the stuff that you have to do a take over and over again. I remember Joe and that slab, where the sword turns into my guitar. I used to play this Ibanez Destroyer. It made that guitar really popular. I had everyone trying to copy it and wanting to play it—again, *the power of the video.* I think there was a seven-inch single, and it was the shape of the guitar as well, which was pretty cool. It just showed you how powerful images were and how it was getting portrayed in the video.

JOE ELLIOTT: We shot for three days for the "Foolin'" video, and the whole third day never got used. I remember thinking at the time how annoying it was. They kept me back. They let everyone else go, for a day off at the beach. I had my day off at the beach ... *riding a fucking horse!* I'd never been on a horse in my life. Saddle sore, my ass was hurting, and they didn't use one bit of it ... probably because I looked like a complete dork. If you want to look graceful on a horse, it helps if you've been riding for ten years. So they put me on this horse on sand, had me riding around on a beach in New Jersey I think it was, and it never got used.

There's a shot somewhere during the beginning of the guitar solo, I believe, where I'm running sideways down this corridor, and pyro is going off. It singed all the hair off my arm! I came out of that video shoot literally, physically, and mentally scarred. The smell of burning hair just doesn't go away, no matter how much you shower off. I had no hair. It was all gone, because I was wearing a sleeveless shirt. I'm surprised my arms didn't actually go up. The opening shot of me laying on my back distorts your face, so there's not much about the "Foolin'" video that I thought was too clever. There's one shot where we [jumped] into a hole, and they ran it backwards, which makes you look completely ridiculous. Again, the nice touches for the director to go, "Oh well, I got this machine. It's 'the wicky-wacky-back-wards-machine!' Press this button, and it will go backwards." Great ... but it didn't really put us in a great light. I think out of the three videos that we did with David, it's by far the worst.

CARMINE APPICE: I remember seeing Def Leppard at the Whiskey, when they were young. And then when they started being played all over MTV ... it was like, *enough already!* [Laughs] They had a tendency to just play it over and over, until you were done.

PAUL DEAN: I have nothing but the highest regard for those guys as people and as musicians. We've toured with them, we hung with them, we've done a lot of shows together. To be honest, I don't remember any of their videos. I just remember their albums being incredible. I don't know if their videos were anything special, but it didn't matter, because their songs were great. I still go to *Hysteria*. I love that album. I don't listen to a whole lot of '80s music, but I still go there and *Pyromania*.

JOE ELLIOTT: My first-ever tantrum! [On the set of the second version of the "Bringin' on the Heartbreak" video] We were shooting it at the Jacob's Biscuit Factory in Dublin. It was February, and it was six below freezing. It was the coldest I can remember in a long time. We were shooting through the night, so it got down to about ten below when 3:00 or 4:00 a.m. kicked in. We were on this lake, and it was windy, and the wind and torn shirts ... Steve and Phil had to climb these ladders up these gas tankers to play their guitar bits. They weren't wearing those clothes for fashion. Steve was wearing this big, old fur coat because he was freezing his head off. I'm surprised he wasn't glued to the outer wall of the tank.

And then there's these ridiculous shots of Sav and Rick wearing these monks robes and hockey masks, rowing the boat while I'm "crucified" to this cross! David had this thing about tying young boys up at the time. I was tied to a pyramid in "Foolin.'" I was just wearing this torn t-shirt, and I had to keep going off. We had a car parked on the side of the lake, with the engine running and the heaters on full. And I used to dive into the backseat into this, like, *oven* of a car, just to thaw out. It's ridiculous, it's over-the-top, but the band was over-the-top at the time. We were a bombastic bunch, just out of our teens. So we just went along with it.

I had a lot more fun doing "Me and My Wine." We directed it ourselves. Mallet shot it. We came in and said, *"This* is what we're going to do. There's an English comedy show called *The Young Ones*, where they all lived in one house. This is how it's going to be, like kind of an extension of that, the Monkees and the Beatles." We wanted to get that feel across, of like a gang. You wake up in the morning, the alarm clock goes off, you hit it with a hammer, the Virgin Mary goes off the thing. That actually got the video banned in Ireland. If you look at it carefully, there were so many in-jokes done. There's a rubber glove stuck on top of a washing-up bottle, flipping the bird. You don't really notice it until somebody points it out to you. I slapped Phil on the stairs. He didn't know I was going to do it, so his expression was genuine. And pulling the shower curtain across to reveal Phil doing his "ballet pose" was kind of pre-worked out, but on a very loose "Let's have a drink and do this" basis. I think that video cost $5,000. We all got to do things ... I used to sing into a vacuum cleaner as a child, because they look like microphone stands. I had to do it in the video! It was a lot of fun that video. It really was.

PHIL COLLEN: The biggest rock album before *Pyromania* came out was *Asia* or something like that. John Mellencamp and stuff like that, but no *rock bands.* Before [MTV], you had the mystique of Zeppelin and the Stones, which was cool. They managed to keep their mystique. With a lot of bands, it was like, "These guys really aren't doing it." But we did the opposite. We were young guys, and we embraced it. Just in the typical cycles that they go through anyway, so I think something would have happened. And MTV just came at one of those starting points, as a result of things getting a bit staid.

MARK WEISS: I thought it was a slicker version of Led Zeppelin. Definitely more poppy, but that's what fit the mold. I guess you could say Bon Jovi followed that, but Bon Jovi took it to a whole new level, whereas Def Leppard are still playing old Def Leppard songs, while Bon Jovi do songs that I don't even know.

ANN WILSON: They were probably the first of the big hair band videos, right? They kind of laid down a formula for what was going to be, for years afterward. Just the really good-looking, made-up guys with huge hair, trying to get girls. So I think they were probably influential in starting the whole hair band movement on MTV.

FRANK STALLONE: I think they're excellent. Joe Elliott is a great singer. What I like about the group is they're still buds. They still hang out. They've been together over 30-something years. They've got a good mindset on it. I like the camaraderie.

PHIL COLLEN: You can say the Police, Madonna, and Michael Jackson, all these really young artists had very definite images. We didn't really consider that we had an image, but I think looking back, we actually did. The Police were kind of from the British punk scene ... obviously not really, because they're some of the best pop songs I've ever heard in my life, Sting being just an amazing writer and the band having this great chemistry. Their look was one thing, and then you had Prince's thing, and Madonna, Michael Jackson, and Duran Duran.

And we were completely different. It wasn't a sweaty, greasy, leather metal, which again, is what we actually came from in England. There were a lot of bands, like Motörhead, and that's all they did. Now, looking back, we actually had a little niche that we found, that reflected what we were doing musically, and we were unaware of it. There was something that was a bit more clean-cut than your average Motörhead fan ... but it wasn't as glossy as Duran Duran. Which was perfect, because the music wasn't that. *We were a rock band that took showers.*

BRUCE KULICK: Certainly, when you look at a Def Leppard record, they were put together by Mutt Lange, who's such a brilliant producer and so meticulous and well-crafted. Well, now that sets the bar really high, and you better make your stuff very high quality, or you don't stand a chance.

ERIC BLOOM: There's Mutt Lange's fingerprints all over what those guys do, from the background vocals to the production to songwriting to everything.

JOE ELLIOTT: Working with Mutt ... I don't know. Have you got three weeks? Where do you start? When we first started working with Mutt in 1981, it was a year later than we wanted to. We wanted him for the first album. A lot of people misinterpret our relationship with Mutt as being us going, "Oh, we want that AC/DC thing." Yeah, we did, but we were into Mutt Lange's productions a long time before everybody knew who he was. I'd bought singles by Supercharge. The Records had a single called "Teenara-ma" that Mutt did that was just a phenomenal song. He did City Boy, who had hit singles in Britain. He worked with XTC, and all the hit singles the Boomtown Rats had in Britain were Mutt Lange productions. "I Don't Like Mondays" was the first one he didn't do. There had been about ten songs that I'd bought that were all Mutt productions. He just made their records stand out a little bit more than the average record. He was like the "Chinn and Chapman" of the late '70s, if you like. So when we actually did get a chance to work with him, which was by virtue of our manager, Peter Mensch, looking after AC/DC. He bribed Mutt to watch the opening act, which was us. And he said, "Yeah ... not perfect, but I can work with this." And that was how we wound up getting him.

GREG HAWKES: The bands he was working with at the time—the most famous would be Def Leppard—which was *huge* back then. In fact, it was really the AC/DC records that got Ric in particular interested in working with Mutt [on the Cars' *Heartbeat City*], because he liked the AC/DC records and just liked the way all the guitars and drums sounded. Then when we first started working with Mutt, he's like, "We've got to make this really *modern-sounding* record, and we're going to use a lot of keyboards." [Laughs]

JOE ELLIOTT: The first album [*On Through the Night*] we did in three months. It seemed like, at the time, three years. We couldn't believe what he did differently to Tom Allom. We enjoyed making the first record and can't stand listening to it. Hated making *High n' Dry*, but I can listen to it, no problem. Didn't have much fun making *Pyromania* either, but it's a great record to hear. He made me a better singer. He pushed me harder than I would have pushed myself. The whole thing was like being in the Army. *"Drop and give me 20!"* You wouldn't do that, unless somebody was shouting at you. And that's what he does.

He would say, "You could do it better than that," and you're thinking to yourself, "I don't think I can." And he'd talk you out of your own negativity. He's a great referee as well. But he's just fantastically tuned-in sonically. He's got "bat ears." He can tune out frequencies that other people leave on their records, and that's what made ours stand out. You listen to "Photograph" or "Rock of Ages" or any track off *Pyromania* played loud on a stereo in a car with all the windows up, and you're on the pavement, and the car's parked. You can hear our snare drum from 30/40 feet away! You can tell it's a Def Leppard record. That's what he was good at doing, giving you an identity.

PHIL COLLEN: He's the best producer and most perfect musician I've ever met. He's just got a great amount of vision and being totally open-minded. Even with different genres of music, letting it all in, combining it, and taking the best of everything. I think certain people stick to their own genres, but with Mutt, it's just like a totally wide open radio signal. He just lets it all in. It's amazing. It was great working with someone that talented, as a songwriter, producer, and everything. It added a different take on stuff, which again, was very inspiring. We were trying to find our sound, and he directed us there. He said, "Let's have some hit singles here, and let's make it different. Let's make it special. Let's make it memorable, and let's make it classic." And that's really what we set out to do, and it worked.

THOMAS DOLBY: I was asked to play on [*Pyromania*] by Mutt Lange. He was a producer that I had worked with previously on Foreigner 4. He was a friend, and he often used to tap me up for keyboard work on his projects. I was very happy that they broke that way. They blended hard rock with more of the pop sensibility. And they were nice, Northern English lads, and quite self-effacing. Mutt was 100% "hands on" that album. Mutt goes over everything in microscopic detail, and he's just got the most sensitive ears I've ever come across. He's such a perfectionist that, instead of playing guitar chords, you had to play each string *individually.* People thought he was completely crazy. It took him ten days to get a kick-drum sound. And this did drive people completely crazy, like Bryan Adams, for example. I think it had never taken him more than about three weeks to record an album, and it took Mutt that long to get a drum sound on the first album they did together [*Waking Up the Neighbors*]. So did the Cars. But the end result was something really special and magnificent. He is one of the world's great producers.

GREG HAWKES: I really liked working with Mutt. He's really a talented guy. But, he's definitely like a micro-manager, and there's no detail so small that he wouldn't happily spend working two or three days on. [Laughs] With little keyboard parts, the detail work was ... even to me—and I had always thought of myself as somewhat of a perfectionist—I was astonished by his sense of perfectionism. And I remember doing background vocals. We would go out there for days after days after days. My ears would be red and sore from wearing earphones. We'd be out there singing background parts, y'know, "Who's gonna drive you home." "Ah ... not breathy enough, man."

"Who's gonna drive you home." "Not breathy enough!" "Who's gonna drive you home." Until it's almost all air and barely a note coming out. "That's the vibe ... but now it's out of tune. Do it again!" It seemed it took days to do the background vocals on that record. Much different [than working with the Cars' earlier producer, Roy Thomas Baker], just in as far as scope and how long it took to make. Before we did Heartbeat City, I think the longest any Cars record had taken had been a month and a half. And then with Mutt, I remember we did it in London. It seems like I went over in the spring and just had a spring jacket, and didn't get back until Christmas ... and the record still wasn't done! [Laughs]

MIKE RENO: We told our manager, Bruce Allen—who manages Michael Bublé and Bryan Adams—"We have to get a hold of this Mutt Lange guy, because he's producing every band that we love." He said, "How the hell am I doing to do that?" The best he could do was he got a hold of somebody that got a hold of Mutt. Mutt Lange was just about ready to do I think Def Leppard's new album [*Hysteria*], so he was unavailable for two years. But he said, "I have a song for you." So he proceeded to play us the song ["Lovin' Every Minute of It"] on the telephone. We proceeded to take out a little recorder and record the song from the telephone. You've got to imagine, this is before cell phones, so there was no other way. We were actually in the studio cutting a record, so we needed to get this done. We tried to figure out what all the parts were just from listening to the song. We could kind of figure it out, even though you couldn't really hear the bass.

So we started recording, and he offered to send us his engineer, Mike Shipley, who, if you look at all the album covers that we loved, he was the guy who mixed all these records, like the Cars, Foreigner, and Def Leppard. We ended up going to a studio in Quebec, outside of Montreal, where a lot of groups recorded, including Rush, called Le Studio. We had Mike Shipley with us, and he proceeded to strap on triggers to the drums. This is before it got all the way it is today, and the trigger would trigger off a sound. And that was the sound we wanted, that cool, big snare drum sound, and the bass drum was the same. And that took about three days to do. So we were sitting there, ready to record, and all they were doing was taping stuff onto drums.

We slowly started looking at each other, like, *"What the fuck is this?"* Because we're a band that get together and create something as a band of guys together in a room, y'know? And it's the fourth day, and all we hear is, "Boom, crack, boom, crack." Five days later, our drummer sits down to play them, but he likes to play with a little finesse. He might want to do a roll. And you can't do a roll with this pad thing, this trigger. You do a roll, and it just goes [makes noisy sound]. So he wasn't allowed to play like he normally plays. After about the tenth day of us trying to do this, we just pulled the plug on the whole thing and said, "Thanks very much." We brought all our gear and set up at Little Mountain, where we usually record, and proceeded to cut the song without him. That's the closest we got to working with Mutt Lange.

PHIL COLLEN: A lot of people just don't understand what he's trying to go for. He's trying to get things special. It's not really perfection. He's just trying to get something out. If it was that easy to get special stuff out, we'd all be doing it all the time. Most of the time, it's trial and error, and you pick up things on the way. That's the whole fascinating thing with that. You stumble on something, and with Mutt, he's got this great track record, and he's very open to stuff. He really pushed it, but managed to keep the integrity of a rock band. But I think that was a big difference, crossing over into the pop thing. It was more "Duran Duran" than "Metallica."

The original five MTV VJs: L-R: Nina Blackwood,
Mark Goodman [top], Alan Hunter, Martha Quinn, and JJ Jackson.
[Photo by Mark Weiss—markweissgallery.com]

Rod Stewart
[Photo by Richard Galbraith—
myspace.com/richardgalbraith]

Todd Rundgren
[Photo by Richard Galbraith—
myspace.com/richardgalbraith]

Queen's Freddie Mercury,
"Bohemian Rhapsody" era
[Photo by Richard Galbraith—
myspace.com/richardgalbraith]

Queen's Freddie Mercury,
"Mustache" era
[Photo by Bev Davies—
bevdavies.com
& flickr.com/people/bevdavies]

The Tubes' Fee Waybill and friends
[Photo by Richard Galbraith—myspace.com/richardgalbraith]

Hall and Oates' Daryl Hall and John Oates (GE Smith in middle)
[Photo by Bev Davies—bevdavies.com & flickr.com/people/bevdavies]

The Talking Heads' David Byrne
(Tina Weymouth in background)
[Photo by Richard Galbraith—
myspace.com/richardgalbraith]

The Ramones' Joey Ramone
[Photo by Richard Galbraith—myspace.com/richardgalbraith]

Joan Jett
[Photo by Bev Davies—
bevdavies.com
& flickr.com/people/bevdavies]

The Go-Go's: L-R: Charlotte Caffey, Belinda Carlisle, and Kathy Valentine
[Photo by Bev Davies—bevdavies.com & flickr.com/people/bevdavies]

The Police's Sting
[Photo by Richard Galbraith—
myspace.com/richardgalbraith]

The Police's Andy Summers
[Photo by Richard Galbraith—myspace.com/richardgalbraith]

The Police's Stewart Copeland
[Photo by Richard Galbraith—myspace.com/richardgalbraith]

Rush's Geddy Lee
[Photo by Richard Galbraith—
myspace.com/richardgalbraith]

Blue Öyster Cult's Eric Bloom
[Photo by Richard Galbraith—
myspace.com/richardgalbraith]

Judas Priest's Rob Halford and Glenn Tipton
[Photo by Richard Galbraith—myspace.com/richardgalbraith]

Pat Benatar
[Photo by Richard Galbraith—
myspace.com/richardgalbraith]

Duran Duran: L-R: Andy Taylor, Nick Rhodes,
Simon Le Bon [top], Roger Taylor, and John Taylor
[Photo by Bev Davies—bevdavies.com & flickr.com/people/bevdavies]

Wall of Voodoo's Stan Ridgway
[Photo by Bev Davies—bevdavies.com
& flickr.com/people/bevdavies]

The Dead Kennedys' Jello Biafra
[Photo by Bev Davies—bevdavies.com &
flickr.com/people/bevdavies]

X's John Doe
[Photo by Bev Davies—bevdavies.com &
flickr.com/people/bevdavies]

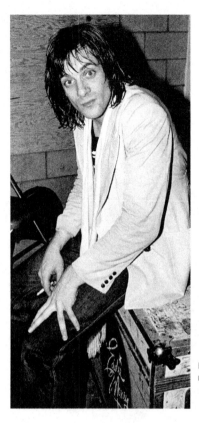

Eddie Money [Photo by Richard Galbraith—
myspace.com/richardgalbraith]

Michael Jackson
[Photo by Bev Davies—bevdavies.com &
flickr.com/people/bevdavies]

Lionel Richie
[Photo by Bev Davies—bevdavies.com
& flickr.com/people/bevdavies]

Phil Collins
[Photo by Bev Davies—bevdavies.com & flickr.com/people/bevdavies]

Def Leppard's Joe Elliott
[Photo by Bev Davies—bevdavies.com
& flickr.com/people/bevdavies]

Quiet Riot: L-R: Rudy Sarzo, Frankie Banali,
Kevin DuBrow, and Carlos Cavazo
[Photo by Richard Galbraith—myspace.com/richardgalbraith]

Ozzy Osbourne
[Photo by Richard Galbraith—
myspace.com/richardgalbraith]

Carmine Appice
[Photo by Richard Galbraith—
myspace.com/richardgalbraith]

Mötley Crüe's Vince Neil
[Photo by Richard Galbraith—
myspace.com/richardgalbraith]

Kiss' Paul Stanley and Bruce Kulick
[Photo by Richard Galbraith—myspace.com/richardgalbraith]

Van Halen's David Lee Roth
[Photo by Richard Galbraith—myspace.com/richardgalbraith]

Van Halen's Eddie Van Halen
[Photo by Richard Galbraith—myspace.com/richardgalbraith]

Van Halen's Michael Anthony and
video director Pete Angelus
(David Lee Roth in background)
[Photo by Richard Galbraith—
myspace.com/richardgalbraith]

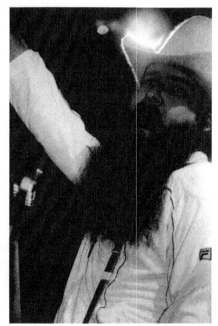

ZZ Top's Billy Gibbons
[Photo by Bev Davies—bevdavies.com &
flickr.com/people/bevdavies]

Bruce Springsteen
[Photo by Bev Davies—bevdavies.com &
flickr.com/people/bevdavies]

Madonna
[Photo by Bev Davies—bevdavies.com &
flickr.com/people/bevdavies]

Tina Turner
[Photo by Bev Davies—bevdavies.com &
flickr.com/people/bevdavies]

Heart's Ann Wilson
[Photo by Richard Galbraith—myspace.com/richardgalbraith]

Van Halen

ALAN HUNTER: It was all about David Lee Roth, wasn't it? I mean, that's where you could do a concert video, and it worked just fine, to see David Lee Roth flopping around in his spandex. David Lee Roth was into mugging the camera. He worked the camera like an audience. But that was just sheer, raw musical power there.

RUDY SARZO: People think of Van Halen as "an '80s band." No, they were actually a '70s band. For all intents and purposes, this was a band that already succeeded and made their mark in the '70s. You had a frontman that was so charismatic, that this guy was *made* for video. Forget about it. I mean, if he took his performance to a certain level in arenas, once you put the camera on David Lee Roth, that was a whole different animal right there. That made him the seminal frontman of the '80s. Nobody even comes close. And it's not that he's got an incredible voice. No. He is an entertainer. And that's what you have to be when you make a video. You're entertaining. And there's nobody better than David Lee Roth. He's in a class all by himself. Van Halen's videos were always fun. You can't help but smile when you watch those videos, because everybody else is smiling! They're having fun, which is what making music is all about. Let's face it—this is rock n' roll. We're trying to escape here, entertain, and brighten up our day. I mean, if you want to get depressed, turn on the news. [Laughs]

MARK WEISS: I met them in '78 and started working with them in *Circus* magazine. David once in a while would fly me in, and I'd just take pictures of him, flying a kite or whatever. So I'd be in his little world. [Backstage] he'd basically turn down the lights, have the little party going, and only girls would be allowed in there. They would have the security guard start giving the speech to the girls. "You've got to be over 18 to get in. I want to see ID, or you've got to leave." And Dave would go to the back room with one or two girls. It was a bunch of flashing lights and music, your typical sex, drugs, and rock n' roll. He would actually give passes out to the roadies. I'd even get them, too. He would [put] your initials on, and if the girl ended up with him in the end, you got a little bonus. I was in the photo pit the whole time, so Dave would give me a little signal, like, *"Five rows, center,"* and I would get it to them.

RIK EMMETT: Their tour was like a traveling Roman bacchanalia. If there weren't strippers and midgets at every party, it wasn't really a Van Halen concert, apparently.

PETE ANGELUS: I was actually doing a lot of different things. I was designing the album covers with Warner Brothers, I was designing the merchandise, I was the lighting director, I was the production designer. And of course, as Van Halen became more successful and quickly started headlining, those lighting productions and stage productions got fairly substantial. And I had complete creative freedom in that regard, to design what I thought best-suited the band. And to follow it up to the MTV and video era, when MTV reared its ugly head in the early '80s, I had spent most of my time in high school making short films. It was actually how I got through a lot of my classes, presenting short films. So when MTV came about, I thought, "Well, I can direct these, if we want to do it." So I rolled into it that way.

MIKE RENO: I think at that time, if I were to think of California, I would think of David Lee Roth and Van Halen. They were the bad boys. They were the hardest rockin' guys out there. I just went, *"Unbelievable."* And Eddie's guitar playing and his brother's drumming and the bottom end from Michael Anthony ... I'll tell you, David Lee Roth became a friend of mine, Eddie's a friend of mine. These guys I really looked up to. I couldn't believe some of the outfits they came up with! They were crazy, crazy ahead of the time, and it was awesome. That to me was a big wake-up call. I said, "Dude, you've got to buy some clothes and get into it." They really impressed me. I tried to take it up a few notches after watching some of their videos. And that's when we started trying to be a little more involved in coming up with some concepts for videos. The first video, we were just told what to do and where to go. And then we started getting into it, shortly after watching these guys.

ERIC BLOOM: Dave is Dave. He's very flamboyant, and "I want to hump your leg." [Laughs] Especially as a young man back then. It's just great, and he got away with that stuff, whereas many other acts couldn't, because he wore his sexuality on his sleeve, and the videos played that up. Plus, on top of that, he's one fantastic frontman, so he could carry off in the videos what he did live. There's one example right there. They could back up the video with a great live performance.

GEDDY LEE: I think those were more song-driven, and the fact that David Lee Roth was a flamboyant character, that worked on the small screen. He was larger than life.

ALAN HUNTER: I'm watching this "(Oh) Pretty Woman" video ... I totally forgot this! This was when the conceptual, story-driven video was at its most absurd. *But it was Van Halen.* They could do pretty much what they wanted to. It wasn't like the Hooters or "nobody bands" that came out and did these concept videos that were shot like mini-films and just fell flat. It had David Lee Roth and his Napoleonic complex, and oh how absurd it was. Eddie's a cowboy ... with the "female" at the end. [Laughs]

PETE ANGELUS: ["(Oh) Pretty Woman"] I did not direct myself. I was on the set with Dave and Van Halen. I think it was kind of a group effort. I think everybody was kind of involved with that. What I remember specifically about that video was that the primary cameraman quit in the middle of shooting it, so that was a problem. I don't remember why he quit. I don't know if we were driving him insane, the subject matter was driving him insane ... I don't know what he was appalled by. But I remember him leaving in a huff.

And then, the other thing I remember about that video is always having to send people around the set to try and find the "little people." We could never find them. People's megaphones were always screaming for them to come to the set, and we could never find them. I later discovered that I think the reason that we couldn't find them was because they were dealing mushrooms on the set, and they were so high that they had disappeared into some field and were having some hallucinatory trip. So I remember that being a problem.

And I also remember at one point, again, searching for the little people and going into the trailer of the transvestite, who was playing the "pretty woman." And all I remember was opening the trailer door, and one of the little people had on a black cape, he was nude, and he was like doing a Mick Jagger impersonation, *while he was holding the transvestite's penis and singing into it like a microphone.* I thought, "You know, man ... how many times in life are you going to come across *this?"* That's all I remember, because it's burned like some some fuckin' horrible nightmare into my memory. So yeah, that's what happened during that video. That video, really as I recall, was a cluster-fuck. There were so many people involved and so many ideas and so many people directing different segments ... I'm surprised it came together at all. After that, we got it more together.

ALAN HUNTER: [Martha Quinn and David Lee Roth] had a little thing going, just a little on-camera silliness. When she interviewed him, she was so into David Lee Roth that she got nervous as hell, and he picked on her like crazy. He flirted with her so much that she could barely get her shit together.

ROBIN ZORN: I remember her being really excited whenever his videos would come on, and she did get to interview [Roth]. Everybody knew that was her thing. She had a crush on him. It just became known. I know the VJs teased her about it on air. We all just knew that Martha had this crush on David Lee Roth.

MIKE PELECH: They hit it off, because he's really sarcastic and kind of a wise guy, and she really played off of him.

PETE ANGELUS: Dave had a great sense of humor, and she was a good recipient of that. It worked out well, because she was always trying to find her footing with the amount of babble that was coming out of his mouth. It probably was so entertaining because it was so uncomfortable so often.

PAUL DEAN: There's a band that loves to smile! Every video, Eddie would be grinning from ear to ear, every shot of him. There were no bummers in that band ever. It was always totally positive and, "We're having a great time ... so you should, too."

ANN WILSON: Those are funny. They were pretty cool, because they really did translate the band as it probably really was, like a bunch of teenaged boys. So they just came out and were kind of doofuses and funny. [Laughs] I used to laugh at their stuff a lot, the same with the J. Geils Band and that ilk.

JELLO BIAFRA: I've barely heard Van Halen in my life. You're dealing with somebody who realized that unplugging from the pop culture grid at age thirteen made him a much happier person.

PETE ANGELUS: "Jump" really was just about personality, really. It was a very simple video. We shot it for nothing. David wanted to incorporate his karate-flipping that he loved so much into the whole thing. The initial concept was just to film them in a very simple live setting, and let the personalities show through. We did it very quickly. Seriously, I think that we probably spent more money on pizza delivery than we did on the video itself. But that was the intention—make it a very intimate, personal feeling, with a very big band.

NINA BLACKWOOD: I thought it was kind of funny that Van Halen's first number one song was actually synth-driven, even though it was a riff.

GEDDY LEE: ["Jump"] was really good. You could jump around all you want, but if the song wasn't so good, it wouldn't have clicked.

PHIL COLLEN: "Jump" was great, so basic and so obvious. You go, "OK, they're just standing there." But David Lee Roth was *so* entertaining. And again, it really got the character over of the band. I remember the first time I heard them, I was like, "Jesus ... *what is this guy playing?* This is amazing!" But when you add the visual thing to it as well, you could see that it was a fun rock n' roll band, and that David Lee Roth was crazy. It was so perfect. Then you got it. You got what their whole schtick was about. It was great, him jumping around and Eddie smiling and playing guitar. It was just perfect for them.

PETE ANGELUS: ["Panama"] was primarily live, and there were a couple of different people involved. I couldn't even tell you who they were. I think everybody was co-directing it or putting up the ideas for it. Edward wanted to sit down and be playing a piano. I think everybody threw their ideas in the hat, and we were just doing it as we went along. I really don't remember specifically, because they weren't structured videos like "Hot for Teacher," "California Girls," or "Gigolo." [The band members swinging from a cord across the stage] was Dave's idea. He thought it would be funny if people were swinging around on the stage. As I said, everybody was contributing at that time to what we were doing.

STEWART COPELAND: I only remember one, "Walk This Way," and I thought he was cool. [Upon being corrected that "Walk This Way" was Aerosmith, not Van Halen] Shows you how much I can remember! I have no recollection of them at all, either Aerosmith or Van Halen. You know, there's a snobbery of all musicians that I've found. You don't even see the ones that come out right behind you. You see the ones in front of you—the ones there before you, as the target. You want what they have. Then when you get there, the ones right behind you don't exist. And then ten years go by, and now you're feeling a little more benevolent, and you start saying, "Hey that's pretty good. Good luck kids!" But there's a gap from where we were big for about ten years, where I have no idea who filled that gap, any of the artists.

ALAN HUNTER: "Hot for Teacher" was more conceptual than "Jump."

PETE ANGELUS: "Hot for Teacher"—we wanted to take that idea of their personalities and drive that down the road 40 years in the future. So I had the idea of "Where will they all be potentially 40 years from now?" And let's try to make it somewhat humorous. The song title and lyrics itself dictated itself, in a sense, that we were going to be involved with younger kids. I had the idea to get look-a-likes for Van Halen. We spent a lot of time casting that. It was very interesting, too, because when we cast those kids that played the role of Van Halen, when they showed up at the set, miraculously, they started adapting to the personalities of the guys in Van Halen! So the little Alex was fuckin' argumentative all the time with me, the little Edward was very shy, [and] the little Dave was very gregarious and ready to go. It was interesting what happened on the set there with those kids.

And then as I said, I wanted to drive it through their school years and where will they be 40 years from now, with Dave potentially being a television show host, Edward being locked up in a mental institution, Alex being a gynecologist, and Mike being a sumo wrestler. One thing I remember about that video that a lot people don't know or maybe didn't see. When Dave turns into the television show host, we had an idea. I thought, "You know ... *there hasn't been a really substantial urine stain on MTV.* Ever, when you really think about it. So let's pour a lot of water on David's crotch. Let's make it look like he really just pissed himself. And then let's see if anyone sees it when we hand the video into the record company and MTV." And nobody did! I know this sounds absolutely pathetic to say, but we probably pulled off the first and most substantial urine stain in the history of television. So we've got that going for us.

BRUCE KULICK: Think of the escapism in "Hot for Teacher," and them having the "mini-Eddie" and the teacher being a stripper. We were using a vibe like that when I was doing this "Monster Circus" rock band last year in Vegas, where we covered that song, and the girls came out in schoolgirl outfits and were dancing around. Iconic stuff, no doubt. It will be around forever.

PETE ANGELUS: Waldo [the lead character in "Hot for Teacher"] was actually ... I remember specifically a kid when I was in, I don't know what grade. Fortunately, we were doing it behind his back, so it wasn't really hurting his feelings, but there was a very geeky kid, and we referred to him as "Waldo." And I thought, "Let me take that kid further in the video." With the hair and make-up people, I remember saying, "Listen, I really want this kid's hair to be fucked up, as if he's sweating profusely through his entire experience of school." They kept coming out, and it was a little greasy, and I'm like, "No, come on, let's do it up here. I want it to look like he's having a bad experience." And finally, I was like, "Seriously, *would you get some fuckin' oil or something and put it in his hair!*" But then the next day, his mother comes up to me and was like, "Do you know how long it took to wash that out of his hair? Do we have to go through this again? Isn't there any other way to portray him?!" I think they had him in the shower for like six hours, trying to get that goo out of his hair. A lot of those things came from experiences in the past, and we just took them further, or things that suited Van Halen's personalities.

JOE ELLIOTT: The only people that could get away with a dance routine was Van Halen, because they were taking the piss. And they did it fantastically.

PETE ANGELUS: The dancing scenes [in "Hot for Teacher"], the worse they were, in my opinion, the better they were. We had a good time making that video. That was really one of the first bigger videos that we made. I think it was a three-day shoot. And that set the pace for what we did later with "Just a Gigolo," for instance—a lot of different sets, a lot of different casting. And introduced more humor into it as we went along.

PAUL DEAN: Not to mention that Eddie Van Halen is one of the greatest guitar players *ever*. I'm a huge fan of Eddie's. He's a tough act to open for, as you can imagine. He's totally one of my favorite guitar players.

RIK EMMETT: Obviously, Eddie Van Halen changed the face of guitar. And the content of what was going on. I would rank him right up there with the guys like Jimi Hendrix and Jimmy Page and Jeff Beck, in what he did to change the course of rock n' roll guitar.

RICKY BYRD: [Joan Jett & the Blackhearts] did the *MTV Rock n' Roll New Year's Eve Bash* in '85. We're set up to open the show, and I think Martha Quinn was the introducer. David Lee Roth ... it was when David Lee Roth was hanging out with muscle-bound women. I don't know what phase he was going through. We were all set up, he came on, and they were going to introduce us. He and the muscle-bound women come walking out on my side of the stage and *totally* walked over my pedals and broke all the wires. And then introduced, "Joan Jett & the Blackhearts!" We go into "Bad Reputation," but my guitar is going [makes a crackling noise]. Meanwhile, my guitar tech, who is standing on my side of the stage, is watching the crowd. If you see the YouTube thing, I'm making believe I'm playing, but all you can hear is [the crackling noise]. It took me well into the break. I don't even think I played the break. All the girls were in gowns and hot, and I think everybody on the stage was more interested in looking at the crowd than watching the band. So it took me a while to get somebody's attention.

PETE ANGELUS: "California Girls," of course, casting was enjoyable. I'm trying to remember how the idea of the "Rod Serling element" of it came about, *The Twilight Zone*. I don't remember specifically how *The Twilight Zone* aspect came about, other than Dave as a tour guide into this *Twilight Zone*-ish world. And, of course, we wanted to show a lot of different types of females. We shot that at Venice Beach. I think we were down there for two days. That was the thing of it. "Let's give it a weird, cartoon-ish, colorized feel, and let's make him a strange tour guide through this California world."

The "Just a Gigolo" video, there were thoughts of Dave being a television host, which showed up in "Hot for Teacher." So we thought we would create "Dave TV." We thought we would march him through some of the video sets that were very popular videos at that time. And then we decided, "Let's not just *march* through the sets. Let's make something happen in those sets." That's why we "electrocuted" Billy Idol, "hit" Boy George, and Michael Jackson we kind of left alone. That was one of the bigger ones that we did, and I think it took three or four days. There were like 18 different set-ups. Then we put a lot of people in the hallway for those scenes, as though it was a television or film studio, with different people auditioning for different things. We had a good time making that video.

Basically, I was working with a producer, and we turned in a budget. The budgets were instantly approved, and nobody was really saying to me, "What are you doing?" It wasn't really until I turned in "Just a Gigolo" that one of the executives at Warner Bros. called me—they had just seen the video—and said, *"Can you come into our offices for a minute?"* I thought, "OK ... this has to be interesting. This is the first phone call about any video that we've done, so I'm curious to see what the reaction is going to be." I remember him saying to me, "So ... do you think that it's a good idea to electrocute Billy Idol? Or punch Boy George in the face?" And I said, "I personally think it's very funny. I think it *is* a good idea!" He says, "I just wanted to know what your thinking was, because the next video, maybe you and I should sit down and discuss the concept before you just go and shoot it." But interestingly, they never did sit down and discuss another concept. Maybe they just realized that those videos were garnering enough attention that they should just continue what they do and let us do what we do. They never really interfered after that conversation.

CARMINE APPICE: Pete Angelus did all their videos, and he did our video [King Kobra's "Hunger"], because we loved their videos so much. Van Halen I thought were a tremendous group for MTV, because they went out and Pete did some great stuff with them. The David Lee Roth videos were awesome by themselves.

PETE ANGELUS: Like all musical groups, perception is everything, right? There was the perception that they all got along beautifully and hung out. And there were a couple of years that went better than others. But I would say, and I'm sure that Edward and Dave—if they were willing to be truthful about it—would admit that there was always some tension, primarily between Alex and Eddie with Dave. Alex was always very regimented in his approach to how serious the music business was. And Dave had a very different viewpoint of it. And Edward was just completely in his own world musically. I don't really think he cared to get in the middle of those approaches [because] he was so involved in his own music. Everything was music for Edward. Edward wasn't as social a person as anyone in the band, because he was dealing with his thoughts and his ideas, all the time. And usually locked in a hotel room playing the guitar, or locked in the bus playing the guitar, or sitting in his bunk playing the guitar. But that guitar never left his hands. With all groups, there is *some* tension between the members.

In 1985, when they announced the break-up, I was with Dave actually at the time. As I remember it, they had been touring pretty consistently for five years. And the idea was simply to take like a year hiatus. And some of them had things they were interested in doing during that year. Dave wanted to spend the time to make a movie [Pete and Dave were collaborating on a movie, *Crazy from the Heat,* which was never filmed]. When I was on the phone with Alex, Eddie, and Dave, everybody was agreeable to a one-year hiatus. And I can't remember, but it was like a week or two after that I read that Dave had quit the group in *Rolling Stone.* At least that was how someone in the Van Halen camp was trying to present it. I remember being on the phone with Dave, going, "Will you look at this shit?! We just had an agreement and an understanding, and everybody was on board a week or two ago ... *and now this?!"* It rolled into a lot of very negative feelings, because I think Dave felt betrayed. I don't know how the Van Halen's felt betrayed, because they had agreed to it. Maybe they felt betrayed because he wanted to pursue something in film. But it rolled quickly into some very negative areas.

I remember having a conversation with Alex, as to "What exactly is going on here? Because I thought everybody just agreed to take a year off." I remember him being kind of aggressive about it, like, "Oh no, that's bullshit man. We're not going to sit around and wait while Dave makes a movie. You've got to pick sides of where you want to be." I was like, "Well, *wait a minute.* No one is sitting around and 'waiting' while Dave makes a movie. A few weeks ago, we were talking about maybe it was time for Van Halen to take a year off the road, after so much consecutive touring." And it was like, "No, that's bullshit, man. We're not going to be in a holding pattern for Dave's whims." So that was probably how he perceived it, after having agreed to it. I don't know why his perception changed, but it did. And I don't really remember speaking to Edward specifically about it after that. I do remember him saying, "We're going to carry on as Van Halen."

Edward and Alex were always of the mindset that everybody that worked for them was overpaid, in a sense, and they were going to very carefully select their "team." Whereas Dave, at the time, was very optimistic and very open to all creative ideas. So Dave was like, "Will you come with me, and we'll carry on? We'll put a group together. I want to go on the road and I want to keep touring. I don't want this to stop me. I'm not going to sit here in a holding pattern and hope for the best." I was always much closer with Dave, from the very beginning. It wasn't really even a decision as to what was going to happen. Dave and I would continue to work together, as we had in the past. And from there, we put together Steve Vai, Billy Sheehan, and Gregg Bissonette, and we carried on.

HERMAN RAREBELL: Sammy Hagar is a great singer. But David Lee Roth and Van Halen ... that is for me, *Van Halen*. No doubt.

ALAN HUNTER: God, that was a great band. I loved the Sammy Hagar years, as well.

FRANKIE SULLIVAN: They were my favorite. I liked when they did the stuff with Dave and later on with Sam, because it was all based around their performance and what they did on stage. I think that was something that the band was insistent upon. It's like, "We're gonna rock ... and you're gonna film it."

PETE ANGELUS: [Roth's solo career] were great and very successful shows. Unfortunately, what happened later on as time went on—and I couldn't really tell you why it happened, I was just very aware how unfortunate it was that it was happening, and I couldn't really stop it—was there suddenly became a lot of friction between Dave and Steve Vai, and Dave and Billy Sheehan. So one by one, people were exiting the group, for one reason or another. That was very unfortunate, because they came out of the box strong.

Probably what I remember the most about [the videos for "Yankee Rose" and "Goin' Crazy!"] was getting away with a fair amount of comedy prior to the songs starting. Like [for "Yankee Rose"] we had the immigrant grocer inside that strange convenience store, the woman who was having constipation problems, [and] the woman who was about to give birth and ending a relationship. And I remember thinking, "I wonder if the song is three minutes, can the comedy be two minutes? Can the intro be *that long?* Can we get away with it?" And we thought, "Well ... why not? If it works with the video, let's give it a shot." And as it turned out, it worked. People seemed to enjoy it.

Is ["Goin' Crazy!"] the one where the Picasso Brothers come to the studio? I think I'm driving the car there with the women and Dave, and the car tips over, because he's in a 300-pound prosthetic outfit. That was the same. I wrote a comedy intro for it, to get him into the recording studio, and I thought, "We'll have Dave in this obese prosthetic outfit, and he'll arrive as a big Hollywood record producer to the studio." We just wrote the comedy intro and then thought, "We'll film the band in the studio as part of it."

RIK EMMETT: As far as Roth goes, he would do so many kinds of goofy things and say goofy things, because he was more of a type of guy that didn't seem to have any kind of "governor" in his head. As it came into his mind, he would just go ahead and say it, whatever he was thinking ... or whatever he had carefully written as the joke that he wanted to crack. That came to me later. I started to realize he had more substance than I gave him credit for. He was actually a fairly consummate kind of performer. He would go out there and give everything he had, even though he might have been partying a little too hard, so now, it was hard for him to physically give his best. Or for his throat to have stood up to the torture he was putting it through the last week of the tour or before he played the gig we were getting to witness. In some ways, in the early days, my respect for him was diminished, just because I would see him in his "less-than-ideal-ability-to-sing mode."

Later on, I realized the guy really *can* sing. There was a thing that circulated a few years back on the Internet, where it was "Runnin' with the Devil." It was a vocal that had absolutely no other tracks. Somebody sent me a link, and I listened to this thing, and I was blown away. I was super-impressed with the quality of that vocal. When you hear it all by itself—all the whoops, screeches, and whistles that he does—you think, "Holy shit ... *this guy is really doing it!*" And it's not bullshit; this is hard to do. As a singer, I was very impressed and got fresh respect for the guy. I thought, "Holy shit, this guy is not a slouch at all. He's not a clown. This guy can really bring it." That changed my whole opinion of him. And the latest reunion tour they did, he wasn't doing a lot of goofy histrionics. He was standing there and singing, and he was doing a great job. I was very impressed. He had maybe gone through a process of maturing and was maybe a little bit more humble and maybe more respectful of that gift that he has, and that's part of what performing is supposed to be. It's not just a question of throwing a big party for everybody.

PETE ANGELUS: I think [Van Halen/David Lee Roth's videos] showed a lot of personality with each individual band member. I also think that they had a sense of humor, that a lot of artists who take themselves very seriously weren't willing to experiment with. I also had specifically colorized those videos in post-production, to make them look brighter than real life and more bold in a sense than real life. So I think that they had a look and a stamp in and of themselves that kind of separated them. Van Halen was willing to push the boundaries of "Let's experiment with this. Yeah, we can try this."

Their music spoke for itself, and there was no question about the talent of Edward Van Halen and what he was bringing to the music scene. And there was no question to the bravado and the sense of humor that Dave was bringing to the music scene. I think they felt comfortable in pushing some of those boundaries in those videos, with humor, or making fun of themselves, and also showing much more personality than most other videos did. A lot of those people took themselves *very* seriously. There was no smiling. They were very, very serious artists. Now, Van Halen were serious musical artists, but Van Halen was a "good time, big show, party band." And as the shows showed a lot of those elements, so did the videos.

Videos: Heavy Metal

— Judas Priest —

ROB HALFORD: Our label at the time, Columbia/CBS, like every other label, "We have to make videos, because it's going to go straight onto MTV in America." Because let's face it, the rest of the world was playing catch up with this MTV experience. So we were just thrown into the deep end. It was a new medium for us. I mean, we'd had a few cameras film us playing live, but we'd never gone out "on location." We hadn't actually dressed up. We actually hadn't sat down with a director like Julien Temple and had a meeting about the storyboard and the script. Y'know, "Is this going to work for the band? Are we going to look stupid? Is it going to be good for metal?"

In those days, your videos were either in a studio—a cheap nickel-and-dime one—or your label threw some money down, and you went out on location, like for "Breaking the Law." We went to Soho in London. We spent all day in the West End. You start at dawn, you finish at dusk, and you just run from different place to place—the seedy part of Soho where the porno shops are, where KK and Glenn had dressed up as Puritan Monks, feeding pigeons. And then you go to an old, disused Barclays Bank, break into it, and steal your disc. Then you get into an old, gold-plated Cadillac and drive over the Westway, past the famous Hammersmith Odeon Theater. And you have a good day out. Then you wait a few days and get sent the final thing. And this is it. *This is going out.*

["You've Got Another Thing Comin'"] was a pretty simple format. We found this power plant right by the M4 Westway leading into London. It's still there, actually, I think. It was again due to Julien Temple's direction. I know we were rushed for time. The label said, "We need this *now*. You've got to go in, make it, and we've got to release it." So again, it was just basically put together with Julien's vision. It's a very simple, straightforward one, but of course, it's a combination of the way, feel, and texture of that power plant, which is very "metal." The lighting, the lasers, just the band's performance is very strong.

And then you've got "the man," as Dennis Hopper would say—the bowler hat, society, "Mr. Big," "Big Brother"—who was trying to stop the show, trying to crush it. And we kick back by blowing his head up. [Laughs] The funny thing was the explosives guy had been waiting all fucking day. He'd been there for like twelve hours. And by the time he'd got his chance to do his bit, he *packed* that mannequin's head with C4 explosives. So when it went off, it just obliterated the thing. There was nothing left! And then it falls over, and the pants fall down ... which was an unexpected bonus. From a sociological point of view, the people that don't like metal—*this is your payback*. [Laughs] We're going to blow your head up and let your pants fall down.

— Ozzy Osbourne —

RUDY SARZO: "Iron Man," "Children of the Grave," and "Paranoid" were included in the *Speak of the Devil* album. So in order to promote that album, they had us play it live at a different place [then it was recorded]. The video was from the Irvine Meadows performance, and the album was from the Ritz performance. My most burning memory of that was the "extra added ingredients" for the filming of that show was they brought in lasers, which were not part of our production. The laser show was tested at the Oakland Coliseum the night before. Now, the Oakland Coliseum is an enclosed arena. So the laser show looked really sharp, because the more smoke and the more of a volumetric environment/atmosphere you have in the place, the lasers catch that, and they are very pristine in their presentation. Whereas when you go into an open-air venue and there's no smoke and no environment ... because it's in the middle of summer and a clear, beautiful night—I believe it was in the last week of June in 1982—the lasers were washed out, and you could barely see them!

So they did some "post enhancements." They had to reshoot the lasers, bring them in post, and layer and composite them into the video. But Ozzy was really pissed off when he saw the rough cuts of that. Actually, that video, watching myself during that rough cut, is what made my decision to leave the band, because I saw myself for the first time being really robotic. This was within eight weeks of Randy Rhoads' passing when we shot this. In order for me to survive going on stage was to go into "automatic mode" and not look at the audience or the band and just survive the show, basically. It's very hard for me to watch that video, because it reminds me of the state that I was in. But watching it made me realize what I had become—something I would have never wanted to be like. After the recordings of the Ritz, I called up Sharon and told her that I was going to leave the band.

CARMINE APPICE: "Bark at the Moon" was wild, because me and Ozzy were doing the album in New York. I was actually the associate producer on *Bark at the Moon*, initially. And then we flew over on the SST—me and Ozzy—to London. It was like a three-hour flight, so we weren't that jet-lagged. The next day, we were at this old mental hospital, where we did the video. That was a crazy experience, because while Ozzy was getting that make-up on—which took him about four or five hours—we would be on set, walking around, looking around, and checking out the place.

It was a pretty horrible place. It was all falling apart. It was a real mental institution. We found embryos in bottles in the closet. It was abandoned, and it was probably 200 years old, if not more. It was a spooky place to do that video. And then they showed the rain scene. We were standing outside at the funeral, and they were shooting up the water on us, to make it look like rain. It was damned cold out there! We had these top hats on, and you see the rain dripping off the top hats. After those scenes were done, we had to be wrapped in towels. It was hard for Ozzy, because he had to put that make-up on. Any fun that it would have been was killed for four or five hours.

— *Rush* —

GEDDY LEE: The first "Tom Sawyer" video we did was just filming us recording at Morin Heights, and you can see us playing in the studio with the big glass window surrounding us. You can see the winter outside. So that was kind of a "let the camera into the session" kind of thing. And then when we were on tour, we filmed another version of it, and that became another thing that got a lot of airplay. Again, because we were unsure of any kind of image to attach to us, we just went with us playing. "When in doubt, *just play.*"

We recorded ["Subdivisions"] in, appropriately, a suburb of Toronto, in a rehearsal hall. And we used a local production company to gather footage of the kind of environment that we had grown up in, which were these bland suburbs outside of Toronto, and these kind of endless, treeless landscape shots. It was kind of a homemade event, where we tried to show us playing and cut back and forth with these kind of abstract shots of suburban life.

["Distant Early Warning"] was one of the "big-budget productions," and that was really a lot of fun to do. We used David Mallet, who was a fairly proven director, for that. Was kind of the complete antithesis of the "Subdivisions" video. We recorded that in England, in one of his places he liked to shoot. It was a really big set, and he took this whole Speilberg-esque attitude to creating this story and creating this mystery. I really loved what he did. We talked a lot together, and it was one of the first videos where we got very involved in helping shape out the little story of the video. He used his tremendous skills to create this mysterious, and yet kind of fun, video. That was one of our most successful "big-budget production videos."

"The Big Money" we shot in Toronto with a Canadian director, Rob Quartly, who at the time was kind of an up-and-comer. Originally, we had two storylines—this comedic storyline and us playing on this big Monopoly set/stage. And when it came time for them to edit it together, the storyline did not work. It just was not funny. [Laughs] So in the end, we said, "Look, dude, *it's not working.*" So we shot it together with the band playing, and that's what it ended up being.

— Blue Öyster Cult —

ERIC BLOOM: "Burnin' for You" was a hit in '81, and it became evident that the "fledgling video place" we were going to have to jump in, having not done it before. We weren't exactly a young band. Our first album was in '72, so it was nine years later. I think we'd done an album a year, so we were up around our eighth album. We went out to California, and our management found a video company, and we did two videos in 24 hours—"Burnin' for You" and "Joan Crawford." MTV wouldn't show the "Joan Crawford" video, because there was something about it that was too racy for them. But "Burnin' for You" got a ton of airplay on MTV in 1981 and 1982.

We made ["Burnin' for You"] in the storm drains of L.A. If anyone has seen the movie about giant ants, called *Them!*, with James Whitmore, it was filmed in the same place. I can't remember the name of the director, but we had the same video guys do two or three of our videos. We came out to L.A., the script was sent on over to us, we approved, and we went out to the location. I think we were there a good twelve straight hours. We had a bunch of extras and pyro, because we burnt a car. And that was all done as "on the cheap" as possible and with low production values and bad editing. But we had fun doing it, because it was new to us.

And like I said, I think we did the "Joan Crawford" video earlier in the day, on location at some house that was rented. Then straight from there, we had to do the "Burnin' for You" video at night. Some scenes were filmed and edited elsewhere, like the actor driving the car. Some of that was filmed at a different time. We thought [the car on fire scene] was very Hollywood, very cool. They had to have a Hollywood film/pyro guy there, who was licensed to burn shit up. He had propane tanks, and he had to have a hulk of a car to burn. It was fun. It was a little taste of Hollywood for us.

— *Triumph* —

RIK EMMETT: In the band, we hated that whole *Allied Forces* thing [the video for "Magic Power"], where we were riding on a guitar in outer space. We called it "birthday cakes in space," because it just looked so stupid. With the wind blowing in our hair, and we're riding on this ridiculous Flying V guitar spaceship, and chicks are dancing around us. It was high concept, and the record company was happy with it. We thought, "Well, it *could* be cool. You're telling us a star field will be flying by our heads?" But when we saw it, it just was cheesy. It looked *so* bad. The execution of it, the footage of the band—the whole technical side of things. You'd shoot on video, you'd look at it later, and go, "Oh man, this looks like just bad local cable TV stuff." But if you shot on film, it had a grainy, documentary look to it. It looked so much cooler. And then you realize, "We're idiots. We should have been shooting on film all the time." But somebody said, "It will be cheaper. We shoot on video. It will be great!" And you're like, "It's not great ... *it looks like shit.*" We went on a soundstage for a couple of days, and we shot "Magic Power," "Allied Forces," and "Say Goodbye." And we tried to suppress them as much as we could. [Laughs] But MTV was just playing the crap out of the "Magic Power" one.

— The Scorpions —

HERMAN RAREBELL: "No One Like You" is a funny story. When we left the island—Alcatraz, where the video was filmed—first of all, we came there, and the guards opened up the cells for us. But the cells were opened all with one gate and were closed with one gate. Once we were done filming our part, our singer, Klaus, had to continue filming until the early morning hours.

So we all went back and slept in the cells. In the morning, we got woken up, and we all went to the boat to drive over the sea back to San Francisco. And as we were in the middle of the sea, we noticed that our bass player, Francis Buchholz, was missing! He got left in one of those cells and didn't wake up. So we had to go all the way back to collect him.

"Rock You Like a Hurricane" was a great video. It was filmed by David Mallet in London. I always remember the make-up they used for the girl's eyes. In those days, it was something really spectacular. They had real Scorpions fans that were invited to come to the studio. They built a cage around us, and it looked like we were inside the cage like animals, and the audience were outside. They were *really* shaking the cage. I thought it was very cool how David Mallet did this. He made the whole thing surrealistic.

— Quiet Riot —

RUDY SARZO: The "Metal Health" video was pretty interesting. It was filmed at the Cal Arts School. It's a school that was started by Walt Disney, in Valencia, California. It's 1983, and think of the students there, who are today's major filmmakers. Probably people running the studios. The whole set was built by the students at Cal Arts. I haven't had the opportunity to look back to see who the alumni was. As a matter of fact, when I'm finished with this conversation, I'm going to Google it. Also, do you know that padded cell in the video? One day, I was walking into Joe's Garage, which was Frank Zappa's rehearsal place. I look at the back of the stage wall ... and it's the padded cell! It wound up at Frank Zappa's rehearsal place.

It was no budget. It cost $10,000. The Quiet Riot fan club, that existed from the Randy Rhoads days, came over and participated in that. If you look at all the shots, we kept shifting the fan club. Like, if there was going to be a shot from the back of the stage ... something very unique about the Cal Arts Theater is that that whole place is modular. It's built on hydraulics. So there's the stage, and where the audience is sitting is actual bleachers that are hydraulic, and you can make them look however you want, different levels. So we just kept shifting everybody around. If you needed a side shot, it's the same people, but on the side of us, behind us, in front of us, wherever. There wasn't really that much time in the budget to get too fancy or think it over. All the extras that you see chasing Kevin [dressed as the gentleman from the *Metal Health* album cover] down the hallway were all Cal Arts students.

["Cum on Feel the Noize"] was done in June during a break. We were in California. We just shot it, and again, we called upon the Quiet Riot fan club, who came down, and we shot the video. What sticks out is the band doesn't come on until like the second chorus! We watched the intro being filmed, with one of the guys from the crew, who actually became the actor, the kid in the room that is being shaken up. Of course, this is before ... nowadays, you can just stick a plug into Final Cut Pro, and you're going to get the "camera shake" effect. Back then, you had to recreate it. It was a room on hydraulics. It was being pumped, and it made the actual room shake. It gives you a really realistic version of what you're trying to achieve, because then things are falling off the wall and stuff like that. It was maybe one or two passes, and then you're done. Nowadays, everything is digital. It's not as expensive.

"Mama Weer All Crazee Now" we went from $10,000 and $40,000 budgets, to now, there has to be *a storyline*. There was a little storyline before, but now, we need an actor. So they brought in this actor—actually, a really good actor—but at the time, he was going through some personal issues having to do with drugs. He was the "hero" character in the video. And it was a "1984 theme," a very Orwellian theme to the video. So the problems were mostly due to the fact that the guy was too out of it to really cooperate and contribute as much as he could have. So most of his parts, he was just sitting there ... drugged out. [Laughs] Success can go to people's heads, and I would have to say that it went to everybody's head [in Quiet Riot]. I didn't have the right tools to be able to deal with people whose success has gone to their head as I do right now, and I wish I would have had those tools then. So everybody kind of mishandled everybody else's way of dealing with success. It was a little bit messy, but the whole thing was to make the best video that we could. But there was a lot of drama going on.

— *Kiss* —

BRUCE KULICK: We went to England [to shoot the "Tears are Falling" video]. I always love being in England. I remember we were using a video director that knew how to do over-the-top stuff. I loved the fact that he wanted to feature me and use the solo dramatically, even if it made me do "the shower thing," and suddenly, I'm doing what looked like a hair commercial! But that was great. Even though we knew it was a one-shot thing, I followed the direction, and I wasn't really that worried about the guitar [getting wet], because hey, I was a rock star, so we'll deal with the guitar. We'll wipe it down.

I dug the set. I thought it was really cool. I was really happy how it came out. I was very proud of the band at that time. I was glad to be a "video star." The volcano I thought was really funny. Thank God it worked and went off when it was supposed to. Everything just really came together. We went to England because, at the time—in '85—the dollar was stronger than the pound, so a $100,000 video might only cost $75,000. I liked that they used a "girl next door" pretty girl [as the female role in the video], not some stripper.

The only negative thing with the videos of Kiss is that Gene and Paul would do their "count each other's shots." And I thought that that was a detriment, but whatever, it *is* their band. I knew I wasn't going to be on the top of the number count, that's for sure! "Wait a minute, I'm playing a solo ... why is the camera on Paul? Why is the camera on Gene? Surely, I look good when I play the guitar!" But what am I doing to do? I'm not in the editing room, and who's going to say, "But who's hiring them?" Me? No. So that was the one negative about the Kiss videos, and I say that pretty blankly about all of them. I didn't take it personally.

— *Ratt* —

WARREN DeMARTINI: Milton Berle was the first icon that I think any of us had ever met [for the "Round and Round" video]. It was a really cool thing. He was really the first guy to ever have a variety show on TV, and he was a cool person to listen to, because he made his career the same way that he knew that we were going to, which is to get on the road. Because prior to TV, it was just vaudeville. He was telling us stories and talking about those days, when him and other comedians of the period would get on a train, travel all night, y'know, Middle America. Raining, cold, get into a hotel, get up in the morning, set it all up, do the show, and then move on. What he described was great, but it was tough.

It was like, "OK, now we're going to be doing something other than playing live," which was the only thing that we were trying to hone. I remember as we were getting ready to do the "falling through the ceiling scene," we only had one chance to do this. I remember thinking, "I have no experience doing this!" There was that dining room scene that was set up, and because of the union rules, they weren't going to set it up and do it again. Once we did that scene, that was going to be it. I had a real moment of just "standing there at the diving board," and it's like, "Do it perfect—*with no practice."* I got through it, and the shot turned out fine, but it was just one of those one of many detours from the road that we had envisioned.

"Lay It Down" was all concept and not one of my favorites, frankly. There's parts I like about it, but like Robbin Crosby and me were always saying, "Why can't it just be a live bit? It just never gets better than that." The "You're in Love" video was probably because we complained so much about having to do a concept video with "Lay It Down," that the next video was a live piece that we shot in Shreveport, Louisiana. It was just a killer gig and a killer show. I had to re-edit that video for the DVD [*Videos from the Cellar: The Atlantic Years*], because the MTV version had footage of Ronald Reagan and Groucho Marx. It was going to be a licensing nightmare. So I went back and went through the footage and found some stuff that I could put in there—in lieu of all the cameo things—and I was really taken by the things they didn't use. What's in there now, there's a really cool, wide shot going from stage right to stage left and into the crowd.

— Twisted Sister —

MARK WEISS: Twisted Sister—I was at all their videos. It was kind of comic book stuff. It was comical, but it was cool. I did the *Stay Hungry* album cover, and then I was their photographer. I did everything with those guys. I just remember they got Neidermeyer and Flounder [characters from *Animal House* for the "I Wanna Rock" video]. I remember Marty Callner, the video director. That was one of his first big MTV videos. And after he did the Twisted one, everyone hired him.

— Lita Ford —

LITA FORD: Making ["Gotta Let Go"] was awesome. That was wild. The directors and the producers come up with a script for each song, so this one was very different. And I liked what they did, because it was so different. You remember Annie Lennox? She used to dress up in so many wacky different ways, and I really admired her for that. And I thought, "Well ... why not do something on that scale? And do the ironing or whatever, treat it like an 'Annie Lennox' kind of thing." But for me, it was pretty hard. Even the other day, looking at the pictures from the video shoot, I had to do a couple of double takes to see who that was. And my kids were like, "Mom ... *who the hell is that?!*" So it was such an extreme difference. But it works for the video. It ended up being in heavy rotation. It was awesome. It's such a thrill to be a part of that.

— Spinal Tap —

MARK WEISS: I remember when Spinal Tap came on [MTV], and nobody knew who they were. They didn't say who it was, like it was Lenny and Squiggy [It was just Lenny, aka actor Michael McKean, *not* Squiggy.]. I didn't know either, and the VJs didn't even know. So they started asking them questions about how they were in England. I didn't know too much about international bands, so I'm trying to schmooze with them, like maybe get a gig. I didn't know I was talking to *Lenny and Squiggy!* Afterwards, we found out, and it was a good little joke.

— *Mötley Crüe* —

RUDY SARZO: Van Halen was more tongue-in-cheek, whereas Mötley Crüe were sometimes trying hard to be bad boys. That was the image that they wanted to put across. They were *really* working hard at it. [Laughs] And, of course, they succeeded—on stage, off stage, and in front of the camera. Whereas Van Halen was like, "Hey, this is what we do 24/7. Come to our party." It's like the whole world was a big backstage party to them.

WARREN DeMARTINI: When I moved to L.A. to join Ratt, Mötley Crüe had just released *Too Fast for Love*, and they were well-known and established in the L.A. area. That was a very exciting time, because you could still see them in a small place, like the Troubadour or the Whiskey. Back then, they would do two shows a night, and people would line up around the block and stand out there *for hours.* Robbin was friends with Nikki, and we were starting to get known as a group, so we could get in through the backdoor. When we used to see them at the Whiskey, there was maybe a couple thousand people who knew who Mötley Crüe were. And we were one of them. So skip ahead to seeing them on TV—that was great.

HERMAN RAREBELL: I remember in 1982 I walked into the Whiskey A Go Go. And two guys approached me, Tommy Lee and Vince Neil. "Hi, aren't you Herman from the Scorpions? Would you be interested to produce us?" Later on in the evening—the next day, actually—they gave me a tape with some of the songs on it, and asked me to produce them. And because I had to go back to Germany and play drums on the next Scorpions album, this prevented this. Otherwise, I would have produced the first Mötley Crüe album. This was how close I was to it. I loved the band. I always thought they would make it big.

MARK WEISS: I was at [the video shoots for] "Smokin' in the Boys Room," "Too Young to Fall in Love." I was at a lot of their videos. I was one of the first—if not *the* first   photographer who gave them a national layout. I shot Mötley Crüe for *Oui* magazine in 1981. I hired a bunch of girls that went topless, and we went to the Rainbow afterwards, and there was shit going on under the table. They were living the dream. Their videos ... if you look at them now, "Smokin' in the Boys Room" is kind of hokey, but "Too Young to Fall in Love" was kind of cool—the one with an Oriental kind of thing, with gang fighting, geisha girls. That was fun. There were a lot of girls around that one. In between takes, I would grab Vince and just shoot him with some girls, provocative poses. I remember Mick Mars had a thing with ... I don't know if they used it, but there was a sushi thing and him taking the fish and hitting someone with it.

CARMINE APPICE: I thought Mötley Crüe's videos were great. They were better than the band at the time. I thought the best thing in the band was Tommy. I became friends with Mick. Mick is actually a pretty good player. And I became friends with Nikki Sixx. Me and Nikki used to live close to each other, and I played him a song from King Kobra called "Raise Your Hands to Rock," and then Nikki ripped my title off and wrote a whole new song to it! They gave me a credit on the album—"Thanks for the title." *How about you should have gave me some royalties?* I lent them a couple of bass drums for the second album, because Tom Werman, the producer, didn't like the way Tommy's bass drum sounded.

FRANK STALLONE: I wasn't into the hair bands, Ratt and all that stuff. I couldn't stand that shit. Quiet Riot, I mean, Kevin DuBrow, I said, "Kevin ... what are you, on smack? *What are you doing?*" I hated it. I used to hang out at the same place, the Rainbow. They were a little younger than me. I would say probably the best of them all was Mötley Crüe, as far as a band, if you really listen to them. It was just weird, guys with teased hair and black fingernails, and could be in better shape to wear the clothes they were wear-ing. When I see guys walk in wearing skin-tight spandex and they're really in bad shape, like they've got cellulite ... it doesn't work, man. You've got to come in *strong*. Yeah, carrying some cottage cheese on a guy isn't good.

Bruce Springsteen

JOHN OATES: I think Bruce was smart to do a video ["Dancing in the Dark"] that was live, because that's what he was all about. His live performances were the centerpiece of his whole career. So he kept true to his thing.

DARYL HALL: I think, like a lot of his career, it was very calculated, and he needed a hit, because he wanted to be part of that. So he manufactured his only real single and did it and made a video, like everybody else.

DAVE MARSH: He had allowed Columbia to release a video clip in the U.K., I think to *The Old Grey Whistle Test*, of a performance of "Rosalita" from 1978. And then one of the guys at CBS came up with an idea of using still-footage to create a *Nebraska* video [for the song "Atlantic City"]. In fact, they did play that on MTV, and it was quite popular. If you look at my book, *Glory Days*—which is in that *Two Hearts* compilation now—you'll see a discussion between Bruce and me about him and Jon Landau arguing about whether he should make "the big noise," a la *Born in the USA*, or "the quieter noise" of *Nebraska*. Once he made that commitment, then it was pretty clear to anybody that he was going to need videos for the songs, at least the singles tracks. Of course, I don't think anybody thought there were going to be that many singles ... or at least I didn't. I thought two or three, not five or six!

So they went and did that "Dancing in the Dark" video. Jeff Stein—who did *The Kids Are Alright*, the Who movie—tried to go in and make a "Dancing in the Dark" video. That failed, and then Brian De Palma came in and rescued the whole thing, with the Courteney Cox "Dancing in the Dark" video that you actually got to see. Which had its own set of problems. The problem was for a lot of Bruce fans, it seems way slicker than he actually is. It had something done to his teeth, so that his smile was like a totally different smile than he had before. He had dental work done. And it wasn't a very authentic-looking "Bruce crowd." [Laughs] Courteney's role was—not her fault—a jive version of what actually went on on-stage, because he actually did pull people up from the audience and dance with them.

But it lacked all of Bruce's on-stage spontaneity. And I think that he paid a creative price for that. Or maybe it's not even a creative price; maybe it's just an image price. But he was, at that point, having it both ways, in terms of being one of the two or three biggest performers in the world and being still a very serious artist. And this was a chink in that armor, in a sense that he couldn't have it both ways with that particular video. There are other videos. I mean, if you look back at the "Born in the USA" video that John Sayles made, it looks very dated, partly because of Bruce's costume. But he was having it both ways, because he had the big anthemic song, and he had the soldiers. And they did their best to make a statement about, "That's not about politics," and they didn't do such a bad job.

DEBORA IYALL: Great song ["Dancing in the Dark"], but the video to me was all about unveiling the personal physical transformation Bruce Springsteen had undertaken. Dude discovered weightlifting! The video was fun for seeming relaxed, live, and joyful. Bruce got down and danced throughout the whole song. Clarence Clemons was incandescent. I liked that he chose a boyish girl to come dance with him on stage, a very young Courteney Cox. ["Glory Days"] is memorable for Little Steven in his scarf, unabashedly mugging it up, and continues with Bruce's framing of his songs firmly in working class experience. Patti Scialfa plays a mean tambourine, too!

"I'm on Fire" pivots in me from a point of deep longing that I've known almost all of my life. The American edge-of-town landscape I saw transformed into suburbs, to well past the gasoline-scented auto body shop I grew up next to. The Thunderbird is as unattainable and as iconic an object of desire as the woman is for him to most of us, in contrast to our familiarity with "a knife edgy and dull." I have vivid memories of when the auto body shop owner brought a mare for his stallion Appaloosa to a small corral out back that bordered our corrals. There's nothing as primal as those horses' vocalizations in the video or in the song—as human desire is so often deferred and sublimated—but those Western-style yodels he does do get me where my cowboy fantasy lives. When he walks away after dropping the keys to the Thunderbird in the mailbox, I was relieved he didn't mess with that woman from the house on the hill. Maybe he'll be going home to someone more like me.

NINA BLACKWOOD: He was one of the last artists to get on board. He was very skeptical of videos and didn't really want to do them at all. ["Dancing in the Dark"] was a total iconic video, but what I thought of as his first *video,* because it was the first one he "acted," was "I'm on Fire." I remember thinking, "Because he hates videos, is he going to stay under the car the whole time?" [Laughs] And "Dancing in the Dark" really has transcended and has become an iconic video of the '80s. And lo and behold, who would have ever thought that Courteney Cox would go on ... and Brian De Palma, he had the best guy directing it. I'm sure he doesn't mind them anymore because he's done so many. I was really impressed with "I'm on Fire." For some reason, Springsteen reminds me of a young Robert DeNiro. I don't know why, his eyes, and there's something about his face that does. He's very expressive without trying.

CHUCK D: I think Bruce Springsteen's performances went far past his videos. I'll tell you, my most influential Bruce Springsteen video came way later—"Streets of Philadelphia," when he was walking through Philadelphia. I just loved that video. That's my favorite Bruce Springsteen video.

JULIAN LENNON: To be honest, I found those kind of videos a bit too "gung ho" for my liking!

Videos: Rock

— Queen —

ROB HALFORD: I think you can marry Queen with Michael Jackson in a lot of ways, just because of the extraordinary depth and fearlessness of "This is who we are. This is what we're about. We're not really listening to the critics. We're not really listening to curry public favor. *We are Queen.*" Everybody knows that I'm a huge Queen fan. I have one iPod that is just full of everything that Queen ever did. Every one of their videos—much like Jackson—were totally original and unique and told a story and was interesting, exciting, entertaining, funny. They remain, still, a powerful force. Again, we've lost two massively powerful people, Freddie and Michael. But their music lives forever. That's the main thing.

TODD RUNDGREN: "Bohemian Rhapsody" certainly took it to another level, long before there was an MTV. You could say that they lay some sort of foundational element with "Bohemian Rhapsody," that certainly helped MTV. It was obviously a formula that could work for others ... but other "formuli" I guess prevailed. I have to admit that not a lot of Queen videos stand out in my mind, because the thing that you always remember about Queen is Freddie Mercury's performance. That strutting around with the half-a-mic stand. Whenever you recall a Queen video, if it isn't "Bohemian Rhapsody," it's something with Freddie strutting around.

JOE ELLIOTT: They weren't even called "videos" when Queen did that in '75, were they? They were "promos." It *became* a video. When we first saw it ... because Queen made a decision—and bless them—they just broke rank and said, "No, we're not doing *Top of the Pops*. We'll send a film in." And instead of it just being them purely live, with that middle bit, it gave them an excuse to go a bit wacky. It had not really been done much before.

It has often been called "the first video ever made," but that's a load of shit, because I've got the video for "Honaloochie Boogie" by Mott the Hoople from '73, and it's definitely a video. It's got Ian Hunter putting money in a jukebox, the song starts, and then he leans on the jukebox with a cigarette in his fingers, mouthing the words, with half his face showing, and the band carrying on behind him. That was like, "directed," and that's three years before "Bo Rhap."

Somebody else would probably tell you, "Well, I can think of a better one. Frank Zappa did it in '69, or the Monkees did it in '67." You can keep going all the way back to other than just performance. But of course, the Queen stuff was great. "Bohemian Rhapsody" was the best of the lot. I thought "Radio Gaga" was a great video—when they sat in the car and then the bit with the crowd doing the clapping. Again, the hairs on the back of your neck stand up when you see it. We put the hand-claps in "Animal," because we wanted to try and create the same effect ... but we failed miserably.

PHIL COLLEN: "Bohemian Rhapsody" was the first "video video" I think that everyone had access to, really. It was great. It was like a short film. In that case, it really put the song over. A lot of cases, the director would miss the point of what the artist was doing, and were just doing a visual version of what they thought was great. But with that, that was the very first video that hit home. It was a very influential song/video, all the way around.

"Crazy Little Thing Called Love" was almost like an old rock n' roll song, and Freddie doing his thing out there, as camp as ever, it was great. It got who Queen were. It was a fun little song. And the fact that it was covered by Dwight Yoakam—it sounds like a total country song anyway—it shows the power of the whole thing.

"Radio Gaga" I think was a take-off of *Metropolis*. They used images. Great stuff, really good video. Back then, videos actually meant something, so after the initial glut of just putting a performance video out, it was kind of nice when you saw things like "Radio Gaga," which really did represent the song and the band. We all loved Queen. It was a blueprint for Def Leppard.

MICHAEL SADLER: Considering Freddie's flamboyant and theatrical nature, I'm sure he embraced the concept of creating images to accompany the music. I also wouldn't be surprised to find out that he had a lot of input into the concept and execution of the videos. "Bohemian Rhapsody"? Classic. "Crazy Little Thing Called Love"? I can only imagine that he had a great time doing his Elvis thing. "Radio Gaga"? Perhaps a little silly, but appropriate. The people from the film production company probably controlled a lot of the content, obviously using the video to help promote the movie. Having said that, though, the crowd scenes for the chorus gave anyone who hadn't seen the band live an idea of the grandiose nature of their performances. Do I sound like a fan? *Damn right.* Queen with Freddie Mercury was one of a kind.

— *David Bowie* —

JON ANDERSON: I just loved everything David's done. I like his work, I like his style, [and] I like his approach. "Let's Dance" was one of the great moments of that period. Everywhere in the world—and I *was* traveling around the world—you'd hear that music and see the video. He could do no wrong for me.

TODD RUNDGREN: I liked the videos from *Lodger* better. They were nice videos—the ones for *Let's Dance*—but I liked the ones from *Lodger* and *Scary Monsters*. They're just more ... David's always trying to be "ute" in a way, and they just seem more naturally "ute." The *Let's Dance* ones are just too slicked up. They're too "new romantic" for me, I suppose.

DAVE WAKELING: We did two shows at Milton Keynes, and he came in to see how everybody was doing, and to say that he really loved going on stage after us. The night before, the audience was just "ready to rock," he thought. And Saxa—the old Jamaican chap, who was always in search of his favorite beer—said, "Come and look in this fridge" and grabs David Bowie by the shoulder and around the neck and leads him to the fridge. He points in there and says, "Do you see any Red Stripe?" He says, "No, I don't." He says, "You get it!" So David Bowie dashes off, and about ten minutes later, this other guy comes back with a box of Red Stripe beer. Saxa says, "Wow, that guy was quick, wasn't he?" We say, *"That was David Bowie!* We were having a nice talk with him until you came in." Saxa thought he was a waiter backstage! Because he had his "Thin White Duke" stuff on—a black vest, black pants, and white shirt—he looked like a New York waiter. A lovely chap, and I wish we'd done more shows with him.

— *Rod Stewart* —

CARMINE APPICE: "Hot Legs" was done in some little town up near Fillmore, California. It was in the middle of nowhere, in the sticks. That's the one where we're riding on the truck and in an old gas station. It was really hot and dusty, and I remember all the townspeople were just hanging around us all the time and going, "What's going on here?" It was pretty off the wall.

Well, first of all, we didn't know the song ["Da Ya Think I'm Sexy?"] that well. If you look at the video, there's a drum fill at the end. I don't even play what's being played on there. In those days, pretty much my whole career, whatever's played on a record was just played on that particular one. When you played live, things changed. So we had never played the song live, and we never really listened much to exactly what we played on the record. If you look, a lot of the stuff was not in synch with what was going on on the record. But it was a lot of fun.

I remember that gorgeous girl that played the lead with Rod, and she had the one scene where Rod was in the bed with her. You could actually see her nipples. [Laughs] We'd always try and barge into her dressing room to try and catch her with her clothes off. And we had a lot of chicks in the actual video, like in the bar scene, sitting down and talking up a lot of chicks. When we did it, we didn't know it was going to be such a huge record. That was the second album I did with Rod.

["She Won't Dance with Me"] was an interesting one, because we were on tour in Europe. We flew into London, and we did two videos—"Passion" and "She Won't Dance with Me." That was fun because, there again, there was a skylight on the first level roof, looking into the girls' dressing room. [Laughs] I remember we were up there, we call it "bogging." We'd go up there and watch those three girls that were in there get dressed and changed for the video. It was all done on a soundstage, and they squared off a certain area, which had lots of polka dots. I had just a rented drum kit, and we all had on "sex police" t-shirts, which was a thing we used to do in the Rod Stewart Group, where if somebody had a chick, we'd "sex police" them and wreck whatever he was doing.

Actually, I wasn't in that video ["Young Turks"]. That's about the time I left the group. I did do one video on *American Bandstand* with "Young Turks" ... but let's not talk about it.

ERIC BLOOM: You've got to remember. [Rod Stewart] was already well-known and a big star. So, "Here's Rod Stewart's new video" had some cache right from the beginning, before you watched any of it. And he just comes across so likable and to girls so sexy and cool, and he has a great voice. The fact that his videos played that all up—he's a very smart man and a great talent.

— Pat Benatar —

BOB GIRALDI: Pat ... I didn't have much of a relationship with Pat. Michael Peters worked with her very intimately [for "Love is a Battlefield"], because he had the task of trying to get her to change and become less a singer, more a dancer. And I had the problem of getting her to be more an actress. And don't forget, that was the very first time that dialogue started a video. Yes, I've been criticized many times by people who think the music should remain pure. And yes, I am responsible for using my imagination to put onto film what I think the music means to me, way more than what the music was written by the artist about. It's really my interpretation.

But as I told Lionel, "If you don't want my interpretation, you should come up with your own interpretation." I write my own. Like with "Hello," absolutely having nothing to do ... and that video has got as many hits [on the Internet] as any video ever made, strangely enough. People love it and cherish it in Europe and all around the world. And had nothing to do with a blind girl being in love with a teacher, but that was what it meant to me, that was what I kept seeing as I kept playing the record.

And the thing with "Love is a Battlefield" had nothing to do with "dime-a-dance." That was my own ridiculous experiences as a kid, going to a dime-a-dance and being tossed around by women. I loved the video challenge, because I loved the music, and the artists were less important to me personally, but they were terrific. I loved just coming up with my own interpretation. Pat and I only did one video together, and it ended up being a sort of a rallying cry for young girls. I put my young daughter in it actually, as a cameo, and I loved the video.

It was the first time that dialogue ... which, subsequently, was criticized that "There is no room for this kind of ... " It's like I'm doing a showtune, or I'm using great artists' tracks as scores to a movie. And in many ways, you can interpret that. But they seemed to enjoy it now, and it accomplished what it set out to be, marketing a new single or new album. And the thing that I respect the most about Pat is, while she was uncomfortable, she never gave up and ended up doing a fairly good interpretation of dance. And those dancers ... if you take your eyes off Pat and look at those dancers behind her, *those girls kick ass.* Oh boy, do they. Especially when they walk out on the street. They're just slamming. It was wonderful to watch. We did that on Fourteenth Street, which is now called the Meatpacking District, in a bar there. Shot all night long and walked off into the sunset as the sun came up.

— *The Shoes* —

ALAN HUNTER: The first hour [MTV was on the air] was populated with bands that no one ever heard of. "Who the hell are *the Shoes?!*" Because the catalog was limited. I remember the guy looked like Peter Frampton. This was the height of "We can't afford more than just the small club, with the five lights in the background." These guys are wearing clothing that look like a nerdy little band of the late '90s, kind of like Weezer or Wilco, except for the guy with the long Frampton hair. This is definitely like, *"Who in the hell is this?"* Four guys, three guitars, and drums. They were forgettable, I would say, but they had to play something, MTV did. I don't know the story behind who programmed the first 24 hours, except they took every video that they could get their hands on and put it in the mix. Why they wouldn't have made that first hour packed with every big star in the world, I don't know.

JEFF MURPHY: After recording *Present Tense* in England, we saw that they had video music shows, which America didn't have yet, and the label decided it would be a good idea to shoot some videos for the European market. We shot all four songs ["Too Late," "Tomorrow Night," "In My Arms Again," and "Cruel You"] in one day. They were filmed at a soundstage in L.A. in the fall of 1979, September or October. It was a long, 20-hour shoot, and we filmed "Tomorrow Night" last, because it was decided to use fog on the set, to try and diffuse the harsh look of video tape and try to give it a softer "film look." We filmed a short interview before the songs, and the interviewer was inexperienced and extremely nervous—he was later edited out—which also made us very nervous. But the songs turned out OK.

JOHN MURPHY: It was a little surreal—no audience, just stagehands, the director, and a few folks from Elektra. It was the first time we ever lip-synched, so that was a learning experience, seemed odd to be hitting strings but you weren't actually controlling the sound. We figured out quick that the trick is to actually sing along, don't just mouth the words. I don't remember there being any video monitors for us to see how we were coming across, so it was pretty much on the fly. Just as we were feeling a little more comfortable with the atmosphere, it was over. The last song was "Tomorrow Night," and they brought in these smoke pots from a church and filled the place up with smoke. They used a lot of red lights, so it kinda looked like Shoes headlining in hell. I just remember the end of the day feeling sweaty, tired, and our eyes burning from the smoke.

JEFF MURPHY: Despite our pleas to the label to film more videos, they refused, citing the expense and dismissing it's importance as, "a flash in the pan." So we independently filmed our own video, to the song "In Her Shadow" from the upcoming LP *Boomerang*, and submitted it to MTV in early 1982, which MTV aired. Elektra became upset and forced them to yank it off the air, because it didn't come through proper Elektra channels. They reprimanded us that it violated our agreement. Later that year, MTV sent a film crew into the studio with us for an interview for their "music news" segment, but Elektra never funded another video for us.

— Jefferson Starship —

MICKEY THOMAS: ["Find Your Way Back"] may have been the first one that we shot. Grace didn't officially rejoin the band until the next album, *Winds of Change*, but she did drop by and record a duet with me, on "Stranger" for that album. So that was kind of her big debut for Grace's re-entry into the band, the "Stranger" video. I think we shot the "Find Your Way Back" and "Stranger" videos at the same session, probably back-to-back. One on one day, the other the next day. We were just kind of feeling our way around, stumbling around with it. "Well, what are we going to do? We're just going to stand here, pretending to be on stage, and run through the song half a dozen times, from various camera angles." And that was pretty much it. It was a little stiff, a little awkward. It was also new.

["Layin' It on the Line"] was one of the most fun video shoots ever. It was a large shoot, and there were a lot of people involved in it. We used this old turn-of-the-century fire station, down in San Francisco, this real cavernous hall. And that's where we staged our "mock political convention," which was loosely the concept for that—"Mick and Slick" running for president. But then we tried to pepper the whole video with as many odd characters as we could possibly find. We tried to run the full gamut. Bill Graham, Willie Brown, and Pat Paulsen are in it, and underground groups at the time, like the Sisters of Mercy and the Residents. And then Grace and I got to do a couple of different personas in it. We got to do our "rock" on stage, and then we got to dress up as political figures, as well.

["We Built This City"] is a pretty cool video, but I don't like *me* in that video. I felt like I was very stiff and wooden. That was one of the deals where, "Now, *a stylist* is going to come in and tell everybody, 'You're going to wear this for this scene, and then we have to fix your hair like this for this scene.'" We succumbed to that for a couple of videos there, and those are the ones that I don't feel that great about. I just feel like I look kind of silly in that one, as far as my physical appearance.

And that was the time where the video scene was being dominated by a lot of bands, specifically English bands. That was the first time where I felt I was trying to dance, awkwardly, in a video. [Laughs] I'm not a "Thompson Twin." That doesn't work for me. But I gave it a go, and then later on, you think, "God, I look stupid there," or "I wish I had not let myself be under the influence of so-called 'creative hands' on that video." I shaved off my mustache right before that video for "We Built This City." That was something that I had been thinking of doing for a long time, anyway. The facial hair was becoming very passe. But at the same time, I had a mustache for so long that it was kind of a scary thing to shave it off. It takes you a while to get used to looking at your upper lip. But it was a much better look for the '80s, I think.

The video that I may be most proud of overall is "Sara." By then, we had enough experience making videos to get a little more creative control over the project. And we really were able to spend a lot of time on that one. I got to spend a lot of time in advance with the director and talk about, "What do we want to accomplish with this video?" It was our most expensive video, I think. That's the one where we got to be really crazy, like we were actually making a "mini-movie." So we got to spend a lot of money foolishly, like you do in the movies. [Laughs]

In my mind, it was sort of a combination of *Wizard of Oz* meets *The Grapes of Wrath*—Midwest, just that whole look I wanted to have to it, black and white, Dust Bowl days-looking. We did silly stuff like we found a house and said, "This looks like the perfect house ... but we really need *a windmill.*" So they went to another house and found a windmill that looked right and moved the windmill over to the house for the shoot. We got a little self-indulgent on that one. And then you get to the point of where you're making this sort of mini-movie-type video. It's hours and hours of footage you shoot over and over, and then it gets down to the reality of it, that, "Wait a minute. We're making a four-minute song here ... how do we get all this information in?" So the storyline kind of evolves and makes sense ... up until about three minutes and 30 seconds of the song. And then the last 30 seconds of the song, we're trying to get all the footage in that we weren't able to use yet. [Laughs] It becomes like a mad dash to the finish line. But, overall, I like that one the best.

— *Loverboy* —

PAUL DEAN: We had just signed with Columbia, and we were all on holidays. We had been working hard, and we had a week off. We were all down in Mexico—Mike, Matt, and me, with our girls. I think we got a call from our manager saying, "We're shooting a video for 'Turn Me Loose' at a club in New York City, the Ritz." So that was our first foray into that. The director thought the song was a parody. He didn't take the lyrics serious. We wrote the lyrics serious—it was a put-down to this girl. It's all fiction ... that's why they call it "creative writing," y'know?

So anyway, the director, his take was, "This should be a comedy." Who are we to argue? We were a fledgling thing. It played out OK. It was pretty funny. The name of the director I can't remember, but he was a staff guy working for Columbia. We were just thrilled to be asked, because we knew the marketing value of MTV. Basically, it was a live performance with a bunch of cut-outs of silent movies, of the girl getting revenge on the guy. That's what the director's idea was. But they also had another cut-away of Mike sitting at a table and a girl smoking, and I remember seeing his hand shake, because he was so nervous. I don't think they got it on film ...

MIKE RENO: ["Working for the Weekend"] is pretty much the same story. We would play the song over and over again, and we'd bounce around like we normally did. Here's what I thought was kind of interesting. The director would say, "OK, we're going to shoot another song. *Now go get changed.*" "What do you mean?" "You have to put on a whole new outfit, and we're going to change the lighting a little bit." But it was the same stage! So basically, we just had to get some other clothes, fix your hair, take a break, and then jump back on stage and do the same thing over and over again. I really felt like I was being abused a bit, but that's the nature of the beast.

["Hot Girls in Love"] was one of the goofier moments in our lives. It was an L.A./Hollywood set. It was a soundstage. We set up in different positions and played different things. I remember I said, "What are you shooting through that glass?" And he said, "Come here, and I'll show you what it looks like." So I went over, and I looked through the camera, and what they had done is about five feet in front of the camera, on glass, they had painted wooden barrels. If you just walked by and looked at the glass, you'd see a glass half-painted with wooden barrels.

But the camera would shine through that glass, and film through that glass, and would end just where the stage floor was. So it looked like we were dancing on these wooden barrels, while we were performing this song. A lot of the video was that shot, us playing. And then they'd break away and have people jumping on and off barrels. Matty, our drummer, was playing with gas pumps instead of drumsticks. This was all just goofy fun. It was almost to me like a Monkees video. We were the Monkees for a day. [Laughs]

PAUL DEAN: MTV ran a contest for "Queen of the Broken Hearts" [the winner would appear in the video]. We were in the Mojave Desert, and [the winner] might have been there with her kid ... but she was just *plowed*. By the time it was for her to go on, she was just gone. I think maybe she got 20 frames, like a second. It was like, *BAM!* "Oh, there she is. There's the big winner!" But at least it's bragging rights, I guess. That was a really cool video to do. I wasn't really agreeing to the *Road Warrior* look, but in the end, I was out-voted. So I went with it.

MIKE RENO: First off, I wasn't really clear on that contest, because there was so much going on, it was just one little thing in a million things that were happening that month. But at that point, we were almost too busy to watch MTV anymore, because we were always traveling, doing shows, and promoting ourselves. But I remember a helicopter had flown us out to the desert—the Mojave Desert—by these catacombs. Very sandy of course, and hot. It was cold in the morning, then it got hot, then it got cool at night. We were basically supposed to be chased around by "she-women," clad in animal hides. We were the target, and they were watching us. We were out in the desert looking for them, and they were looking for us. It was just a big, huge, sexy, "manly guys and half-dressed women," running around the desert. In some mishmash, macho, *Road Warrior*—the whole thing was devised to be very *Road Warrior*, *Mad Max*-ish. We just played along with it.

PAUL DEAN: David Fincher was the director [for "Lovin' Every Minute of It"]. He's gone on to do *Seven*, *Alien 3*, and so many amazing horror movies. I remember sitting with him, and he's telling me, "Y'know, this is OK for now ... but I really want to do scary horror movies. I want to really get into intense stuff." I remember we didn't have a storyline at all, and we were sitting there—he, I, and the cinematographer guy—trying to think of an ending. It's a three-day shoot, and who knows how much hundreds of thousands of dollars this thing cost to shoot. It was pretty cool. Everyone had their own room and their own "set" of girls. That was a really fun thing to do.

MIKE RENO: We took over a hotel, over by the Hollywood Bowl. The Holiday Inn there in Hollywood. I don't know if we took over the *entire* hotel, but I know we took over the whole eighth floor. It started off with filming in a small, little club, where we were playing as if we were a club band, and some guys are going, *"These guys aren't even close to being Lover-boy."* And then it moved over to showing fantasies of everyone. We were all asked to come up with "a fantasy." If we could have a fantasy for a day, what would it be? And everyone in the band came up with a different scenario.

There were rooms decorated in the Holiday Inn with that particular fantasy. So one guy's fantasy was piano and a candelabra and women in white sheets floating around with blonde hair ... that would probably be our keyboard player's fantasy. Mine was like a circus fantasy—Cirque de Soleil almost, before its time. I had jugglers and little people, body builders with those whiplash mustaches. I think mine was a Fellini dream, like a Fellini movie. It was way out there. And Paul's was in this guitar manufacturing shop that was loaded with half-dressed babes. And there was a poker game with our bass player, Scott. His dream was poker. And Matt had one ... I can't remember what his was. It was a little movie production really. Every scene had to be shot separately. And they'd move the cameras and shoot the end of the scene, even if it was only in the video for seven seconds. I kind of learned how people work out in Hollywood. It's "hurry up and wait." Set the lights, get the smoke, dress the people, fix their hair. It was insane. It probably cost a huge amount of money.

— *The Tubes* —

FEE WAYBILL: "Talk to Ya Later"—we did a video of the entire *The Completion Backward Principle* album. We filmed the entire album and made a home video. We didn't do individual videos. We made a home video product, which we did at Shepperton Studios in England, with Russell Mulcahy, who went on to do a number of movies. He was just a video director then. And our choreographer, Kenny Ortega, has gone on to be a very famous director, with *High School Musical* and the Michael Jackson DVD [*This Is It*].

He pretty much put that whole thing together with Russell. And it was great. We had a fabulous time. We worked hard. It as actually right at the same time they were filming the first *Alien* at the studio. It was so cool to go to the *Alien* set and see the monsters and the spaceship. It was amazing. We did it right before we did a big tour, and we were there for about three weeks at the studio, working every day. Naturally, we had the facilities of a movie studio. We could make a lake, and we could do this, and we could do that. We had everything happening.

I remember we did one video called "Sports Fans." Of course, they could never show that on MTV. It was about a jock who couldn't figure out what sport he wanted to do, so he's wearing all the equipment for all the sports at once. It opens with the sports guy walking into the locker room ... only it's the *women's* locker room. The girls are supposed to be standing there naked in the shower, and we hired these women, and they said, "Oh no, we won't take our tops off." We went, *"What?!* What are you talking about?" So we covered them in whipped cream and foam, so it looked like they were soaping and lathering up, and you couldn't really tell they were wearing clothes underneath. I was so mad that we had hired them and that they wouldn't appear naked that I was supposed to come out in a jockstrap, and I took my clothes off, and came walking out into the dressing room naked. Full-frontal nudity! Russell loved it. Everybody loved it. Naturally, it was a little controversial, so we ended up having to do two versions. We had to do the censored version for the U.S.A., but then for Europe and most of the other countries, we did the naked version.

"She's a Beauty" we did on the A&M lot, and nobody was too happy with it, because they wouldn't let us do what we wanted to. They wouldn't let us do the *Freaks* video, with all the geeks—the chicken woman, the bearded lady. So we had to come up with this sort of tame version. It was OK, but it wasn't great. We had a lot of people there. Rosanna Arquette was "the big sister," and Robert Arquette [who plays the young boy] was young, and it kind of scared him. At one point, he started crying! He was scared of the scary woman in the fish tank. We had a mermaid in a fish tank, and she was kind of evil-looking, and he thought she was drowning or something. He was just a kid. He got scared and started crying, and Rosanna had to come and calm him down.

— Saga —

MICHAEL SADLER: The storyline [for "On the Loose"] was really handed to us. That was a matter of your director will be given the song to listen to and come up with [an idea]. Unless he's really far off base, generally, the artist or band will adhere to it. That was the case with that. He just considered it, "OK, 'On the Loose' ... let's take that literally. Crime, breaking out of jail." So he took that angle. And really, at that stage, I think you walk into it really green, and go, "Sure! I'm sure it's going to be great!"

I remember showing up on the set and putting on the prison grays. It was all shot in a little subdivision in an industrial area of Toronto. It was a little silly—as a lot of the videos were—but that was the genre. It was fun to do and fun to watch. I got to do a little action, like jumping off a fence and pretending that I'm breaking out of jail. It was my first introduction to acting. And I never looked back. I'm waiting for my big break. That's why I'm living in L.A. now. [Laughs]

We shot a video for a song called "Amnesia," and it was about Jim Gilmour, the keyboard player, having a case of amnesia and not remembering who he was. The live part of it is us playing on a stage, and I'm having to cover his keyboard parts, because he forgot to show up for the gig, and he's wandering around the streets.

One of the scenes, the director decided that he wanted to have a pink elephant—but a real one. And what ended up happening is they brought two live elephants to the set. The reason they brought two is the one that they wanted to use couldn't be separated from the other one. They were real good pals, and they would freak out if they were separated. So they ended up bringing both of the elephants to the shoot. They actually painted the one bright pink. They stood there with big brushes, and there's this gigantic pink elephant. And it's just for this quick scene. Jim Gilmour is walking by, [and] the elephant is walking by the other way behind him. The problem was, at the end of the day, they had to take the elephants back to the zoo, and they couldn't get all the pink off! So one of the elephants ended up going back to the zoo more than slightly pink.

— Aldo Nova —

ALDO NOVA: The video [for "Fantasy"], how that came about was my manager at the time—Sandy Pearlman, who managed Blue Öyster Cult—hired this B-horror-schlock-movie film director, Richard Casey. And he had come up with some sort of a thing, because I had a "soundtrack" in front of my song, which was a helicopter and all that stuff. He basically had me coming out of the helicopter, and the laser beam was my idea. It still stands up. It gets played a lot on YouTube. Plus, I had that weird leopard suit. I used to go out with a stripper back then, so the girl that made the costumes for strippers made my leopard suit. [Laughs]

I had a lot of stick from the record company about it, because I was actively involved in the editing. I was not happy with the way the guy was editing the video. I went in there myself and said, "Choose this shot. Choose that shot." The record company would get on my case and say, "Who are you to edit a video? *You're a musician.*" And I said, "I have no limitations. To me, it's all music. It's just what I want to see on it." "Fantasy" sort of invented that genre, that you tell a little story before it—a little "pre-quote" to the song—and then you go into the song. And then after that, you've got Lady Gaga doing that now with all her videos—like "Telephone," when she's in jail. They tell a little story, and then it goes into the video. Back then, there was nobody doing that.

— Peter Gabriel/Genesis/Phil Collins —

MICKEY THOMAS: Peter Gabriel, overall, is probably my favorite artist, *period.* If you just put it all together—stage performances, albums, videos, lyric content, just coolness—Peter Gabriel is right there. His videos, early on, were some of the most interesting, experimental videos at the time. He was really right on the cutting edge of that. "Shock the Monkey" is a great video. It was very striking. It had images that I think we had not seen yet at that time in video. That de-evolution of man, getting back to your primal roots, that kind of thing. And, of course, that goes hand-in-hand with rock n' roll. It can be very primitive. But yet at the same time, using some of the most exploratory and cutting-edge video techniques at the time.

I remember when that record came out, *Security*, I was already into Gabriel, but the rest of Jefferson Starship weren't really hip to Gabriel yet. I brought that album into the studio—we may have been working on *Nuclear Furniture*—and sat the whole band down in the studio and played that whole album, blasting on the big speakers, and "conditioned" the band. But Peter Gabriel was the kind of artist that could change your life, the way you look at the world. And "Shock the Monkey" is a prime example of that.

GEDDY LEE: That was a perfect combo, because Peter Gabriel was such an interesting artist as a young frontman for Genesis, and he brought such an unusual and fresh visual style to Genesis in the early days, and then when he went out on his own, because he is such a creative person. I think he really took the bull by the horns and made it his own and was tremendously successful because his music was so interesting and so high quality, and he had such a vibrant imagination. He was able to bring those two things together and really take the media seriously.

It was obviously the concept of these types of animations that he did—stop-motion animation with clay and other props [for "Sledgehammer"]. Everybody wanted to use that guy, but of course, that concept became pretty much identified with Peter Gabriel. He did other things besides that. He was always very theatrical. The original Genesis, of course, was in that whole prog rock/theater/English kind of deal. I always loved his records because he's very meticulous about the production, the songwriting was great, and I think he just nailed it when he would produce the videos, because they would be so entertaining. You knew when a new one was coming out that you didn't know what to expect, but it was really going to be spectacular.

JON ANDERSON: Peter I do love very much. I follow him very carefully. I think he's always been very inventive and always will be. "I wish I'd have done that video!" y'know? "I wish I had wrote that song!" Him and Sting—it's like, "Oh my God, I wish I had done that."

MICHAEL SADLER: Nothing comes close. He and Freddie Mercury, for me, as entertainers and creative ... just artists in general that no one will ever replace. No one can touch Peter. It's just ridiculous his creative mind, the way it works. It astounds me.

ROGER POWELL: [Phil Collins] took the tactic of reinforcing the music, and they had the budgets to do good stuff. He's certainly a dynamic person. I think he's an incredible songwriter and performer. He did one with Philip Bailey ["Easy Lover"]. That was good, too. I heard it in the supermarket the other day. [Laughs] That's where all this stuff ends up!

GEDDY LEE: Those videos were more about how successful those songs were, rather than the strength of the videos. "In the Air Tonight," which is the song that broke Phil Collins as a solo artist, was such a strong song. I think the song broke the video, not the other way around.

MICHAEL SADLER: Great sense of humor. Again, not taking yourself too seriously. Especially with a band like Genesis, because it's so musical, the video has a chance to say, "Don't take us too seriously," and put a funny image in front of it, and it takes the edge off of, "Well, I like Genesis ... but they get a little too musical at times." I think the videos were a chance to take it a little more tongue-in-cheek and just relax with it.

JON ANDERSON: Phil carried the business of pop music for four years, *constantly*, churning out this incredible amount of hits for his solo album through to whatever. But he just had this incredible run through the '80s, where that's all you heard, [and] that's all you saw.

— Asia —

GEOFF DOWNES: ["Heat of the Moment"] was Godley and Creme, who started to become quite significant players in the game, as far as MTV was concerned. They were doing a lot of video clips. But you've got to bear in mind that when that stuff was being shot, it was being shot by video camera, so it had a certain kind of "look" about it. It wasn't film or anything like that, that had kind of a rough edge to it. People were starting to get very creative with videos then, starting to use a lot of graphics and a lot of things that would make it more interesting for the viewer. Something other than just footage of a band playing. All of a sudden, they were injecting all sorts of effects.

I think ["Only Time Will Tell"] was done the following day. I think we did the first two promo videos on two consecutive days in London. I remember seeing the girl—I think she was about 15—and she was dancing, and I thought, "Wow, this is really bizarre." But when I saw the final article, I thought, "I see where these guys are coming from. They're trying to create something unusual and different."

We went with the director Brian Grant, and ["Don't Cry"] was a video that was very much based on *Raiders of the Lost Ark*. In many ways, we felt embarrassed about it, because we were kind of drawn into doing things that we didn't do naturally. With a band like Asia, we were known as musicians, and all of a sudden, we're in a kind of spoof film. In some respects, that didn't really work for us.

— *Yes* —

JON ANDERSON: We knew the guys who did the filming [for "Owner of a Lonely Heart"], so we got on very well with them. We really hadn't performed as a band [after Yes reunited in 1983]. We made the record as individuals, but we'd never been on stage together. So we were like, "Hi Trevor, nice to meet you, give you a hug. OK, *we're filming."* I think we did the first "movie" with a different keyboard player, and then he had to be edited out, because he wasn't in the band anymore. We were just juggling it around. But the video came out, and I thought it was a pretty good video. I wasn't sort of "blown away," but the record was so good anyway.

And then we did another one, "Leave It," which is a totally surreal sort of video, which I loved. By then, we were number one around the world, so we were immensely famous for ten minutes. That was it. It was, "Oh, we're going to be upside down ... that's cool! Let's do 17 versions. Oh great, that's amazing!" So there are actually 17 different versions of the video, which is perfect. Anything more abstract really reaches me, because it's something that I'll remember, where sometimes you do a video, and you think, "Oh, that looks OK," and ten minutes later, you don't care. But something that's abstract, you can look at it now and think, "That's a damn good video," because it is different.

— *ZZ Top* —

NINA BLACKWOOD: That transition was fairly brilliant on their part. They had the trilogy of "Gimme All Your Lovin,'" "Sharp Dressed Man," and "Legs." And then incorporating the logo with the keychain and the *Eliminator* car. And they are just so odd-looking to begin with! Then you have Paula Abdul, who choreographed them. Granted, they didn't have a lot of moves, but the moves and gestures that she had them do really worked. It completely blew them over the top. They were this little boogie band from Texas. They had a great following, but then that broke them wide open. Even in their shows ... they're like dirty old men! They have girls prancing around, but it was brilliant for them. I'm not really—except for Santa Claus—into long beards. And I always thought it was funny—the one guy that doesn't have a long beard, his last name is Beard!

— *John Cougar Mellencamp* —

DAVE MARSH: "Jack and Diane" was at the drive-in or something, and "Pink Houses" had that great footage of the old black guy sitting on a stoop. Because of what MTV was in terms of race terms, that black guy sitting on the stoop was an insurrection. It's the kind of thing that John in his "perpetual rebel thing" really does right. You said he was Bruce's competition ... I think there were *four*. I was thinking about this the other day, because Bob Seger's birthday was last week. There was really Bruce, Bob, Tom [Petty], and John.

People try to call it "heartland rock" or whatever they called it at that point. What it really meant was *"Not punk, not new wave, not British— American."* And those guys, of them all, Bruce made OK videos, I don't remember Bob hardly making any videos, Tom made videos that were really fun, and John has always been a pretty serious songwriter. He was probably at his most popular, and he was writing the most serious songs he ever wrote in a lot of ways. And the most effective. "Jack and Diane" not so much, but "Pink Houses" ... you could remake "Pink Houses" right now, that lyric, and do a more up-to-date arrangement of it, and it would sound like it was written yesterday. And all of those guys have some songs like that. Y'know, I had two teenaged daughters at this point ... I saw *a lot* of MTV. [Laughs]

MARK WEISS: The thing that sticks out on that is, a few months after it happened [an MTV contest in which a winner received a free house, painted pink with the help of Mr. Cougar], it ended up being on some sort of nuclear waste [site] or something. I don't know if it was rumor or what, but it was on a dump-site, and they ended up selling it. But at the time, it was fun. They "painted the mother pink," as he would say. They got overalls, had a big painting party, and then jammed in the room. It was pretty cool.

GREG HAWKES: John Cougar ... not a fan. All I remember of his videos is him, like, singing on a farm.

— *Tom Petty and the Heartbreakers* —

DAVE MARSH: Tom Petty's videos I remember, because I had stopped smoking pot 15 years earlier, and they made me hallucinate—*because he was so stoned!* Those were the ultimate stoner videos. And I think it really helped Tom, because being stoned in public and being able to laugh at yourself a little bit, if the music's good, that's always pretty good PR. He really pulled that off in those videos.

— *Bob Dylan* —

GEORGE LOIS: I did a music video for Bob Dylan, "Jokerman." Kurt Loder says it's still the best music video ever made. The way that happened is I had convinced Bob Dylan in '75 that Rubin "Hurricane" Carter was innocent and that the Jersey cops framed him. I went to prison to meet Rubin. So I convinced him to join forces with me and Muhammad Ali, because Muhammad Ali was the head of the committee I started, of famous people who were speaking out and trying to tell the world how Rubin was brutally jailed and had been in jail for like 16 years or however long it was. And Bob wrote a song, "Hurricane," and did a concert in prison. And then a couple of days later, he did a terrific concert at Madison Square Garden. So I had that experience with Bob, and Bill Graham came to me when I was doing MTV, and he had been having arguments with Bob Dylan about music videos at the time. Bob was very much against them, and Bill said, "The only way I can get him to do one is to tell him that you'll do it. Will you?" I said, "Of course I'll do it!"

So they sent me his album [*Infidels*], and I chose "Jokerman" out of it, because every line was visual. I saw five or six thousand years of the history of art, in every Goddamned line he said. And also, I devised him intercutting singing the song. I devised this running graphic visual album of some of the greatest works of art in the history of the world. And the coup de grâce, I put the lyrics on the screen, as they're going with each visual. One of the reasons why is I think it's always difficult listening to lyrics on TV or the radio. I can listen to a song, turn to my wife, and say, *"What the fuck was that line?!"* So I put the lyrics on, which really nails the son of a bitch. In fact, when Bob came with Bill Graham to see what I wanted to do, I had a roomful of visuals with the type on them, so it was like a storyboard pinned to the walls in a big room. I explained the lyrics and visuals with it. I went through the whole thing. And I remember Bob said, "You know, a lot of these things I had in mind when I wrote the lines!" He got excited about it. "I wrote that line, and somehow, that line really is what I said."

— *Rolling Stones* —

JOHN OATES: I thought [the Stones' videos] were nothing. [Laughs] They were exactly like ours—*nothing*. They were just a bunch of guys clowning around in front of cameras. There wasn't really any thought put into it, just, "Hey, we've got to do a video, let's do a video, let's get it out there ... and here's our new single."

FRANK STALLONE: I don't think the Stones ever had really good videos. Their videos are pretty cheesy.

— *George Thorogood* —

GEORGE THOROGOOD: We were in England, touring with the Rolling Stones. The English office of EMI were there, and they wanted to do "Bad to the Bone" as a video. I wanted to do it as a card game. I wanted to pattern it after the movie, *The Cincinnati Kid*, with Steve McQueen. And the same time, I'm thinking that there was a director in L.A. that was thinking of doing a video and doing a take-off of Paul Newman's *The Hustler*. We were ready to rip off two classic movies! [Laughs] We got our heads together, and they said, "Do you know any people you'd like to have in this video?" Originally, they thought about BB King to play the part Bo Diddley played, and I said, "BB King might be a bit too dignified for this ... we need somebody that's a heavy rocker." So we settled on Bo Diddley, which was fantastic. Bo had a lot of natural acting skills. He was up for the challenge.

The funny thing that was I went in there and tried to rip off every pose James Coburn did in every movie he ever did. [Laughs] And little things we did that we took from *The Good, the Bad and the Ugly* and *Ocean's Eleven*. And I thought, "This is great. This will launch my movie career. I'll be able to get in movies from this." Well, what happened was we did it with the pool player who taught Paul Newman how to shoot for *The Hustler*—Willie Mosconi, the greatest pool player in the world. And he got a part in a movie, *The Baltimore Bullet*, with James Coburn, and Bo Diddley got a part in *Trading Places*, with Dan Aykroyd and Eddie Murphy ... *and I didn't get anything!* I'm still waiting for a part. Mr. Mosconi was like a gangster. We called him "Mr. Big." We wanted to have credits—Mr. Big, Bo Diddley was "Bad Bo," and I was "The Kid." We made it kind of like an old-time western but pool shooting instead. That was like a mini-movie. And they had footage of us playing in it, at the Peppermint Lounge in New York City.

— *Robert Plant* —

JOE ELLIOTT: People don't seem to ever mention it, but I thought "Big Log" by Robert Plant was a phenomenal video. This was Robert Plant going out on his own. Now, he'd already done a solo record in '82 [*Pictures at Eleven*], and this must have been his second album by then [*The Principle of Moments*]. He was all over America in '83, just as much as a band like us or Quiet Riot. But I liked the Plant one, because it was him on his own. It was all about *him*. He didn't have the, "Oh, I've got to get shots of the drummer!" It doesn't matter who the drummer is on a Robert Plant record. You don't have to do that "balancing act" that you do with a band, where a guitarist goes, "I should be on when it's a solo" and all this bullshit.

It should be about the video, and the director has a much easier job with a solo artist than he does with a band. Because if you take the David Bowie/

Mallet ones, like "China Girl," all you've really got is Bowie up against a wall, the girl with the long finger nails, Bowie laying on the beach mimicking that shot from *From Here to Eternity*. But it's all about Bowie—*Bowie, Bowie, Bowie.* There's no shots of Stevie Ray Vaughan, Earl Slick, or whoever. It's all about Bowie. They're the ones that are probably a director's dream. With a band like us, it's probably a director's nightmare. But that's what I meant about the Plant one. It was a breath of fresh air.

— *Heart* —

ANN WILSON: ["What About Love"] was the first one we did in England. We didn't know what we were getting ourselves into. We were pretty naïve about it. It's this huge, big-budget video shoot that Capitol had planned. David Mallet was the director. They had all these sets. Nancy and Howard Leese had to go up this spiral staircase, and when they got up at the top, they set it on fire. It was burning from the bottom ... and they were up there with their guitars! They had to rely on the fact that, just when the fire got to them, that the stagehands would put it out. They got the shot. And they had me dressed up as a welder, in this impossible outfit, with this tiny corseted waist and this big welder thing going on.

All sorts of strange twists and turns of plot, like I was in the back of a bus reading *Gone with the Wind*, with a big tear rolling down my cheek. [Laughs] And they put the first extensions on our heads that we ever had. Suddenly, one day we had hair down to our waist, where the day before it had been to our shoulders. And it was purple and blue. It was pretty fun. It was like playing "hyper-dress up." It was very scary hours. I think the shoot took a couple of days, and by about 24 hours in, I was starting to get really, really scared, just by how tired I was and how the pressure didn't stop. They were like, "Well, we're holding your close-ups until the end," so you're at your most tired, emotional, and strung-out. "And now ... we shoot your close-ups!" That was the unfairness of a rock video shoot.

I believe we did ["Never"] in L.A., and it was probably Marty Callner. The same type of thing—really huge budget. Lots of different scene set-ups, really outrageous, outlandish ones. I think on that one, they had Nancy jumping off a cliff with her guitar on. And, of course, it was Nancy, because she's the blonde, really pretty one, so they had her do all the physical stunts. I'll never forget, even though they had her in a safety harness under her clothes, I did not like what it looked like to see her jumping off a cliff. I burst into tears, and I had to run off the set, because it bothered me so much. They had to go, "OK, hold it. The other sister is out of control." But they got the shot. It was a stupid idea, and it hit the cutting room floor. But that's just to illustrate what it was like. Nothing was too outrageous; nothing was too trite or silly. They had to try it.

["These Dreams"] was a good one. Jeff Stein was the director, and we did that in L.A. That one I thought was pretty well done. It had a more creative look to it, a more gentle look to it. They created this set that was like another world. It was like a magical land somewhere far away, that was perfect in every way and colorful. And Nancy was wandering, strolling, singing. Of course, there were extensions down to our knees by then, and we could never get enough volume in our hair. *The corsets were tighter than ever.*

— Bon Jovi —

FRANKIE SULLIVAN: Bon Jovi always did great videos. Again, most of his were based around the band, being a rock n' roll band and performances. I saw "Wanted Dead or Alive" the other night on TV, and watching it this many years later, I realized it's a story about a rock n' roll band that was having a hard time. And when you look at it, you can see it. Jon's really tired, and they've been out there pounding it, doing what rock n' roll bands do on the road.

— Dire Straits —

STEVE BARRON: I was doing quite a lot of post-production videos. I was working at a company in London. They had what was an early CGI computer graphics machine called the Bosch FGS-4000. It was a big machine that could generate these three-dimensional graphics. It was doing quite a lot of big logos for corporations like IBM. I'd keep walking past this guy, Ian Pearson, who was working away on these logos, and said, "Could you create characters out of these lumps and blocks?" And he's like, "Yeah. There's nothing you can't do." At the same time, Warners was saying, "We've got this track, 'Money for Nothing.' But Mark Knopfler hates videos. Would you want to do something with it? But he might be resistant to it, because he doesn't want to do anything other than see the band playing. It's all about the music."

So I took the effects of that FGS-4000 machine and another machine called Paintbox, which I was starting to see, which painted the images. And I thought, "Well, instead of just having the band directly playing, you'd have them 'painted' as well." The irony of all this is that these two characters in this song are slagging off MTV. There's a layer of irony I can put on it by having them be part of television, having them be the pixels that make up television. I thought, "There's a good motivation. Maybe I can sell that to Mark." But I had nothing to show him. I couldn't show him an IBM logo. He'd be like, *"Whatever."*

So I flew to Budapest to do the live part of the shoot, and I think in retrospect, Warners had told them that that was all they were doing. "Oh, there's this guy flying over to do this live thing." And they pushed it into my hands to tell him over dinner that actually what I wanted to do was completely mess with the live performance, and create these two characters! So I pitched it to him over dinner, and I remember a sort of sinking feeling, as I pitched him something that had never been done before, that I had nothing to show him what it would be like. It was obviously in his power in the end. And, in the end, there was actually someone else at the table—his girlfriend at the time—and she had been watching a lot of MTV. I pitched on about how [MTV] needs a real "refresh," and how this would be the way to do it. And she was like, "You're right. It's getting really stuck." So, anyway, it prevented the "no" from Mark ... but it didn't get a "yes" either. Because it got neither, I just took the footage back and began the process of the concept. So out of that, we did those characters.

Madonna

ALAN HUNTER: If you wanted to talk about style and fashion, you'd point to Madonna solely, singularly, as the head of that. I'm not saying that young girls adopted fashion quicker or more heartily than boys did back then, but certainly, little girls watching MTV were more apt to go to the store and either find or demand some trendy fashion they saw Madonna wearing. There's no doubt that the new wave invasion from the U.K. influenced people's style of dress. They started wearing different kinds of shirts and maybe putting more gel in their hair. The mohawk didn't come from "Joe Dirt rocker" as much as it did from the new wave people.

Madonna certainly made MTV more about trends, lifestyle trends. Her clothing was one factor of it, the style of her videos, after "Lucky Star," which was her against a white backdrop, and her bangly, jangly clothes, which were a totally big trend in fashion. After people saw Madonna with all of her bangles, bobbles, and wraps, all the little girls were dressing totally like her, with the scarves and the bandana look. But that video was so simple. After that, she got a lot more conceptual with stories.

She was absolutely at the top of the heap, when it comes to setting trends—both fashion and style. And there's no doubt that she helped motivate "the strong female" in the rock n' roll business. Short of the Joan Jetts of the world, who were sticking it in the eye of the punk world, Madonna said, "You can be at the top of the *entire* heap, not just as a female." She made a lot of little girls feel like they could be empowered. She sat with Mark Goodman in an interview a year or two later and talked how she was looking for her new "boy toy," so she was in charge.

EDDIE MONEY: She had a big influence on kids and fashion. The girls started wearing that real "moppy look," with the big bows and very '80s. But to tell you the truth, I was never really a Madonna fan. I never thought she was much of a vocalist, but she was definitely an entertainer. She knew what she was doing.

DEBORA IYALL: She fascinated me. And her fashion caught on almost immediately. When "Lucky Star" came out, suddenly, everybody had the cut-off leggings, the wrestler boots, the short skirt over the leggings, and the hair tied up however she did it. That really influenced fashion. And I was attracted to it. It was simple. It was her dancing with two people. It was amazingly effective for how simple the shoot probably was. But she was also very charismatic and compelling, and the camera knew how to get in there. And they lit her to love her skin. I thought it was kind of embarrassing, though, when I saw the video for "Like a Virgin," of her in Venice, writhing around on the gondola. I was just embarrassed for her. [Laughs] But what do I know? And I liked "Borderline," because I was really attracted to the graffiti community, and it seemed like she was hanging out in the Bronx and being kind of a homegirl. I thought, "Well, that's kind of interesting. In one video, she's a dancer, and then in this one, she's a homegirl ... *OK.*"

STEVE BARRON: I did Madonna's first video as well ["Burning Up"]. She was a new artist that Warners were very excited about. I also remember it was one of the tracks I was not too fond of. I really liked some of her other songs, like "Borderline," and over the years, tons of other tracks. "Burning Up" didn't inspire me visually.

We nearly killed her, on her first video, because we had a cherry picker, looking down at her on a lake. We weren't quite over the top of her, and I asked them to push out the arms so we could be over her. As we reached over her head from 50 feet—with 22 tons of metal—I looked back and saw as we were extending, the back wheels of the crane had lifted off the ground, and we were totally on the tipping point. And the guy hadn't even noticed. So I said, *"Stop!"* He stopped and did the little bounce thing, and we were going to come down on her. She would have totally been dead. We just held our breath, and I said, *"Take it back. Take it back."* If he would have pressed the button the wrong way—one more inch—we would have been down on her. We just moved it back inch by inch, until the wheels sat back down on the ground, and I said, "Alright ... we do that shot another way!"

I remember her being a real character. I met with her in this squat in Manhattan, before we started filming. She was doing all this sort of, almost sort of "tease-y type talking," with her head on the side. That's where I got her to "roll around on the ground sort of thing," with her head down on angles, because our first meeting was a bit like that.

STEWART COPELAND: I remember having great respect for her, because she was around the "Studio 54 days," and she was a scrubber, without much going for her. But just through tenacity and strength of will, she forced herself onto the world and had a big career. And I have enormous respect for her, because she wasn't drop-dead gorgeous by any means—she wasn't even that great a singer—but she just had a mind like a rock. We were all happy to see she used her force of will to succeed. Other girls were prettier, other girls were better singers ... *other girls were actually guys,* but Madonna had none of that going for her. She was just a scrubber who was determined to conquer the world.

MIKE RENO: Sexy. *Very desirable.* I have a funny little story. I was in the studio cutting a track, I think on my second album. And there was someone on the phone. I could see through the glass. So, finally, I stopped singing, and I said, "How come you guys were on the phone for like the last half an hour?" And they said, somebody is calling for you, but you're busy." And I said, "Well, who is it?" And they said, *"Madonna."* I thought it was kind of curious, because she hadn't had an album out yet. It probably could have been her. Maybe I was somebody she looked up to, I don't know. She came out with her bunch of songs, and I thought, "Wow!" She kind of reminded me of a "New York girl," all bundled up, and you couldn't tell if she had clean clothes or dirty clothes or if they were from the night before. But it worked for her. She was something to watch. Some of the stuff was a little light, but you know, it doesn't mean I have to love it. I loved what she was doing. She definitely changed the way things were done. When that camera was on, she knew she was working, that's for sure.

ALAN HUNTER: I remember distinctly, about '83, we'd be sitting around the green room, shooting the shit, and a producer would come in and say, "Someone has to go interview this 'Madonna person' tonight at the Limelight." Before we all got to know an artist or before they were big, it was like,

"Oh crap, I've got dinner tonight." You know, everybody running not to have to go do the interview, unless we had a desire for that particular music or something. I didn't know her very well, and before I could say, "No," Martha and Mark had already said, "No." They had something else to do, so I got the gig. *Lucky me.*

I remember it was really hectic. The club was hopping. The Limelight was the best dance club in town. I had kind of a long day as I remember, and I didn't get as much chance as I would have liked to have to bone up on her. She was relatively new, so there wasn't this massive history. It's not like you're going to interview Pete Townshend, y'know? So I didn't have a whole lot of prep. I then had the producer yelling in my ear. We were backstage, but it was still pretty loud. She was trying to prep me by yelling, "She just did this, and her song is that." "Borderline" was the tune. So I just had to wing it.

Again, when you were interviewing a new artist, it was a little easier to say, "Well, tell me about yourself." The world doesn't know you quite yet. I was very green at the time still. Interviewing people was definitely a chore for me, because I didn't have quite the chops. I wasn't a journalist. I was a music lover, so I tried my best. But we got along great. She was very accommodating and accessible, but cool. You could tell that she had a "force" going, and she was not going to suffer fools easily. And she had a real focus. She didn't have a lot of idle chit-chat in between takes.

I remember standing there waiting to get the camera rolling, and that was always the worst part, when the camera guys had to load in a tape. You're totally ready, and the artist is sitting right there, anxious to go on. And you're like, "OK guys ... *got the tape yet?*" You're trying not to make small talk, and you're trying not to ask any of the questions you're going to ask. But she was sweet. She was certainly not as "coiffed" as she became later. An artist starts off with the clothes that they can grab, and the hairstyle is not quite what it will turn out to be. I remember she could probably use a little "eyebrow plucking."

BOB PITTMAN: Madonna—the same thing as Michael Jackson—she has to go down in history as one of the first real video performers. She put on *a show* and always put on a show. Don Ohlmeyer used to be the head of programming at NBC, a legendary sports programming guy, retired now.

Don was at RJR and Nabisco, and ran the agency that did all the buys for it. So we did the [1984] Video Music Awards show together. Don was in there directing the creative, because he himself was a director and a fantastic creative guy.

And I can remember that Madonna was almost an unknown artist. We had put her on, and she jumped out of a wedding cake in rehearsal, and her top came off. And at that time, you go, "My God ... *her top came off!*" And you realize, probably, she took her top off. But she had the sense of how you create an event. And did it again and again. I remember Don going, "Oh my God, *who is this girl?* Where did she come from?" And what we were looking at is the first of these people that really knew how to use the medium.

BOOTSY COLLINS: Now this girl was just what the doctor ordered for MTV. She did for MTV what Elvis did for rock n' roll. It is something about her that is simply sex-rated, but at the same time, the kids got away with watching it, and they all love her rebellious ways. Who wouldn't? She knew how to get what she wanted, and she did.

JELLO BIAFRA: One woman I was close to said she liked Madonna because she brought back pretty bras and vintage lingerie. I couldn't disagree with that one.

ANN WILSON: *She dominated.* When she came along, she was a real actress. Maybe she didn't succeed in movies as an actress, but in rock videos, she was queen. And she knew how to talk to the camera. God, her fashion sense, she could dance—she did it all. She was like a "twelve-trick pony." She was amazing.

TONI BASIL: Fabulous. But she was a dancer. And she's a drummer, which I think is very interesting. It contributed a lot to her dancing, her rhythm.

JOHN OATES: I remember having an argument with Madonna a few years later. We did a conference somewhere. We were both on a panel, and the subject of music videos came up, and I said, "I was never interested in being an actor. I always wanted to be a musician." For me, videos were just a means to an end, to expose the music. And she really objected to it strongly and said, "Well, you're wrong. You just don't get it. *The video itself is a medium. It's a new medium. It's a whole new thing.*" And I understood exactly what she was saying, because video really was part and parcel of what she was. It became just as important a component of her career, or her art, for that matter. But for us, who had been around for 15 years before she made her first record, we thought differently. She really embraced it and used it for its fuller potential.

LITA FORD: She had some beautiful videos. Really well-thought-out. Every one was so different. You never knew what to expect from Madonna. The earlier videos, they're really different. I mean, all of a sudden, she changed. There was a huge change in her life, where she became thin and very muscular, and her whole body, everything changed about her. But her earlier videos ... sometimes the simplicity of a video is better than spending tons and tons of money and making it really complicated. And sometimes, it doesn't always turn out that great.

But if you can take the simplicity of, say for instance, Whitney Houston's "I Will Always Love You" video, where she just sits on a chair and sings the song, and that's it. It's magic. It's simple. It shows the beauty of the song and herself. I think Madonna could do the same thing. She didn't need all this stuff buzzing around her. But back then, I think she was doing the appropriate thing for the time, because maybe she was a little weight conscious or whatever. Which women do get. I know I do. If I put on two pounds, I'm like, "Oh my God, I've put on two pounds! Give me a sweat-shirt and cover it up!" But the videos themselves were great. They're simple, basic, great videos.

GEDDY LEE: Madonna is very smart. She really understood her opportunity. And I think she maximized those moments to become this chameleon, image-wise. She really got it. She really understood what MTV could do for her and came up with these ever-changing visual styles that had a tremendous impact. Probably the biggest factor in her success was the way she was able to manipulate her image successfully. Many people tried, but she was really good at it. She hired the right people, and she was right on top of it.

PHIL COLLEN: With Madonna, she realized she could create "Madonna," and that's really what she did. She said, "OK ... I can sit in this pool of mediocrity"—because there were a lot of artists out there that were doing her thing—"Or I can take this whole image thing and *really* go for it." And you saw her image change, and also, musically. It all changed at the same time. That was really cool on her part. I think she just changed the whole thing around. She was like, "I can create an image. I can create an iconic character." Which she really did. If you look at the early videos ... like any artist, they're still trying to struggle to find who they are, their identity. But I think especially in Madonna's case, she actually saw it as an opportunity to totally change—to do a 180—and go somewhere completely different. It was just a great, calculated move on her part. She saw what she could actually create and become.

KATHY VALENTINE: Madonna is really the one who took MTV and ran with it. I think MTV created her. I mean, there had to be *something* there to create. I don't think there had been a woman ... maybe her and Cyndi Lauper—a single, focal point woman. It's easier for an audience to glom onto a single focal point like that. When I think of Madonna, still what pops into my mind is the "Borderline" images.

ORAN "JUICE" JONES: Madonna was "the Lady Gaga" of that time. Lady Gaga is Madonna right now. It was strange at first for me ... see, I didn't realize that white people could get down like that. [Laughs] I mean, I knew they had soul, they had rhythm, but I didn't really think they could just let it all out. They could just get loose with it. I'm going to tell you something strange. It might not make sense—it still doesn't make sense to me, even now—but for some reason, when I saw Madonna, I realized that we're all connected. I don't know why; it just dawned on me. Black, white, there ain't no difference. We're all connected. We're all the same people. She just had a swagger with her that was like a breath of fresh air. I really didn't identify with the music, but what I did identify with was her willingness to express herself *her way.* And uncompromised. No guard, just, "This is me. This what I do. Love it." That fearlessness, that desire to bare all—tastefully—I would hope that all artists will embrace that.

DAVE MARSH: Madonna was, by far, the most controversial thing on TV at that time. I don't even think there was a second place. And she played that for all it was worth and did a great job of it. She made, in many ways, very interesting videos. In my own life, the most important thing that MTV did for me was Tipper Gore [head of the 'Parents Music Resource Center'] had come out in favor of "Papa Don't Preach," so naturally, I was feeling exactly the opposite. And my kids said to me, "You know … you don't understand 'Papa Don't Preach.' You don't understand this 'I'm keeping my baby' thing. *You need to see the video.*" And in the video, it's revealed that "I'm keeping my baby" means I'm keeping my boyfriend, not that I'm not going to have an abortion, is what Tipper and company thought. And that kind of dialogue between parents and children, I was very lucky to have kids who would think it was worthwhile saying it to me and would feel free to. And I'm not bragging about my parenting; I'm bragging about my kids. They had a lot of guts.

I can remember it was a real eye-opener for me, what she did with that video. Because she just turned the thing around. I don't know whether she knew she was going to get the anti-abortion crowd on her side and then turn around and smack them in the chops, or whether it sort of came up when the video opportunity presented itself. That was a really important video. Madonna's videos were very, very good. They dealt with the race issue, they dealt with the sex issue, and they dealt with them very forcefully and not in any terms of terribly conventional thinking. And I think, probably, they were, if not a liberating, at least a *freeing* force. So those I remember as being important. I don't remember very many other important videos … except that it was important that I leave the room, usually.

RICK SPRINGFIELD: I actually stopped watching TV by that point. [Laughs] I know Madonna was really pushing the same thing Prince was— the outrageous thing, trying to shock people. But I don't really have a big awareness of that stuff. I was more into the bands.

TODD RUNDGREN: *Yuck.* [Laughs] Almost every Madonna video to me is, like, "Yuck." It goes along with my opinion of the music.

MARTHA DAVIS: The girl knows how to work it. She's definitely one of those people that will study, whether it's going to be Marilyn Monroe or whatever, to get the concepts going. And then she plays them off beautifully. David Fincher worked with her after he worked with me, and did some wonderful stuff with her. But it's an interesting thing. I think that transition between more of an entertainer than just pure artist, she probably spearheaded that, in a huge way. She's absolutely great and wonderful, but I don't think of her as the singer/songwriter. I think of her as more of the consummate entertainer, even though I know she writes from time to time. Cyndi Lauper I don't think took it to the stadium level. I mean, she was huge, but there was something about Madonna that was very much purposeful and planned, and the next step was planned, and the next step. Each step was bigger. I think she had a very grand plan from the beginning.

PETE ANGELUS: You have to give Madonna credit where credit is due. She has done an incredible job in the music business. And she's an incredible business woman.

FEE WAYBILL: She was very hip, very cool, very cutting-edge. She probably pushed the envelope more than anybody, which made MTV a little bit hipper, and not quite so "family." She definitely pushed it right to the max.

Videos: Pop Rock

— The Buggles —

GEOFF DOWNES: I think [the filming of "Video Killed the Radio Star"] was September of 1979, just before the single was released. We felt at the time that the nature of the song and title of the song, that the stops were pulled out to try and pull off something quite original. We got together with director Russell Mulcahy, and the rest is history. I think he had a wacky idea of how he wanted to make the video, and he was using a lot of the lyrical content—the band in studios, girly vocals, and that kind of thing. It was almost a parallel of what went on in the lyrics. I think it was all done in a day. You'd spend six months making an album, and then you'd spend a day on the video. At the time, no one really knew the impact of videos' connection to records. Radio was still very strong at the time. No one ever thought that radio would really be usurped. So I think you could do these promotional videos later in the day, kind of a postscript to making the album. We had the album, *The Age of Plastic*, and that's how we saw the band, a product of a technological generation. So the idea of the plastic, the man-made fibers, was very much included in the nature of what we were trying to provide.

— The Human League —

STEVE BARRON: "Don't You Want Me?" I remember Virgin Records came along and said, "This is a really strong band. We want to do something a bit stronger than your average video." And they gave us $25,000 or something like that. I said, "If we could get that budget, then we could use 35-millimeter." Everything before that had been done either on video or 16-millimeter, because 35 was unaffordable in terms of the camera size, the film stock, the developing process. So we got 35-millimeter and wanted to do "a film within a film." I was also very influenced by that François Truffaut film, *Day for Night*. I'd been watching it, and I fell in love with Jacqueline Bisset, who was an actress in that. So I was a bit obsessed with that film at the time and thought, "We've got 35-millimeter. Let's do a film within a film, like the Truffaut film." And then I thought, "Wait a minute ... it's a music video. We're trying to push things further. *Let's do a film within a film within a film!*" So even in the cutting room is a set.

— *Tommy Tutone* —

TOMMY TUTONE: ["867-5309"] was a great time. The director had the whole crew from the movie *Eraserhead*. They thought that we were funny naturally. My partner and I were characters of our own right. He was very preppie, and I was kind of a Midwest guy. And they said, "We're going to make the most of it." If you watch our other video, "Which Man Are You," we wrote that together about our contrasts and made a story out of us. I was the kind of guy that was really shy—except when I was singing—and my partner was pretty urbane and from New York. We made three videos for twenty grand or something ridiculous, just churned them on out. Making records was really boring, and this was pretty effortless and a great experience.

That's still a scene [where Tommy is a "peeping tom" and gets busted] that I was really embarrassed by. That look on my face is just ... my mom would have laughed at that! Biting my cheek or something. "Get in there and look wistfully," and I didn't know what to do. I think that was the first take. I thought I looked really dumb there, but I guess it had its charm. I liked the way when I turned around after I got the number. I thought that was pretty funny, my double-take. I thought that was good acting. We did that at Perkins Palace in Pasadena, and fortunately, we had already played there a couple of times. It was an old theater. They said, "You're going to play it three times through. We're going to be out here the first time, up close the second time, and the third time, we have these things going around in circles around you. And that's it." We went on through it, and we had a natural interaction on stage. We were just ourselves.

— *The Romantics* —

WALLY PALMAR: "What I Like About You" was in the top 20, going into the top 10 in Germany and the Netherlands. They had pictures but no footage, so they sent a film crew from the Netherlands to film us. We were doing a show in L.A., I believe it was at the Whisky, and we were doing a soundcheck. They filmed us during that soundcheck, two songs—"What I Like About You" and "When I Look in Your Eyes." We're talking 1980, so at this point, there still is no MTV. We were surprised that they were sending a film crew over from the Netherlands to film us. We more or less dressed up in what we were going to wear later that night. They set up maybe two cameras, and it was a straight-ahead performance video shoot. A very simple, straight-ahead cut. No talking, no acting, no nothing—being yourself, performing the song. And that's it.

Once again, ["Talking in Your Sleep"] was climbing the charts at a pretty decent speed back then. That was the last song recorded for the album *In Heat*. All we had was a backtrack, the instrumental part of the song. And we realized it was too good a track to leave unfinished. So everybody put their heads together, and in a couple days, we finished up the song melodically and lyrically. We were out touring, and we needed a video clip, so they set it up, where we filmed it in Detroit. I think we were coming in to play Detroit, so we got in a day or two ahead of time, on a soundstage, very early in the morning. We did our performance piece, and then there was also the added attraction of having a lot of girls in their "sleeping attire" in the video. Starting to film that 8:00 in the morning is not really "rock n' roll hours," but it was interesting, and in itself, was very effective.

— Rick Springfield —

RICK SPRINGFIELD: I didn't really know why we were doing that [filming a video for "Jessie's Girl"]. There was talk that there was this channel that was starting to get some notice, MTV. And RCA gave me 1,500 bucks or something to just do the video. I didn't really know what would happen with it. I storyboarded it, and then we just shot it "guerilla warfare style"—y'know, without getting permits and shooting it in Hollywood alleyways until cops came. It was really fun, and once it started getting played, everyone started seeing the value of it. It certainly heightened your identity. [The scene when Rick smashes a bathroom mirror with his guitar] was my idea. Actually, that was our big expense, the 24 mirrors I broke.

SERGEANT BLOTTO: I love Rick Springfield! I was just singing "Jessie's Girl" the other day. He was great. Those videos ... I can't say I ever watched him on *General Hospital*, so I didn't know him as an actor. But he certainly was a cute boy, and he made the most of it. *And he rocked.* "Jessie's Girl" was one of the keys, one of the "door-openers."

RICK SPRINGFIELD: ["Don't Talk to Strangers"] was kind of the first big-budget one. It wasn't actually *that* big, but we had the money to rent cop cars and rent out a motel. It was shot in one day and night. It was never an extended shoot. You felt like you were kind of on the cutting-edge of something new and wonderful, and it felt kind of "movie-esque," to a degree. At this point, it was more kind of the director's vision than mine. I still wanted a performance video, which it was, but there was a lot of people trying to make complete stories out of three-minute pop songs, which sometimes didn't work. I think they were trying to "tart it up" a bit, because they had some extra money, and we could afford a breakaway window [in reference to a scene where Rick jumps through a window]. At that point, I think they were still just trying to interpret the song pretty literally.

["Affair of the Heart"] was the first video that I really thought looked cool. The guy, Doug Dowdle, who became a good friend of mine, he shot the next three or four videos of mine, but "Affair of the Heart" was the first one. And it was the first one where we had an actual preproduction meeting, and they sat and laid out what they thought of doing and talked about it. More money was being put into it, and I was really happy with the final result of that one.

["Love Somebody"] was another Doug Dowdle one. I look at that one and cringe a bit. They were starting to get really into the over-the-top stuff now. Everyone was really high on the videos and throwing the kitchen sink in. We were all starting to get a bit carried away with what we thought the power of it was and what we could get away with. That one really had absolutely nothing to do with the song. Now, I would have shot it completely differently, because "Love Somebody" was one of my favorite songs of the hits I've had. And it was a tougher song, and we kind of tarted it up with this weird tribal/goddess thing. I think we were starting to lose our mind at that point.

— Toto —

STEVE BARRON: "Rosanna" was one of the first sort of "dance videos" that I did. And I was really lucky. Kenny Ortega choreographed that. He found a space and brought this dancer [Cynthia Rhodes] in to show me, and she was just great. We said, "She'd be perfect for 'Rosanna.' We'll get her doing a *West Side Story* thing, spinning and twisting through." Actually, off of that video—and this happened a bit during that period—that girl was cast as the lead in *Staying Alive*, the follow-up to *Saturday Night Fever*. Stallone was directing it, saw that video, and said, "Unless that girl is a mute, she's in *Staying Alive*!"

Memories of ["Africa"]—there was a great map painter, the guy who painted in the old-fashioned way, used to put glass in front of the camera, and you'd paint a part of the scenery on the glass, directly in front of the camera. In "Billie Jean," we couldn't afford to build above the first story of the street, so the second story was done by a guy named Eric ... I can't remember his last name. A really good paint artist. The second story was put in there, and doing that, I think I was doing Toto three weeks later. I thought, "It would be lovely to have a pile of books bigger than one can do, so let's do a 'glass shot painting.'"

— Survivor —

FRANKIE SULLIVAN: [Sylvester Stallone] was—and still is—really good friends with the president of our record company [Tony Scotti]. Stallone was pretty much done with *Rocky III*. Where we entered the picture was he wanted something a little bit different, and [Scotti] was very business smart, and saw this as an opportunity. He said, "I have a young band. Maybe you'd be interested in seeing what they would come up with. I can put you in touch with them, and you guys could talk. Maybe they could hit the mark or come up with something you like." That's really where it started.

My stories with [Stallone] went back to *Rocky III*, because when we put the music to the film, he wasn't happy with what was going on. There really wasn't a lot of rock bands doing soundtracks back then. Sly was a guy that really liked a lot of balls and punch. He liked the demo version a lot. He liked the rawness of it. I got a call, and he said, "Will you come out here?"

He was struggling with what they were doing, because they were sticking to a standard. By then, you'd get into a soundstage, and they'd have a big screen with two VU meters, and they'd play it really safe, because they don't want the stuff to get printed on the film, and then it ends up in the theater, and it's all distorted. Sly wanted that song *slamming*.

So I was there for about two weeks. I stayed with him. He was very cool, very easy to work with. He put me in the hot seat. That was a wake-up call, because I was 24 years old, and Donny Zimmerman, who's won like 22 Oscars, was sitting in the driver's seat, and Sly was like, "This isn't it. *I want more balls!*" I said, "Well, we do things differently. These guys like to keep it in the black. We like to ride it up into the red, the VU meters. The more the better. You get the tape compression, you get that low end, you get the drums, [and] everything kind of pops out. And if you get it to the right sweet spot, it gets huge." And he says, "Sit down there." He had the guy get up. He was a big star and had a lot of power, so they're not going to argue with him. He said, "Just do what you do. Pretend they're not here. Whatever you did when you did the demo and mixed it, do it here." I looked at the VU meters and did what I would do if we were mixing a record. He said, "Now we're getting there." We finally got to a point, and he said, "Print it." They were arguing with him, but he'd just say, "Hey, who's movie is this?" They hushed up pretty quick.

He played the whole four minute and 58 seconds of the song at the beginning of the film, so that in itself was a video to me. That was my favorite video version. He did that little montage that he wrote, where he did all those commercials for American Express. If you watch the beginning of *Rocky III*, you'll notice that. To me, we had a "60-million-dollar video" out there, and we had a guy at the time who was just a *huge* Hollywood star. He was out there promoting the film and loved the tune, so he was promoting the tune. It was like a double whammy. Our version of the video, I was never really a big fan of it. There are parts that are cool, and there are parts where we're walking around the streets of Chinatown in San Francisco, that I look at, and say, "That doesn't really make much sense to me."

FRANK STALLONE: My brother had used that phrase in the movie. It's just a great record, the perfect record. Again, *a shit video*. My video ["Far from Over"] is better than that video! I said, "Frankie, you and Dave look like you have a stick up your ass walking down the street. It's the worst video I've ever seen! Your record was bigger than mine, you had a bigger budget ... and your video *really* sucks."

FRANKIE SULLIVAN: I had a couple of conversations with [Sylvester Stallone], but never about that [writing a song for *Rocky IV*]. Tony kind of put that together. He said, "You've got to have a song in this film. Why not?" I remember thinking to myself, "Well ... why wouldn't we? It would only make sense." But then coming up with the song, that was the hard part, because you don't want to rewrite "Eye of the Tiger." You've got to write something new. My favorite song on that soundtrack was not ours. I thought Robert Tepper did a phenomenal job with "No Easy Way Out." ["Burning Heart"] was fun. We did it where they filmed the fight scenes. Sly was going to come down that day, but he didn't make it. Which is not a diss. He was like that, because he was really busy at the time. We just got up on the stage and performed. Nobody's acting a part or playing a role. There's no script to follow. They're just filming the band performing the song.

— *Billy Joel* —

NINA BLACKWOOD: I really liked the video for "Pressure," maybe because I could relate to the whole concept, both the song and the video itself. I was living in New York at the time, and New York is pressure-filled. I thought it was clever. A lot of his other videos, it seemed his persona was a flashback to early '60s and the groups that inspired him. And this one was different. It probably is my favorite of his videos. It has elements of his early music, that Beatles-esque melody that's running through it. And then he also has the "Russian thing" [a Russian-sounding piece of music]. I thought the video went along with that very well, because sometimes, these concept videos, you look at them, and go, *"What the hell?* It has nothing to do with the song!" And this one did. I think it's an example of perfect meshing of video to song.

— Men at Work —

COLIN HAY: The videos that we did were very inexpensive. I think "Who Can It Be Now?" cost $5,000. It was shot by two guys, primarily John Whitteron and Tony Stevens. They were two guys who were responsible for a lot of the other videos that we did. It was a case really of finding a good location and coming up with a couple of ideas that would be interesting. Primarily, Greg Ham and myself came up with what we would shoot, in collaboration with John and Tony. We never went to the cops and got permission or anything like that. We just went in, shot, and got out of there as quickly as we could, if we weren't supposed to be somewhere.

"Down Under," we had to fight for another $1,000 from the record label. That one cost $6,000. The great thing about that I think was just finding the sand mine at Cronulla, which was a suburb of Sydney, that great location at the end of the video, that we use to come over the top of the hill. I think that was a beautiful shot, that clip, which is a strong visual and really worth doing. It was kind of an inspired location to find, that sand mine.

ALAN HUNTER: Certainly, Men at Work were a novelty band. I interviewed Colin Hay and don't remember any of the other members. He was "the guy." I think I did interview them, because I remember asking about Vegemite. That was the only pertinent question, "What is Vegemite?" I think all of America learned a little bit more about them and how nasty Vegemite was. Again, I think the video helped those images. The video helped maintain a sort of frivolous image. They were all dancing around in little tennis shoes and hopping around, and he was such a funny character on camera. Mugging the camera and being lighthearted. That was probably what undercut some of the real good songwriting that was going on.

COLIN HAY: The young kid we found to play "Johnny" [in "Be Good Johnny"] was great. I think more than anything, our videos had our personality to them. Because, as I said, we didn't have any money for effects or fancy locations or extra stuff. It was just very much, "OK, here's the band, and here's a few ideas." It was pretty much just do everything ourselves, because that's all we really had at our disposal. It was an enormous amount of fun doing them. We really enjoyed putting them together.

["Overkill"] was more introspective. That was around a place I lived, called St. Kilda. There were a couple of different techniques that the cinematographer used and employed in that video. And I think it featured me a lot, that clip. It was really the start of fracturing within the band. During the last tour of the States, it was not a band that had a lot of unity or soul in it. It was probably the start of the end, and even visually ... I mean, you can't really see it, but from my memory, there was a tinge of sadness involved with that, because you could almost see what was going to happen in the next couple of years.

"It's a Mistake" was a great video. That involved really cool claymation. There was a huge fire that happened then, Ash Wednesday, which was a horrible bush fire. We actually used that tragedy—a few days after the fires had burnt out—as a location for shooting the stuff, which was to simulate a warzone, which was pretty tragic for the people involved, but an opportunity for us to shoot a video that looked pretty authentic.

— Hall and Oates —

DARYL HALL: The first videos we did, we didn't have a clue of what people wanted or what to do. We just stood in front of curtains and jumped around. I felt like Sid Caesar in *Your Show of Shows* or something back in the '50s. It was an era that nobody knew what they were doing. They didn't even know where to find these "video directors," so they would get people who were sort of underlings in the commercial business. People who had no track record at all. They had a camera or two, threw some lights up, they put the song on, and we'd jump around a few times, and then they edited it together. That was early video. And then it went into the "auteur state," where everybody thought they were Cecil B. Demille, and went into these outrageously over-extravagant, expensive videos, that had very little to do with the music. I always tried to stay out of that world as much as I could, and I—to some degree—had a running battle with what was going on at the time. I'm a purist.

JOHN OATES: What happened was, here again, we were asked, "Hey, MTV needs stuff. Content. And we want you to make a video." So, basically, our first reaction was, *"What's a video?"* Because we didn't really know what to do. There was no direction really. It was just, "Play the song, lip-synch the song, and perform it." Both those videos ["Private Eyes" and "You Make My Dreams"] were shot at SIR on Fourth Street, I believe, and we were in there rehearsing for our tour. It was the final day and our final rehearsal. I think it was at least midnight, if not even later. The bus was out front, idling, ready to go, and the trucks were being loaded with our equipment.

Some guys came in and hung black drapery behind us, and we put on these stupid "private eye" trench coats and fedoras. They brought in the cameras, and we basically mimed the video. That was the video. It didn't take very long. We didn't know what we were doing, and just goofed around. And the moment we were done, we took the clothes off, got on the bus, and went on tour. It's funny, if you look at the Rolling Stones video from that exact same time ["Start Me Up"], they did *exactly* what we did. They put up a black curtain and jumped around in front of the camera. They probably did the same thing we did because no one was really thinking about anything else at the time.

The "Maneater" video was further along. It was shot in L.A., with much higher production values, shot on a soundstage. We had a live leopard. [Laughs] In L.A., you had the infrastructure for the movie, film, and television business, so you had better camera, better lighting, better facilities. So that's where the videos are starting to get a little more elaborate.

DARYL HALL: ["One on One"] was a Mick Haggerty video. Mick was living in New York. We were all living in New York. He was a pretty good friend of mine. And I just wanted to do a video that really ... I was trying to get close to reality with it. I lived across the street from Village Cigars on Seventh Avenue, and we started the video right there and moved up the road, to Times Square. It was a real "New York video." We tried at least to describe the lyrics visually and stick close to the idea of the song, the mood of the song. Which I think Mick was pretty good at.

JOHN OATES: ["Out of Touch"] was the end of us going crazy with videos and budgets. You have to remember, in the context of the time, we were having huge hit records, one after the other. The record company was basically happy to do whatever we wanted. We shot that in New York, out in Queens. Here again, that was the time where videos were becoming "more and more is better." The mid-'80s, it's kind of like Gordon Gekko. "Greed is good." [Laughs] The guy who dies with the most toys wins, y'know? I just remember Daryl and I being sealed into this giant drum at about 3:00 in the morning, looking at each other, and going, "What the hell are we doing? How did it come to *this?!*"

— *The Go-Go's* —

JOHN DOE: [The Go-Go's] were charming. They were adorable. Nobody in L.A. ever felt like they were selling out, because the whole concept of them is just really poppy. They were pretty inventive, I think.

MARTHA DAVIS: We used to rehearse together in the same room, under the Pussycat Theater on Hollywood Boulevard, in a place called the Masque, which was a famous punk rock place. They rehearsed on one side of the room, and we rehearsed on the other. We got signed first, and they said, "We're going to move our equipment to your side of the room ... maybe we'll get lucky and get signed, too." And they certainly did. [Laughs] I played with them recently, and they're still great. They sound amazing.

KATHY VALENTINE: As we did later videos, we would meet with directors, and they'd have storyboards, and you'd do all this stuff. ["Our Lips Are Sealed"] wasn't like that at all. It was just this real free-forming thing. I don't even remember who directed it. I just remember them saying, "We have this idea of getting in the convertible, and you guys drive around." It was kind of a free-for-all. Everybody threw in ideas. The biggest thing about that video was when we went to the fountain in Beverly Hills, somebody had the bright idea if we were splashing around in the fountain, maybe a policeman would come and give us a citation. And we thought how cool that would that be in the video. But as it turned out ... nobody paid any attention.

DEBORA IYALL: I loved the one where they're driving in the car, and they're singing and splashing in the fountain—"Our Lips Are Sealed." I just thought, "I'm in love with the girls." They were sexy and attractive in their own way, but they're also being themselves, and I love that.

KATHY VALENTINE: ["Vacation"] was a blast. We had the best time. There's a lot of waiting around, and it takes a long time, so we got pretty juiced up. We were drinking lots of champagne. So when it came to do the water-skiing, the fun and silliness is real. We're just having a good time. We've been drinking champagne *for hours*. [Laughs] ["Head Over Heels"] was a very dark period in the band's life. When I see that video, I just think about what we were going through, and it kind of makes me sad. To me, it looks fake. The kind of "happiness"—I know it's not real. Charlotte was really deep in her addiction, and maybe we already knew Jane was going to quit. She might have already quit and just agreed to do that tour. So we were frazzled. It was frayed. Everything was unraveling. And yet, we're supposed to look like we're the same happy band that's having fun, fun, fun.

— Culture Club —

MIKE SCORE: I didn't particularly like Culture Club, but I didn't particularly hate them. I felt they were just a "pop thing," with a good figurehead. I don't think they were a huge touring band, which was the traditional way to make it in America—to be a big touring band and gather fans that way. MTV made Boy George what he was in America. He deserved it—good songs, great biography. [Laughs]

STEVE BARRON: Punk had stamped its authority and thrown down the gauntlet and said, "You don't have to conform," which opened up the door for the new wave world and extraordinary things. It opened its eyes to say, "Different is OK. Different is better. Just do your own thing, and if people want to come along, they come along. If they don't, you're being unique and creative." He was one of those people in London who was doing extraordinary things musically and visually. A lot of that comes out of the fact that videos came along and said, "You can't all just stand there with your guitar and bass on a stage with a few colored lights. Things in this new world have to say a bit more and do a bit more." He was fantastic for that. "Do You

Really Want to Hurt Me" is just a brilliant song. He's a pop genius of that era.

ROB HALFORD: I suppose because of my sexuality, I accepted George instantly, because that's just by my nature. I'm a very unprejudiced person. I accept everything, because I understand what goes behind putting something together. So when I saw George, I thought, "This is cool. This is exciting. This is different. *This is what rock n' roll is all about.*" When I say "rock n' roll," I mean it as a broad label. I thought it was really powerful. And especially when I heard him doing his interviews, as articulate and intelligent as he is.

I thought it was a breath of fresh air when Culture Club came on the scene. Driven by him, obviously—he was *the man.* He took it to its extreme. Because in the gender-bender thing, we had Bowie in his dresses and Bowie as Ziggy, but Bowie was a lot of things. He was the Thin White Duke one minute, and then he was Ziggy the next, and something the next. But here was George coming out in such a flamboyant, androgynous way, that everybody was curious. But he could back it up by the main feature—his voice. He has the most amazing voice. If you close your eyes and just listen to that voice, it's a really unusual, beautiful voice. So again, just an extraordinary moment. It's important, if you look across the decades of rock n' roll—starting with Elvis and I don't know who we're ending with right now in terms of extremity—Culture Club and Boy George has his slot in the "shock and awe" moments in rock n' roll.

COLIN HAY: He's fantastic. I loved those songs, loved his voice. Loved everything about him. He was really a star. Cool songs and different.

DEBORA IYALL: I was fascinated by Boy George. I was from San Francisco, so the whole transgender thing was something that I had experienced first-hand. I had some drag queens helping me get dressed for an important gig on New Year's, for instance. Miss X and Doris Fish were pals of mine, who were dressed as women. I liked it that he still kind of looked like a man ... and then he didn't. That was kind of neat. That hybrid—I appreciated that. And what was so strange was he looked like that, and he sounded like something else. He had a very soulful voice. And I liked the attitude and content of some of his songs a lot, what he was saying. All props to Boy George!

MICHAEL SADLER: Brilliant, absolutely brilliant. Because, not to be taken seriously, and the videos come off that way. And him in all his glam glory. I was not a massive fan, but not being a musical snob, I tend to give everything credit if it's of quality. Everything they did, again, very controlled and image-conscious, as most of the '80s English bands were. Boy George took it to another level and created this "alter ego or is it?" kind of thing. I can just imagine the kind of person he was and realizing that he got to play "dress up" for a living every day. He was in his glory. He probably had a lot of control over the videos that they did. I'm pretty sure he had a lot input into the final product and how the band came off looking on screen.

— *Toni Basil* —

TONI BASIL: I was doing a video album deal, so I was looking for several ideas. The day I shot "Mickey," I think I shot part of "Time After Time" and "Little Red Book" that day. And then I came back and shot the other half of the other video, because I used a different backdrop. They were almost all on white or black backdrops, with very minimal furnishings or set piec-es, because I was shooting so many in a day, and I wasn't doing locations, because that takes a long time. It eats up your time if you're doing locations and if you're changing sets. I shot more like you would a musical number on a TV show, on a variety show, with the more progressive idea in the editing.

I wore my cheerleader outfit from high school for "Mickey," and I got real cheerleaders from Carson High, and there's real cheerleaders from Dors-ey High singing the chant on the record. I think that was maybe something that people didn't expect to see, which was real cheerleaders. At the time, mostly you hired jazz dancers, and normally, *they* would be cheerleaders. But I hired real cheerleaders, and nobody had really seen mounts, when they climb up on each other like a steeple. And most of the girls and the women that they had seen on videos looked different than these girls, especially the girls that were on the bottom that held up the other girls, which were kind of husky/strong-looking girls. It was just a different look, because it was real. It wasn't fake. I was a choreographer before I really started to record, and I also made films. I always made 8-millimeter and 16-millimeter films as a hobby. So between being a choreographer, making films, and understanding editing, my video work looked like it did. My videos were a product of my history. "Mickey" was a product of my history, because I was a cheerleader all my life.

GERALD CASALE: We knew Toni since 1977. She came backstage with Iggy Pop, Leonard Cohen, and Dean Stockwell at the Starwood. She walks in, and she's wearing a gold lamé vest with nothing on underneath it—black toreador pants and three-inch heels—and says, *"Who choreographs you guys?"* [Laughs]

— Eddie Money —

EDDIE MONEY: We made two videos. I think it was $77,000—the "Shakin'" video with Apollonia and the cars bouncing up and down. That was the first thing Apollonia ever did in show business, before *Purple Rain.* She had a boyfriend that was a karate expert, and the guy was always ready to break my arms in half. He was a very jealous man. I never would have hit on her, because I had an old lady at the time. You know how it is. Some people think you're hitting on the ladies even when you're not. You get in all kinds of fucking trouble. It happens to me year after year after year. The storyline is Apollonia gets out on the streets and starts the cars, and we were racing the cars. It was actually the first video where the cars are bouncing up and down. And one thing I remember specifically was that Apollonia might have been a very pretty girl, *but she sure couldn't dance.* "Think I'm in Love" was great, because the whole thing was me as Dracula, and my ex-wife was in the video—a very pretty girl. It turns out the whole thing twists around, where she's biting my neck instead of me biting her. It was a cute video. We shot it in a castle.

— Joe Jackson —

STEVE BARRON: Joe Jackson's "Steppin' Out"—he was an artist who was not all together comfortable with the world of videos. He felt often that they just didn't represent the music in his head. It was always difficult. What do you do with the artist? Do you have them try to act? Do you just have them play and detached? And what I was trying to do with that was really have him as being the narrator and moving through the scenes and do a little kind of Cinderella story. It's a chambermaid in a posh hotel, who, for a moment, gets lost in one of the rich patron's closets. "Wardrobe of possibility"—what it would be like to be glamorous and successful. So she goes into a little fantasy with him narrating. I remember we shot it at the St. Regis Hotel in New York. At the time, computers were fairly new. And in [the hotel's] computer, they hadn't quite figured out how to deal with a film crew that would pay them $3,000 to use the hotel. I remember I went back to the hotel about a year and a half later, and they said, "Oh ... you've got a *$3,000 credit* here at the hotel!"

— The Motels —

MARTHA DAVIS: "Only the Lonely" was shot in downtown L.A. We were very "renegade" in those days. Cast and crew would huddle together down in some abandoned building. We wanted to give the bar the look of the bar in *The Shining*, kind of eerie and weird. So it was lit from underneath. The old man who was the bartender in that ... the way we cast videos in those days was the PAs would run around and look for people on the streets that might want to be in a video. And this old man had literally just gotten off the bus—from I believe Oklahoma—and he gets approached by these young kids, "Do you want to be in a video?" And he's like. "Uh ... *OK.*" He was hilarious. He was having little drinks back there. Actually, he was hitting on me most of the night.

"Take the L" was Russell Mulcahy. That one was a lot more intense in terms of costume changes and different set-ups. It was also shot downtown. It was a great crew. Just fun. It was a blast. [The album cover coming to life] was all Russell's vision. In fact, David Fincher kind of did [it] again with the billboard coming to life in "Shame."

"Suddenly Last Summer" was one of the ones that I had storyboarded and had all the concepts for. That one was not as much fun, in the sense that I was being produced by Val Garay that time, and he decided that he wanted to direct the video as well. He wasn't really a video director, but there were some hilarious things about that, though. He said, "We need to have you have a co-star that's a real hot guy," so they get Bobby Carradine ... whose next role was *Revenge of the Nerds*. [Laughs] That video was a lot of work, because I had to run up and down sand dunes a lot, and if you've ever done that, it's not really easy on ya. I don't feel that what I was seeing in my mind got captured in that, so that was frustrating, for various reasons.

— *Bryan Adams* —

JOE ELLIOTT: My memories of Bryan Adams was just this gum-chewing punk, and I don't mean "punk" in the English sense. I mean the American '50s sense. Kind of the greased-back hair, leather jacket, tight blue jeans turned up at the bottom sort of thing ... and a low-slung Telecaster. It wasn't bombastic like a band. It wasn't ever going to be like Poison. But for that reason, it was going to have a bit more longevity, I think. The Poison/Mötley Crüe/Guns n' Roses videos were bombastic. They were like watching a Vietnam film. They were "napalm" in comparison to Bryan Adam's "hand grenade," if you will. Bryan Adams was like a league up from Eddie Money. He was walking the same path as John Mellencamp and Tom Petty. He was a singer/songwriter. It had balls, but it wasn't metal. *It was Americana.* It was like a division down from Springsteen.

STEVE BARRON: "Cuts Like a Knife" got some real stick. It was like '83, and there was a girl who was probably naked, and it was like, "Is this what videos are going to be in the future? Is it going to be all about sex?" Of course, you look at videos now—especially R&B videos—it's absolutely not hidden in the slightest, in a way that we were starting to do then. I remember it was the same year as "Billie Jean," because the girl in the bed in "Billie Jean" who disappears and is on the poster, is the girl from "Cuts Like a Knife." There's a little trivia connection.

— *Stray Cats* —

SERGEANT BLOTTO: The Stray Cats were very cool, because that was sort of the first rockabilly stuff going on. And that was a lot of fashion. There weren't a lot of bands using stand-up bass back then. That really made an impact and broadened the musical personalities.

— Eurythmics —

LITA FORD: I'm a huge Annie Lennox fan. I think she's awesome. I remember she used to change her hair a lot. She keeps herself covered. She's not a sex symbol. There was nothing there that your parents wouldn't want the kids to watch—any cleavage hanging out, butt cheeks hanging out, or anything like that with Annie. She had nothing to do or show off but her voice, and that was enough for her.

— Billy Idol —

SERGEANT BLOTTO: Billy Idol—those were videos capturing the energy of the song. They made him a personality, which I guess you could say that pretty much for everybody. But he came across as a larger-than-life personality in the videos.

— Huey Lewis and the News —

EDDIE MONEY: Huey Lewis came out with some pretty good videos. Huey Lewis was very poppy to me. He's a good buddy of mine. I've known him for years. He was definitely out there doing all those videos, and for some reason, his music really fit television. It was very "up." It wasn't moody, and there weren't a lot of interludes in it. If you look at my video, "I Wanna Go Back," it's harder to film a ballad than it is to film a fast song. It just is that way. I don't know. I was pretty out there back then. I didn't know what the fuck I was watching. [Laughs]

—Julian Lennon—

JULIAN LENNON: [For the "Too Late for Goodbyes" video] Martin Lewis, a mad English producer, decided to hook me up with Sam Peckinpah, whom I'd knew of, through his movies, but never figured how it was going to work between us. Anyway, I'd seen this guy dancing very uniquely on PBS and decided, "Maybe I need a few original moves, for either video and/or stage." So found out who this guy was—Moses Pendleton from Momix [dance troupe]—and decided to go and "train" with him at his dance studio in Connecticut.

I went to meet Sam in Montauk, Long Island, with a terrible hangover via seaplane from New York. We met, and he was an amazing character, who loved to play tricks on people. So much so, that he almost had Martin Lewis in tears, thinking we'd had an argument, and it was never going to work out, after all the expenses laid out by Charisma/Atlantic Records, run by, at that time, Tony Stratton Smith/Ahmet Ertegun.

We arrived at Bear Track Studios, and I had no idea how we were going to do this and what we were going to do. All I knew was that it was going to be a kind of "live performance"-looking piece. Sam had no idea who or what Moses was doing or why he was even there. I didn't either, really, as I wasn't dancing as such. Nonetheless, Moses bizarrely ended up looking like dad's ghost in a doorway in the background, which was never ever part of the plan, but c'est la vie. I was young and very shy, so [I] didn't voice my concerns.

Er ... not entirely clear on [the "Valotte" clip], whether we filmed it at the same time as "Too Late for Goodbyes" and in the same studio. But again, I was told it was going to be a chilled performance piece, which is what it turned out to be. Shame I was so nervous. I couldn't play the piano and sing at the same time, with a whole film crew around me and Sam there, observing from the dark corners of the room, shouting, "CUT!"

Again, I kind of knew the basic storyboard [for the "Stick Around" video], but it didn't really hit me as to what we were really doing, until we actually went through the process. It was a crazy/hazy video shoot, which was constantly moving and changing, and I was instructed to follow through with the ideas of the director, which I did. It was fun. Met lots of new friends through the process. It was a fun video, looking back ... but what was with the hair-do?!

— *a-ha* —

STEVE BARRON: I had worked with Jeff Ayeroff on a couple of things, and he said, "There is this new band. They're from Norway. We did a $15,000 video in London of just them playing in a blue studio-type thing, and nobody played it, and nobody played the song on the radio. We just can't sell them. They're really good looking guys, but there's no catch. There's no 'hook' to it." I always said to him, "If you give me enough time, we can do animation. Just give me three or four months instead of two weeks to deliver a video, and we can do some frame-by-frame animation." He came and said, "I've put the release on hold because it's not working. You've got enough budget to do something, and you can take as long as you like. It just needs a good concept."

He showed me some animation by this guy, Michael Patterson, from film school, and said, "This is a style that could be good." And it was. I said, "We've got to motivate it somehow, and then that will make it stronger. Because if there's a reason for it to be live animation, we're going to have a stronger video." So I went away to think and came up with the idea of the comic book, sort of based on a comic book I had read when I was five or six years old about these sidecar racers, and goodies and baddies. And then I thought, "Well, the love interest is a girl reading a magazine, and then there's a hand," and then the image came to mind of this hand reaching out—this comic-drawn hand. And I thought, "That's a pivotal image. I can build the video around that image." I structured a little story around it, and we went and shot it. You had to shoot everything, including everything that's animated. We went off and shot for a few days with these guys, and then everyone waited for months while the animators got to work on all the animation, and we put it together digitally.

— *Cyndi Lauper* —

LITA FORD: Cyndi wasn't a sex symbol, but she had such an awesome voice that she didn't need to be anything but just an awesome voice. And making the videos that she did in the beginning were wonderful. They were very simple, basic.

DEBORA IYALL: I think I cried watching "Time After Time." Just the song, for one thing—the narrative of it—and the misty-eyed train waving goodbye. Something inside of me really identified with her and her little trailer and her having to leave home. It was like the story of "smalltown boy." That video was sort of the story of that, from the girl's side. And then "Girls Just Want to Have Fun"—I never understood the Lou Albano thing, so that was kind of like, *"Whatever."* I did like that she had actual friends of hers in the video. I remember reading that and thinking, "Good. Get some neighborhood girls in the videos."

MARTHA DAVIS: I loved Cyndi. Cyndi and I were in *Look* magazine or *Life* magazine, one of those big "L" magazines. We ended up in the magazine at the same time as "women in rock." We ran into each other at some music awards show, and she's like [adopts New York accent], "Mawtha, oh my Gawd, we're women in rock togetha!" She was so sweet and hilarious. She's a gas.

KEN R. CLARK: Cyndi Lauper was always a favorite to have in that studio. That woman is generally funny. We always knew we were going to laugh hard when Cyndi came in. She's a salty New Yorker. She takes her craft seriously, but she doesn't take *herself* seriously. And that was I think what made a big difference with a lot of celebrities, is whether they took themselves too seriously.

ALAN HUNTER: Well, she was our first "fun girl," wasn't she? She was to the left or the right—I don't know which—of Madonna. Madonna took herself *very* seriously, and you could tell she was going to be a superstar. Cyndi came from almost a fresh, breezy approach. She was very accessible. And she was part of the trend for fashion, with her crazy little dresses and her bobble things. And her persona—there was no one like her. She was very asexual. You couldn't tell what she was about. [Laughs] That was a very alluring with a lot of the artists, certainly the male artists from overseas, against a rock n' roll Loverboy video or something. I liked Cyndi Lauper because I got along with her well. I interviewed her first, and I was part of the "rock and wrestling" thing [which Cyndi was a part of, too]. So she did "Girls Just Want to Have Fun," then she backed it up quite smartly with "Time After Time," the serious side of Cyndi. And it didn't come off disingenuous. It wasn't like, "I want to change my direction now. I'm not that frivolous girl." It really was a good mix. You felt that Cyndi was well-rounded. She had fun, but then she could do a nice ballad, and it seemed to work.

Devo

ART BARNES: *The best.* Barnes & Barnes worked with Devo and hung with them in those days. Mark Mothersbaugh did some "Booji Boy" appearances in Barnes & Barnes projects. Those guys are serious artists. They were/are the real deal. I love their early videos. Creepy and strong.

SERGEANT BLOTTO: I loved Devo. They were "the Dadaists" of the whole movement ... and managed to make flowerpots cool.

KATHY VALENTINE: My all-time favorite videos were Devo. They captured the essence of the band—how smart they were, how funny, how twisted. It just came through. You would watch a Devo video, and you got it right away. You got who these people were.

TONI BASIL: They were brilliant. Everybody copied them. They were the first of that style of video and music. They were absolutely groundbreaking. I knew them when they first came out here, because Iggy Pop and David Bowie had told me about them, and I think Iggy and I went to see them at the Starlight Lounge. They were doing videos on the wall while they were performing. Which again, was groundbreaking. Nobody was doing that. "Whip It" came later. They had some really great early videos. It's their cynical take on the world, which is pretty funny.

STAN RIDGWAY: I thought Devo were brilliant, and what they brought to the "video party" was really original. When they first got to Los Angeles, they played the Whiskey A Go Go, and I remember seeing them for the first time there. They played some of their videos. They were really actually films. They weren't shot on video. Nothing was shot on video back then. You shot on film and then converted it to video. "Jocko Homo" and some of the other earlier things—it was very avant-garde, smart, and entertaining at the same time. It appealed to your intellect, but also, to a quality that wasn't pretentious. I thought that was really exciting.

DEBORA IYALL: Oh, I love Devo. The first time I saw them in San Francisco, it was so exciting. This tiny, sweaty club, and they came with their outfits that all matched, and they showed a film during their show, of Booji Boy—that character in a playpen—and they had the Bruce Conner *Mongoloid* film. Their music was really catchy yet really edgy at the same time.

JOHN DOE: The first introduction to Devo was through their films in L.A. They sent some copies of their films—the Booji Boy films and stuff like that—to play before punk rock shows, before they ever came out to L.A. to play. They had some MTV/pretty heavy rotation. "Whip It" was a little bit later, but the first stuff—"Jocko Homo" and "Satisfaction"—those were great. They were delivering on the promise of what video could do.

GERALD CASALE: We did [the "Satisfaction" clip] in Akron, Ohio. We pulled some favors and shot the performance on the stage at the Akron Civic Auditorium, which, at that point, had fallen into disuse, like the rest of Akron, was kind of half-shuttered. And we shot at this old strip mall, the scenes in the car with General Boy. We shot that in West Akron. And then we shot the interior scenes at Mark Mothersbaugh's father's house, the guy that played General Boy. We shot the whole video in two days, on 16-millimeter film, and it cost $7,850. [Laughs] I remember when we got to "Whip It" in 1980, it cost us a whopping $15,000. We thought, "Oh my God ... *we're really going too far!*"

GREG HAWKES: The Cars ... that was right in the middle of our big run. So we were part of the whatever you want to call it, "new wave bands." But it seems to me, I remember Devo being *the* band, which were really the pioneers, as far as video stuff. They were the first real "video band," and videos were part of their shows. They made such creative use of video and just the way they incorporated it into their shows. They did one tour with the treadmills and the video screen, and I thought that was great. It was beyond just being a rock concert. It was almost heading toward a Broadway show or something—not Broadway as such, but some sort of more theatrical element had been ignited.

MARTHA DAVIS: I love Devo. That's one of my favorites of all time. They were just absolutely brilliant. As soon as you say "Devo," the video for "Whip It" pops into mind. It's just classic and brilliant. I cannot come up with enough accolades for them. They were brilliant musically, so funny, and so tongue-in-cheek. It was that sort of "serious funny," where they did it very seriously. I remember when I went to see them live, Mark Mothersbaugh was marching around with a pouty face on, and then just dives into the audience. You're just like, *"What the hell is going on?!"* And we hear Mark Mothersbaugh every day, at least 30 or 40 times a day, if you have your television on. He's become so successful as a commercial guy. And he's still absolutely lovely, a wonderful guy.

GEDDY LEE: They were funny. I loved them. "Whip It" I think is really good. Ironically, we ended up working with Jerry Casale many years later. He directed a couple of videos for us. He went on to become a very good video director. Their visual point of view and their humor—their tongues were planted firmly in cheek.

GERALD CASALE: The way ["Whip It"] happened was Warners had never focused on that song, and frankly, neither had we. We weren't sitting down going, "Let's write a hit." We just wrote songs we liked and only put the songs on the record we liked. The record company said, "'Girl U Want'— *that's your hit!"* And, of course, it went nowhere. So they had us make a video for "Girl U Want," and then somebody at the label said, "'Freedom of Choice!'" So we made these two videos. They released "Freedom of Choice" when "Girl U Want" tanked, and "Freedom of Choice" went nowhere.

We were on tour for like three months, and while we're out there, "Whip It" starts being played by Kal Rudman, who was a major programmer/radio mogul in the Southeast. Back when people could start things regionally, he did, and it grew out of there and went up to New York City, and the "Rudman Report" had it on fire, so all these other stations started picking it up.

So in the middle of our tour, they had to keep changing venues, canceling shows and putting them in other places, because suddenly, we were playing to twice as many people ... and sometimes even more than that. And when we got back off that leg of the tour, they go, "You've got to make a video for 'Whip It.'"

We were rather burned out and really on a schedule, and Chuck Statler, the cinematographer that had been my college friend that we shot everything with, was busy. He was working with Elvis Costello. So I planned the whole video with my friend, John Zabrucky, who is a prop designer and an artist. We planned the whole thing out, and Mark and I storyboarded it, and we cast it and built a set out of a rehearsal space we had in a warehouse outside of Beverly Hills. Chuck flew in with just a four-man crew, and we started shooting at something like 7:00 in the morning, and we ended at like 1:00 in the morning. We shot the whole thing in like 16 hours. And then the editor, Dale Cooper, followed the storyboard, we tweaked it a bit, and it went out. It was one of the quickest videos we ever made. Other than "Beautiful World," it's the most favorite Devo video I ever directed.

DEBORA IYALL: "Whip It" was kind of weird. [Laughs] I'm basically a feminist, and him whipping the girl's clothes off is a violation. It made me a little uncomfortable. Now, I'm like, "Well, I'll never really get all they were trying to do with that one and the crazy West." And I also thought, "Well, I'm just not seeing what they're alluding to, with this Western theme and the exploitation of the West against the native woman." I probably over-think things a little bit.

GERALD CASALE: ["Beautiful World"] is like our pièce de résistance, because even when Mark and I were writing the song, and I wrote the final line, "For you, but not for me," we already had in mind using archival footage to slowly go from really funny to really dark. The kind of way *Bonnie and Clyde* had. And we loved that. We thought, "If we use archival footage, we can really make the point, because this archival footage will carry so much iconic and cultural impact. We could never shoot enough stuff to communicate that. So we'll just shoot us in a way that we can integrate us with archival footage." And I spent a long time with Chuck's help, going to all these stock footage places and archival footage places, before the big boys bought up all the mom-and-pop places. Before it got congealed into big bucks, where it was monetized, when people realized how much they could make from stock footage. Literally, some places would sell us *bags* of film.

So we'd find these little canisters of 400 or 500 feet of this and that and nothing more than a description of what it was. We spent weeks and weeks watching this stuff. And then we went to New York, to some of the more expensive film libraries, where it's really cataloged specifically, and you're paying by the minute and paying for viewing, when we needed the really powerful stuff, like racial protests in the South in the '60s. And the editing was the most fun in the world. You took all this great stuff we found and started building a story, like a collage, with the existing moments that you could afford. The whole thing in the end cost $25,000. It was the most labor-intensive video I ever made in my life ... but I loved every minute of it. And I even like the kind of lo-fi quality of the whole thing, because there's a certain crude power in that. It holds up. You watch it now, and you're like, *"Jesus!"* It's just as unnerving as it was in 1981.

ROGER POWELL: They're hopefully in Dr. Demento's list as well. And that's what I liked—the band to do something bizarre or creative at least, with the visual medium, rather than just film a concert. There's certainly nothing wrong with filming concerts, but it's like, "You just finished making this cool, wacky record. Why not do something visually thematic? I always admired those guys as being pioneers. They took the legacy of Frank Zappa into the video age.

GERALD CASALE: "Peek-A-Boo!" was part of a trilogy, where we had this great idea, which now, you can see Nine Inch Nails or U2 do, and a few other bands with money. We said, "We're going to create a video that approximates what people are going to see us do live. So when they see the video on television, that's what they're going to see when they come to see us live. And they'll know from watching the video what can happen." So we created backdrops in sync with the music, using really crude computer graphics at the time, mixed with live action and animation. And with the express intent of rear-projecting them on a screen, which at that time, the best we could do was 25 feet wide by 17 feet high. And then develop the lighting system and a matte black floor, so that light wouldn't bounce, so we could be lit standing about ten feet in front of the screen and be the same color temperature/exposure rate as the screen. So we're not brighter than the screen, we're not darker than the screen—we're matched. And then we would project that, and that would be connected to a 6-track, 35-millimeter film dubber, with the sound mag [having] the click track we had cut to and some effects, and we would play to that click track—bass, drums, guitar.

We'd be totally in sync with these films. So the first 25 minutes of the show, that's what it was. The people went nuts, and we loved it. Back-up singers would come on screen at the scale where they looked the same size as us, and Mark would turn around with a prop laser gun and blow up these computer girls that were dancing in a line, like a duck shoot. People went nuts ... *and critics attacked viciously.* Even though the next part of the show was more traditional, early *Are We Not Men?* songs in yellow suits. Especially guys like Robert Hilburn. I still remember how mean he was. We played two sold-out nights at the Universal Amphitheatre, and the people never sat down once. And he writes, "Hey Devo, if I wanted to see video-games, I'd go to an arcade. *Rock n' roll or stay home."* It was nasty. We were definitely "the let-no-good-deed-go-unpunished guys." Y'know, like the pioneers who got scalped. Now, it's like you're almost expected to do something like that. Stealth video curtains and Quicktime films and laptops allow anybody with any money to do that so much more easy than we did it, and less labor. And so much more refined, high-tech, and high resolution. But we were trying to do something that hadn't been done.

JELLO BIAFRA: I was mainly into Devo before Warner Brothers got a hold of them. And Klaus Flouride, our bass player, was really into them throughout. But a lot of the hardcore kids and pioneer bands of the early '80s just hated them. Almost irrationally, where if you *really* wanted to put something down—this was an Orange County slang term—you called it "Club Devo." Maybe it was because it was the first new wave-related band that was really unusual that the people they hated in school got into. I have no idea. Or, Devo was the first band that they got into, before they discovered hardcore, and became like *Mary Poppins* to them. When you're seven years old, you love *Mary Poppins*. When you're eight years old, you hate *Mary Poppins*. And then when you get older, you start liking it again.

Because now, I've noticed a lot of people who came up a little after I did—like the guys in the Melvins—they love Devo. Devo has definitely been redeemed in a lot of people's eyes since then. I did see some of their early films they made—even before they put out records—and I thought they were pretty cool and pretty demented. Their whole original theory, if you remember, Devo stands for "de-evolution," and a subhuman species called "Jocko Homo." And boy, was that species in evidence at some of the later big hardcore shows in southern California. I renamed them "The Flintstone Children," because they all seemed to be like Pebbles and Bamm-Bamm and know about four words of the English language—"Uh-huh," "Uh-uh," "Gimme," and "Fuck you." Now, they're in Congress ... and look what's happening to our country!

ALAN HUNTER: Devo were certainly groundbreaking. That was up there with "Fish Heads." They seemed to have a real good knowledge and handle on what they wanted to achieve from a video, and it wasn't what Michael Jackson wanted to achieve. Theirs was not about glamorization; theirs was de-evolution. They had a real vision for the video medium. Their whole bit was about the mystic and fun attitude that they created. For them, video was so integral to who they were. It wasn't like they were an artist having to do video for promotion. They always had a good sense of humor. I gravitated towards the bands that had some sort of self-deprecating sense of humor about the whole thing. I would not have expected that from Bono or Peter Gabriel. They didn't need to. They were bigger than the other ones, like Men Without Hats and Madness, some of the English new wave bands. They were "of the medium," not above it, necessarily.

"Weird Al" Yankovic

GEDDY LEE: I love "Weird Al"! Funny stuff. He was the first guy to go out and take the piss out of everyone else, on an MTV level. He did it well, and he was the only guy doing it, so he broke through. I saw him last year at a premiere. It was funny to see him.

ROGER POWELL: I always loved anything that "Weird Al" did. I actually got to meet him once at an accordion seminar, somewhere out in Colorado. I always looked forward to anything that he did from a record point of view. And, of course, the videos were just hysterical. The humor thing, that definitely translates well from record to video.

ART BARNES: Al's been a pal since before MTV. His videos are always brilliant. He's a really hard worker and a very nice guy. One of the good guys. I'm very happy for all his successes.

SERGEANT BLOTTO: He made it OK to be funny, which was good for Blotto. It's one thing to take a song and come up with a clever parody of it. It's a whole other animal to try to create a whole film that does the same thing. You're not only parodying the song; you're parodying the video of the song. And stuff like "Fat," that's a work of art. That is classic stuff.

STAN RIDGWAY: His career is something of an accident, a "happy accident." I don't think Al set out to be the "king of parodies." He just had an accordion, started to play it, and said, "Goddammit, I can't play any more of this polka music my parents taught me!" I think he deserves all that success, because nobody really had any idea to do anything like that. No one would have wanted to. He had very little competition at all.

JELLO BIAFRA: "Weird Al" Yankovic? I know nothing about him, except for the name. A friend of mine who collects novelty records and lives in rural Illinois, the only live shows he's been to in years is me and "Weird Al" Yankovic. I don't know what that means ...

ALAN HUNTER: "Weird Al" was great. I never understood why "Weird Al" had such easy acceptance by all the artists. Once he had taken on Michael Jackson ... and as I remember the story goes, Michael had no problem with it, for "Eat It" and "Fat." "Weird Al" was *so* gonzo. He provided the comic relief for MTV. MTV was all about creating an atmosphere and eclectic nature from going from serious "U2 bands," to Devo, to David Byrne, to then "Weird Al" Yankovic. I mean, the good, the bad, and the ugly was what MTV was all about in the '80s. And it was kind of what I revel in now on the radio show. I'll come out of a Debbie Gibson song or an REO Speedwagon song and go, "Well ... *I went to the bathroom on that one.*"

It was the good, the bad, and the ugly, and it all seemed to work. But it worked in the context of 24-hour video, because you needed relief occasionally from the seriousness of things, the overly pretentious '80s. To have a good David Coverdale and Whitesnake bullshit video with Tawny Kitaen writhing around, to break the bubble of pretentiousness from Ultravox or Simple Minds. But it all seemed to work in the context of the rest. Pick them all out individually and watch them on YouTube, and it's like, "Oh my God, how did people get into this?!" But it was part of the fun, because when you're three or four beers down, watching that, it makes sense. [Laughs]

"WEIRD AL" YANKOVIC: "I Love Rocky Road" was shot on an abandoned airstrip in Agua Dulce, California. I remember we had a lot of technical problems on that shoot. For whatever reason, a lot of the film got ruined, so we couldn't use some of the best takes. Also, it was shot in one long 22-hour day, so everybody was completely burnt by the end. And there was a group of accordion-playing kids that we were going to shoot for a scene but for some reason never got around to it. I still feel bad about that.

"Ricky" was my first real music video. I think we spent a total of about $3,000 on it. It was shot—on video, not film—at somebody's house in the

San Fernando Valley. It starred me and Tress MacNeille, the multitalented voiceover actress, who played the part of Lucille Ball. I played myself, as well as Desi Arnaz, after I shaved my mustache and put on the appropriate wig. The shoot wasn't very well-organized. I was supposed to be shaking maracas in one critical shot, but nobody had thought to bring any…so I found some bowling pins and shook those, because if you were really drunk, they might look kinda like maracas.

"Eat It" was my first "big-budget" video, although still extremely modest by today's standards. We shot for two days on a soundstage. Michael Jackson's original locations didn't exist anymore, so we had to recreate everything from scratch. Michael's choreographer, Vince Patterson, reprised his role as a gang leader for my video. This was before I was directing my own videos, so my manager, Jay Levey, was calling the shots. I remember things got a little stressful on the set. For one set-up, when it was determined that the top of a street sign wasn't in the frame, instead of waiting for the DP to adjust the lens, someone bent the pole down so that the sign would fit.

"Like a Surgeon" was filmed in an abandoned hospital, where apparently a lot of other hospital-themed TV shows and features were also shot. My main memory of this shoot was that we had an actual live lion roaming the halls, which was a reference to the lion in Madonna's video. At this point, we lost a lot of extras, who decided that they weren't getting paid nearly enough to deal with this.

GERALD CASALE: Well, that's exactly what we did *not* want to be. It's kind of like Dr. Demento. As soon as you wink and nod at the audience, like, *"This is all a joke,"* you become a clown, and you're letting everybody off the hook. You're not making them think anymore. It's like, "Oh, this is going to be a funny parody." It's in the name—"'Weird Al' Yankovic." As soon as you say "weird," "Demento," "goofy," or "crazy," you've just pulled the plug on anything real that can happen.

FEE WAYBILL: Not a big fan of "Weird Al." It's just kind of too hokey. It's strictly comedy, strictly novelty band. Not really a player.

GREG HAWKES: Some are funnier than others. Sometimes, it's a parody of a song that I don't even like in the first place, so it's hard to get excited about the parody in that case.

"WEIRD AL" YANKOVIC: I don't remember exactly how [special "AL-TV" segments on MTV] came about, but after the success of "Eat It," MTV agreed to occasionally give me four-hour blocks of programming to basically do anything in the world I wanted to. Can you even imagine them doing something like that now? That's how MTV was back then. It was seat-of-your-pants stuff...exciting, dangerous, very cool. MTV almost seemed like a weird local UHF TV station, but of course, it was a national phenomenon.

Anyway, on AL-TV, I played a bunch of my favorite videos, I made disgusting sandwiches, I introduced "my best friend in the whole world," Harvey the Wonder Hamster, who would do horrifying stunts. I would provide running commentaries for music videos. I would do fake interviews with celebrities using clips taken out of context. It was a lot of fun. The conceit was that I was using my pirate satellite broadcasting transmitter to take over the airwaves. So during that time, MTV wasn't even mentioned. All the promos and IDs just said "AL-TV." Again, can you believe they let me get away with that? I still manage to do AL-TV every few years, usually with the release of a new album. But these days, *it's on VH1.*

CARMINE APPICE: I lent a bass drum to "Weird Al," to do some of the hits that he did on their first album, that Rick Derringer produced [*"Weird Al" Yankovic*]. I was doing the DNA project with Rick at the time, and Rick was producing "Weird Al." "Weird Al" had a lot of great videos; in fact, his videos were *killer*. When Rick started producing him, he was playing accordion, and they did that "Ricky" song. Little by little, you kept seeing these videos he kept coming up with—"Eat It," "Fat." I thought he found a great niche. And it's amazing—he still goes out and plays for 3,000 people. When I met him, I said, "So what do I call you for a first name? 'Al' or 'Weird?'" He's always been a cool guy. And then he went into movies [*UHF*]. I said, "Wow, it's amazing how you go from goofing with an accordion to being a rock star."

"WEIRD AL" YANKOVIC: Even though it's a grey area and legally I don't necessarily need to, I always make a point of getting permission for each and every one of my song parodies. I'm not sure that we ever approached Joan Jett, because she wasn't one of the writers for "I Love Rock 'n' Roll," but we did approach Jake Hooker, who was. Jake also happened to manage guitar legend Rick Derringer, and he suggested that maybe Rick and I could work together. So because of that contact, Derringer wound up producing my first six albums. Toni Basil was great about letting me do my parody, as was Michael Jackson, to my utter disbelief. Michael loved the parody videos and was always very supportive of them. Madonna didn't write "Like a Virgin"—that was Billy Steinberg and Tom Kelly—but she indirectly gave me the idea for my parody. As legend has it, she was talking to a friend of hers in New York one day, and wondered aloud, "When do you think 'Weird Al' is gonna do 'Like a Surgeon?'" Her friend happened to be a friend of a friend of my manager, and when word got back to me, I thought, "Hmm...well, sure, *why not?*"

Videos: Oddities

— *Barnes & Barnes* —

ART BARNES: Well, I grew up working with some of the greatest film and TV talent ever [Art—aka Bill Mumy—played Will Robinson on *Lost in Space*.]. Making "Fish Heads" as a film was total guerilla filmmaking, on a cheapo, cheapo budget for the most part. We spent money where we needed to, on editing and transfers, but the making of it was done really low-tech. And I love that about it. We purposely wanted it to look scratchy and be a bit disturbing, while still serving that nursery-rhyme-type melody. We shot it on both super-8 and 16. There's nothing "video" about it. We used a hand-cranked Bolex camera for most of it and a couple of cheap super-8s. It was a collaborative project between Bill Paxton, Rocky Schenck, Joan Farber, me, and Robert Haimer.

Billy really had the most energy and was basically the director. He's the one who pushed hard and got it on *Saturday Night Live* right after we finished editing. Rocky did the cinematography and was absolutely brilliant. Joanie did the design, make-up, and wardrobe. If you think it's easy putting false eyelashes and lipstick on fish heads ... *think again.* Robert and I produced it, helped outline it, and set the tone. All of us suggested scenes that we filmed. We were like a tight little band. Those were good times. It was a lot of fun, and I like that we incorporated so many styles into it, yet it feels like it flows naturally. We started off in a black-and-white film noir homage, then used some cheesy animation, then cut to color. "Fish Heads" has been a positive thing in my life. I think the song and the film hold up as a genuine art project that works on a primitive melodic sense and has an adult wink built into it. It was very popular on MTV. *Rolling Stone* magazine named it "the 57th best video of all time." We continue to make money from it.

ALAN HUNTER: It was so bizarre and underproduced and art school. It was kind of like the art graphics that MTV put in between all the videos.

MTV was really groundbreaking when it came to the kind of art and visual graphics that was the glue and the interstitial material between the videos. They went to the best art design houses in Manhattan to get all that stuff. And they were just constantly experimenting.

So to have something as underproduced and as bizarre as "Fish Heads" ... *that was true drug music.* Again, I think there was so many styles of videos. That's why the audience was so large for MTV. Everybody enjoyed *something*. If you really did like the headbanging stuff, you had it. If you liked the new romance and the new wave from the U.K. Great. You got it. But if you just wanted to smoke pot and have a giggle at 2:00 in the morning, Barnes & Barnes gave MTV street cred for that.

But it's bullshit to see four fish heads singing. [Laughs] We also had the Residents, with the big eyeball heads. It was sort of the "New York-centric art house school" video that made MTV cool. But you put "Fish Heads" up against a Rod Stewart video, it made it all better. The "Fish Heads" video and Devo videos were band-aids for all the other bullshit. It's kind of like, "Where else could you see that?" Early MTV was all music-based, but it was all different styles of artistic expression. I liked that.

— *Blotto* —

SERGEANT BLOTTO: We didn't even initiate [the "I Wanna Be a Lifeguard" video]. That was something that some kids from ... I think Plattsburgh, were in video/film and needed to do something for their senior project in college. They loved Blotto and thought, "Let's make a music video." This was well before MTV was on the air, obviously, since the video aired on the first day. They were just doing it for a fun little school project. I think our total budget for that video was $11, which I think we spent on ice cream and donuts in one scene, when I'm walking down the street stuffing donuts into my face. We didn't get permits to do any of the shooting. We just went and did it. All of the concert footage was done at a club here in Albany, called JB Scott's, which has long disappeared.

And we did other stuff. We got permission from some shoe store to go shoot the "shoe store scene," but the other stuff, we went down to the Empire State Plaza, which is the New York State Offices, and went in with the camera and did some shooting on this escalator. We'd go down to Central Avenue and film some stuff. I can't even remember whose house we used for the Allied Van Lines moving scene, where we were carrying some enormously heavy sofa down some stairs. The thing that I remember most is the beach scenes, which we filmed in Lake George. We were filming in I think it was April, so if you look at the video, you'll see there are no leaves on the trees. That water was *cooold*. But hey, it's for art. So we're in it.

The "Metalhead" video was fun. It was a bigger project. We hired somebody and storyboarded the whole thing. The concert footage for "Metalhead" was filmed at The Chance in Poughkeepsie, which is still in operation. We also filmed a lot of that over at Union College in Schenectady. We commandeered somebody's room at a fraternity house for the "metalhead room." I remember vividly sitting there on the bed with these headphones on. It was so low-tech, it was beautiful. We wanted to get a smoking headphone effect, so what I had done is taken some headphones, gutted the speakers on them, drilled holes in the back of each earpiece, and taken some clear plastic tubing and stuck it in there. So when we were filming it, I'm holding onto the headphones, and as I recall, Broadway and Bowtie were sitting on the floor—to the side of the bed, just out of the camera view—smoking these big cigars, and blowing the smoke through the plastic tubing.

One of my favorite shots in that video—that we also shot at Union College—of standing out on one of the campus roadways, and we had these bikers that were fans. I'm standing there with my legs wide apart, and somebody's helmet fell off the back of their bike, and one of the other bikers kicked it, and it went rolling right through my legs! It was a total accident and not planned at all. I think we went back and tried to do it again and couldn't get it, and said, "Alright, let's hope we got that first one." That was more of a production and less of a "Gee, what the hell's going to happen?"—which is what "Lifeguard" was.

Just yesterday, the *Today Show* was doing some segment on tanning or something, and five people called me up. "Hey, I just heard 'Lifeguard' on the *Today Show!*" The beauty of it is there are thousands of songs about love ... *there is only one song about lifeguards.* [Laughs] Every year, it's one of those perennials that just pops up and starts getting more airplay at the beginning of every summer.

— *Utopia* —

TODD RUNDGREN: At this point [circa the "Feet Don't Fail Me Now" video], we're making videos because we have the space to make the videos in. We see them, to a certain degree, as a promotional element. We're still doing the songs that could or would be released as singles. But our expectations are somewhat different. In that particular instance, we're conveying to people the underlying sense of humor and irony that the band is all about, and that some people may or may not be familiar or aware of the existence of. [Laughs] Doing this kind of almost live-action cartoon was a way to convey the lyric of the song, but more than that, our skewed way of seeing things.

ROGER POWELL: That was really somewhat astounding. [Laughs] First of all, Todd had the equipment to do this blue screen stuff. It was his concept to do this, with the bugs and all that. The thing that I would say about all of our productions was that they were certainly low-budget. They were sort of medium-tech. They always had a home-spun, "Let's-go-out-and-put-on-a-play-in-the-barn" kind of a quality to them. They were not super-polished. But I think they sort of fit the vibe of Utopia. Our videos, there would be a lot of volunteer people that would just come and do things, like sew costumes together. Or at one point, we hired a bus and brought people up from New York City to be an audience for "Rock Love."

For "Feet Don't Fail Me Now," which, by the way, I think ended up in Dr. Demento's list of the "Ten Most Demented Videos of all Time," the costumes were pretty interesting. I had to get in this funky costume and then go against the blue screen. And that got to be awkward, because there was a bunch of shots where we're in different contorted positions. I remember one, where I had to look like I was upside down. I had to hang from a bar, in this costume, while trying to hide parts of my body that didn't have the costume on, and having to curl up into a spider position. This, along with another video we were doing, "You Make Me Crazy," I had come back from a European visit to promote my solo album, *Air Pocket*, and while I was over there, I was in a traffic accident and had cracked ribs. I had been home for a while, but every now and then, if I moved the wrong way, I'd get these spasms. And I remember having those because of all this awkward body contortion. And in particular for "You Make Me Crazy," there's a scene in the end when all hell breaks loose, and we're jumping over furniture, and they actually had to take me to the hospital after, because my whole chest was just shaking in spasms!

We were trying to be as inventive as we could with what limited props and limited resources we had. We were lucky enough that we had our own video studio, which meant we could take our time to do things. We weren't under someone's watch, where it was burning a thousand dollars an hour or something. On the other hand, that was about all we had—the studio and the equipment. We didn't have the budget for high-tech special effects. We made it more about the story and what we could get away with. But "the bug video" ["Feet Don't Fail Me Now"] was interesting because we always were surrounded by art people and costume people. We had the talent that we needed. These people made us a sofa out of a hot dog bun and cigarette butts! We had this whole miniature set. It was literally a foot and a half wide, with all the furniture emulated, as if you were in a bug's home. And then we would shoot the other stuff against the blue screen, and when the miniature set was in the background, it looked like it was full size, and there we are in those scenes. I thought it was a very clever use of our medium-tech approach.

Fun at MTV

ALAN HUNTER: Nina posed for *Playboy* magazine in the '70s. I got wind of it in the dressing room one day. Mark and I were totally blown away that Nina appeared in it, but none of us had seen the pictures. On one of my personal appearances my first year, some kid comes up with the magazine, plops it on top of the table of where I was signing autographs, and says, "Hey, I thought you'd like to see Nina's spread." I was like, *"Holy cow!"* There were like hundreds of people waiting to step up. I couldn't just sit there to ogle it for a while. But I took mental snapshots really quickly, came back, and told Mark I had finally seen the prized pictures of Nina. It was pretty bold. She was not bashful in those photos, I'll tell ya.

NINA BLACKWOOD: I did it way before MTV. I think viewers started writing about it. I think how it came up was *Playboy* decided to re-run the photos, which they always do, when somebody starts to get any degree of celebrity. *Penthouse* did that with Madonna. Because I had signed a release, they had the permission to do that. So it was like, "OK ... *here it goes.*" I got brought into the office of the executive producer. When I did [the photos], I worked as a model. I was quite naïve, and I didn't really think of that as seriously as what it is.

And then, all of a sudden, it seemed like I had done something bad. It was just weird. They were trying to decide how to handle this. What am I supposed to do? I didn't release the pictures. Really, what was I supposed to do? They never threatened to fire me or anything like that—that wasn't it—but they did call me into the office. What can I say? I can't even say I'm sorry, because I didn't release these things. And then later on, look at where they are! Come on, I mean, Jenny McCarthy was one of the people they hired after I left [who had also posed for *Playboy* before joining MTV]. And certainly what I was wearing was much less risque than the girls prancing around in the videos, y'know? That didn't help with the "video vixen" thing. It really pushed it in that direction. And I still, to this day, get mad at my manager [Laughs]

KEN R. CLARK: In the very beginning, everybody took cabs, and everybody complained about that, because some nights, we would get out late, and they'd want to have a car sitting at the curb. So they contracted a town car service. The first one was kind of a lower-class town car company, I think it was called XYZ. And all the town car companies back then worked on a voucher system, so you actually had to have the damn car vouchers when you rode in the car. You had to find the voucher, and the driver would put "to and from" and give you a copy of it. That's how MTV got billed for it. There was always tension between the VJs and MTV about Communicar usage. It got to the point where I was only allowed to issue a certain amount of vouchers, one for each direction, and ten if they had extra things to do that week, because people would take them to clubs, and that wasn't part of the contract.

Mark had gotten into a town car to come down to the studio one morning, and part-way down, realized he didn't have any car vouchers. Which had happened pretty regularly. They'd forget them, so I'd have to wait for the car to pull up and run out with a voucher. And most of the drivers were fine about that. It took an extra ten seconds. *And this guy went apeshit!* He started turning around and driving Mark back to the apartment, and Mark was up in Riverdale, in the Bronx. I have somewhere in the vault a memo that Mark had written, probably to Bob Pittman, about this horrible experience. It was like two pages, overly dramatic, like his life had flashed before his very eyes. I'm sure it was a bummer, but it seemed a bit embellished. But the guy had at some point taken a screwdriver and was attacking Mark over the front seat! [Laughs] And Mark finally bailed out of the car. It was either moving or stopped at a light, and he bailed out and ran. We remember him calling the studio from a payphone somewhere, all pissed off, because he was stranded on the Upper East Side, and he probably didn't have any cash, because VJs never had any cash. We ended up firing the XYZ car service and went with Communicar.

ALAN HUNTER: I remember being called to task about an Andy Warhol interview that I did. I was interviewing Andy Warhol after he directed a Cars video ["Hello Again"] down on the Lower East Side. So I was interviewing Andy and had a great interview. Those were the kinds of interviews that I liked. People in that world I felt more comfortable with, than being "the rock journalist." I remember shooting the shit with him in the middle of a tape change, and I had bought an Andy Warhol poster a week before, a 20-dollar poster. I brought it and said, "Would you sign this thing?" And I said, "Alright! I bought it for 20 bucks ... *and now it's worth 30!*" He thought that was funny. I was just kidding.

And one of the VPs at MTV called me about a week later, because he'd seen the tape. And he said, "Look, we can't be making fun of the artists and celebrities we have on MTV. You might offend Andy Warhol ... I'm afraid you did." *Are you kidding me?* It was overkill. The more corporate it got, the more money they started making, the more audience we had, the more they were being looked at by the industry, the more all the execs were getting phone calls from all their buddies in all the other parts of the industry. You go out to dinner with the head of Arista Records, and he goes, "Look, don't let those VJs make fun of this new girl I'm about to hand you. Would you tell them to lay off?" We'd get the memos.

KEN R. CLARK: Nina was my best friend of those original VJs. Nina and I struck a bond immediately. I think it was because we were both from Ohio, perhaps. But Nina was genuinely just the nicest, most down-home gal in the world. Here's a funny little insight into the VJs. Everybody thought Martha Quinn was "the cute little girl next door," and that Nina Blackwood, with the bleach-blonde hair and the whole get-up, was some kind of crazy, wild, party girl. And, in fact, nothing could have been further from the truth.

NINA BLACKWOOD: Adam Ant, he came down, and I used to get teased about that, because Adam invited me to his concert. He invited me to his hotel restaurant to have rice pudding with him. *That's it!* And for months, I never heard the end of it. Nobody ever believed that nothing else happened. I chose to be professional. There were times when the artists that came in would ask me out, and I wouldn't go, because I thought that it was unprofessional. And, consequently, a lot of the events that I was invited to, I was with my friend, who's a publicist, Ida Langsam. So I heard one rumor. They go, "She's gay." And I'm like, "I am not!" They either think you're some rock n' roll groupie, and if you're not, then you're gay. *And I'm just Nina*, who likes long-term relationships. I don't know how these people in the public eye deal with the scrutiny that happens nowadays. I wouldn't be able to handle that. I'm so glad that wasn't around when we were there, so you could actually have a semblance of a private life.

KEN R. CLARK: Nina was so shy and so humble. She would come into that studio in a tracksuit with her hood pulled up over her head, so that nobody would ever recognize her. Although she did date a couple of music biz people—she dated John Waite for a while and a video director—but Nina was so quiet and un-celebrity-like in any way, shape, or form. And Martha was the one who was dating Stiv Bators from Lords of the New Church! Martha was a rude, crude, little girl. When a bunch of people work in close proximity for years, you get to know each other very well, and frequently during our hour lunch break, I don't know what would set them off, but we would have "belch-offs" on the set. And Martha would win every one! Martha's like 4'10" and weighs like 90 pounds. Very big burps come in small packages.

STEWART COPELAND: [Martha] was going out with a real degenerate at the time, which we all thought was kind of cool. Who was she going out with ... Stiv Bators? She was a nice girl, clean-cut. And the idea of her with Stiv Bators was kind of intriguing.

ALAN HUNTER: I can't remember when Martha reportedly started dating Paul Stanley. It was like, *"Paul Stanley dates women?"*

KEN R. CLARK: I don't think Martha ever dated Paul Stanley. Kiss were a regular staple of MTV for quite a while. Paul and Gene in particular were at the studio really regularly. We used them as fill-in VJs a lot, when one of our guys was out or sick or on vacation. Paul and Martha were friends, as was Paul and Mark Goodman and Mark's wife at the time, Carol Miller. No, I don't think they ever dated. The only rock star I can recall Martha actually "dating dating" was Stiv Bators. People were always surprised that she was dating hardcore punk rockers. And although he's not a punk rocker anymore, she married Jordan Tarlow from the Fuzztones, who was an MTV alternative rock star of the day. So, Martha liked the bad boys.

KEN R. CLARK: There were a couple of funny sex stories. Sometimes, the fact that a high-end MTV executive was caught getting "oral" from a female early MTV star—in someone else's office!

ALAN HUNTER: I remember probably three years into it, we started getting different memos from the head guys. Whereas before, they just let us do our own thing. We started getting memos about what we were saying and, "Be careful about this." We'd get memos quite frequently about the way we were talking about some of the bands. "Hey, make sure not to make fun of ... " "You mispronounced this guy's name." "Manager of so-and-so called up and said you were ragging on the guy." It was a funny corporate thing that started happening. Instead of 2 million people, there were 20 million people watching. Stakes were rising daily around year two or three.

The other thing I remember happening was all five of us got shipped off to a communication coach. We had to take lessons from a lady who coached the likes of Tom Brokaw and President Bush Senior, on how to speak and communicate. And there we were, once a week, each of us going with our little air checks, plugging the three-quarter tape into the deck and having this woman watch us talk rock n' roll. *It was excruciating.* Helpful, but the kind of language we were using was a little clipped, and it was the kind of vocabulary you'd use when you're talking about a cool video or some rock n' roll ... *but not making a speech at a National Governor's Association.*

NINA BLACKWOOD: At first, I didn't know what to think [about Julia Louis-Dreyfus' *Saturday Night Live* spoof on Nina]. And it's funny, because I have never used that [phrase], "Hot!" But after she did that, people would come up to me, and say, "Say 'Hot!' the way you do." And I never did!

Everybody was saying, "You should really be flattered," and I would like to see it again, because I haven't seen it in a really long time, since it was on. Of course, I love Julia Louis-Dreyfus, what she's gone on to do. So yeah, it's cool. It was funny, with the head going back and forth. Yeah, I really do that, so I was like, *"Oh damn."* [Laughs]

KEN R. CLARK: During the course, we worked at Unitel—and I think it was increasing towards the end, maybe it would only happen every few months—someone would take a shit somewhere! It never happened in MTV-leased space; it was always in the Unitel building. So we knew it wasn't a disgruntled MTV employee, rather a disgruntled Unitel employee. But there had been turds on the reception desk, turds on the sofa in the waiting room, somebody had left a turd on a digital mixing console in one of the editing suites, which had everybody in a complete fucking uproar. We'd all be having coffee and donuts in the morning, because that was one thing about MTV in those days—they always catered the set, so the whole crew would gather for morning coffee, bagels, and donuts. We'd be mingling around, ready to make rock n' roll television, and the Unitel gestapo would come raging through, looking very stern-faced, and they'd be questioning people quietly. We'd be whispering, "What's going on? Oh ... *the shitter struck again.*"

Bad Rockers, Good Rockers, Strange Rockers

ALAN HUNTER: I loved Frank Zappa—I was a huge fan of his—and I was glad to get the gig. I studied hard for him, and I remember I was coming back from Mardi Gras, and I had to take the red eye back to make this interview happen mid-morning in Manhattan. And Moon Unit was coming on with Frank. I was interviewing them about "Valley Girl." I was sleepy, tired, a little punchy. And I remember asking questions, when I started getting into Frank's life, he was just answering "Yes" and "No." Being really mean. I'd ask a question, and he'd go, "No. *Why do you ask that question, Alan?*" And Moon Unit would elbow him and say, "Dad, why are you being so mean to Alan?" The interview went downhill. The producer kept stopping tape and whispering in my ear. I was very disheartened by that. A few weeks later, Dweezil and Moon Unit came on to do a guest spot, and Pop came along with them and hunted me down and apologized. He said, "I was just feeling kind of perky that day. Sorry if I ribbed on you."

NINA BLACKWOOD: One name—*Frank Zappa*. Oh, that guy. You know how I said they were matching people up with the artists? They should have put him with JJ, because he wouldn't have pulled the stuff he pulled with me with JJ. I don't even want to talk about it ... just Frank Zappa. To this day, it remains the worst moment in my broadcasting career.

ALAN HUNTER: Ozzy Osbourne was the hardest for me, because he was the "Ozzy" that we see in all the clichés. Sharon was saying that he had a trip, and on the plane, he was sick and was taking medication. But he didn't make a lick of sense. Again, that was early in my days as an interviewer. I was very reverent to all the artists. I didn't have the sense of my stability, so when I would ask a question, and he didn't even come close to answering it, I was just thrown for a loop. It was really his fault. I could have kept going.

I interviewed Billy Joel in Russia towards the latter part of my career. In fact, I think it was the first freelance gig I did after I left MTV. I went to Russia for almost two weeks, in 1987, and that would have been right when Perestroika was happening. It was just an amazing time to be there and then interviewing Billy Joel in ... at the time, it was Leningrad. He had been drinking like crazy the whole time, and he and Christie [Brinkley] apparently were fighting like mad. So he showed up for the interview with his sunglasses on, and nobody knew how to ask if he would take them off. He took them off, pointed at the saddlebags under his eyes, and said, "Gentlemen, *I don't think you want these on camera!*" I was a huge Billy Joel fan, and to interview him was sort of the pinnacle of my '80s career.

MIKE PELECH: Devo. Jerry Romano—the other cameraman—and myself ... I don't know who came up with the idea to wear green flowerpots on our heads behind the camera, when they came into the studio. *They were not amused.* These guys were really into their whole persona, and we thought it was hysterical.

KEN R. CLARK: Paul McCartney—I've read over the years that he has a reputation for not always being so nice. But that's not what I witnessed, at all. When I tell you this story, it's going to jump ahead a little bit, because it ties into one of the most *unpleasant* people I ever met. [Laughs] Ringo Starr had come to plug one of his All-Starr Bands ... *what a jackass.* He came in with a flotilla of five stretch limousines, and bodyguards, make-up artists, security people, managers, and publicists. It was the freaking Ringo Star Battalion. We had to clear the halls. We were not allowed to "look at Mr. Starr," "speak to Mr. Starr," "no photos with Mr. Starr," "no autographs with Mr. Starr." In order for him to walk from the green room to the set, we had to clear the hall, including MTV staff. You know, we had worked with the biggest of the big ... *kiss our ass.* [Laughs]

We didn't have a lot of patience for celebrities who came in and acted like that, because the majority of them weren't. The majority were just professional and very nice. Especially newer celebrities were very excited to be at the MTV studio. They were as in awe of being there as we were of them. But that was the "Ringo Starr experience." It was just like, *"Jesus."* He was the lesser Beatle anyway, come on.

So a week or two later, Paul McCartney was scheduled to come in. We were ready to batten down the hatches for this one, because we figured if Ringo had been such an ordeal, this one was going to be a real hinderance in the flow of our day. And nothing could have been further from the truth. That man showed up in a yellow cab with his publicist or manager, did the interview, and spent probably a good hour after the interview—he wanted a tour of the studio, the sets, and the control room. He hung out, had lunch, took pictures, signed autographs. He asked questions about MTV and how we managed to produce 24 hours a day/seven days a week of television in a Monday through Friday, 9:00-5:00 work week, which was pretty much an assembly line in of itself. He was just a very gracious person, and that always stuck with me.

NINA BLACKWOOD: A cool event that I got to do—I got to fly on the maiden voyage of Virgin Airways and interview Richard Branson. I love Chrissie Hynde, Ray Davies. A fun one that sticks out was George Clinton from Parliament-Funkadelic, because he was just so "out there." Somebody that I felt a real poignancy behind—and sadly, he passed away not too long afterwards—was Phil Lynott. I thought he was a very interesting soul. He put out a poetry book at the time, and that's what I was talking to him about. I remember him just *affecting me.* There was something that I felt from him that was very poignant. A kindred spirit maybe, at the time. But I'm a person that, if Van Gogh were alive, I probably would have gone out with him. [Laughs] The "tortured artist"—that's what I was picking up. One of John Mellencamp's very first times he came down—his nickname, "Little Bastard," well, that's what he was! But he was great. I loved him right from the start. I just had a feeling he was going to go places.

ALAN HUNTER: Interviewing Kevin Bacon. He came on and was a big fan of the channel. I liked talking movies. It was fun to do those Hollywood premieres. I had the chance to interview James Taylor one time at one of his concerts, and I was just such a big fan of his, the record company guy said, "Do you want to talk to him?" And I said, "I don't think I can. *I think I'll just throw up!*"

KEN R. CLARK: Tina Turner was probably the first big celebrity that I personally had to interact with. I may have still been an intern at that point, but David Bowie and Mick Jagger had done a video for "Dancing in the Street," and she was good friends with both of them. The video had just come out, and she hadn't seen it, so she had come into the studio to do an interview and heard that we had an advance copy of the video, so they brought her down to the screening room and asked me if I could screen a copy of it for her. She sat there about five feet away from me, sort of dancing in her chair, singing along with it. That was like my own, "private Tina Turner conference." I was the only other person in the room with her. I just sat there and quietly died. It was one of those mind-blowing moments for a kid from the Midwest. It was like, *"Holy shit!"* And when she was done, she gave me a hug and said, "Thank you, cupcakes." I'll never forget [that] she called me "cupcakes!" and went on about her business. Just throughout her whole time there, and watching her interact with people, she was a genuinely pleasant, gracious, lovely woman.

Jimmy Page from Led Zeppelin—quietest, most low-key, soft-spoken, pleasant man. I had really been prepared for something weird there, because I had grown up a big Zeppelin fan. Robert Plant had been in numerous times, and although he had been a nice guy, he was not terribly approachable. He always had a lot of people with him and was sort of "rock royalty." You didn't just walk up to Robert Plant and say, "Hey, can I get a picture?" [Laughs] I think Jimmy Page came by himself—in a cab—with an acoustic guitar and a stack of photographs. While we were either waiting in the green room for him to go on or afterwards, he actually sat in the green room with four or five of us and played the guitar. He actually played a little "Stairway to Heaven," which again, was one of those "Holy shit, I can't believe I'm living through this!" moments. And I think for the VJs, too, those moments were pretty crazy.

David Lee Roth was in regularly. He actually lived in New York for a while and would always jog around Manhattan, wearing those God-awful multicolored stretch/spandex pants that he used to wear on stage. So you'd run into David Lee Roth in the deli next to the studio in those damn things, and the bandana tied around his head. David Lee Roth is David Lee Roth—

on stage, off stage. It wasn't an act; *that's Dave*. Dave was the sort of guy that would just stop in the studio. There were a couple of celebrities that would occasionally drop in for the hell of it. We wouldn't even know they were coming. Jon Bon Jovi, when he was first getting started, I think right around the time of "Runaway," which was his first video to hit the channel, he would just come in and hang out at the studio. Watch tapings and stuff like that. There were a number of people back then that were part of the social entourage.

Mötley Crüe came in a lot of times over the years. They were never any terribly debaucherous stories with Mötley Crüe. They were just high-energy guys, who are ball-busters. They're certainly not quiet and meek, that's for sure. Y'know, "The 'Crüe Circus' has arrived." They were always a lot of fun and barely under control. We had a guy that worked in our staff, Andy, who by day was a PA with MTV, but by night, he was a "rock n' roll magi-cian" named Arioch. Martha loved Andy, too. She featured him on a couple of segments with her, where he came on and did various tricks. But Andy could shove a six-inch spike up his nose. [Laughs] I'll never forget—I think it was Tommy Lee and Nikki Sixx were sitting there in the green room—and Andy said, "Hey you guys, do you want to see something cool?" And took that nail, banged it on the pool table a couple of times to prove that it was a real spike, and then just slowly shoved it up into his brain. Tommy Lee in particular I thought was going to faint. He was really, really grossed out. The blood left his face. He was like, "Oh my God. Dude ... *that is the sickest thing I've ever seen!*" So we were proud of the fact that we could actually shock Tommy Lee. That probably doesn't happen too often.

KEN CEIZLER: The most memorable stuff, that I got really excited about, was when Dan Aykroyd came to us and was promoting *Ghostbusters*. I think that was the first time I recognized that MTV might have had some influ-ence, in that we were attracting people who were looking to promote their movies. For us, the directors, there was nothing more thrilling than an artist that wanted to come down and do a Christmas song, because it gave us a chance to do something besides just a "talking head" kind of thing. And then it was just the series of rock n' roll stars that came through. I always tell this story, when Madonna was first brought in, and she was just beginning at that point. I remember her promoter or manager said, "Do you think you can get her on?" And I said, "I don't know, but I'll try. Just have her sit over there." And we had this little diner area. I remember her patiently waiting. There's moments like that.

KEN R. CLARK: Frankie Goes to Hollywood weren't too nice. I don't remember much about that, other than the fact that sometimes it was the one-hit wonders that were the most terribly most unpleasant people to work with. It was the people who had been in the business a long time and had been up and had been down and had seen it all [who] were truly the best people to work with. There were never really a whole lot of odd requests from celebrities when they came through. It's not like there was a concert, and there was a dressing room rider with requirements.

There were some shenanigans ... do you remember Vinnie Vincent? He replaced Ace Frehley in Kiss, and then after that, went on to the Vinnie Vincent Invasion. He was one of the first big glam, over-the-top, almost to the point of full drag. Apparently, Vincent was a very neurotic man. [Laughs] He ended up locked in a janitor's closet! He ended up locked in an honest-to-God broom closet, with this manager and publicists all banging on the door, trying to get him to come out. [Laughs] We were all in the halls going, *"What the fuck is going on?!"* As I recall, someone was let in there with him, and then a while later, he came out. I don't know what went on in there. Nobody probably knows but the other person that went in there.

Portrayal of Women in Music Video

DAVE MARSH: People talk moralistically about hip-hop and metal in terms of their exploitation of women. Well, who encouraged them more than anybody else to do it? Not radio. Not really the record companies. The encouraging factor was MTV, and they never get put on the hook for that. Or at least not very often. There's a difference between "Roxanne Roxanne" and what came later. MTV didn't have nothing to do with "Roxanne Roxanne." That was an empowered woman there.

DEBORA IYALL: A lot of the videos that came on probably post-when we got started, especially once the more mainstream artists were making videos, then the women were just like "props." Totally. *Well-dressed* props. But when it first started out, there was, in my mind, a lot of creativity about women being artists. In "Video Killed the Radio Star," the girl was an individual personality. She wasn't dressing herself to be a sex object. And Bow Wow Wow was like that, and Altered Images were on real early, and Joan Jett and "I Love Rock n' Roll." Before there was more of the pop music or mainstream rock on it, it was "showing the new way." You can be a musician and be yourself. And not a commodity so much, but as an artist statement.

ANN WILSON: They were portrayed as sex kittens or dragon ladies, but always from an extremely hyper-sexualized standpoint. That seemed to be the only arena that was open to women on MTV, then and now. It was kind of like that old Marilyn Monroe movie, where she gets stuck in the porthole. She's stuck because her hips are too big to get out, so she has to stay in this tight little place. She has to stay there, flop around, and look gorgeous.

MARTHA DAVIS: The whole "women" issue is interesting, because I'm a child that grew up in Berkeley, California, and saw the whole '60s thing, watching women fighting for their rights. And then, all of a sudden, it's back to a *Girls Gone Wild* kind of situation. Especially with the big hair bands, there was definitely the gratuitous sex, which hasn't gone away since. I guess maybe gratuitous sex is here to stay. I have no idea. I think it's all everybody's comfort level. It doesn't bother me ... but it's not something that I would do. I don't know if it's "forward" anything, but it's rock music. It's about sex, basically. So I think it's all good.

DAVE MARSH: Women didn't exist. "Girls" existed, to start with. I mean, maybe there would be a mom once in a while or an older school teacher. There weren't any "women." It was basically a world of teenaged sluts. The Whitesnake videos, the ZZ Top videos, Duran Duran videos. There was a cluster of them. There were bands that prospered on the basis of doing sort of sub-*Penthouse* video shoots. And the problem with it wasn't that young women were being "sexualized." Young women do a fine job of sexualizing themselves, or even that they were being stereotyped. The problem was that it was so one-sided. Very few female artists, for instance. And absolutely no female perspective, unless you count Nina and Martha ... and that would be ridiculous.

FEE WAYBILL: Compared to today, they were treated much better back then. Today, it's a bunch of misogynists. If you look at rap videos or stuff like that, it's a bunch of hookers. There was an R-rated version of "Girls on Film," the Duran Duran video, and then they did the tame version for MTV. Compared to today, it was pretty tame. Women were treated pretty decently. Now ... of course it depends on the genre, but it's a lot more misogynistic now.

LITA FORD: They sure weren't portrayed like they are now, with all the money and the gold and the shaking their booty around in their bikinis. I mean, even wearing a bikini ... like if I were to slap on a bikini and got on MTV, that would have been a big no-no. People wear bikinis every day, so it's a normal thing. But, for some reason, I believe they wouldn't have allowed it. They would have said, "Can you put on a dress over it or something?" They just didn't really want that back then.

TONI BASIL: I didn't think about it, because they were being portrayed how they were in commercials or anything else. I didn't really analyze it, because if I wasn't interested in the music, I didn't watch the videos. If the videos didn't have dance in them, I didn't really watch them. Even now, I'll just surf. If I see dance, I'll stop. If I don't, I don't stop.

KATHY VALENTINE: Probably pretty much how they wanted to be. That's kind of the band's call, or the artist's call. I don't know [if] the artist can be portrayed in a video in a way other than they want to be. You can say, *"No."*

CHUCK D: There hardly were any black women in it as far as women were concerned. It was just like, "Get as much make-up and hair as possible."

ORAN "JUICE" JONES: They were dogged down, man. They were dogged down. What amazes me is how a lot of young men think that they have to solidify or maintain their manhood by being—as far as women are concerned—acting crazy or being barbaric. At that time, women—especially black women—were portrayed ... I mean, they had tits and ass, you had to be in the street. It was a particular type of woman. It wasn't the type that you'd bring home or you'd introduce to your mother. It was the type you go out, and you have a good time. You spend some money, and you get freaky with her.

One reporter told me that she was particularly thankful that we came up with "The Rain." It still got the point across, but it allowed women to maintain their dignity. Which I thought was very interesting. I've always been happy or proud of the fact that you could still get your point across, a man could still get his point across, and you don't have to beat up, act like a fool, or act crazy. There's ways to do it more cleverly, with more wit, with more class. And get your point across, and still allow her to retain her dignity. At least that's what one reporter told me about "The Rain," and I was particularly proud of that.

But as far as black women were ... not were, still are, still now, women aren't really given a fair shot as far as ... even in hip-hop, female rappers don't really last that long. They come; they go. But they don't have the same impact as their male counterparts. Which I think is unfair. But that's the world we live in. Hopefully, it will change.

JOE ELLIOTT: Probably like they were portrayed before the suffragette movement. I mean, you look at the "Photograph" video, and it's one of the many examples where there are hot chicks caged up with torn clothes on. [Laughs] It was before the full-PC thing kicked in. So, it wasn't exploitive in the sense of ... look, we didn't shove them in there against their will. They willingly took the money to be paid to do it. And it wasn't prostitution. It was role-playing. It was tragically sad by today's standards. But you see, it's such a macho-fucking-business. Let's think about it—throughout the whole MTV thing, other than Pat Benatar, I'm scratching my head to think of another female that was actually ... Janet Jackson came much later. I never saw that much of Joan Jett. I mean, she was great, but I didn't see her videos as much as I saw Billy Idol's, you know what I mean?

PETE ANGELUS: That was a very sexual time, really. Listen, I know that there were a lot of videos that portrayed women in a very negative light, but not any more so than how some of the women are portrayed in rap videos to this day. I remember when we did "Hot for Teacher," getting a phone call that some organization—I can't remember what it was—but females were appalled, disgusted, insulted by the fact that these "teachers" were dancing on desk tops and that the classroom had been turned into a strip club. But listen, this is meant to be humorous. We are certainly not trying to degrade that woman in that role. Those were attractive women. I can't speak for all young men, but I can tell you that I personally had a lot of those fantasies when I was in school. I didn't think it was such a far stretch, and it certainly wasn't done with the intention of being insulting, by any means. It was speaking more towards those kids' fantasies and thoughts.

I can understand why some people got upset, but here's the bottom line. People are always upset about *something*, no matter how you handle it. At the time, I remember there was a lot of media about how those women were portrayed in "Hot for Teacher," but in reality, it just garnered more attention to the band and to the video. I've seen some things on MTV where I was like, "Wow, that's going pretty far with that woman there." And is it necessary? Probably not. I mean, basically, *she's fucking the television.* Is that good for younger people to see? Maybe, maybe not. I don't know. I'm not sure exactly what the message is of all these asses in the camera, but apparently, these people are trying to send a message ... and I'm not going to spend a lot of time trying to figure out what it is. MTV was an art-form. It was a blank canvas, and some of it was handled well. And some of it, the paintings just weren't that attractive.

MICHAEL SADLER: Generally, they were portrayed—especially in Whitesnake videos or Ratt or Cinderella or Poison, that whole genre—as "the groupie," as the subservient fan that would do anything for the band. And, generally, that was the case. Maybe art imitating life, I don't know. But I know that that was the lifestyle with those kinds of bands, the "hair bands" of the time. But they were portrayed as a lot of them ... unfortunately, that was not that factitious. That was pretty much what was happening at the backstage doors and hotel rooms.

MARK WEISS: I think they were the way it should be in rock n' roll—girls with big boobs and scantily dressed and sex. To me, that's the way they were designed for in the '80s. I mean, the '70s, there was the groupies, and in the '80s, there were the bimbos. Everyone used to hang out with the rock stars, and you took it to the max. I used to pull girls out of the crowd all the time and photograph them—naked, half-naked. I'd say, "Do you want to take a picture with the band?" And they'd take their top off and have their backs to the camera, whatever.

JOHN DOE: It was just as revolting as it is now. But that was why the hair bands succeeded and punk rock bands didn't, because they were willing to play that game. They were willing to play that card, and not be mentally challenging. And that played into MTV. Pretty antifeminist point of view. The kind of rap artists and urban artists, that came later ... maybe not. I don't remember Grandmaster Flash and the Furious Five videos. I do remember Kurtis Blow, but that was kind of shots of the street, as far as I remember.

JELLO BIAFRA: I think it was a deliberate throwback. I mean, how many of those videos were ever directed by women? It's the same old Hollywood we've had for decades, where generation after generation of hypertalented female actresses can't get a job because of the way they look. Remember, Jane Fonda was ordered to get a bunch of her teeth pulled, because Hollywood didn't think her face was skinny enough, and she resisted. I mean, that still goes on, only we have boob jobs, nose jobs, and thanks in part to "eMpTyV" and *American Idol*, now we have aspiring L.A. chicks getting boob jobs from their parents as a high school graduation present.

I have very, very deep objections to this whole way the "fashion police" beat up on people—both guys, but especially, young girls. Where no matter how smart, creative, or interesting you are, what you really have to worry about is you're too fat, or you don't look enough like Britney Spears, or your friends might not like you, or somebody might think you're weird, and, "Oh my God, you're an ugly duckling unless it's the *90210* world or *Dawson's Creek* for you." Both of which I think were pitched at MTV viewers, and the influence crept in on those, too. Granted, I did watch the "prom" episode of *90210* with a room full of drag queens all in prom dresses once. I thought that was pretty amusing.

The pin-up girls of the '40s and '50s could never get jobs in Hollywood today, because they're not emaciated enough. "We want a bulimic body with a great big boob job on top, or you don't get on camera. Because the only roles we're going to bother writing for you in our stupid movies and our stupid TV shows ... the guys can play *characters,* but you're going to play *the girl.*" And there are a few over the years that have been able to break out of that, but considering how few of them have been able to establish themselves, a la Meryl Streep, Julia Roberts, Rosie O'Donnell, or Sarah Silverman, versus how many guys can break out of that, it's still "Exhibit A" on how far we have to go in the way that women are treated not only in culture but also in daily life. A friend of mine who worked in that scene in L.A. had a great term for what they do with women in a lot of videos. She called them "wiggle girls."

JOE ELLIOTT: But with the women thing, I don't think there was ever a sexist stance. I just don't think that generally that many women got into it. I wish the Runaways would have started seven or eight years later. I would have loved to have seen them do a video for "Queens of Noise" or "Cherry Bomb."

LITA FORD: I had to change lyrics. I had to change a few things—clothes. Especially being a woman, women can be extremely sexual ... as well as a man. But for some reason, they have to pick on the women. I did get some attitude from the record company. "Lita, don't wear so much make-up," and "Maybe you should cover yourself up a little bit," or "Don't wear black nail polish." I was always being told what to do and what not to do. I never listened to any of them. I just went ahead and did what I wanted to do. If they wanted to sign somebody like Britney Spears, then they should have signed Britney Spears if they didn't like me. But I didn't want to change. I wanted to be different. I wanted to be one of the first to do what I do. Being a female guitarist, the sexuality thing is part of the act. Sex attracts. And that's what I wanted to get across. It wasn't the fact that I was just trying to be a sex symbol or anything. I was just trying to sell records.

Kmart, Target, Wal-Mart, all those kind of stores refused to put *Out for Blood* in their stores because of the guitar being broken in half, with the guts hanging out and stuff. I was wearing a g-string. I don't remember what I wore in the video ... I personally think it's decent. Women wear a lot less these days than they did back then, and that was an issue, because of the things that I was wearing ... or not wearing. I remember having to do re-do the album cover, so I didn't look so "undressed," and holding the guitar in front of my crotch, so you didn't see the g-string so much. Just stuff like that I had to deal with. I went ahead and did a lot of it anyway. How many times are they going to tell you, "No, no, no"? Because each time they do, it costs them a ton of money. So I just tried to stick to "Lita." That's who I am, and that's who I wanted to portray. I didn't want to put on some pink dress or whatever. It really was an issue, and I had to fight it.

JELLO BIAFRA: Even after the Go-Go's broke, women were completely commodified in the eyes of the major label machinery. There was a really talented, kind of a melodic post-punk band from here, called the Contractions, who were three women, and I believe it was their manager who told me at one point, when she was knocking on doors of major labels trying to get them a deal, what they came back with was, "We've already done the Go-Go's. Girl bands are dead." As if gender was a novelty. It would disqualify everybody else of the same gender. And this was definitely more of a "women's band," that wrote about issues of women who worked in downtown San Francisco. It was a completely different thing, but, "Oh no, one Go-Go's is enough. That trend is over. *Bye.*"

KATHY VALENTINE: I still see "women in rock" issues and books come out. I think that there's a mystique still, for some reason, maybe because the rock n' roll pioneers were men, that it's such a wedged-in thing, that it's always going to seem a little bit special and unique. I don't know if it will change. It's still here. I'm not saying I don't like my "guy rockers," but if I see a band and they have a girl bass player, that's where my eye tends to go more. I don't know why.

ANN WILSON: I guess it's a story to tell. It makes it more interesting. It makes it less threatening to people who maybe are afraid of women. If you go, "Wow, there aren't very many. There's only a few, so don't worry!" Also, I think rock n' roll has traditionally been invented by men to get girls and impress girls. So for women to come in and find a way to take up the dialogue themselves, they've got to be *really* original. I think Annie Lennox was really original. And we have always tried our damnedest to be authentic and to go by the question of "Why aren't there more women in rock? Because women aren't strong enough?" If you want to do it, *you can do it*. That's the answer. Look at Patti Smith or Debbie Harry. She was amazing on MTV. And she looked like *herself.*

DEBORA IYALL: There's always got to be a frame. And the frame can either be one that you totally jive with, or it leaves too many people out. It's funny, because there's a "women in rock" compilation LP that came out, that had myself, Pat Benatar, and Olivia Newton-John on it. [Laughs] It's like, "Yeah, we are all women. You've got *the ovaries* right." It was kind of hilarious. As music fans, we saw ourselves more in camps of our intentions, our music, and what was driving that, rather than just being women. Although I do have to say I totally enjoyed the Go-Go's. We got to play a party for them after they played, at Mabuhay Gardens in San Francisco. And I was totally thrilled, to have a band full of wild girls. I always had lots of girlfriends I'd hang with, and it only seemed like a natural thing to get the girls you hang with to learn songs and start to make some noise.

MARTHA DAVIS: It doesn't matter if you're a woman or a man. It matters if you write great songs. It should be about your art. It shouldn't be about your gender. I never thought about it. I never approached it that way, and thus, I don't think I ever felt it. I think some of that stuff, you create your own situation. It was the one question that got asked every five minutes back in the day. It was like, "What does it feel like to be a woman in rock?" I'd say, "I'm just a musician trying to make good music. *That's all.* It doesn't really have to do with that."

Kiss Unmasks on MTV

ALAN HUNTER: That was an amazing day [September 18, 1983], and JJ [who was the host of the segment] was really excited. He was good friends with Paul Stanley. I thought it was pretty major. Again, it was another example of how MTV was a platform for any kind of announcement that a band wanted to make. Kiss decided to "unveil," and they chose MTV. Of course, there was no other choice. There was nothing else to do it on. They weren't going to do it on late night television or *The Today Show*. JJ was pretty pumped. I remember hanging on the edge, watching.

I remember everybody from the office of MTV came down. Whenever something big happened, all the secretaries and everybody came down from the office. [Laughs] It was like, "What are you all doing down here?" *"We want to see Kiss unveiled!"* So the hubbub and the entourages and the publicists and the record company people—it was just packed. The pressure was on. And I remember we only really had one shot at it. It's not like a drawing, you couldn't screw it up. And I remember JJ would get very sweaty under those circumstances. As much as a pro as he was, he'd get real tight and nervous.

MARK WEISS: I think I did [take photos that day]. JJ was "Geraldo" discovering Al Capone's safe, uncovering it. But instead of Geraldo having nothing in there, JJ had the prize of uncovering rock royalty for the first time. I know they did the whole hype-up, and then they did the unveiling. It was a good lead-up, but it was kind of anti-climactic.

JOE ELLIOTT: They obviously saw MTV or the medium of video was a great opportunity to do this en masse, rather than just do it at a press conference in New York, hoping it would sneak into all the broadsheets. It was a smart thing to do, actually. As it was in '96 to put it all back on again.

WARREN DeMARTINI: It was pretty shocking to see what those guys really looked like. You're just so used to the make-up. It really did conceal their real faces. It was just a total, unforgettable TV moment.

RIK EMMETT: The Paul Stanleys, the Gene Simmons's, and these kind of folks, they are just performers. And at some point, you have to say, "OK, forget all the artifice, the imagery, and all the histrionics of show business. Now I'll just show my talent. I'll show my ability. I'll write a song, and I'll present the song as best I can." It gets down to that elemental kind of thing. And I do think television and big rock shows, they tend to take you away from that. But that core value, that never goes away. No matter what happens in the music business, it will always boil down to when you distill it to its pure essence. It's still going to be a songwriter who has written a song that is being performed by a good musician. *Period.* A lot of the bands that I've always respected are bands that always understood that.

NINA BLACKWOOD: I thought it was great. In fact, that was the period I liked them the best. Because it was real, and I thought Bruce Kulick was a great guitar player. I just liked that approach. When they put it back on, it was like, *"Oh come on."* It's like "the band that just keeps going."

ERIC BLOOM: Looking back, it didn't hurt. It certainly made a buzz. But then they put the make-up back on and retired ten times. In retrospect, they never made a mistake. I love the original version, with Ace and Peter, and the Bruce Kulick era was great. Early on, Kiss opened for us [on New Year's Eve, 1973]. When I saw them that first night, they were an opening act jammed onto our show. It was us, we were the headliner, Iggy and the Stooges was the special guest, and Teenage Lust was the opening act. And Kiss was *under* the opening act, as a favor to somebody. They came out, did their thing, and it was like a *holy shit* moment. They've stood the test of time.

CARMINE APPICE: I don't remember if I saw that or not, but I knew those guys. I knew them without the make-up, so it wasn't that big a deal to me. I used to hang out with Paul Stanley. In L.A., we would sort of be a team. We'd go see Angel in Long Beach and sit in the audience. I'd be mobbed, and nobody would know who Paul was. We'd go to Midas Mufflers to fix my Jaguar, and nobody would know who Paul was. A guy there asked, "Hey ... *are you guys in a band?*"

RUDY SARZO: It was a ballsy move, something that they felt they needed to make. What was really interesting about that, everybody in the industry thought, "Well, that's it. They cannot go back to wearing the make-up again." Which actually was not it. The make-up is kind of like that Superman/Clark Kent alter ego thing. Now, they can do both, with the make-up or without the make-up.

MIKE RENO: I thought it was not a very good move, just because they had created this *illusion.* I personally would have rather kept it that way. The illusion was created. It's kind of like finding out the magic you just watched was actually just a trick. I liked the illusion. I wouldn't have done an "unmasked" situation, but that's just me. I just thought it was a very cool illusion. But it was almost as big as watching the Super Bowl when they came on TV. It was big. That's why they did it. It was probably a "Gene Simmons idea."

FEE WAYBILL: No, I didn't watch it. I remember it. I remember the whole incident. But I'm not a Kiss fan, not a fan of Gene Simmons. Possibly the greediest man on the face of the Earth.

GEDDY LEE: No, I didn't see that. I already knew what they looked like. [Laughs] I didn't really think about it, and frankly, I haven't thought about it. I don't think it was such a big deal.

LITA FORD: I think it was too late. I think people just didn't really care. They just loved their music, and that was it. Wanting to see what they looked like without the make-up, I think that wore off. And when they did take their make-up off, people were like, "Eh ... *they should have done that a few years ago.*"

PHIL COLLEN: I thought, "Oh man ... *don't do that!*" That's what every-one really wanted, for them to be the characters that are Kiss. But it's cool. That's what you do in a band, you constantly change ... or you should. You try different things. It would be really boring if you've done the same thing over and over again. You have to mix it up a little bit.

BRUCE KULICK: It was pretty interesting. I mean, I knew what the guys looked like, so it wasn't like, *"Ooo!"* But it was more like, "How are they going to handle it? How are they going to present this?" And I thought it was really cool. The only odd thing to me was I was always going to keep my eye on the position that I wanted ... *which was Vinnie Vincent.* He didn't look like he belonged.

PETE ANGELUS: I might have thought, "This is interesting, because they have created such a substantial brand." And now, this is almost like when the curtain comes down on *The Wizard of Oz.* Now you're seeing the guy behind all the smoke and mirrors.

ANN WILSON: I think everyone had the same kind of response to that. [Laughs] I think it was, "Put the make-up back on." Not because of them personally, but just because they were so much more interesting with the make-up on. They had come out with that as their "cartoon." Their whole thing was that. So for them to suddenly not be that, there were tons and tons of other bands that were just like them. That set them apart.

MIKE PELECH: When Kiss decided to take their make-up off, I think Scott Fishman was directing, and he said, "Now we know why they put their make-up on in the first place." They were the four ugliest guys.

GERALD CASALE: I thought, "Jesus ... *put it back on.*"

1984 MTV Video Music Awards

LES GARLAND: The MTV Video Music Awards show kind of started off as another one of our jokes. We'd all gone through award season, and "My God, the Oscars, the Globes ... wouldn't it be fun to do a spoof on awards shows?" We thought, "We'd get this funky place, we'll have some funky award, we'll give it to people, and just let people get up and rant and rave. Just make it complete anarchy." That was the idea, to spoof and make fun of the real awards shows. So we set a date in September [September 14, 1984]. And we were smart enough to know that we should probably go to the outside and get some people that have had some experience, which would make it even funnier. So Don Ohlmeyer, as you might remember from sports [*Monday Night Football*]—he is one of the guys that helped develop instant replay—we hired Ohlmeyer's organization. And they "got it." They understood the sensibility of what we wanted to do.

I'll never forget Ohlmeyer making a really brilliant statement one night. He's like, "The one thing I learned about sports—*it's not contrived.* There's no script. The great sports events on television captured the sport. We need to capture the award show. Just let it happen, don't contrive it, don't fake it, let it happen, and we'll try and capture it." So it started out as a joke, which is why we got Dan Aykroyd and Bette Midler [as hosts], two of the funniest people around. I remember Aykroyd was dressed as the moonman.

How about the Moonman Award for openers? That was a joke. At the top of every hour for 24 hours a day [sings MTV's top-of-the-hour music], that rocket ship taking off and the astronaut planting the MTV flag, we were convinced that we probably poisoned the minds of a generation of young people that thought that we actually sent an MTV flag to the moon! So when it came time for the award, what would be a better award then a moonman? In fact, I'm looking at the first one ever made—right here, right now, I'm touching it. It sits in my office. It's beat up, but I'm sure it would draw a handsome dollar on eBay. Put that in the category of a stunt, but it was such a big hit, we did it every year.

BOB PITTMAN: The Video Music Awards came about because Don Ohl-meyer had a big budget at RJR Nabisco, and he said, "I've got money if you do an awards show." I said, "I want to do an awards show, because I don't want somebody else to do 'The Academy Awards,' and MTV will just be one of many players—MTV, *Friday Night Videos*, everybody. We should be the umbrella over *all* video music, not part of music video in somebody else's umbrella." So we thought it was important to try do it. I couldn't figure out quite how to finance it and get it going. But Don stepped in with the money, and also creative help. Don had done big-time TV, knew how to do an award show, and knew how to organize it.

The problem was we didn't have enough carriage, enough reach of America to make enough money on advertising. So I went to a guy named Dick Block, who ran the Metromedia TV stations, and worked out a deal to simulcast it on the Metromedia TV stations, which became the Fox stations later. And for the first few years, I think we simulcast it on broadcast TV, cable, and radio, so we could get enough reach for the advertisers to make enough money to pay for the show. It's obviously become an annuity now and a big moneymaker for them, but that was the early days.

ALAN HUNTER: I remember getting the meeting with our senior pro-ducer, Julian Goldberg. He sat us all down over lunch, and we were all very excited to hear we were going to have a Video Music Awards show ... and that Dan Aykroyd and Bette Midler were going to host it. We were always a little miffed. At some point, as the years went by, we just did our stuff, and we had this weird, sort of schizophrenic feeling of things that happened on the channel. On one hand, we just wanted to be left alone, do our gig, party, go out, and didn't want to work much more than what we thought we needed to. But when we didn't hear about stuff, and they had invented and constructed some new program, we were all very offended that we weren't in on that from the beginning. [Laughs] And before you know it, now, it's a Video Music Awards show, it's happening in Radio City Music Hall, and Dan Aykroyd and Bette Midler are hosting it. And we were like, "Well ... how long have you all been meeting on this shit?"

Our biggest deal was, *"We're not hosting it?"* That was a really interesting turning point for us VJs. That was probably when we started to understand that all this stuff was … we were the faces of the channel, no doubt about it. Bob Pittman and the higher-ups' philosophy was that none of us hosts would get too big. They, in fact, kept us from doing movies and stuff. I remember I was going to be in this movie, *Girls Just Want to Have Fun*, and they asked me to play a music host type. I was all excited about it. And Bob Pittman said, "No, you can't do it." And I asked him why—I begged him—and he said, "You don't want to do that Al. That New Line Cinema company isn't going anywhere, anyway. And this movie is not going to be the right vehicle for you." He was very patriarchal about it. And it was really because they just didn't want to pay us anymore.

His philosophy was that "nothing should be bigger than the music." It was almost like I couldn't fault him for that. So the hosts should not be too big for their pants. And we weren't. We weren't as rich or famous as the artists, but all the artists knew who we were. We were as recognizable as they were, so there was this weird symbiosis that we had with the artists. But as far as the channel goes, it was like, "Nah, you've got a shelf life here." And when they said, "You're not hosting the Video Music Awards show. We're getting movie stars," *we were stunned*. I can remember the gigs that we had for the show was I had one little report from up in the balcony, and the same goes for Mark, Nina, Martha, and JJ. We had these little reports we did, one-offs. And the rest of the night, we sat out in the audience, like everybody else. It was kind of a wake-up call.

KEN CEIZLER: It was a tough pill for them to swallow. It was a tough pill for all of us to swallow.

BOB PITTMAN: We knew we needed star performers. It's the "Academy Awards." Who's our star who's going to be doing it? It shouldn't look like it's the everyday programming. It really had to look like a big event. We needed the biggest names we could get. And the reality was the guys were great at what they did, but that wasn't their specialty, and they weren't known beyond MTV. If we were going to do the Video Music Awards show and simulcast it on broadcast TV, we needed something that said, "We've arrived. We're big. The big people are here."

KEN R. CLARK: That was the first thing ever on the channel that wasn't really hosted by the VJs, because back then, even the news segments were done by the VJs. There were no Kurt Loders or John Norris's with *MTV News* at that point. The VJs did everything. And there was no concept of programs. At the time, the whole philosophy was "television without a beginning, middle, and an end." You could turn it on at any time and turn it off at any time. That was really the first program on MTV that wasn't hosted by the VJs. I don't recall a ton of tension about it at the time. Maybe some of them wondered what was going to go on down the road, but I think everybody realized how cool it was to have the people hosting it that were hosting it. They were creating a television extravaganza, and all the VJs were realistic enough.

NINA BLACKWOOD: It was fun, and Madonna doing her thing, that now, is *so* tame. But then, was so shocking, shockingly provocative at the time. But you know what's funny? I was watching, but I don't remember being shocked. I didn't go, "Oh, what is she doing?!" I'm not jaded. It's just like, *it was a performance.* I wasn't as shocked as the press seemed to be. So that sticks out. Those were always fun. You get to wear a designer outfit and get driven around in a limousine ... in New York. Come on, that's cool!

GREG HAWKES: I thought [Michael Jackson's videos] were great. Is that what the Cars was up against? [The Cars' "You Might Think" won "Video of the Year" over Michael Jackson's "Thriller," Herbie Hancock's "Rockit," Cyndi Lauper's "Girls Just Want to Have Fun," and The Police's "Every Breath You Take"]. Wow. I'm surprised we won over "Thriller." But see, that's because "Rockit" and "Thriller" kept winning the other awards, so I was sure that they were going to take the big one. I remember thinking we weren't going to get it, because we had been nominated in six or seven categories, and we kept losing all night. So I figured, "Well, that's just the trend, just the way it's going to go." So when we actually did win for "Video of the Year," I was like, *"Whoa!"* That was a surprise. I think Eddie Murphy was up on stage with us. Maybe he was just a presenter. And I think both Jeff Stein and the Charlex guys were there, too.

KEN R. CLARK: A lot of those events—particularly when you're doing live television—went by in a blur, because you were so focused on whatever your task was at hand. Mine was always making sure that the right VJ was in the right spot at the right time and knew what they were talking about. You don't really have a perception of the show itself, because you're not watching it. And so much of what's going on on stage, you never see, because you're running around in the rat's maze of Radio City Music Hall. The first events like that, it was cool, but it wasn't until the second or the third year that they started getting bigger and bigger.

I remember a lot more about the New Year's Eve Balls rather than the VMA's. The New Year's Eve Balls were always a big deal for MTV. It was a genuine really cool party and a really cool concert. It was originally at the Manhattan Ballroom. Celebrities galore, and for a kid who grew up in Ohio and Michigan, you're turned loose in the middle of every rock star you ever admired. You're working for the coolest thing on cable television. We all realized that we were really lucky people. [Laughs]

LES GARLAND: I got Eddie Murphy to host the second award show. He came out, and as many times as I told him what he could and couldn't do, he just took off on a tirade, [about] partying and this rock n' roll scene. The punchline was he'd gotten "something," and he says, "I'm not going to say my penis was burning, but flames were coming out of that thing!" Or something like that that. Oh my God. Pittman is like, "Garland! *You've got to stop him!*" I'm like, "What do you want me to do? Go on stage?"

He comes off, and I'm like, "Eddie ... *what are you doing?!* I told you what you can do and what you can't. I can't believe you did this." He says, "You told me I couldn't say 'shit' or 'fuck'." I go, "I meant you couldn't say *all of them!*" [Laughs] We lost a bunch of TV stations. They were clipping it off right and left. I don't even know if we had a delay back in those days. As bad as that might have been when it was happening, it turned out to be a great moment of anarchy, and it had a little rock n' roll edge with this crazy comedian of his time. Those are the stories that I hope are part of the legend of MTV.

ALAN HUNTER: You can certainly say that is what made MTV the platform for all sorts of different types of entertainment, when we had the Video Music Awards show. We were seen as the hub of all things movies and music.

VH1

BOB PITTMAN: A lot of changes and fighting with the cable industry, because we were originally going to give it to them for free, and then we wanted to charge them. And, of course, when that happened, John Malone, who ran a company called TCI, the biggest cable operator, and Joe Collins, who ran ATC Cable, went to Ted Turner, and got him to start the Cable Music Channel. And then we had to launch VH1 as our fighting brand against that and negotiate with the other guys.

ALAN HUNTER: There was suddenly almost competition. When Ted Turner started talking about his video channel, that is the reason VH1 was invented. There was no plan on the books. There might have been some plans for a more "adult" channel from MTV, but they were not thinking about it until Ted Turner made that announcement, and the higher-ups at MTV scrambled very quickly to construct VH1. And indeed, they did, and that killed [Cable Music Channel]. *Friday Night Videos* was apples and oranges. That was *Friday night*. We were so big at that point. We were the only game in town. No one could beat us. MuchMusic was in Canada. It didn't really reach into our world at all. I don't think any cable channels had it in America. *Top of the Pops* across the ocean was sort of the model for MTV, but that was a once-a-week show. So nobody made a stab at it at all.

LES GARLAND: We did it to fight off Ted Turner's music channel that he started. We had been in development on—way ahead of its time—a shopping channel. We had invested some of our resources and were about to invest more into a launch of a shopping channel on television. And we had been in talks with JCPenny. It was going to be like a "JCPenny shopping channel," because we had had some success with a system out in Ohio that was owned by Warner, called QUBE. Interactive TV.

So we had this idea about shopping, that was the next network we were thinking of launching corporately. Ted Turner came to us sometime before that and asked if our ad team could represent CNN, on Madison Avenue with the ad agencies. If we could sell MTV on the young demo side and CNN on the older demo side, and they wouldn't compete with each other and our sales people could get better commissions. We had a deal with him, representing his ad time on CNN. If not one of his channels, maybe two—TBS.

About a year or so later, he came forward and wanted to know if it would be OK to launch a music channel for the older demo. We were kind of reluctant, but there wasn't much we could do to stop it. We said, "OK," and it was launched. The channel lights up ... *and they're playing MTV music.* We couldn't believe it. The old competitive nature in all of us, from our radio days, came out quickly, and we said, "Whoa. If anybody is going to do music on television, *it's going to be us.* We really shouldn't let him do this. We need to compete with that."

GEORGE LOIS: I got a call from Bob, and he says, "The shit is hitting the fan. Ted Turner is starting a middle-of-the-road music channel, following MTV." Turner or his people said, "If MTV is successful, why not do a middle-of-the-road one, where even more Americans would go to it." It made some kind of marketing sense. I run over there, and there's a bunch of us talking, and they're going, "What the fuck are we going to do?" And we were looking at each other, and three or four of us in the room said, "Why don't we announce that we got one?" And everybody was like, "What do you mean? We *don't* have one." I think it was more than me saying, "Let's do some advertising and say that we have it. Let's come up with a quick name and cut them off at the pass. It'll probably be so successful that we'll have to do it." And Bob and everybody said, "Why the fuck not? Let's give it a shot." It took big fucking balls for Bob to do that. It's one thing to suggest doing that; it's another thing to squeeze the trigger.

BOB PITTMAN: You're always worried about the competition, and Ted was put in business by ATC Cable and TCI and encouraged to do it. They made him big promises about the carriage they'd give him. And I had my head handed to me by Cinemax when I ran the Movie Channel. I learned about fighting brands, flanker brands. When you have a big service like HBO, you don't want HBO to fight the Movie Channel. You'd rather start another service to fight the Movie Channel. We decided, "We're going to invent another service to fight Ted Turner, so MTV doesn't have to go into battle." So we started VH1. And VH1 was completely a flanker brand.

From day one, we had to do it as cheaply as possible. Originally, we didn't think we could even do videos of the VJs. We'd do audio. And then our head of engineering figured out a way to do it on cheap 3/4-inch, fixed cameras. I went out and hired some big DJs—Don Imus, Scott Shannon, and Frankie Crocker as the VJs—just to get us attention on the radio. It's interesting. We were carried on Manhattan Cable at launch. Everybody said, "How the hell could you get a brand new service on Manhattan Cable?" And the way we got it on was there was a guy named John Gault, who ran Manhattan Cable. And Don Imus would go on every morning on his radio show and say, "We're going to be launching VH1, and I'm sure John Gault is going to be carrying us." And John would call me and go, "I can't carry you!" And I'd go, "Would you want me to tell Don you're not going to carry us?" "No, no, no, don't tell him that!" So Don kind of boxed Gault into carrying us.

NINA BLACKWOOD: Poor VH1 was like the bastard stepchild. [Laughs] I went to their studios once for something, and it was this teeny-tiny thing. There was no money involved in that. We never had interconnection really with VH1. It's not like we would have "MTV parties" and VH1 would be there. We didn't. It was really—and I hate to say it, I'm not trying to be mean—kind of a non-entity at the beginning.

LES GARLAND: I must admit now, 25 years later, we did go to the music companies and let them know that it would be frowned on if they cooperated with another music channel, that we would consider it an act of betrayal. And we came guns a-blazin'. 37 days later, they shut that down, and now we were in the position that we have to launch a music channel. So coming up with a name is always fun. We thought, "Video Hits—VH. And there's only one number one, [so] let's grab the number one." So it was going to be Video Hits One. Our greatest fear was that we would cannibalize MTV. So we intentionally tried to make it *not* great. Am I going to say we tried to make it horrible? No. But we didn't want it to be so good that it would hurt MTV.

It was all over the road. It wasn't even middle-of-the-road. It was *all over* the friggin' road. This network—with very little direction—took on its own life. Like a plant getting out of control. People liked it. We couldn't believe it. We were surprised, and we decided, "Well, it's time to take it seriously," and we brought in some people to do that. Kevin Metheny got moved over there from MTV. Lee Masters, who went on to do cool things, and VH1 became the real deal. It truly was not planned. It was really done more out of defense than it was as an offensive move on the field.

"We Are the World"/Live Aid

NINA BLACKWOOD: Band Aid's "Do They Know It's Christmas?"—to this day, I don't feel like it's really Christmas until I hear that song. I thought it was beautiful. Of course, very sad that there's situations that we have to do that. In the idealistic world, we wouldn't have that. But that's not the real world. I thought that was absolutely stunning, and the same goes for "We Are the World." I'm sorry actually that they did a new version of that [in 2010]. I wish that they would have written an entirely new song. I'm happy that it raised funds. That part I'm very glad about, so I'm not poo-pooing the whole idea. But I thought the first one was perfect. And now, with Michael gone, even more poignant.

DARYL HALL: The recording of "We Are the World" was one of the most bizarre experiences I've ever had in my life. I don't think I'll ever top it. It's sort of a surreal moment. It all came out of this idea—Quincy Jones said, *"Leave your egos at the door."* And by meaning that, he basically locked the door. Everybody has their posse—their entourage, your tour manager, your assistant, your hairdresser ... whatever it is. They were all barred out, and it was just the artists themselves in a room with Quincy. And that put people very much out of their comfort zone. All they had was each other.

Musicians have cordial relationships with each other, but they're not friends, because we all live in our own "solar systems." Very seldom are we close friends with other people on our level. It happens, but not with a lot of frequency. We were all people that knew each other, but not really. And didn't know what to say to each other. So everybody sort of reverted back to eighth grade in high school chorus—I think that was the common denominator with everybody—and Quincy Jones was "the choir director," and they treated him that way. Suddenly, everyone went to him as if he were "the adult" in the room. It actually generated into a really interesting, natural thing that was totally out of context with the people that were in that room.

JOHN OATES: Bob Dylan was off to my one shoulder, and Ray Charles was in front of me off my left shoulder. I remember Ray Charles being really cool and a lot of people deferring to him in a lot of ways. It was great to be in the room. There was a real purity of spirits. Nobody had ever done anything like that before. I had the presence of mind to go around with the sheet music and have everyone sign it. I have it in my studio. Whenever people come into my studio, the first thing they notice is the "We Are the World" sheet music, with all the signatures, and they freak out.

DARYL HALL: Ray Charles was funny. He kept cracking jokes. Billy Joel kept wandering over to Ray Charles and peeking over his shoulder, because Ray Charles obviously couldn't see what he was doing. Ray Charles was play-ing the piano, and Billy Joel was stealing all the licks from him. Michael Jackson told me he stole "Billie Jean" from "No Can Do" and asked me if that was OK ... and then pretty much hung with Diana Ross for the rest of the time. Lionel Richie and I were talking. We became pretty good friends. I was talking a lot with Bob Geldof and became friends with him. Cyndi Lauper was nervous. Bruce was kind of quiet.

ALAN HUNTER: Live Aid certainly made people take notice that MTV could be the platform for paradigm-shifting things once again.

BOB PITTMAN: A guy named Chip Rachlin, who did our music acquisi-tions, came in and brought Bob Geldof to see me. He said, "Bob wants to do this show and is looking to sell the rights." We convinced Bob that instead of selling the rights to it, what he should do with Live Aid is try and get every-body to carry it, and do donations on air. Which nobody had really done, except the *Jerry Lewis Telethon.* We said, "We'll carry it 24 hours." ABC said they'd carry it during primetime, and at the end of it, they would cut it and sell it to HBO or somebody.

So we put together this whole package, and the reality is we didn't have enough money to be competitive to buy the thing. But what we knew was we could get our audience very engaged, and I think they raised something like $60 million in donations, which at the time was an enormous amount of money. Really a defining moment for MTV. We sort of "arrived" with Live Aid. We produced the whole show, and we were producing it from both England and Philadelphia [Wembley Stadium in London and JFK Stadium in Philadelphia on July 13, 1985], which was pretty remarkable for us. I still remember running around back there and the camaraderie of it, making the last-minute decisions about what we would do if things didn't turn out quite as we expected. We were very much on the fly, a big live event.

ALAN HUNTER: I think it was the height of [MTV's] "social responsibility quotient." Whether they were doing that for ratings or it was the right thing to do, that's the question with any big corporate entity doing anything like that. I just think it made so much sense for MTV to be the lead outlet for that. It was fairly massive. I would certainly say it was a very uncynical and sincere approach to televise to the world something that big. For us to broadcast that for 17 hours was pretty massive.

NINA BLACKWOOD: A very eventful day. *Amazing.* Work-wise, for me, it was very intense, because it was live. I remember being really serious that day and being on my toes. The only time I would leave our "home base" was to run downstairs, go to the bathroom, and run up real quick. I don't even think I ate all day. It was just amazing to be a part of that event, because in the world of pop culture, that really was a historic moment. The whole thing was a blur. I don't remember any one particular interview that stuck out, because it was just continuous.

ALAN HUNTER: I found it difficult when I had my hosting duties in little two-hour windows—we all rotated in and out—to come out of such a momentous collaboration and capsulize that in 30 seconds, it was definitely more JJ and Mark's forte. Me, words like, "Wow, that was great!" was all I could muster up, because I just wasn't a journalist. *I was a fan,* awestruck by the whole thing. I wasn't there to talk about the first blast-off to the moon, y'know? I wasn't "the Walter Cronkite of music." But it was awesome to be there, no doubt.

ROB HALFORD: We were in the Bahamas recording *Turbo*, and we'd been asked to take part in this event. We just knocked together a quick set-list in the studio, had a quick run-through, flew directly from Nassau to Miami, Miami to Philly. We wanted to get there early, because it was just phenomenal, the talent. I think Priest and Sabbath were the only metal bands on there. I remember doing an interview with Martha Quinn, and I'd had one or two "beverages," and I was in a happy state of mind. I think I kept saying, "Can we start again?" And she kept saying, "No ... *we're live.*"

One of the things I remember is Priest had covered "Diamonds and Rust" by Joan Baez, and it had been quite a successful release for the band. And we never ever met Joan Baez. I'm sitting outside the trailer before we go on, and I see this gal walking towards me, and I'm like, "Oh my God, *that's Joan Baez* ... and she's walking over towards us!" We met halfway, and I said, "Hi Joan, it's really lovely to meet you. We're huge fans, much respect for what you do." And she goes, "I just wanted to say thank you for covering my song. It's the only song that's been covered, that my son"—her son was a teenager at the time—"my son loves Judas Priest's version of 'Diamonds and Rust.'" And I thought, "How cool is that? That this iconic legend would come and thank us for covering that beautiful song."

CHUCK D: I thought Live Aid was fantastic. I was really happy when Run-DMC was a part of it. Run-DMC was my rap heroes.

RICK SPRINGFIELD: We were on the road, and it was just another big event. The "Woodstock syndrome," where everyone knew it was going to be big, but didn't realize it would have the place in history that it did, as really the first big, televised, "let's change the world" music. It was a very brave attempt and said a lot about the state of mind of doing something with the power that successful musicians had, rather than just using it to get laid or buy a bigger house. I thought that was really admirable and probably one of music's finest moments.

GREG HAWKES: That's really the only thing I can compare to the US Festival, as far as its scope and scale. It was really exciting to do Live Aid. Boy, *was it big*. David Robinson had some electronic drums, and some of his things might have been triggering on their own. [Laughs] Unintentionally. Sometimes, some of those big shows like that, I tend to feel a little "detached," almost. The audience is so big, that it's hard to really connect in a way. It gets a little surreal.

ALAN HUNTER: At Live Aid, I was just wandering around backstage, and Crosby, Stills & Nash were sitting at a picnic table. Our producer wandered over there and asked if we could interview them, and I just happened to be the guy on call. I was a huge CSN fan because of my brothers. The producer whispers in my ear, "Ask David about his drug problems." He had just gone through rehab. It came out of my mouth, and he goes, *"You don't want to go there, Alan."*

DARYL HALL: It was sort of an extension of the same thing [as "We Are the World"]. You had all of these ridiculously significant artists all backstage, bumping into each other and walking into each other's dressing rooms. It was a very strange backstage.

JOE ELLIOTT: Rumor has it that Queen rehearsed for an entire week, and that the Who rehearsed for 20 minutes. And if that is true, it's a great example to any band that thinks you don't need to rehearse. *You're wrong.* And I love the Who ... but they were awful. They were much better at the Super Bowl [in 2010]. In fact, they were great at the Super Bowl. They'd obviously spent a long time saying, "Let's not do what we did at Live Aid." But I thought Queen were great. They even managed to pull off "Is This the World We Created?" when all the sound started screwing up, because they're professionals. Between them and U2, they were the best things on.

GREG HAWKES: One of my favorite moments was smoking a joint with Paul Shaffer while watching Madonna's show! The other thing I remember is for the TV show, while we were playing "Drive" is when they cut to Phil Collins' airplane landing at JFK, because he did the London show, and then took the Concorde over. When they were showing the Cars playing "Drive," most of the footage was of Phil Collins' airplane landing at JFK!

BOB PITTMAN: My son, who is now 26, was at Live Aid, backstage, as a two-and-a-half-year-old. My son looked up and said, *"Phil Collins!"* And they go, "No, no, Phil Collins isn't here. He's in England, little boy." And, of course, Phil Collins had taken the Concorde, had made it over, and was there, and was the drummer for Zeppelin. In my view, Zeppelin is the greatest rock band of all time, and at that time, I really thought that was true. That was one of the great moments of the whole show.

ALAN HUNTER: I'm sitting there in 1985, and we were 20 yards from the center of the stage, *watching Led Zeppelin reunite.*

JOE ELLIOTT: It's not really fair to tell, because the sound was so bad. When they started playing "Rock and Roll," the distortion coming out of either Phil Collins' or Tony Thompson's high-hat, that just ruined it all. Robert's voice is cracking a bit, Pagey I think was all smacked up. It's a hard one to call. I think most people were just glad they were on the same stage. It wasn't as bad as everybody made it out to be. Most of it was technical problems.

JULIAN LENNON: I'd only been living in London for a year or so, when I was watching Live Aid on TV. They mentioned this subject [a rumor that the Beatles were going to reunite at Live Aid, with Julian taking the spot of his late father], while I was sitting in my apartment with my friends. We were all in shock with the announcement. I felt like a spotlight had been put on me, and felt really flushed at even the thought of it! I wished it had happened, and was saddened that it didn't. But hey ... I honestly think in retrospect, that I wouldn't have been up to the challenge at that point. I was way too young and way too shy. All too much.

JOHN OATES: We were performing with Mick Jagger and Tina Turner, and also with Eddie Kendrick and David Ruffin from the Temptations. But we closed the show that night. We were the final group. We did our Hall & Oates set, brought out Eddie and David, and did a medley of the Temptations stuff. And then Mick came out and brought out Tina, and that was the end of the show. I remember hanging out in the dressing room area, which were a series of trailers, arranged in a big circle. Everyone was there—Dylan, Madonna, Duran Duran. People were really cool. It was an amazing event.

ALAN HUNTER: Kurt Loder in *Rolling Stone*, reviewing the whole thing and our coverage of it, thought the MTV VJs were a bunch of airheads. It's ironic that Kurt would join MTV years later. [Laughs]

FRANK STALLONE: I wasn't really into that, and I'll tell you why. I almost had the Bob Dylan thought, when Bob went on stage and goes, "Y'know, a lot of farmers could use the help" and then went into the song. In other words, he goes, "All the American farmers are losing their business, but everyone cares about the other countries but their own." That's why I think Farm Aid is so much cooler. I believe in taking care of business at home first. I mean, I think Live Aid was good, but the thing is, take care of your own backyard. Let's see what's going on.

But the performers, I don't think half of them could have given two shits about it. I mean, they figure, "Hey man, I'm sitting next to Michael Jackson and Diana Ross, and we'll go in the bathroom and do a line of blow and come back out and sing 'We Are the World'." That's what it reminded me of. I'm not a real big fan of musicians talking politics. *Shut up.* Because all of a sudden, now you go, "I really like his music ... but I hate him so much now. I don't even want to listen to him."

GERALD CASALE: For me, it was ambivalence, because we really did have a social consciousness and a humanitarian concern about fairness and justice and what's going on with people. But we weren't really associated with that, and we never even got asked to participate in any of these things, at all. Like Amnesty International, when they were doing those big concerts, when they bring in Peter Gabriel. And we would have done so. We realized that it was all just about "the royalty of rock" being invited to a private party. Like, Devo wasn't selling enough records, wasn't "in." They only want the "multimillionaire club" to be there. It's funny. When you watch "We Are the World," you can believe that the people that are singing it there together, *do believe that they are the world.* [Laughs] It was ironic.

ROB HALFORD: The other moment was hanging out with Jack Nichol-son, who was—and still is—my hero. He was with all the bands everywhere, and we were hanging out together at a party, in some penthouse in Philly. We just talked about this, that, and the other—about fame, music. He's still a big rock n' roll fan. Whenever I see Jack—like I did last night on the side-lines watching the Lakers, and he loses his mind and he's flipping everybody off [laughs]—it just takes me straight back to that day at Live Aid.

ALAN HUNTER: I remember when it was all said and done, we went back to the hotel, and I partied all night long with Paul Shaffer. [Laughs]

When Music Video Attacks

JOHN OATES: It became a one-upmanship contest at a certain point, with budgets and ridiculous concepts. And we got caught up in that—the "Out of Touch" video. And we also did a more obscure video, for "Adult Education"—*completely ridiculous.* It was an English director who had this vision of this post-apocalyptic world underneath the city of New York, with fire and people in loincloths. It was just completely stupid. Yeah, we got caught up in it as well. I guess as long as the record company was willing to pay for it, we went along with it.

JOE ELLIOTT: I think we all tolerated certain indulgences in videos, because it was still a new medium. But there was a lot of stuff that we watched and went, "You can't do that." It's dead easy to keep picking on the rock bands, like Twisted Sister, Bon Jovi, or Def Leppard. But truly, if you watch VH1 Classic, when you see Kool & the Gang's stuff, *that's* where the crimes were committed! Oh boy ... silver or gold lamé suits, keytars, dancing around the stage, doing this awful boogie stuff. It was just the worst.

WARREN DeMARTINI: I saw [music video] as a double-edged sword. It was something that you could take huge steps forward. But the other side of it was you could also wreck your career very quickly. TV could be a very detrimental thing at the same time. Some artists ruined their careers through their TV image. I noticed that, if an artist made the wrong video, and it was putting out the wrong image, it would sort of reinforce this thing that was not what the fans liked about the artist, and it would just poison the whole affinity.

ALDO NOVA: I was a big fan of Billy Squier's, because he had "The Stroke" and all those songs. I think Billy is a big example of how video had impact, because he did one video where he was dancing around in his bedroom

380 MTV Ruled the World

["Rock Me Tonite"], and that killed his career. It goes to show how powerful video was at this time. It could either make you or break you. I think they weren't expecting that sort of like ... I don't want to put to put my foot in my mouth, but that "effeminate" quality. I do remember that a little bit after that, he sort of took a back seat. I don't know what he's doing now. I mean, he was *huge*. His records were produced by Mack, the same guy that produced all the Queen stuff. He was a huge artist, and he definitely influenced me. I remember playing air guitar to "The Stroke" and "My Kinda Lover."

JOE ELLIOTT: That's the one when he was crawling around the bedroom, with pink sheets over him? *We were watching it through our fingers.* I remember saying at the time, "Mick Jagger can get away with that ... Billy Squier can't." Sadly, I was right. It's just one of those things, where it's like, "Oh man, no, please, don't do that!" We all loved the *Don't Say No* album. Things like "The Stroke" are fucking great. But then he goes and does that, and it's like, "You've got to be kidding me."

PETE ANGELUS: I remember seeing the Billy Squier video, with him dancing around the bedroom by himself, in some slingshot t-shirt or something. I remember thinking to myself, "What the FUCK are you doing?! Oh, I know what you're doing. I might be wrong, *but I think you're destroying your career."*

BRUCE KULICK: The album I did with him [*Tale of the Tape*] I don't think he did any videos for. But by the time he started to become a star, he started doing the videos, and that one where he was crawling around on the floor, I realized—even though I didn't think of him in any way as being homosexual—he came off that way enough that it really hurt him. Which is pretty interesting, because he has an effeminate thing, but so does Paul [Stanley] in a way. He came off in a bad way. So it can damage you. It can hurt you. You had to be careful about that.

ROGER POWELL: You do something which you think, "Oh, I'm on TV. I've got to do Vegas." And if it's not actually cohesive with the music that you're doing ...

MICKEY THOMAS: It goes back to what we were saying about "falling prey," to being at the whim of stylists, people that come in and you allow them to be in complete control of your image. And that can be a dangerous thing in the world of rock n' roll. I experienced some of that same feeling, but maybe not to the extent that it happened to Billy Squier, where it's like, "You're supposed to be this tough rocker. You're supposed to have this credibility." And then, all of a sudden, you're there with your little hairspray and little poofy shirt. [Laughs] But for some people, it worked, and for some people, it didn't. They were even able to talk Bruce Springsteen into wearing a little white, short-sleeved shirt with rolled-up sleeves. [Laughs] *But they couldn't corrupt Bono.*

FRANK STALLONE: Billy ... I mean, his moves were always a little questionable.

WARREN DeMARTINI: We were opening for Billy Squier during that period. We were right there when he went through that whole thing. When you compare that to the video that preceded that—it was jeans, a t-shirt, and a Les Paul Junior. And it worked. It was great, hard to beat. You're not necessarily going to get better with anything different, and why would you want to? We almost never sound-checked, so we were laying around the hotel room, just passing our time watching TV. I was seeing him on local TV channels complaining that he used the wrong director, [that] he was really talked into doing that. The thing that I could never understand was why it wasn't changed or stopped, because it was clearly something that was detrimental. I remember thinking, "Why is this being allowed to continue?"

MARTHA DAVIS: I remember seeing it and going, "Oh my God, what has he done?" It's one of those, "Whoops!" But the thing is like any art, any time, anywhere, you can have a very concise picture in your head, and sometimes when you go ... even if you're writing a song, you'll start out with this one thing, and it will go its own way. And, sometimes, it will go in a glorious new direction, and sometimes, not so much so. By the time you get to 1984, these videos are *not* cheap. I mean, we went from doing two for $60,000 to

$100,000/$200,000. If you're locked in, you've spent a lot of money. I can see, even if he had second thoughts about it, it's kind of like, *"Uhhh."*

JOE ELLIOTT: Pat Benatar came out of this era stinking of dead fish, but she went into it smelling of roses. When she did that dance routine stuff that Michael Jackson had done, it started to kill her. But "Love is a Battlefield" wouldn't have been a hit had it not been for MTV. It wouldn't have been a *bigger* hit, let's put it that way.

ALDO NOVA: "Love is a Battlefield" is another example of something that could either harm you or make you. When she did "Love is a Battlefield" with the dance routine, I don't think that helped her career at that point. There's the robotic dancing in the middle. She went from "Hit Me with Your Best Shot" ... "Love is a Battlefield" is a great song, don't get me wrong. You hear it on the airwaves, and it stands out. But if you see the video ... I don't think it helped her at all.

MARTHA DAVIS: ["Love is a Battlefield"] was kind of bizarre, because you don't think of Pat breaking into moves. You think of her as the ultimate singer. And I'm sure at that time, there was the pressure, because there was emerging this combo of dance. Before, if you were a rock n' roller, you sang and you played. But then, between Madonna, Prince, and various people, this "dance element" started coming into it. I'm sure somebody said, "You've got to throw a dance thing into it," or who knows, maybe *she* said, "I've got to throw a dance thing in."

MICHAEL SADLER: I thought it was brilliant. I thought it was handled really well. Because I think the dance routine was choreographed in a "rock way," in a very tough way. I don't remember having a reaction like going, "Oh my God, they're doing a dance routine in a Pat Benatar video?!" I thought it was appropriate. I thought it was handled really well. It was like that whole "girl power" thing. It really drove home the "we're in charge" kind of vibe. It came off the right way to me.

PETE ANGELUS: It's like somebody came and said, "We have to have choreography." And by the way, speaking of choreography—that is specifically why I had Van Halen and the idea of, "Let's have the group do a choreographed dance in 'Hot for Teacher.'" Knowing that they would never be able to pull it off. Interestingly, we had a choreographer on the set with us to teach them the fundamentals of those moves, and while we were filming, the choreographer would be pulling his hair out and losing his mind, saying, "Oh no, Alex fucked that up! We have to do it again." And, in my opinion, the worse it was, the better it was. So I never really allowed for that "second take," to try to tune it up. I thought, "This is a statement about everybody who's got to have some dancing in the videos. Here's our take on it."

BOB GIRALDI: Why would I say something to defend a video that has gone on to be as popular in history as "Love is a Battlefield"? I mean, really, why would I now say, "Well, those people are wrong"? They're totally entitled to their opinion and totally correct in their own opinion, but look at the opinions of the billions who have accessed that video over the years and used it in movies and skits in as many ways as they have. The success of those five videos stands on their own. Once in a while when I'm bored, I'll go on and see what they say about them, and a lot of times, people will say, "Oh, that was so corny." Whatever it was, it's still good. I watched *Glee* the other night, only because somebody told me they were going to do an interpretation of "Hello," and it was marvelous. It brought back such great memories.

JOE ELLIOTT: The poor guys in Styx have got to live with that fucking "Mr. Roboto" thing for the rest of their lives. They can blame the singer who's gone now. I always hated Dennis DeYoung. I thought he was a complete nob-head. But the rest of the guys are lovely. Thank God they've got Lawrence [Gowan] in the band now. I mean, I've sat down with Tommy [Shaw] over a cappuccino, and said, *"What the hell were you guys thinking, man?"* It's just fucking ridiculous. There's no redeeming factors to it at all. Styx were a great band. But grown men wearing robot suits and walking around like a robot ... what the fuck is that all about? It's more ridiculous than anything we ever did.

FRANK STALLONE: By the time anything happened at all in my career, I had been in the business 21 years. I didn't get to do my first video until 1983, and that was for *Staying Alive* [the song "Far from Over"]. I think it was voted "the shittiest video." It was horrible, it was just really bad. Don Zimmerman directed it, and Don was an Academy Award-nominated film editor, but he really couldn't direct. He wasn't a director, unbeknownst to me. It's almost like one of those things they used to use when they sold bad records, a bad infomercial-type thing. But I didn't know any different. It was a big mistake. I was getting a lot of airplay because the record was huge.

It was a bad video, but compared to a lot of other ones, it couldn't be any worse than "99 Luftballons," with little flash-pans and a girl with hairy underarms. *That* was a bad video. ["Far from Over"] was a bad video, and in spite of it, the record did OK. It really wasn't my video, because I was at the mercy of the movie business. There's a lot of stuff from *Staying Alive* and a little bit of me in between.

["Far from Over"] was filmed on a little stage. I don't even know where the hell it was. Some backlot somewhere. But I remember they had tinsel behind me. There's no camera moves. It's just me standing on a stage by myself with my guitar, wearing black leather pants, a red headband, a leather jacket, and playing my song. It's very uninspired. It's not like it's a great production with a lot of people around. I think there was maybe five people there, including the crew. Put it this way—VH1 Classic doesn't really show it too much. My second one, "Darlin,'" you can see on YouTube. It's done pretty good. I'm dancing, jumping all around, doing spins. I never had a great-looking band. They're kind of shleppy-looking guys, but they were good friends and good players.

After that ... oh man, this is a nightmare. My next single was going to be "If We Ever Get Back." So I convinced my brother to direct it. He was the biggest actor in the world at the time. They were very excited about it. So he showed up with all this fanfare and had some girlfriends at the time of his that were like strippers. He put them in the video, which had nothing to do with the Goddamn song at all. So I'm sitting there, and I'm doing the video. I'm getting excited about it. Now, this is a whole different scene. We've got 50/60 people there, Sly's there ... it's a big thing. *And he didn't show up the next day.* We were supposed to shoot, and he never showed up. Just disappeared. So that didn't really look too good for me with the label, and I wasn't really too happy about it. And we didn't get to see the strippers anymore. But that was really messed up. I show up to do the shoot, and they go, "Where's your brother," and I go, "Isn't he here?" And they go, "No." So that didn't help my career too much at that point.

JOE ELLIOTT: There's a "literal version" of "Total Eclipse of the Heart." You have to watch it! Go onto YouTube, and put up "literal version" of Bonnie Tyler's "Total Eclipse of the Heart." Watch and listen, it's hilarious. That sums up a lot of those videos in the '80s—they were there to be mocked. It took the Kurt Cobain "irony videos" to really turn the whole '80s into "it's the emperor's new clothes, and he's not wearing any." Now that I've seen the literal version, I can't even think about the proper version. It's beyond over-the-top. I mean, we've done arty-farty things, but I think because, again, it's not a solo artist where there's this indulgence, and it's not necessarily on Bonnie Tyler's part. It could be the director.

When we did the "Hysteria" video, it's a very "adult video." Y'know, dancers on the dance floor, we're all wearing buttoned-up black shirts and jackets, because it wasn't a "metal song." We wanted to do a video that tastefully represented the visual side of this piece of work that we'd recorded. Most songs, they don't necessarily need a visual kind of guide or compass. But you had to do it, because it was that time. It was the '80s. If it was going to be a single and you thought the song was good enough musically to go on the radio, you had to make a video, or it wouldn't be as big a hit. So you were always whoring yourself up to a point.

I can understand why somebody like Roger Waters would go, "I'm not fucking doing this." Because in fairness, [Pink Floyd] don't do "songs." You listen to the whole album. We weren't the same kind of band. You could see why it doesn't fit certain artists, and other bands thrive on it. But I think our "Hysteria" video, you can't really mock it, because it's a very tasteful video. There are plenty of other videos we made that you could mock. "Total Eclipse" and videos like that are just way too self-indulgent and way too much money spent on them. But they got the job done. The song was a hit. As I've always said, I must add the disclaimer, "Who am I to slag anybody else's work off? Mine is not perfect."

FRANK STALLONE: But you know, I'm not the only one. There are some guys that had some big records but bad videos. I mean, look at Billy Ocean's shit videos! They weren't good either!

ORAN "JUICE" JONES: I remember that video for "Party All the Time." It was a hoot to see Eddie Murphy singing. [Laughs] That was priceless. He was singing like he meant it, too, Jack! It was cool, because let me tell you something, artistic expression is supposed to be given. It's supposed to take place. You can't judge art. You can either appreciate it, or you don't. A lot of cats had comments and opinions about Eddie Murphy when he was doing that, and we knew Rick James. He used to come by, and we'd smoke blunts. He was a cool cat ... a little strange, but overall, a cool cat. But Eddie Murphy, he was a comedian, and he was singing. You had to appreciate his fearlessness. That was courageous. He jumped out of his comfort zone and did something that was so far to the left, you couldn't even see it. *It was around the corner!*

PETE ANGELUS: I just saw that recently, as a matter of fact. I just thought, "Jesus Christ, man ... somebody pull him aside and say, "Please ... *stop!*" To me, it was how serious he was taking himself, and Rick James dancing in the background like he was creating some Vivaldi piece or something. I just thought, "Wow, they are very, very seriously into this concept of partying all the time." And it's not that serious of a concept when you come right down to it. I felt the translation of the lyric, the expressions on their faces, and the camaraderie of "partying all the time" was just fantastic.

FRANK STALLONE: *Oh please.* It's just Eddie. "OK, gee I'm famous, let me do a really bad song. And I'll get Rick James to produce it." It's just dreadful. It's like Don Johnson from *Miami Vice.* Jesus, come on. David Soul, "Don't Give Up on Us," but he was a singer. I mean, they'll do it. Telly Savalas did an album, but he talked. William Shatner does records. John Tesh, Jim Nabors ... *I want to kill myself.* ["Party All the Time"] was just a dreadful video. You have real artists out there that want to get a chance to do something ... in other words, if he wasn't a movie actor, you would have never seen that. It was not like he would have gotten a music deal from "Party All the Time."

But there's some videos that are horrible, like Men Without Hats' "Safety Dance." Now, I would have liked to have come in there with a daisy cutter and mowed everyone down. It was just all these cretins. The dwarf looked like he took a dump in his pants. It's just a creepy video. It's like, "Where the fuck did these guys come from?" They're Canadians or something like that. You had this dwarf that looked like he had a load in his diaper or something, chasing him down the hill. I hated that.

Like "99 Luftballons." *Come on, man.* You got all these German guys sitting there on "a battlefield" ... it's just a soccer field with flash pans. It's supposed to be Verdun or something, like you see the Eastern Front or something. But she had her shot ... *she blew it.*

JON ANDERSON: A lot of musicians and artists would make the wrong video, and they'd be one-hit wonders. Very sad.

PETE ANGELUS: I also remember—which I wasn't very fond of—David Bowie and Mick Jagger's "Dancing in the Streets" video, with the two of them dancing around each other. And with all due respect to both of them, because they're great artists ... I couldn't help but say to myself, *"What the fuck is wrong with you?* I mean, seriously, you're one step away from wearing a Speedo ... I don't know where you're going with this." I understand that both of those artists want to incorporate some level of femininity into who they are, but it is a bit of a stretch. But that was the beauty of MTV.

To me, as great as some of the videos were from a lot of artists, there were also these fantastically *horrendous* videos that were trainwrecks, that you just couldn't stop watching, going, "Seriously ... the manager, the director, a friend of the band, a wife, nobody came on the set and said, *"What the fuck are you doing?!"* Nobody thought of that? I just think it's fantastic, that a band would be led around by some director, who really wasn't connected to them in any way, other than he had been hired to come up with some bullshit idea, and that the band was following their lead. To me, that was as interesting as the great videos.

I don't think what I think of other artists videos is important. I thought some were very creative and innovative, others I didn't pay much attention to, and some I considered fantastically horrendous. When I created and directed videos, I didn't view myself or my work as being in competition with, or compared to, other videos. Basically, I simply figured if the concept made me laugh or smile, it might have the same affect on some other people. I wasn't attempting to create "art" for a rock n' roll audience. I was just trying to grab the viewer's attention, burn a visual into their minds, and put a dirty little grin onto their faces.

PHIL COLLEN: The great thing about these videos is they would get you to do this really geeky stuff. But we were so young and green, we'd go, "Oh ... *OK!*" When we'd done the "Animal" video in Holland, we'd hooked up with a circus. They said to me, "We'd like the knife thrower to throw stuff. If you're playing guitar, just stand still, and he can throw knives." And I'm like, "Uh ... no. *I don't think so.*" So they talked Joe into it. And if you see the video, you see him stand up against this pole and wincing as this guy dressed as an Indian chief is throwing knives at him. It was all excess, and it was kind of virgin territory. It was "Spinal Tap to the extreme" in a lot of cases.

JOE ELLIOTT: But what you have to understand is you can't plan your life around "What people might think in ten years." You've got to do it for what people are going to think tomorrow—and suffer the consequences. Some of us are lucky to get through that ... and some of us aren't.

PMRC and Censorship

DAVE MARSH: This is the period of "the great music censorship panic."
MTV was funny. They instigated some of the criticism with some of the
stuff you were talking about, about sexuality. It was an open-invitation that
way. I don't remember a lot of violent videos. Am I wrong about that? I don't
think they got a lot of violence criticism; they got a lot of sexual criticism.
That's probably proportionately what you would expect.

JOE ELLIOTT: I wasn't aware of that at the time [the 1985 Senate hearing
which sought to label "offensive" records, lead by the PMRC, Parents Music
Resource Center]. We were in Holland from '84 to '87, so whatever was
going on in the States was coming at us at a very slow rate, over the phone.
MTV Europe didn't launch until August 1, 1987. We were there at the party,
because it was in Amsterdam. Elton John sang "Happy Birthday" to me on
a barge. It was amazing. But all this stuff, we were hearing it second-hand. I
wasn't even aware that they had a problem with the *Pyromania* album cover.
If they did, they are sadder than I thought they are. In fairness, I had a problem with it on 9/11. The second that happened, I went, "We should maybe
withdraw the sleeve from further pressings." And after six weeks, people
went, "No," because everybody realizes it's just coincidence.
    But as for pre-9/11, somebody going, "Well ... this building's on fire."
It's like, "So?" It's hardly *Appetite for Destruction*, where there's this like raped
chick with a robot next to her or whatever it is [the initial pressing of *Appetite*
was originally to have a controversial Robert Williams painting as its cover].
People do take the "comic book element" of rock a little too far. And Tipper
Gore [PMRC co-founder] is the prime example—fucking moron. God bless
Dee Snider [who spoke at the Senate hearing]. Irrelevant of what I think of
his records, he was an absolute genius, standing up for the entire music business, going, "You guys are just pathetic." And he was very eloquent in his
speech. I thought Dee Snider did everybody a big favor.

DAVE MARSH: I don't remember how much they interacted with MTV. Specifically, I led the charge from the other side, and I'm the one who broke the story in the *Voice* that, in fact, this group of housewives in the D.C. suburbs—every single fucking one of them—turned out to be to related to either a senator, a congressman, or in one case, a cabinet member. That was *one* thing. I did a bunch of stories about their connections to right wing preachers and stuff. I was the one who stood up at the press conference. They kept trying to get these warning labels on the records, which worked out exactly the way that I predicted it would work out. Metal and hip-hop acts are the only people that have had labels on their records. *Ever.* So they come up with this press conference in D.C. They're all about, "This is going to be a voluntary label thing." But if you really listen to it, what they were saying was, "The record companies were going to do it voluntarily."

So in the question period, I stood up and said, "You keep saying these stickers are voluntary, but there aren't any artists up there. Can you tell us which artists volunteered?" You never heard such hemming and hawing in your life. It was hilarious! To me, it was like the most obvious journalistic question, and nobody else was going to ask it, because everybody else had been snowed by the idea. And I said, "Well, wait a minute, I guess I have a different understanding of 'voluntary,' because does this mean you can 'volunteer' for me?" [Laughs] Actually, Dee was even better than Frank Zappa [who also spoke at the hearing], and Frank was at his best. The big lie that came out of the PMRC Senate hearing was during the presidential campaign [in 2000], Al Gore said, "I was hardly involved in this, and really on the day, I didn't say much." He was the only senator who never left the room. And it's on video. C-SPAN ran the whole thing.

HERMAN RAREBELL: *Lovedrive* got banned. As you remember, there was chewing gum put over one of the breasts of the woman sitting in the back of the car. That cover got banned, but at the same time, it was voted by *Playboy* as "The Best Cover of the Year." And because of this, a lot of kids bought that cover, because it was banned. *Love at First Sting* also offended a lot of emancipated women and women for women's rights, who felt that it revealed too much. So, therefore, they wanted to ban this one, too.

LITA FORD: I think there's ways to make things happen, and I personally don't think what I was singing was very rude. So I think it was uncalled for. It's not like I was cussing and swearing up a storm. The worst thing I said was "I want to taste your sweet thing. I'm hungry for your sting." [Note: The actual lyrics to the song "Hungry" are ... "I want to taste your sweet thing, I'm hungry for the sting of your sex"]. I mean, *it's dumb stuff*. Why would anybody censor that? It's dumb. I guess they're trying to keep everything clean. The songs now, they're *really* overboard.

DAVE MARSH: It was hip-hop and metal right away, and hip-hop more universally. Because they were the most defenseless. You realize that these record companies—I don't know if they still have them—at the time, they set up lyric-screening committees. Actual censorship boards within, which they denied for years. Until finally, somebody leaked a memo or something—probably to *Rock & Rap Confidential*—where they're actually talking about, "This record got through," and "This record we have to change the following." It promised no censorship, which is hallucinatory, right?

JELLO BIAFRA: One of the few silver linings of being Tipper Gore's pigeon in the attempts to beat up on and censor music was when I was charged with obscenity because of Dead Kennedys' *Frankenchrist* album—I got to spend some time with Frank Zappa on a few occasions. And, at one point, he came to me with an idea, where he said he was going to go to MTV and ask them to give him the "dead time" of the wee hours of the morning, when nobody was really watching them, and see if they would let him do whatever he wanted. To make it a much more free-form, creative, wide-open medium, that it should have been in the first place. And he told me he wanted me to be his "Andy Rooney." I barely knew who Andy Rooney was. But I realized what he wanted was occasional bits of editorial commentary. I thought, "Well, if it's something like that, sure, I'll go on TV." All kinds of ideas popped into my head. I made a whole file of ideas on the subject. But then, Frank's idea never happened.

NINA BLACKWOOD: I understand where they were coming from, but I thought it was really stupid. They obviously did not win the battle or the war, because rap makes anything that the PMRC was even considering awful look like nothing. I didn't give it a lot of weight, I just thought, "Oh God, here we go again." It's the history of rock n' roll. There's always some entity saying, "It's the work of the devil" or Elvis Presley and his hips swiveling. And it's weird, because I ended up being a very strong supporter of Al Gore. I go, "It's weird that he's married to Tipper." Of course, now they're getting divorced. "Oh, maybe he saw the light!" Because she was coming from such a different place than what I felt Al Gore always stood for.

LITA FORD: The only thing back then that bothered me was the censoring. Now, everything seems to be so open about sexuality. You couldn't just sit down, write a song, and say what you feel. You had to pretty much write it around what you think they might play and what they might not play. At least now, we have a bit more freedom.

Losing the Plot

GERALD CASALE: We quickly realized what MTV was really all about, and it didn't surprise us where it went after that. What would seem brilliant to a naïve artist, like a new art form—where artists could have audio/visual/multimedia self-expression—quickly turned into a commercial assembly line where all the videos looked alike. And then slowly, for advertising dollars, they had to keep playing videos less and less and create horrible programming ... until they played *no* videos. And, of course, the whole experience was like *Animal Farm*, where the rules kept changing on the side of the barn. It's like, "But why didn't Madonna have to the do that?" *"Because she can, sport!"* It was extremely frustrating, exasperating, and sad. We went from being the cool art darlings to somebody shoved into the cut-out bin, because the world was safe for Bon Jovi now. It was a typical experience of an artist travailing corporate business agendas.

ALAN HUNTER: I'd say that two to three years into it, what happened was that MTV—the three letters—began to be used in articles of all kinds and used as a generic term. They started using it as a "Kleenex term." "That commercial is very *MTV-esque,"* "That movie is *MTV-like."* They were referring to the edit style, fast-paced video montages, and the short attention spans. When that started happening, we said, "Ugh. MTV is about to become 'big business.'" And there was certainly a corporate-down thing that started happening.

BOB GIRALDI: In our business—the media and advertising business—when you become successful is when it's no longer fun. Because then you have a lot of requirements, a lot of things to live up to. Now all of a sudden, people say, "You have to do this. You have to do that. You can't do this. You have to do this." Why? Because it's been proven that, if you do that, it will be successful. In those early days, it wasn't like that. It was everybody collaborating, trying, and experimenting, and "Let's see what happens." The same with MTV—was all about "Let's see what happens."

DAVE MARSH: There's this whole ideology that came out of the "greed is good" period—which is very much the "birth of MTV" period—that confuses "big" with "good." It confuses "size" with "excellence." It's, "Steven Speilberg is the best director because his movies grossed the most." "Michael Jackson is the greatest artist in history because his records sold the most." And MTV was very much a purveyor, both in terms of movies and music and lots of other things, of that idea. Sometimes explicitly, but more often, just implicitly.

And I think that that's a risky game for any media enterprise to play, because you may have been number one for a long time, and you may be number one for a while into the future, but eventually, you ain't going to be number one. And if what you're pedaling is that everything under number one is worthless in descending or ascending degrees, that ain't no way to create a culture with lasting value, is it? And I do think that is part of their periodic identity crisis that they have. "OK, let's not do videos. Let's do reality shows ... let's do videos for a while ... let's do game shows." But that's part of their identity crisis. "How do we stay big?" It's such an anachronism.

ERIC BLOOM: Some people's perspectives was, "These guys really suck ... but they have a great video." Like somebody would put too much money in a video, which could be an amazing video, and the band takes off from it, people go see them live, and they're not very good. But all of the above happened. You could have a shitty video, but be a great band.

GEORGE THOROGOOD: It got to a point where, before you'd even make a record, people would say, "Well, what's the video going to be?" And that soured me a little bit. I was saying, *"Nah.* Let's make the music, and if there's a good video there, we'll make one. If not, then we'll pass." Then it became a promotional vehicle for launching records, as opposed to breaking it on radio and television.

DAVE WAKELING: I sat behind two teenagers one day, and they were talking about "that song," and they were like, "Oh, what about this?" "Yep, seen it." "What about this one?" "Yep, seen it." They were ticking the songs off by which ones they'd seen the videos of. For my favorite songs of the '60s —like "Downtown" or "Walk Away Renée"—I had my own "videos." Every time I hear that song, my own little show-reel gets dusted off and taken out, and I replay my own "videos." Some of this a little racier than you could ever be allowed on MTV. So the downside could be that video was either particularly bad or particularly eye-catching, and especially if it was both, you'd never be able to hear a song you liked again, without seeing that midget on the motorcycle with the champagne. That was it. You wouldn't be able to see nothing else.

JELLO BIAFRA: I wrote a song called "MTV Get off the Air" for a reason. There were a few "I Hate MTV" songs kicking around by then, but I knew from our "Moral Majority" song and others that, once I made my lyrical mark and put some really cool music to it, that the Dead Kennedys song was going to be the one that everyone remembered. And there was so much to make fun of there. How could I resist? But part of the message of the song also was "Keep your bullshit detectors on, people. You don't have to automatically be sucked into this. If you don't want to buy, you don't have to."

That's what I've told people since, when they've said, "Punk is so awful now, now that Green Day, Rancid, Bad Religion, and the rest got so big." And I keep telling them, "Well, if you still love punk and you're so troubled by that, why don't you ignore what those bands are doing, and go out and support something you like?" Life's too short to waste my time to listen to bad music or watching bad television. I wish more people would realize they have more of a choice on that. All you have to do is stop being afraid of your own creativity and intelligence, and then you'll never be bored.

STAN RIDGWAY: Videos went through a period of time where they became more and more ambitious in the storytelling department. A lot of videos turned into bad versions of a soap opera or something, pasted over a song that really had no story to begin with. Or the song didn't have much to say, but the video was very ambitiously put together, as if it was *Gone with the Wind*. That became kind of stupid. But some people enjoyed those.

I think the whole thing as it evolved over time, the tables turned, and all of us artists were kind of "at the knee of MTV," having to placate to them. It became really frustrating, because it began to cost more and more money to make these things. Then record labels started to say, "Hey, we don't want to pay for all this. So now, we're going to have the artists pay for at least half of it."

And then you started getting into situations where you could make a video, it could not be played very much, and you're in the hole for 50 grand. Or more. The whole thing got larger and larger, and even more gargantuan, in terms of budgets and spending. But I think, even now, there's something obscene ... maybe the word "obscene" is not right—"unseemly"—to be able to spend so much money on basically these advertisements for a song, or a culture, or a lifestyle in a band, when really, they're just too damn expensive. I say feed the poor. It's just too much.

LITA FORD: That's what I liked about the earlier videos. They didn't have a lot of effects and a lot of crap that takes away from the music. Sometimes people will pay tons and tons of money—and I've done it myself. I've been there, done that, and I look back and think, "Why didn't I just sit in a chair like Whitney Houston, and sing the damn song? Why do you have to go out and spend $300,000 on some fancy video?"

GEOFF DOWNES: Record companies in those days had a lot of money, and they could get a director and spend $400,000 or $500,000 *on one video*. It was that crazy. And then people realized that was more than they spent making an album.

JON ANDERSON: It just got crazy, where I remember the last video that we proposed to do was going to cost us $150,000, and the last two we'd done hadn't been picked up by MTV. So the argument was, "Why make a video if there's nowhere to play it?" And, of course, at that time, it was like us against them—the musicians against the corporate—to make you into a commercial entity like ketchup, y'know? What's the point? That's why I was always aggressively against wasting money on something that might not get picked up. I might as well go to Vegas with a hundred grand.

GEDDY LEE: You're sitting there going, "Wait a second ... we have to fight to get a decent recording budget, yet we can get a video budget that dwarfs it?" It didn't make any sense to us.

DAVE MARSH: The record companies were really left holding their ass in their hands, because first of all, probably upwards of 60%—maybe even 75% or 80%—of what they made as videos never got showed anywhere. And they became enormously expensive. $250,000/$300,000 was sort of the buy-in price, not the high price. They got very little for it, and it cost them career development. And for a long time, they didn't know what to do with that. And then they figured out they could just make stupid shit, rotate Jessica Simpsons, and it would work out well for them. It did for a while, and they reaped the whirlwind. But that's what happens when you sow it.

TONI BASIL: I started to see when I would be working for people, "the director's cut." And I would look at this director's cut and think, "This is a cut that makes the director look good, *not the artist.*" We went back to the record company in one particular instance and said, "This director is making this video for himself, not for the artist." And quite frankly, it's the artist that pays for it. I mean, "Hey, let's get the better shots of the singer." *Please.* It's shocking what goes on. It's not a world I really want to be in. Unless you're really a major star and you can keep people out of your hair, it's everybody's video but the artist.

GEDDY LEE: We went through a number of years where we really struggled with the idea of how we wanted to present ourselves on video. And it was always uncomfortable, and we always used to talk to these directors and say, "Look, *just show us playing.*" And, after a while, that wasn't enough for what MTV wanted out of their bands. They wanted little movies. So it was a strange time for a band like us, who were forced to deal with that whole issue.

DAVE WAKELING: What we did best really was just to try and have a bit of a story going around what we did normally, which was play the songs. Because of the list of the "30 things," you could imagine what would happen if you ever came up with a good idea for a video! It just got emasculated to the point you wished you never mentioned it. Which was embarrassing, because I had plenty of friends who had managed to make very exciting, homemade short movies—three or five minute clips—for very little money. And had managed to do something that moved you.

I used to be embarrassed, because they could make such great short films for $5,000 or much less. And for $100,000, we couldn't seem to do anything that excited the band or the director by the time it had been finished editing. So we generally tended to do a live performance-ish kind of thing and make up some cute-but-simple story around it—that never included a woman with big hair, packing her suitcases on the bed, and a lamp swinging. *Menacingly.* You know she's leaving this time ... she's going straight down to the car, she's going to roll all over the car for a couple of minutes, then she's off. And that's it.

RICKY BYRD: After a while, the years went by, and all the videos started to look the same. Everybody just ran out of ideas. It's like a sitcom. How many times can you do the same thing? And then, after a while, it didn't even have anything to do with the storyline. It was just gratuitous girls or muscle-bound guys, depending on who it was.

ROGER POWELL: You had the overexposure thing. It was "a danger" we never experienced ourselves. [Laughs] I would have liked to have been in that position, where it was like, "Oh no, stop playing it ... *it's hurting sales.*"

CARMINE APPICE: It got ridiculous. It was always the same bands. You'd see the same however many there were, 20 bands. Def Leppard, Judas Priest, Ratt, Mötley Crüe, Journey, Foreigner—it was always the same bands. They never gave airplay to the other bands after a while. I remember when it first started, it was always these guys calling my manager, saying, "When Carmine's in town, can he do an interview?" So they used all of us to help get it going, but then when it got going, it was like, "Oh, *forget about you guys.*"

RICKY BYRD: When I was a kid, everything was different. The only thing we knew from the stars that we loved—like the Stones or the Who—was the stuff we read in *Rolling Stone* or *Circus* magazine. We didn't know people's deep, dark secrets. We knew Keith was a junkie, but we read that. There was an aura of "cool" that was around when I was a kid. Everybody wanted to be a rock star. Maybe not *everybody,* but the kids I hung out with. Everything was so mysterious. It was like movie stars. "What do they do in real life? What are they like?" With the onset of MTV, videos, and *Behind the Music,* now you know everything. You know what shoe size the person wears. You know how many girls he's screwed. It all became this other thing.

FRANK STALLONE: I came up in the era of the Beatles, the Stones, Crosby Stills & Nash, Joni Mitchell, Cat Stevens—all that good stuff. And now, I'm trying to communicate with guys who know nothing about music. They're just sitting there, sampling with a synthesizer. So the music went like that. The music got cheesy. People like Madonna—I can't put her down, she's successful. I don't really particularly care for her music, but she would have been stoned off stage when I was coming up. If you came on stage like *NSYNC, they would have stoned you and killed you. You couldn't play the Fillmore, guys out there dancing in syncopation? *Forget it.* Or Madonna dancing ... the girls we were listening to were Janis Joplin, Tina Turner—hardcore stuff. I mean, choreography? That was like Broadway.

ANGELO MOORE: I remember going on MTV, and I had just had this zoot suit made. It was a marijuana/hemp zoot suit. It was made out of hemp. It had purple stripes that were horizontal, and it had glow-in-the-dark marijuana leaves on the pants and the jacket. I had a hat with a marijuana glow-in-the-dark leaf that spun around. And they wouldn't let me wear it. I said, "Why?" And they said, "Well, it has marijuana leaves on it." I went back-and-forth with the programmer for a while. I was just like, "Well, come on man. *It's a nice outfit.*" Long story short, they didn't let me wear it. I had to change my clothes. Which really upset me, because I thought, "This isn't what art and music is all about. It shouldn't be about censorship."

DAVE WAKELING: Why MTV moved onto television without the music part ... for a few years, you could have a laugh flicking on when the commercials were on the station you were watching, and see how many times they were playing a video. But after a year or two, the game got kind of sad, because you could get all ten hits with quite easily never getting a music video. So that was the end of it, really. What was it, the Internet killed the video star? Or was the list of 30 transgressions that made it that there wasn't enough to capture the imagination? It was already a cold medium, and with the broadcasting rules, which have always been about what 40-year-old people think 14-year-old people are offended by. And they're usually *totally wrong*. The combination of all that meant that it was a very shiny edifice, like the beautifully polished car, but it didn't have no engine. So we just looked at it ... and that was that.

STAN RIDGWAY: Videos are garbage after a while. They all just become like garbage. I'd much rather see a performance of somebody. Something that just came out recently was the rerelease of *The TAMI Show* from the early '60s. *The TAMI Show* was a show that was made in 1964, that probably has James Brown's best filmed performance you've ever seen in your life on it. And there's also performances from the Rolling Stones, Jan and Dean, the Beach Boys. It's all filmed in one night. That is something to me, the beauty of being able to capture things on film or video, that becomes very valuable. These other things, videos and things like that, become nostalgic moments for some part of a memory that I might have been going through at that time.

FRANK STALLONE: MTV had changed quite a bit. When I first started, it was Pete Townshend going, "I want my MTV!" and no commercials. And then slowly but surely, commercials and political crap. So I didn't even pay attention to it anymore. I think it ate itself.

DAVE MARSH: The record industry figured out at some point along the line that having replaceable stars was ultimately more cost-effective than having stars with longevity. Because even though the stars with longevity sold a lot more records, at the back end of that were royalties being paid. And since their only business model ever was stealing from artists, now, it's pretty conscious that they're not interested in having acts that last more than a couple of records. And that really was generated from the MTV kind of, "Let's go back to top 40." It was really an attempt in some ways to go back to the early '70s or even late '60s top 40 radio. There was a superficiality about it. They'd rather have the Archies than the Stones, it seemed like.

STAN RIDGWAY: Nothing lasts forever. It was a bright moment. For one bright, shining spell, we had Camelot.

The Team Breaks Up/JJ Jackson Remembered

KEN R. CLARK: The original VJs started leaving in '85. Nina Blackwood was the first to go, followed shortly thereafter by JJ. The two of them left pretty close together. Mark, Alan, and Martha stayed on a bit longer. It was a bittersweet time. I think the channel didn't renew everybody's contracts and felt that it was time for some fresh blood on the air. Other people like Martha, there was such a public outcry after they didn't renew her contract that they wound up bringing her back. There were a couple of shows that we brought Martha back from L.A. to host after that.

BOB PITTMAN: Suddenly, [the VJs] were being talked about. People were coming to them, saying, "You could be a movie star. You could host *The Tonight Show*." And some of them had to try it. They believed it; they wanted it. They were only going to make so much money as a VJ. So I think they went out and tried their hand at it, and understandably so. They began to replace some of the VJs. And one of the big decisions we had to make was, *Rolling Stone* grew up with its audience. Originally, it was younger, and now, people my age read *Rolling Stone*. We made the decision to do the opposite, consciously.

We said very early on, "Strategically, we're not going to get old with our audience. We're going to let them go, and we're going to replace them with a new audience, so we're never 'your older brother's channel.'" And, by the way, one of the reasons that *Saturday Night Live* would stop doing bits that were working was they had done it. And they had to do something new. I think the challenge of MTV is to give up what they're doing that is a big success and continue to do new things, so that they turn over the audience and never look like they've been around too long or like they're the last generation's service. And I think that required turning over the faces on the air and getting rid of shows that work, because they'd just been around too long. It's counterintuitive, because most of us work toward getting it just right and then hanging on to that. And at MTV, mentally, you have to get in the idea that we're always going to be changing. And I think the VJs became a part of that.

NINA BLACKWOOD: I was broached a year before I actually left by *Solid Gold*, to co-host with Rick Dees. I was getting a lot of offers through my agents. I was getting offers for a lot of things that I had to keep turning down—commercial sponsorships, worth thousands and thousands of dollars. I actually had a television show that I was given permission to shoot the demo for. It was Merv Griffin, and it was *Live from the Hollywood Palace*. I was the host. And his words were, "I don't care who we get as the co-host ... *as long as we get Nina.*"They let me do that, and they put a lot of money into that, even took it to the big convention where they sell TV shows to sponsors, NATPE. They had the brochure with me. My name was on the marquee when we did the shooting. Those guys at MTV ... again, I got called into their office. [Laughs] They gave my manager permission for me to do this. And then, when push came to shove, they reneged. They said, "You have a choice—either do that or do this. You can't do both." And I'm going, "You gave me permission!" I picked MTV. Because of the camaraderie and the family that we had, I wasn't ready to leave MTV yet. So I turned down a lot of things.

That last year I was there, things were changing. You could feel something in the air. They were taking a lot of the duties that the VJs had before away from us. They had Doug Herzog in there. There was now a "news department," whereas we always did the news before. And they again didn't let us expand—if we wanted to produce a special show, we weren't allowed. That wasn't part of the plan. So this is my fifth year. With all that going on, my manager is still out in L.A. with my agents, and he had kept the fires going on a couple of these offers. So now, Paramount Pictures upped the ante. They really wanted me, and they said, "Not only do we want her to co-host *Solid Gold*, but we want her to be the music correspondent for *Entertainment Tonight*. So those two offers were on the table, plus another one for a syndicated radio show through United Stations, and then another one through I think CNN. So all those things were happening, and my manager and I had decided, "OK, now is the time to jump." I was ready. So that is in reality what happened.

I didn't just get thrown off MTV. I had three jobs that I went to, immediately. Howard Stern—who worked with some of the executives at NBC—somehow sussed out what was going on. I didn't tell anybody. But somehow, *he knew the truth.* And I remember him calling me and having me on his radio show, because he was giving "the finger" to the MTV executives. I'll never forget that, and I was always very indebted, in thinking, "Thanks, Howard." It was pretty cool. It really hurt me that they spun it around, like, "We're not renewing her contract." "Well, no. *I'm leaving.*" And they forbid me to talk to the press. I was not allowed to speak my opinion or say anything. But I did Howard, because that wasn't press. That was a radio show.

ALAN HUNTER: I remember when Martha was told that her contract was not renewed, we were all dumbfounded. When JJ and Nina were not renewed, the writing was on the wall. Both of them were let go. That was year five, and Mark, Martha, and I went, "Holy cow. *This really is happening.*" That was good motivation for us to begin to think about our careers thereafter! I just signed a three-year extension on my contract, so I had been given sort of a vote of approval. I don't know why. But I was pretty happy about that. When JJ and Nina were let go, we thought, "Well, let's start looking around." When Martha was let go a half a year later, I just didn't understand that at all. And then Mark and I looked at each other and said, "There really is a final window here on this."

I was already ready to go. I was ready to get out of my contact and go out to California. Mark and I were the very last ones to leave. I was the very last to leave by three weeks. Mark left in early August, and I left in late August [1987]. It was very moving. It was like breaking up a family, no doubt about it. It was bittersweet. I was totally jazzed to move on, because after six years, I was burnt out, to be honest. I couldn't introduce another video. I thought, like everybody that moves on, that the future was ahead of me. Little did I know that I would move to L.A., and the writers would go on strike! I wish I would have stayed on MTV for another year or two, just to keep the bucks coming.

NINA BLACKWOOD: There was one woman who I really thought was my friend, who was on the executive level of the public relations department, and I felt like she stabbed me in the back. I don't ever say that, but she was probably the one time in my life that you'll hear me say that. She was right with the program. She was the one doing the blackout and doing the spinning. It's like, *"Why?!"* But the feelings didn't last, because I had many other things I was going to. And then people could *see* where I was anyhow, so it was no big deal, because they could actually see it wasn't the truth. You don't just magically get a job as soon as you walk away from another one, unless you were planning on it.

KEN CEIZLER: I think there was a real sense of insecurity that [the VJs] had, as far as their place in the channel. But on the other side, they were also getting notoriety, and that fine balance, where you start to get people from outside agents and managers saying, "You're terrific. You're phenomenal. You could be doing this. You could be doing that." I think you had instances where they would go, "Hey wait, I'm worth something. I want X amount of dollars." And Bob Pittman would always say, "The VJs are not the face of the channel." Actually, it depended on when he needed to say it. Sometimes, he would say "The VJs are the face of the channel," and sometimes, he would say how completely indispensable they were. With the end of contracts came contract negotiations, and it probably was a matter of dollars and cents. And also a sense of what they individually thought their own personal value was, where they thought their future was, and where they wanted to go beyond that.

KEN R. CLARK: It was like losing a family member. They weren't even "going off to college." It wasn't like they were going to come back and visit on holidays. We threw big parties. I've still got big boxes with party invitations for Nina and Mark. We knew it was the end of an era. And around that same time, the channel started to evolve a little bit. I think they had to, because the novelty was wearing off. Those original years, people just sat and were willing to watch for five/six/seven hours, just stoned out on music videos. After a while, the novelty wore off a bit. It wasn't something so new and exciting. And MTV began looking for ways to capture people's attention and hold them for longer periods of time.

Music videos were changing, and the music world was changing profoundly, and MTV started categorizing music. If you look at those original years, everything was all mixed up. You didn't have all the dance music together, and the hard rock together, and the alternative together. It was all just a mishmash of everything. And they started doing specialty shows, like *120 Minutes* for alternative, and *Headbanger's Ball* for heavy metal, and they hired a news anchor. They realized that packaging everything kept people in for a half-hour or an hour. *Top 20 Video Countdown, Dial MTV*. The whole schedule started to have a structure to it, which originally it never had, with these big five-hour blocks. There were VJs, and then there were program hosts, like Riki Rachtman, Dr. Dre and Ed Lover, Dave Kendall. Everything started to change. Everybody knew that the innocence of those very first years was over.

LES GARLAND: I don't know if you can be an MTV VJ for ten years. I don't know if the lifespan is that. It's a funny thing about television. Glen Campbell said, "Be careful of television, Garland. It has this weird ability to chew you up and spit you out." I never forgot that, because I think Glen Campbell's TV show was once number one, and then it went to the basement. So he was talking from experience.

KEN R. CLARK: MTV was no longer owned by Warner-Amex, which when I started, we were owned by Warner-Amex Satellite Entertainment Corporation. I think for a brief period of time, MTV bought themselves away from Warner-Amex, and was "MTV Inc." for about a year or two, and then Viacom came in and snatched it up. Everything became about making money, everything became about selling product, and it was all a scramble to get those ratings. The ratings had just been there in the beginning, and then they actually had to start working and employing honest-to-God programmers, who started structuring the free-form. And the staff started to turn over, the VJs started to turn over. It was still good I think for a while. There were some big successes during that time. There were a couple of really good VJs—Downtown Julie Brown and Adam Curry were two of the greatest VJs

MTV had. Certainly the most famous and well-paid. I doubt they're still paid what they were for a while there. The pay scale changed considerably, too. I think the original VJs were lucky if they were getting paid $50,000 a year when they signed on in 1981. By the late '80s to early '90s, we're talking quarter-of-a-mil/half-mil contracts, with make-up artists, security, limos, agents, and managers.

BOB PITTMAN: We tried to buy the company. American Express wanted out of the Warner-Amex joint venture. We had gone public, but the majority of the stock was still owned by the Warner-Amex joint venture. So that put us in play. It wound up that Warner Communications bought out American Express in a buy/sell. They wound up the acquirer. So they owned 100% of the joint venture. And to pay for it, Steve Ross needed to either sell cable or sell MTV Networks, because Atari had failed, and the balance sheet was bad. He didn't really have that money to reach like that. And he originally worked out a deal to sell half of MTV and half of the cable company—in other words, half of Warner-Amex—to Viacom. And we, as the management group, wanted to buy MTV.

We worked with Teddy Forstmann's brother, Nickey, and Brian Little. Steve called me in to say, "I want you to do this Viacom deal." And I go, "Steve, look, I'm very loyal to you, and I appreciate what you've done for me, and I will go do whatever you want to do with MTV. But only if you will first listen to a pitch from Teddy Forstmann." So he goes, "OK, I'll do that." And Teddy came in and pitched him, and he agreed to sell MTV to us. So we had a deal. And then at the last minute, Teddy and Steve got in a fight about something, and a guy named Alberto Cribiore went over to Viacom and told them, "You make a big offer on MTV, and you can get it." They made a big offer to MTV and also to buy Warner out of their half of the Showtime-Movie Channel joint venture ... and Viacom got it.

I was disappointed and sad, although I made for the first time in my life, real money, because I owned a piece of the business. So as a seller, I got cash in my pocket, and the Viacom guys gave me a nice five-year deal, a signing bonus, and stock in Viacom. But at the end of the day, I had lost the company. And somehow, it just didn't feel right that Viacom owned it, and we were "the stepchild." So I was open to ideas, and MCA-Universal came to me, and said, "Why don't you start a company. Go buy whatever you want to buy. We'll be the check book. You'll own half; we'll own half." And I decided, "You know ... *it's time*. It's time for me to do something else. I've done this." I was a young guy, 30/31/32. I wanted to do other things in my life besides just MTV. So I decided to leave. I think some of it was the emotion of being let down that they got the business instead, and suddenly, I'm living in the house of the people that stole my business. It was the end of '86. I actually stayed as a consultant until '87, but I really gave up the day-to-day at the end of '86.

KEN R. CLARK: Up until a point, there were the original five VJs, which was like the "original phase." And then, the second batch of VJs, which also brought something to it. After that, they kind of came and went like a revolving door, and there haven't been very many of them that have had a lasting impact, with the possible exception of Carson Daly. There was never another group like the original five VJs.

MIKE PELECH: JJ is missed. We're all kind of dumbfounded that it's been six years [JJ passed away on March 17, 2004, from a heart attack]. It's just impossible to believe that. He was a really cool guy, funny. Just have lunch with him, tell stupid stories, and make people laugh. So entertaining. Every time I went out to the west coast, I always made it a point to have dinner with him. We would pick up the conversation and continue laughing. That's how I remember him. But I think everyone remembers him the same, as a wonderful person.

KEN CEIZLER: What a great sense of humor. He was just a sweet guy. I made him laugh. He thought I was the funniest fuckin' person in the world. And nobody cheered me up more than he did. He was quick to laugh, and he loved the music. He's the type of person that gave you a hug. You didn't shake hands with JJ; *you hugged him*. He was a true lover of music and people.

NINA BLACKWOOD: He was the elder statesman. Just a very loving man, very classy, very knowledgeable. He was a wonderful club man. Our rock n' roll beacon.

KEN R. CLARK: Of the original five, JJ was the notorious partier. He was one of the smartest people in rock n' roll that I have ever met in my entire life. He was also the oldest of those VJs. He was significantly older than the rest of them. I don't think people realized at the time that he was older. He'd been around doing radio since the '60s and had been involved breaking Led Zeppelin in this country. JJ had a music resume that would impress anybody, and he loved to talk about music. If there was anybody that would end up sitting in the green room or in his dressing room talking about bands and albums, it was JJ. He truly was an incredibly knowledgeable person. Everybody liked JJ and respected him. He was a really sweet, big guy, with a fun sense of humor. He liked to go out and party—*a lot.* [Laughs] He is the one that would come in late, with puffy eyes and dark shades on, and he wore this floor-length black mink coat. He looked like a pimp getting out of that car to go to the studio, with a model on either arm! [Laughs] No one else carried on like that. Everybody else was pretty low-key. But JJ liked to go out and do the nightclub thing. He was also the only VJ ... I mean, Nina would put the hood over her head and slink in that, but JJ actually wore *disguises* towards the end. He had fake mustaches and stuff, so when he would go out and walk his dog around the neighborhood, no one would recognize him.

ALAN HUNTER: JJ was a beautiful spirit. A classy man. He was sort of a big brother for the whole crew. He kept us all together. Whenever there was an issue with MTV or fights that we had with the higher-ups, he was the leader. He wouldn't take shit from anybody. He had a big old laugh and a big old heart. We loved him for his big heart. Ultimately, that's exactly what killed him. He had a heart attack and died on the 401 Freeway in L.A. I just loved his passion. He was so passionate about everything. It showed on television. It showed about the music that he loved. We all really appreciated that. I was sort of irreverent about things, and JJ liked that about me. What I liked about him was that he was sincere and passionate about stuff.

ROBIN ZORN: JJ just had a big, huge heart. When he died, it left a big hole in our family. JJ was just "one of the guys." He kept everybody's spirits up. I don't think there's anybody that would talk about JJ and not mention his smile or his laugh. Just really special. JJ caught me in a compromising position with one of the people that I worked with—in a doorway on the street outside the studio—and JJ kept that secret long past its time that it needed to be kept secret. JJ was great to everybody. Took care of everybody, was always there, and was always happy to answer questions and talk to people. A really warm, loving man. Huge smile, big heart.

LES GARLAND: He had a lot of credibility with people. He was a man of dark skin who came from a rock n' roll world, so he had a great place at MTV. Funny, I used to think, "How can a bunch of guys accuse us of being racist, when we have a person of color as one of our main hosts?" And we were very early in doing that sort of thing. We didn't even look at [it] as any sort of a barrier. We never thought like that. That wasn't our mentality. But I would like to think that people knew him on radio, they knew him on television. He had a lot of credibility.

BOB PITTMAN: A really down-to-earth, nice guy, who was passionate and knowledgeable about music. A prince of a guy.

MTV Today

DARYL HALL: I don't think anything of it. [Laughs] There's a name called MTV, but there is no *MTV.*

NINA BLACKWOOD: Oh boy. I never thought it would end up being the way it is. And it has nothing to do with sour grapes, because I would say if I thought it was really cool. I am not a fan of reality TV on any network, let alone MTV. And the fact that they dropped "Music Television" [from the MTV logo in 2010] ... OK fine, you're making money. Great. But you completely destroyed the whole reason that MTV started. It's gone. It's like, "Why don't you just take the whole thing away and rename the channel 'Reality Garbage?'" It appalls me. I'll read about something—because I'm not watching it—about some new show that is going to air, and I'm like, *"You're kidding."* It's like the most asinine ... horrible. For a while there, I'd actually try and see if there was anything on there. Now, I don't even stop on the channel.

It worries me about the entire state of the nation, if these shows are watched. I really wonder how the intelligence level has fallen. Because it's not just escapism. It's awful. It shows the worst—other than war—the really worst part of humans. Not even the common denominator. It's below that. I'm not saying it should be "back in the old days," but stick to the music. The Video Music Awards I actually liked this year [2009]. I don't know why. I usually turn it off after 15 minutes. I don't know why this year I ended up watching the whole thing. But it's like, "How can you have these awards when you don't even play music?" I remember a few years ago when they did it in Miami, Florida, all these artists are pulling up in their yachts. I'm going, "Oh my God! What is this?! I *think* rock is alive ... you're just oblivious to the fact that it is." *Ugh.*

ALAN HUNTER: I tune into it every so often. I believe that they have evolved over 30 years. They dropped the "Music Television" slug line this past month, if you noticed, which is telling. They are not about music, necessarily. They are about the lifestyle. I've got no beef with what they've done because they knew they were all about lifestyle. I think they still try to be the place where they break ground, even though I think they've gotten stale with the reality television programming. I think they're going for the lowest common denominator. Still seems to make them money, but seeing the ratings degrade, they're having to rethink their attitude a little bit.

GEOFF DOWNES: Reality probably killed the video star!

GERALD CASALE: My God, I have to be honest—I don't even watch it. Their "reality programming"—which is not really different than any other reality programming—is just hard to watch, and total proof of de-evolution. I'm watching a bunch of people that are proud to be stupid, with really bad values ... like indulgent/entitled brats acting horribly, where I just want to take a laser gun and get rid of all of them. If I was like Alex in *A Clockwork Orange*, if they wanted to put me in hell, they'd put those things on my eyes, watch those fucking reality shows, and I would definitely go mad. Imagine being strapped to a chair and not being able to go homicidal? *You'd just want to die.*

"WEIRD AL" YANKOVIC: I'm disappointed, because I remember how great it used to be. It's such a cliché to talk about how there's no music on Music Television anymore, but that's still the obvious problem with the channel. The last show that I enjoyed on MTV was *Human Giant*, which was brilliant. But frankly, I haven't really been following their line-up lately. The last time I looked, the bulk of their programming consisted of reality shows, and I'm really not a fan of that genre.

GEDDY LEE: It seems to be all reality shows every time I click onto it, while I'm sitting in my hotel room. I see some depressing scene of people that shouldn't be on television being filmed. I find the whole reality aspect that they've gone to really low quality, so I don't really think much of it.

PHIL COLLEN: The thing about MTV is it was the first place to see reality TV, so they were definitely ahead of the curve there. I'm surprised at the level the public are still interested in reality TV. It's way out there. People are not just fascinated with celebrities, but some kind of reality. And MTV started that off, with *The Real World*, and even VH1 with *Behind the Music*. It was real, and people were just clamoring for it. They were just loving it.

STEWART COPELAND: My understanding is that they don't play music videos anymore. Somebody once told me that the minute they play a music video, their viewership just *dives*. They've changed their format many times, and MTV has been a different entity many times over the decades. I remember the days before MTV, and then it was what it was when it started, and then it turned into something else, then it turned into something else again, and it has been through several incarnations since then. I have no idea where they're at now.

BOB PITTMAN: I don't watch it, because I'm way out of the demo. I mean, I'll pass by it occasionally. I think they've done a fantastic job to keep something as a cultural icon in the mainstream of the youth culture for 30 years. So I think they've done great. I hear friends go, "They're not as good as when you were there." And I go, "That's because you're old! It didn't get bad, *you got old.*" And I think that's true, whereas I was 30 years old or 27, I could intuitively understand where it was. I think there's zero chance I can intuitively understand where it is today. But I think I'm smart enough to understand they are still there and are still the voice of young America.

ROB HALFORD: It's MTV as it should be in 2010. Everything changes. I think it's still important and still valuable. It still reaches people the way it needs to. There are like five or six different ones now, aren't there? You've got the main one, which doesn't play music anymore. It's reality shows. But you can't discount it at the end of the day. It's Viacom, and it's cash. But at least the spirit hasn't been totally destroyed. You still get *Headbanger's Ball* and one or two other important moments. But it's a different world, a whole different world. MTV is still here, and I think always will be.

TONI BASIL: I still watch all those channels. I can't tell the difference between them, but I surf them everyday. I look, and if I see Chris Brown I stop, and if I see Ciara I stop. I'm always looking to see what the new steps are, what people are doing, because I continue to choreograph, so I like to see what everybody else is doing.

ANN WILSON: Which one are you referring to? It seems to have turned into quite a spider with many legs. Last night, I was watching MTV, and they showed *Into the Wild*, and I thought that was probably the best of what MTV is today - where they really can go in and show rock movies. They can go into rock in a way that's not necessarily a reality show. I don't really prefer reality shows on MTV. I like the other side of the coin.

KEN R. CLARK: I think that MTV has finally successfully reinvented itself as something viable. And I almost can't believe I'm saying that, because for many years, I truly despised what they had become. I just didn't pay any attention to it. They really had lost their identity for a while and floundered around, trying to figure out what they wanted to be. The programming wasn't particularly appealing. This is going back a ways, but *The Osbournes* was one of the first shows on MTV that I thought, "That's just plain, *damn fucking good*. It's funny." Now, I think they have a ton of shows—between MTV and VH1—they've got some really engaging programming. It's not about music anymore. It's about youth culture. If you accept that and don't hold on to what MTV was—and look at it for what it truly is now—I think it has become something that has become viable once again.

MIKE SCORE: Now it's just like ... who cares what kids do on spring break? It's probably the last thing I want to see. But for some reason, it must have worked. To tell you the truth, I haven't seen one reality TV thing and gone, "Wow, that was great." *Not one.* I'm sure it's cheaper for them to make it, and they have God knows how many hours of filming they have to fill in, so whatever they have to do. But as far as entertainment goes, reality TV is at the low end. It's almost like fart jokes. "The fart joke of television."

EDDIE MONEY: It's very dramatic, with a lot of kids crying on it and a lot of girls breaking up with guys. And girls beating each other up. It's come a long way from music, y'know? My daughter is 21. I feel like I'm living in MTV, because she's always breaking up with her boyfriends! It's crazy. I don't have to watch MTV anymore—I have five kids that are all teenagers, drive me out of my mind.

BOB GIRALDI: The television culture is so glitzed, so maneuvered, so manipulated that it doesn't interest me. I'm more interested in the real deal. I'm real interested in what young people are *really* like, and not how they're portrayed to be like. So I don't watch it, and I know very little about it. The same with VH1. That was then, this is now.

JELLO BIAFRA: When pop culture gets stupid, I just ignore it. Every five years or so, people come up to me—"MTV used to be really good, but it really sucks now." And I'm like, "Hey, wait a minute ... didn't it always suck, and you just outgrew it?" Some people complain that there aren't enough clips anymore, and it's just one dumb reality show after another that they don't really want to watch. But that doesn't motivate me to watch those shows, just for the sake of watching those shows. There's a lot of things that turn up in popular culture that I saw no reason to watch because I was never interested in it. To this day, I've never seen *Charlie's Angels*, I've never seen *The Brady Bunch* or *The Partridge Family*, never saw *Moonlighting*, I've watched about five minutes of *Seinfeld*, and decided I had better things to do. That's just the way I am. Again, why keep up with bad pop culture when there's so many other interesting things to keep up with? I just don't bother.

RICK SPRINGFIELD: It's a completely different animal. I'm not bemoaning the loss of MTV. Like I said, it was distasteful to me the posing ... and I was certainly guilty of it myself. But there were also some great moments. Honestly, I haven't seen a lot of videos. I think most of them now are performance videos in kind of an odd setting, on a city street or something. I've seen a couple of the newer ones, where they do concept videos, and there's nothing really new that's being done. Everything was done back in the day, when everyone was experimenting. So there's nothing really new to be done, I don't think. It's probably very smart that they morphed into what they're doing now.

JOE ELLIOTT: I moved on to VH1. That's what we all did, at our age. It's sad that this generation will probably go, "We started with iPods and don't even know what a cassette is." There are a lot of people that will really genuinely never experience the kind of excitement that we did.

BOOTSY COLLINS: The feeling it has for me is just like everything else nowadays. It has no feeling. The cell phones have souled us out, and the smart phones are not saving us from making dumb decisions. And that, my friend and funkateers, is what my next album will be about, the very thing that you are writing about in your book. Times have changed technically, but we are still as stupid as it gets with our choices. We are all a by-product of our desires and choices.

CHUCK D: They're totally all over the place. The only reason I would watch MTV is because of *MTV News*. That's it. There would be no reason, whatsoever.

FRANK STALLONE: MTV's gotten real jive. It has no soul anymore. Not that it really did ever have great soul, but it's pretty bad now. See, I don't watch TV shows like I used to, because I'm not into this thing where rappers are fighting and carrying guns. I'm like, "What the hell is going on here?" In my era, it would have been, "Hey man, you better watch out. *Ray Davies is going to pop Mick Jagger.*" What kind of shit is that? I think it's a crashing bore. It has no credibility anymore. I mean, I guess if you're going to listen to Justin Bieber or whatever his name is—I don't even know what he does or who he is. To me, Justin Timberlake is still a "boy band guy." Guys with their five o'clock shadows, acting like they're all tough. I don't get it. I'm really open to a lot of stuff. I really like Kings of Leon. I think they're great. Because they're like a real band, aren't they?

PAUL DEAN: The "new video channel" now is YouTube. All you need is an Internet connection. I'm on YouTube all the time. That's an awesome "MTV." Way better, because it's viewing on demand.

THOMAS DOLBY: In a way, the most comparable experience for kids today is YouTube. I think, as was the case in the early '80s, when teenagers would be doing their homework with MTV on in the background, I think these days, I see teenagers doing their homework with YouTube in the background. So I think that legacy has been taken up elsewhere.

STAN RIDGWAY: I'm in a media transition at home, where I'm trying to get rid of my television and get rid of my broadcast or cable, and make the change over to just having a computer in the living room with a large monitor, and be able to watch whatever I want, whenever I want to. I'm not interested in what some bail-bondsman in Hawaii is doing and what he's doing with the extensions in his hair today.

LES GARLAND: When I heard the Rolling Stones do "Satisfaction" in 1965, nobody would have had the balls to predict that the Rolling Stones would be the highest grossing tour band between 2000 and 2010. That, to me, is just extraordinary. And that's what MTV is. MTV is an extraordinary phenomenon around the world. It's bigger than life. When we created it, we wanted it to live and breathe. And today, it's living and breathing.

ALAN HUNTER: I think it's such a worldwide phenomenon now, that's what amazes me, how ubiquitous they are around the world. That has everything to do with youth. MTV is so much "the pacifier" for young people around the world. I think that's probably my biggest worry—what I'm not sure they're doing is motivating young people above and beyond just entertaining themselves. But they sure have a big enough following that they can make changes and "pied piper" these youngsters along.

When they do the occasional social event, they can sure get a lot of people come onboard that. And some people think that's a little disingenuous, like they're keeping their cred up a little bit, by doing these one-offs every so often.

I think MTV surely must be at a place where they have to evolve again. And they've got to rethink spotlighting only the dumbest and meanest among us. If they can do that, than maybe "year 31" will be worth watching again. Certainly, it will never be for an older demographic. They know who they're talking to. But they're a lot more about merchandising nowadays than anything else.

DAVE WAKELING: We were just talking about it last night. We even talked about it on stage. We sang a little of "Satellite Killed the Video Star" ... or "Internet Killed the Video Star." It's interesting. We thought the world had changed forever, but it was only a short change. Things were going to change even more after that. It turned out our "Lady of the 30 Rules" wasn't going to be ruling the artistic universe for as long as we thought.

SERGEANT BLOTTO: I wish there was somebody that was doing what MTV used to do. I think that's still a valid ... I don't know how it could be commercially successful. But maybe that's why I'm sitting here, and Bob Pittman is sitting somewhere else. [Laughs]

MARTHA DAVIS: Sometimes, I'll look back on the '80s and go, "Was it all frivolous? Was it all crazy?" A lot of it was just *fun*.

Where Are They Now?

JON ANDERSON: Performing with the Cleveland Youth Orchestra, the Vermont Youth Orchestra, and the San Antonio Youth Orchestra. Recording with students from the Paul Green School of Rock on a project. Still performs solo shows, as well as shows with former Yes bandmate Rick Wakeman.

PETE ANGELUS: Manager of the Black Crowes and Truth and Salvage Co. Has a film project in the works.

CARMINE APPICE: Performs as part of a drum show called *Slamm* [from Carmine's site—"Described as *Stomp* on steroids, Appice and four young drummers rule the stage and make rock music playing buckets, sticks, oil cans, drain pipes, even Dixie cups, as well as drums"]. Does drum clinics, performs with bands, and working on an autobiography.

ART BARNES: Continues to record with Barnes & Barnes, who released *Opbopachop*, in 2009.

STEVE BARRON: Working on a sci-fi show, *Slingers*, for a games company, Sleepy Dog. Developing an '80s set movie, *Slow Down Arthur, Stick to 30*, written by artist Harland Miller, for the U.K. Film Council.

TONI BASIL: Completed two years of choreographing and serving as dance director of Bette Midler's *The Showgirl Must Go On*, at Caesers Palace. Also was associate director and choreographer of Tina Turner's last world tour. Writing a book of the history of American street dance, and judges and teaches at street dance competitions.

JELLO BIAFRA: Records/performs as part of Jello Biafra and the Guanta-namo School of Medicine. Released *The Audacity of Hype* in 2009. Head of the Alternative Tentacles record company.

NINA BLACKWOOD: Hosts a daily show on Sirius XM, *80s on 8.*

ERIC BLOOM: Continues to tour with Blue Öyster Cult.

SERGEANT BLOTTO: Is a music and arts writer for the *Albany Times Union.* Also writes for nippertown.com. Still performs sporadically with Blotto, and is a member of a four-piece acoustic jug-band, the Ramblin' Jug Stompers.

RICKY BYRD: Finishing up a solo record with producer Ray Kennedy.

GERALD CASALE: Continues to record/tour with Devo, who released their ninth studio album, *Something for Everybody*, in 2010.

KEN R. CLARK: A real estate broker with RE/MAX.

KEN CEIZLER: A freelance director.

PHIL COLLEN: Continues to record/tour with Def Leppard. Working on guitar designs with Jackson Guitars. Writing songs with his songwriting partner, CJ Vanston, for Def Leppard and his side-band, Man-Raze.

BOOTSY COLLINS: Launched *Bootsy Collins Funk University*, "the first online funk bass university of its kind," via bootsycollins.com, and is work-ing on a new album, also titled *Bootsy Collins Funk University*. Works with the Bootsy Collins Foundation, whose motto is "Say it Loud, an Instrument for Every Child."

STEWART COPELAND: Reunited with the Police for a tour in 2007-2008. In 2009, penned the book *Strange Things Happen: A Life with The Police, Polo, and Pygmies*. Writing a symphony for gamelan and orchestra for the Dallas Symphony, writing an opera for the Royal Opera in London, and working on *Mikrokosmos* for percussion.

CY CURNIN: Finishing work on a new Fixx CD. Also runs a solo label via cycurnin.com. Is working on a music project with Nick Harper.

CHUCK D: Continues to record/tour with Public Enemy. In 2010, released a solo album under the name "Mistachuck," *Don't Rhyme for the Sake of Riddlin'*.

MARTHA DAVIS: Released three albums in 2007—*Beautiful Life*, *Clean Modern and Reasonable*, and *This*. In 2010, released a children's album, *Red Frog Presents 16 Songs for Parents and Children*. Recording a group of torch/jazz/ballad songs with original Motels saxophonist/keyboardist, Marty Jourard. Has a podcast with manager, Gaye Ann Bruno, and Berlin's Terri Nunn, called *Between the Sheets*.

PAUL DEAN: Continues to record/tour with Loverboy. Released *Just Getting Started* in 2007.

WARREN DeMARTINI: Continues to record/tour with Ratt. Released *Infestation* in 2010.

JOHN DOE: Tours as a solo act and with X and the Knitters. Working on a new solo album. Last release was 2009's *Country Club*.

THOMAS DOLBY: Releasing his first new album in 20 years, *A Map of the Floating City*, in 2010.

GEOFF DOWNES: Continues to record/tour with Asia. Released *Omega* in 2010.

JONATHAN ELIAS: Working on a score for the film *Son of No One*, a new album, and is the head of Elias Arts, which does TV commercial music.

JOE ELLIOTT: Continues to record/tour with Def Leppard. Launched a side-band, Down 'N Outz, releasing *My Re Generation* in 2010.

RIK EMMETT: Reunited for shows with Triumph in 2008. Released *Greatest Hits Remixed* in 2010. Plays in an acoustic guitar trio with Oscar Lopez and Pavlo. Records/releases solo albums via rikemmett.com. Plays solo acoustic shows. Plays in a duo, with Dave Dunlop, called Strung-Out Troubadours. Teaches a music business course and songwriting course at Humber College in Toronto.

LITA FORD: Released her first new album in 14 years, *Wicked Wonderland*, in 2009. Working on a family reality show.

LES GARLAND: Runs a consultancy business, AfterPlay Entertainment. Working with Michael Cohl on building a new entertainment company, "Soon to be Named" (aka "S2BN"). Does voiceover work for commercials.

BOB GIRALDI: Shoots TV commercials, develops films, does short films, teaches a graduate short film program for the School of Visual Arts, and owns ten restaurants.

ROB HALFORD: Continues to record/tour with Judas Priest, who issued *Nostradamus* in 2008, *A Touch of Evil: Live in 2009*, and *British Steel: 30th Anniversary Edition* in 2010. Touring with his solo band, Halford, as part of Ozzfest in 2010, and released *Halford IV* the same year.

DARYL HALL: Continues to record/tour with Hall & Oates. Does his own Internet show, *Live from Daryl's House*.

GREG HAWKES: Toured with Todd Rundgren's band in 2009. Also plays in Flo & Eddie's band and does occasional solo ukulele shows. In 2008, released *The Beatles Uke*, an album of ukulele/Beatles covers.

COLIN HAY: Tours/records as a solo act. Released *American Sunshine* in 2009.

ALAN HUNTER: Runs a film company with his brother—Hunter Films. Runs a music venue in Birmingham, Alabama—WorkPlay. Hosts a daily show on Sirius XM, *80s on 8*.

DEBORA IYALL: Teaches art on the Navajo Nation and in community centers, jails, and boys and girls clubs. Working on new music [which can be heard by going to reverbnation.com and entering in "Debora Iyall"].

ORAN "JUICE" JONES: Is considering making a new album and is helping his daughter and son with their music careers.

BRUCE KULICK: Released his third solo album in 2010, *BK3*, which featured guest appearances by Gene Simmons, Nick Simmons, Eric Singer, John Corabi, Doug Fieger, and Steve Lukather. Also is the guitarist for Grand Funk Railroad and often participates in "Rock n' Roll Fantasy Camp."

GEDDY LEE: Continues to record/tour with Rush, who is finishing work on their 19th studio album. A documentary, *Rush: Beyond the Lighted Stage*, was released in 2010.

JULIAN LENNON: Working on his first photo exhibition. Released the book *Beatles Memorabilia: The Julian Lennon Collection* in 2010 [with a share of the proceeds going to The White Feather Foundation, which is tied in with the "White Feather: Spirit of Lennon" memorabilia collection]. Preparing a solo album, *Everything Changes*, for release in 2011.

GEORGE LOIS: Still does ad campaigns. Released his latest book, *George Lois: The Esquire Covers @ MoMA*, in 2010.

DAVE MARSH: Hosts four shows on Sirius XM—"Live from E Street Nation," "E Street Radio," "Kick Out the Jams with Dave Marsh," and "Live from the Land of Hope and Dreams." Still writes and is currently working on a book about *American Idol*.

EDDIE MONEY: Eddie's life story is told in a play, *Two Tickets to Paradise*, which was premiered at the Dix Hills Performing Arts Center in New York in 2009. Is planning on doing an album of songs from the play.

ANGELO MOORE: Continues to record/tour with Fishbone. Has a solo project, Dr. Madd Vibe, and a side-band, Madd Vibe Experiment, and does comic books. Has his own record label, Mooremapp Records [mooremap-precords.com], and released *Madd Vibe En Dub* in 2010.

JEFF & JOHN MURPHY: Continue to play sporadic shows with the Shoes. Jeff released a solo album, *Cantilever*, in 2007, and wrote a book the same year, *Birth of a Band, The Record Deal and The Making of Present Tense*. Both have been interviewed for an upcoming book about the Shoes, titled *Boys Don't Lie: A History of Shoes*, by Mary E. Donnelly. Compiling a DVD release.

ALDO NOVA: Has recorded a rock opera, *The Life and Time of Eddie Gage*. Has written songs for Faith Hill, Celine Dion, and Clay Aiken.

JOHN OATES: Continues to record/tour with Hall & Oates. Is launching an annual songwriters festival in Aspen, Colorado—7908: The Aspen Songwriters Festival. Also working on a solo album.

WALLY PALMAR: Continues to record/tour with the Romantics. Touring as part of Ringo Starr & His All-Starr Band in the summer of 2010.

MIKE PELECH: Is the operations manager for *CBS Evening News with Katie Couric*.

BOB PITTMAN: Co-founded a private investment firm, Pilot Group LLC, which has controlling investments in such companies as Thrillist, Tasting Table, and Casa Dragones Tequila, among others.

ROGER POWELL: Released his fourth solo effort, *Blue Note Ridge*, in 2009. Toured with Todd Rundgren's band in 2009.

DEREK POWER: Manages Stewart Copeland. Is head of the Derek Power Company and a partner in Kahn Power Pictures.

MARKY RAMONE: Hosts a weekly show on Sirius XM, "Marky Ramone's Punk Rock Blitzkrieg." Still tours and records, and launched a pasta sauce, "Marky Ramones' Brooklyn's Own Pasta Sauce." Working on an autobiography.

RICHIE RAMONE: In 2007, did a score of *West Side Story*, where he played the drums with an orchestra, titled *Suite for Drums and Orchestra*.

HERMAN RAREBELL: Released his second solo album overall, *Take It as It Comes*, in 2010.

MIKE RENO: Continues to record/tour with Loverboy.

STAN RIDGWAY: Records/tours as a solo artist. Finishing work on his latest solo album.

TODD RUNDGREN: Records/tours as a solo artist. Working on a DVD of his 2009 live performances of *A Wizard a True Star*.

MICHAEL SADLER: Records/tours as a solo artist. Recently performed with a big band, doing big band/swing versions of Saga material.

RUDY SARZO: Plays bass in Blue Öyster Cult. Participates in Rock n' Roll Fantasy Camp. In 2008, released the book *Off the Rails*, which focuses on his time playing with Randy Rhoads in the Ozzy Osbourne band.

MIKE SCORE: Continues to record/tour with A Flock of Seagulls.

RICK SPRINGFIELD: Records/tours as a solo artist. Released *Venus in Overdrive* in 2008. Releasing an autobiography, *Late, Late at Night*, in 2010. Takes part in a yearly "Rick Springfield Cruise" and continues to act, including a role in the TV show *Californication*.

FRANK STALLONE: Records/tours as a solo artist.

FRANKIE SULLIVAN: Continues to record/tour with Survivor. Working on Survivor's first all-new studio release in over 20 years.

MICKEY THOMAS: Continues to record/tour with Starship. Released a solo blues album in 2010, *The Blues Masters Featuring Mickey Thomas*, and is working on a new Starship album and solo album.

GEORGE THOROGOOD: Continues to record/tour with George Thorogood & the Destroyers, who released their latest album in 2009, *The Dirty Dozen*.

GLENN TILBROOK: Continues to record/tour with Squeeze. Also records/tours with his side-band, the Fluffers.

TOMMY TUTONE: Records/tours as a solo artist. Working on his latest album, *Soul Twang*.

KATHY VALENTINE: Continues to record/tour with the Go-Go's, who in 2010 launched a farewell tour. Produces other artists and plays in an "all-girl blues-rock band," the BlueBonnets.

DAVE WAKELING: Continues to tour with the English Beat, or, as Dave describes, "I'm sitting naked in the back of the tour bus, staring out the window, at a very clammy and muggy day in Indianapolis. It hasn't rained yet ... but it looks like it's destined to. And I can't think of an item of clothing that goes with this weather at all. So I'm stuck here in the back of the bus ... until something gives."

FEE WAYBILL: Continues to record/tour with the Tubes. Released an archive album in 2010, *Mondo Birthmark*, and is working on an anthology of all the Tubes' videos, *White Punks on Dope*.

MARK WEISS: Continues to still photograph rock stars. Is promoting weissguygallery.com, which contains a gallery of his classic pictures from the '70s and '80s.

VERDINE WHITE: Continues to record/tour with Earth, Wind & Fire. Was inducted into the Songwriter's Hall of Fame in 2010.

ANN WILSON: Continues to record/tour with Heart. Released their thirteenth studio album in 2010, *Red Velvet Car*.

"WEIRD AL" YANKOVIC: Records/tours as a solo artist. Working on a new album.

ROBIN ZORN: Is a freelance producer/director.

Printed in Great Britain
by Amazon

29227439R00264